Praise for *Alvin Ailey: A Life in Dance*

"[Dunning] brings to the difficult task of telling Ailey's story long experience covering his art, sensitivity to his secretiveness about his homosexuality and a good understanding of how racism circumscribed his life. Candidly, she presents his frailties as well as his strengths."
—*The New York Times*

"[Dunning] unravels the complicated weave of Ailey's private and professional life with knowledge, skill, and tact. . . . Dunning sheds a much-needed light on racism in the dance world." —Lynn Garafola, *The Nation*

"Finely researched and beautifully written." —*Chicago Sun Times*

"Jennifer Dunning's eagerly anticipated biography manages the daunting task of portraying a person famous for his work, but compulsively private and unreconciled in his personal life. This readable, often moving book describes a man who made enormous emotional sacrifices."
—*Philadelphia Inquirer*

"Painfully honest yet affectionate. . . . Dunning brings a broad and balanced knowledge of dance history to this book. . . . Thanks to Jennifer Dunning, Ailey's complete story is now told." —*Pittsburgh Post Gazette*

"Jennifer Dunning's new biography . . . is the first profile of Ailey that captures both his choreographic achievements and his personal tribulations. . . . [Dunning] tells the story of Ailey's life with openness, objectivity and care. . . . [She] paints a portrait of Ailey that weaves discussion of his sexuality into the greater ebb and flow of his extraordinary pursuits as a dancer, actor and choreographer. . . . [A] biography of stunning openness and dignity." —*Washington Blade*

"Exhaustively researched . . . [*Alvin Ailey*] provides as much information as anyone would want about the brilliant choreographer and dancer. . . . Dunning has done an astounding amount of reporting, especially on Ailey's years in Los Angeles, digging up elementary-school teachers, high school classmates, and dance students. She has also interviewed many of the people who were early supporters and who helped build Ailey's company. . . . The book paints an honest and complex portrait of the man." —*City Books*

"Dunning offers a new perspective on the tension between Ailey's public and private lives." —*Chicago Tribune*

alvin ailey

A LIFE IN DANCE

JENNIFER DUNNING

DA CAPO PRESS • NEW YORK

The *New York Times, Dance & Dancers, Dance Magazine*, and The Black Archives of Mid-America have generously given permission to use extended quotes. Further permissions appear in the chapter notes.

Many of the designations used by manufacturers and sellers to distinguish their products are claimed as trademarks. Where those designations appear in this book and the author was aware of a trademark claim, the designations have been printed in initial capital letters.

Library of Congress Cataloging-in-Publication Data

Dunning, Jennifer.
  Alvin Ailey: a life in dance / Jennifer Dunning.—1st Da Capo Press ed.
    p.   cm.
  Originally published: Reading, Mass.: Addison-Wesley, c1996.
  Includes bibliographical references (p.) and index.
  ISBN 0-306-80825-0 (alk. paper)
  1. Ailey, Alvin. 2. Dancers—United States—Biography. I. Title.
[GV1785.A38D85 1998]
792.8'092—dc21
[B]   97-42644
                                                  CIP

First Da Capo Press edition 1998

This Da Capo Press paperback edition of *Alvin Ailey* is an unabridged republication of the hardcover edition first published in Reading, Massachusetts by Addison Wesley Longman in 1996. It is here reprinted by arrangement with Addison Wesley Longman.

Copyright © 1996 by Jennifer Dunning
Text design by Karen Savary

Cover photo of Alvin Ailey dancing "Hermit Songs," 1961,
© Jack Mitchell

Published by Da Capo Press, Inc.
A Subsidiary of Plenum Publishing Corporation
233 Spring Street, New York, N.Y. 10013

All Rights Reserved

Manufactured in the United States of America

For my father, John, and my friend Núria,

with loving thanks for the gifts of dance they gave me

CONTENTS

ACKNOWLEDGMENTS

This book is also dedicated to the memory of Talley Beatty, Charles Blackwell and James Truitte, men of special dignity and grace whose witty, loving and perceptive contributions to this book made them seem like friends and inspirations as well as helpful sources of information. It is dedicated, too, to the memory of Ivy Clarke, all durable shell and a heart that bloomed at the slightest attention. And it is dedicated to the dancers of the Alvin Ailey American Dance Theater and Repertory Ensemble—past, present and future—who give so much to their audiences, with the hope that the day may soon come when training and hiring in all dance is color-blind at last.

I would like to give extra thanks to Judy Cameron, Blanche Sutton, Pam Crow, and Elliot and Margaret Goodwin, who were so generous with their time in helping me to know Los Angeles, Rogers and Navasota in ways I would not have without them. Edele and Al Holtz not only opened their extensive archival collection to me but their home in Swannanoa as well. Dorene Richardson got me started on my research with her personal archives. I was touched and encouraged by the kindness and helpfulness of Calvin Cooper, whose generous gift of one of his brother's African artifacts brought Alvin Ailey into my everyday life in a new way. And I am in debt to Sylvia Waters Jones, who never lost patience through endless requests for help, to Mickey Bord for guiding me through the wonderful Ailey archives and to William Hammond for his unfailingly cheerful aplomb.

My thanks also to the people I interviewed for this book: Miguel Algarin, Sarita Allen, Frank Andersen, Evelyn Clayton Ashford, Clive Barnes, Mary Barnett, Mikhail Baryshnikov, Talley Beatty, Laura Beaumont, Ruth Beckford, Fred Benjamin, Charles Blackwell, Marilyn Bord, Dan Butt, Thurston Carlock, Vinnette Carroll, Nicola Cernovitch, Raquelle Chavis, Masazumi Chaya, Ivy Clarke, Carol Coe, Calvin Cooper, Lula Cooper, Billy Ray and Pam Crow, Ulysses Dove, Richard Dow, Eddy J. Duckens, Matty Duckens, Carmen de Lavallade, Katherine Dunham, Frank Eng, George Faison, Lois Framhein, Marianna Gates, Maxine Glorsky, Lelia Goldoni, Juliet Goldsmith, Elliott and Margaret Goodwin, Meg Gordean, Rusty Graham, Allan Gray, Cynthia Gregory, Robert Greskovic, Anna Halprin, Lavinia Hamilton, William Hammond, Ves Harper, Ella Hurd Harris, Bob Harris, Gary Harris, Lawrence Hatterer, M.D., James Henley, Mary Hinkson, Dustin Hoffman, Geoffrey Holder, Al Holtz, Edele Holtz, Lena Horne, Nat Horne, Dawn Lillie Horwitz, Darcell Jackson, Judith Jamison, Louis Johnson, Mari Kajiwara, Milton Katselas, Linda Kent, Anna Kisselgoff, Albert Knapp, M.D., Herman Krawitz, Pearl Lang, Cristyne Lawson, Ellen M. Levine, Harvey Lichtenstein, Don Martin, Keith McDaniel, Donald McKayle, Anne McKnight, Clyde McQueen, David McReynolds, Arthur Mitchell, Jack Mitchell, Ella Thompson Moore, Mio Morales, Michele Murray, Dennis Nahat, Joe Nash, Sandy Neblett, Gladys Nelson, Walter Nicks, Rodney Nugent, Hilary Ostlere, Marjorie Perces, Brad Perry, M.D., Ruby Alexander Phillips, Stanley Plesent, Charles Queenan, Charles Reinhart, Al Reyes, Arthur Reynolds, Desmond Richardson, Dorene Richardson, Dwight Rhoden, Louise Roberts, Herbert Ross, Kelvin Rotardier, Elizabeth Roxas, Harry Rubenstein, Donna Wood Sanders, Brother John Sellers, Lynn Seymour, Gil Shiva, Michael Shurtleff, Norman Singer, Sherman Sneed, Anna Sokolow, Blanche Sutton, Marian Sylla, Paul Szilard, Claude Thompson, Onella Travis, Walter William Travis, James Truitte, Matt Turney, Glory Van Scott, David Vaughan, Larry Warren, Sylvia Waters and Dudley Williams. Extra thanks to those who bravely shared with me difficult memories of a man they loved and admired, sometimes anonymously. I hope they will feel that what I have written, with something of the same love and respect, repays their trust.

Many people helped me with research problems, photographs, shorter interviews and encouragement. I would like to thank Judith Jamison and the generous staff of the Alvin Ailey American Dance Theater (among them Suzann Abdool-Lee, Molly Browning, Algernon

Campbell, Ronni Favors, Calvin Hunt, Minda Logan, Sharon Gersten Luckman, Heather Mangrum and Sathi Pillai), the staff of the Black Archives of Mid-America, Inc. (Renaldo Andrews, DeAnna Austin, Ruby M. Jackson, Bill Livingston and Douglass G. Walker), and Everett Aison, A. Peter Bailey, Peter Brook, Delores Brown, Tine Byrsted, Masazumi Chaya, Gwin Chin, the Dance Collection of the New York Public Library for the Performing Arts at Lincoln Center, Tommy De Frantz, Alexander Dube, Martin Duberman, Reverend Sylvester Duckens, Frank Eng, Dr. Judith Ginsberg, Lelia Goldoni, Meg Gordean, Allan Gray and the Kansas City Friends of Alvin Ailey, William Hammond, John Edward Hasse, Jane Hermann, David High, Chauncey Jones, Walter Kattwinkel, Peter Koepke, Herman Krawitz, Cristyne Lawson, Harold Levine, Naomi Nomikos, Sharon Pavlovich and Class 4/5 201 at Public School 191 in Manhattan, Sidney Poitier, John S. Pulliams Jr., Rosalie Radomsky, Arnold Rampersad, Tony Randall, Janice Ross, Richard Shepard, Blanche Sutton, James Truitte, Barry Ulanov, Julia Walker, Myrna White, Clark J. Whitten and Nancy Wright.

I am grateful to the friends and colleagues at the *New York Times* who made this book possible, among them Anna Kisselgoff, Gwen Smith, Jack Anderson, Constance Rosenblum and Robert Berkvist, Wade Burkhart, Max Frankel, Arthur Gelb, Paul Goldberger, Warren Hoge, Eugene Lambinus, Joseph Lelyveld, Daniel Lewis and Alex Ward.

Thanks to my family and friends—among them Joan Acocella, Leah Ben-David, Gwin Chin, Kenneth Fay, Robert Greskovic, Ellen Jacobs, Judith Levin, Núria Olivé-Bellés, Curtis A. Robertson, Nana Simopoulos, Dinitia Smith, Helen Miranda Wilson and my brouha Dellora Hercules—for listening for so long and with such convincingly unwavering fascination to all my talk about The Book. Thanks also to the Roosevelt Island Gardening Club for understanding that book work was responsible for all those weeds, and to Hamish Macbeth, Agatha Raisin and Miss Zukas for the pleasurable distraction of their company.

I would also like to thank Judy Gitenstein for her enthusiastic help with research and Curtis A. Robertson for his sensitive help with transcribing interviews. And last but never least, thanks to my agents Elise and Arnold Goldman, to Tiffany Cobb, production coordinator, and, most of all, to my editor Sharon Broll for her bracing clarity, optimism and extraordinary patience.

one

"BUSY AS SOON AS HE WAS BORN"

The sky is open and endless in Southeast Texas. Green-brown fields and dirt roads run straight out to the brim of the horizon and over, the green punctuated by grazing cows, the small groves of trees smudges against the blue. Man-made cattle ponds, or "sinks" in Texas talk, curve up toward the sky they reflect like the palms of hands. Towns are the barest clusters of buildings, with names like Red Ranger, or Joe Lee, or Zabcikville, where Czech and Bohemian farmers settled.

And always the trains, crisscrossing the countryside, keeping company with the horses, buggies, cars and trucks as they travel along country roads. The Santa Fe and Southern Pacific announce their approach with a distant cry of warning at countless dirt-road crossings along their route. The cry grows louder and more urgent, then suddenly diminishes, spent in a whir of steel bodies headed somewhere else—followed by the eyes of silent children playing by the tracks, heard by the drinkers in the Dew Drop Inns along the way, sensed by the Sunday worshipers calling out their love for God and their hope for salvation in throbbing, exalted song.

The world into which Alvin Ailey was born was, and to some extent still is, one of harsh and arbitrary extremes. Given a certain kind of

1

attention, a black child could flourish there despite adversity, yet never quite feel he belonged in the larger world. In the 1930s, when Alvin was a child, public facilities were segregated, and "colored" facilities were almost always humiliatingly inferior to what whites could expect. Decades later, Alvin's mother could still see and smell the toilets and eating areas for the colored that were hidden at the back of bus-stop cafés along routes from one Texas town to another, as much out of view of white eyes as possible. She remembered, too, the stop where the stench of nearby white urinals filled the air around the table where blacks were sent to eat.

Blacks and whites lived in mostly peaceful coexistence in the small segregated rural towns where Alvin lived for brief periods of his earliest years. A 1929 directory for one town lists two "colored cafés," one "Mexican" and one "colored and white." But everyday life was a matter of hard work for the Aileys of that world, work that started before the sun rose and ended after it set. White children went to school, Alvin's mother remarked many years later, and black children picked cotton.

Rogers and Navasota, the towns where Alvin lived longest, are on the wide, muddy Brazos, one of the largest rivers in the state, where the first crops of cotton, planted in 1825, had been harvested by slave labor. In 1930, 62 percent of the black population of Texas lived in rural areas, although that would begin to change within the decade as blacks and whites were lured away by the promise of good industrial jobs far from dying farms and drowsy towns.

For the blacks who stayed, life held the promise of extended families, long Sunday dinners and even longer Sunday church services during which one repented the sins of the Saturday night before. The children had pastures and wooden sidewalks to race across, ponds to plunge into, horses to ride and snakes to torture, and pecans, peaches, pears and plums to harvest and sell. Few instances of bad behavior went unseen and unpunished, for almost everyone was part of a large, extended family of kinfolk, neighbors and friends.

This was the life lived by whites, too, whose comings and goings were duly recorded in the *Navasota Examiner*. "Mrs. Lockett Kennard of Anderson was shopping here this morning," a 1934 personals column reported. "Dr. Beatrice Hammons will leave tomorrow for Houston to spend the weekend." Stories about two-headed calves, pickle collections and eggplant fields competed for space with news of war, international celebrities and escaped convicts. "Jiggs is the meanest animal in the ape house," a zookeeper announced in newspaper filler titled

"Chimpanzee Turns Sissy," "but give him a mirror and he softens up at once."

One issue offered news of the visit of an African evangelist to "the colored Methodist Church." A long front-page story is devoted to the death of an "Old slave of Navasota man," "Aunt" Easter Barry "as she was known to her many many white friends. Both white and colored alike will be sorry to learn of 'Aunt' Easter's death."

Black lives were as peaceful and secure as racism and poverty would allow. The number of lynchings had dropped steadily during the second half of the decade, with the Tuskegee Institute in Alabama reporting a total of three in 1939, in Florida and Mississippi. But there was muted talk among the grown-ups of murders, the Ku Klux Klan and imprisonment, all of which were feared realities in the lives of most black males. Some were afraid to live in the small wooden "box" houses peculiar to southern towns, for it was too easy to be shot in the back while running along the straight hall from the front to the back door if unwelcome visitors arrived.

Matty Duckens, one of Alvin's many cousins, tells of a night when she, a child clinging to her father's shirt, watched him face down white men who suddenly appeared at their door. "They had guns, and they told my father that if he didn't stop talking up they'd tar and feather him. He told them to start heating up the tar."

It was a world that Alvin's mother, Lula Elizabeth Cliff, knew intimately, though from the perspective of someone who did not entirely belong. Born in 1912, she was the light-skinned granddaughter of a white man and a black woman. Unable to live together legally, Louisia and Jenkins Cliff—Lula's paternal grandparents—were forced to meet in clandestine visits on Friday nights in Milano, Texas, where Louisia lived with her children, and for a time with Lula, whose mother, after whom she was named, had died when Lula was two. One of the earliest of Lula's vivid memories was of her grandfather Jenkins's long arms wrapping around her in an embrace, with treats for all the children stuffed into his pockets.

Lula's father, Norman Jenkins Cliff, was a farmer who grew squash, persimmons, apples, pears and chickens in a life that sometimes seemed idyllic to his youngest child. He was also tough, strong willed and unswerving in his morals.

Lula was five when her father took a new wife, "a beautiful Indian lady" named Ardela Fantry. The marriage ended tragically when Norman caught her with another man, an incident Lula remembered many years later in vivid detail. "I was playing. Papa came back and asked me where my mother was. 'Probably in the bedroom,' I said. Papa knocked on the door. Nobody said nothing. He took out his key and opened the door. There she was in bed with this man. 'Get up and put your clothes on and go home,' Papa told him. He didn't raise his voice, and that really hurt her.

"It was still early in the day. Papa just went about his work. She had a corn on her foot. The doctor was treating it with antiseptic tablets he said would kill forty-eight mules, but it didn't seem to get any better. She was writing. I thought she was probably writing her folk. Then she took three tablets and she killed herself. She was writing to her family, 'Norman didn't get upset.' "

Lula was only sixteen when she married Alvin Ailey, a good-looking young man she had met in church and gotten to know at picnics and other community events. Norman objected to their marriage on the grounds that Alvin and his impoverished family had no "get-up-and-go." Doomed from the start, their marriage began, at her father's insistence, with a wedding night in the bride's home in a room with a lamp that was to remain lighted all night.

Looking back, Lula could not remember if her husband was present at their son's birth. Eighteen at the time, she went into labor on the afternoon of January 4, 1931, in her father-in-law's wooden cabin, in a room that contained only the bed she lay on, a cot and a potbellied stove.

Dr. F. F. Flanagan, an imperturbable white family doctor in Rogers, arrived when called that afternoon but promptly read the signs of a delayed delivery and made himself comfortable. He called for a spit cup, dipped some snuff, then kicked off his boots and fell asleep on the cot.

Alvin Ailey Jr. was born during the dark, icy morning of January 5. The doctor awoke an hour before he arrived and, calling for hot water, delivered the child without further delay. The baby seemed unremarkable, at least for the first few moments after his birth. "Look at that kid," the doctor suddenly cried. Alvin had strained up to stare around him, resting on his pudgy elbows as if to survey the world. He had moved so little in the womb that Lula wondered if her first child was dead. "But he got busy as soon as he was born."

He was a big baby, with so large a head that his mother wondered whether he might be hydrocephalic. He also displayed a profound reluctance to walk on his own, so Lula carried him everywhere, walking slowly with him slung on her hip for the first year and a half of his life. "I wouldn't let him walk anywhere," Lula remembered. "I just thought he couldn't. But one day I told him, 'You sure are getting heavy. I'm going to have to put you down.'

"I put him down on the ground. And that little boy spun around like a top. I said, 'I thought you told me you couldn't walk.' He said I didn't let him. He made two or three flips like he'd been experimenting."

That the child was so large and active seemed something of a miracle. Cradling Alvin in her arms just after his birth, his undernourished mother found she was unable to breast-feed him. "One of Alvin's great-uncles, Uncle John, was a minister, and he had a club," Lula recalled. "When people got babies or were sick or something, everybody in the group that belonged to his church had to bring this person a pound of beans or flour or sugar or something." Sugar from the Benevolent Society was wrapped in a cloth to create "sugar tits" for the roly-poly baby until he was able to eat table food that his mother crushed with a spoon.

With thirteen men, women and children living in the cold, single-walled cabin, there was as little room as there was food, so when Alvin was three months old, his parents moved with him to a one-room cabin of their own. Just outside Rogers, the cabin was on the property of Horace Crouth, a white landowner with a reputation for tightfisted-ness, who allowed them to live there in return for working on his farm.

What their new home made up for in privacy, however, it lacked in comforts. The only furniture was a cot and a pot-bellied stove for warmth and for cooking. Meals were milk from a farm cow, bread made from hand-crushed corn and water that came from a muddy, dirty tank.

Alvin Ailey Sr. fled three months later, abandoning his wife and son. With the fierce determination that would rule her life and that of her child, Lula decided she would remain on the farm and make a better life for herself. She was soon taking in washing and ironing, the time-honored work of black women. And she planted a bean garden that fed the two—and indirectly prompted the first of many moves.

One day when Alvin was two, Lula put on a pot of beans to cook for dinner that night. She left for work at Mr. Crouth's, looking over from time to time to make sure that her son was playing safely in the yard. But when she went home to check on the beans, which were just beginning to soften, there seemed to be fewer in the pot. She asked

Alvin what had happened to them and he told her he didn't know. But that night, after dinner, he began to groan and Lula noticed that his stomach was distended. He had eaten the half-cooked beans.

She gathered up the child, propped him on her back and began the eight-mile walk into Rogers to Dr. L. E. Etter, a white doctor who treated blacks. It was late, and the country roads were not only unpaved but dark. Trees and bushes reached out over the road, scratching Lula and her baby as they hurried along, Lula watching for the hidden attackers that black women had good reason to fear.

Lights appeared in the distance. They had arrived at last. Would Dr. Etter even open his door to them? Lula knocked at the back and he appeared, dressed in pajamas, and took the two into his consulting room. Castor oil was prescribed, as well as a good night's rest in the doctor's house. The next morning, horrified that Lula had walked all the way to his house, Dr. Etter drove them home and was even more shocked to see their bleak living conditions. He returned the following day. His wife needed help, he said. Would they move to his home, to servant quarters behind his house? After deliberating for a week, Lula packed their possessions in a flour sack and walked back into Rogers with her son.

Life with the Etters was pleasant until Alvin Sr. returned in May 1935. The reunion was not a happy one. "He was a big, fine-looking guy, dark skinned with black curly hair. He was a good man. He wasn't rude to me. He was a straight well-dresser, but he just wasn't a well-worker. He just didn't have the education to take care of a family. His family was the same. They depended on Mr. Crouth all their lives. So I just made up my mind I was going to do something about this.

"I told my father I was going to separate from him. And my daddy told me, 'You married him, you're going to stay with him. There will be no divorces in this Cliff family.' I said to myself I'd fix him." At the time she was earning $3 a week, her highest salary during the Rogers years. "I started saving it up. I didn't tell anybody what I was going to do."

Lula left the Etters and her husband four months later, in early September. At the railroad station in Rogers, she asked the clerk to sell her a ticket for as far away as the $8 in her pocket would buy. She and Alvin boarded the midnight train and left for Wharton, Texas, arriving very early the next morning to find themselves stranded with no money on the station platform. Maggie Earl, a gentle, observant black woman who had been traveling on the same train, invited Lula to live with her until Lula found her bearings in Wharton. There were chores to be done in the Earl household and cotton to be picked in the fields beyond.

Alvin picked with his mother, although his work consisted mostly of an occasional, rather lordly separating of the unopened bolls that had found their way into the sacks of cotton. Mostly, Lula recalled, he slept on top of the sacks.

Lula had a sharp tongue and was, as she would later laughingly describe herself, "a tough old hen." She could be just as unbending to her little boy, who in his earliest years was often left alone or with unfamiliar relatives. At times, weary from working, Lula would drink too much.

She was also a living, thrilling embodiment of theatricality. Tall, thin and graceful, with glowing dark eyes and a teasing smile, she had the kind of clear, casual beauty seen in white models of the 1940s. She was fanciful and unpredictable, and not the most comfortable mother for an introspective and uncertain child. But though she would brush off the suggestion many years later, her behavior fed the kind of youthful fantasy and imaginative thought that breeds artists. And she accepted her son as an equal.

"Alvin and I, we kind of listened to each other. He'd say, 'Lula, let's do so-and-so' and expect me to do it. He was kind of bossy. He'd call me Lula until I started teaching him to call me Mama when he was eight or nine."

She began to suspect that her toddler son might be unusually bright when Alvin, who followed her everywhere once he began to walk, found an unusual Christmas present for her and gave it a name that Lula found intriguing. "He picked up everything on the street. One time, he found a stick, made like a chicken breast." After stripping the bark and polishing the forked stick, he presented it to his mother. "Gee, how beautiful," Lula told him. "Well, I thought you'd like it," he answered. "Now I'm going to give it a name."

" 'I said, 'What's the name?' He said, 'A cottee.' And I've looked everywhere to see what that means, and it's nowhere."

The two shared precious times of closeness, telling jokes and reading stories from "some old books" Lula had bought. They took turns retelling the stories to each other, and from day to day Alvin never forgot whose turn it was. He sat with Lula while she quilted, threading needles for her and telling her about his day. They took long walks in the woods, where a favorite activity of Alvin's was picking bouquets of wildflowers and weeds for his mother, some of which they saved and dried. "That little boy nearly picked himself to death," Lula said. "Anything that bloomed—wild onions, Crow Poison, dandelions, whatever."

On one such walk they passed a deserted old wood-frame house peering out at them through the trees. Built on stilts near the Brazos River, the shack was livable. The roof didn't leak. There was a potbellied stove. Lula guessed that somebody had moved on to Houston or Dallas once the children were grown.

Alvin stopped and turned to his mother. He loved the house, he said. Couldn't they live there, in a home of their own? Lula agreed. For the past nine months they had been staying with Fannie Warfield, a black woman who lived in nearby Wharton. It was time to move on. Mrs. Warfield helped them furnish the house, and they moved in. As always, though, it was not to last.

Lula was now earning enough money picking cotton to afford three full meals a day, but she soon realized that her little son was carefully putting parts of his meals aside. " 'You're supposed to clean your plate,' I told him, because we didn't have that much food."

She noticed that Alvin was taking the leftover food and disappearing with it outside the house. One day she followed him quietly and discovered that he was hand-feeding the most enormous chicken snake she had ever seen. She knew it was not poisonous, but the sight of the huge snake, along with a frightening shower of praying mantises that her son had shaken free one day from a tree near the front porch, made up her mind to move.

Lula slipped back to the house and announced to her son that they would leave for Rogers the next day, returning later for his pet. They never did return. She found work cooking and cleaning for Mrs. Dorothy Ball, a white woman in Rogers who had a cabin where Lula and Alvin could live.

Almost five now, Alvin was able to cross town by himself to play with his twin cousins, Franny Lee and Tranny Lee. It was a relatively carefree time at first. "Mrs. Ball was such a sweet woman," Lula recalled. "Our house was in the back. She used to come to the window and sing 'Walking My Baby Back Home' when the time came for me to come in and work." One day, hanging laundry to dry in the sun, Lula looked up and across the road to see a young white woman watching her from beyond the picket fence. Their eyes met, and the woman waved and disappeared. Lula later learned that she was Bonnie Parker of Bonnie and Clyde fame, hiding out with members of the Parker-Barrow gang who lived in Rogers.

Violence of a much more personal nature was to follow when, on her way back to the house after work, Lula was raped. Her face contorted with disgust, decades after the attack, remembering the old white man who raped her. Stumbling into the house, battered and weeping uncontrollably, she could not tell her little boy what had happened as he tried to help her, running for a wet rag to wash her face.

Alvin did all he could think to do to calm and take care of his mother, so suddenly and uncharacteristically helpless. But a five-year-old boy could do little for such pain.

He found out what had happened, almost before he knew what the word *rape* meant, when he overheard adults murmuring about the attack. His mother never discussed it.

Three moves followed in quick succession. Lula and Alvin went to live briefly with Nettie Corouthers, Alvin's aunt on his father's side and the twins' mother. Then it was south to Milano and the home of Lula's sister Inez Douglas. Finally, the two returned to Aunt Nettie's place again. There Alvin followed the girls, who were slightly older, into kindergarten and was allowed to stay, although he was too young to enroll in the church school. To the teacher's surprise, he was soon singing his way through the multiplication tables.

The days passed in ordinary pursuits. A chubby child nicknamed "Big Head," Alvin shot marbles in the road and had a brick lobbed at him by a little girl with whom he played. The amount of blood was frightening, but the injury left only a small vertical scar on his forehead that would later add a touch of extra character to the faunlike beauty gazing out of photographic theater headshots.

Many hours were spent watching trucks and trains go by. When the children got carried away one day and sat on the track as a freight train approached, Lula appeared in the nick of time and "whupped" them with a switch torn from a handy peach tree for the punishment.

Sunday mornings were spent in fervent song and prayer at the tiny Mount Olive Baptist Church on a dusty, unpaved road across from the railroad tracks. The one-room, white-frame building is one of the few landmarks of Alvin's childhood still standing in Rogers.

The air inside the tiny church is musty on a scorching July afternoon, sunlight filtering through the windows that range the length of the room. Today everything has a worn but cherished look—stick-on stained-glass patterns that cover the windows, tufts of faded plastic flowers sprouting here and there, paper fans and wooden benches and folding chairs, an upright piano and simple wooden pulpit and altar.

On either side of the altar are straight chairs, covered with blue cushions, on which the devoted sit facing the congregation and publicly "get right with God."

The thrilling power of ·vhat went on here, of songs and personalities lovingly remembered by an observant little boy, is not so hard to imagine. Not only were there mesmerizing four-hour services but also the sense of growing up in the faith and in an enduring community of the faithful.

Alvin was mischievous and a bit of a rebel. His church pennies were dispensed a few here, a few there, in various collections. Once, a nickel somehow remained rooted inside his pants pocket. "Mama," he whispered to Lula, reverting to babyhood, "I was baaaad. You gave me a nickel to put in the church and I got a nickel left. I wonder how it got into my pocket."

Sister Hattie Taplin, president of the missionary society and wife of the pastor, would sometimes ask the children to lead a prayer. "Which one of you youngsters would like to pray?" Miss Hattie asked one Sunday. Alvin waved his arm but another child was called on and made his way through "Now I Lay Me Down to Sleep." Miss Hattie asked for another volunteer. Again, Alvin's arm shot up and again he was not chosen. A second child cantered through the Lord's Prayer for the congregation. "All right, Alvin Ailey Jr.," Miss Hattie finally called out.

Irritated at having to wait so long for his turn, Alvin knelt, cleared his throat loudly and stood up, without uttering a word.

"Well, you did one thing right, Alvin," Miss Hattie said. "You got down on your knees." The congregation exploded into laughter. Had anyone ever heard of a prayer like that? Miss Hattie asked rhetorically. "Alvin had his way, or else," Lula recalled. "It was the longest time before we could stop laughing."

Baptisms were an integral part of the life of the church. Down a slight incline from the church was a pond ringed with thick grass, scrub and a few trees, where the sacrament took place. Deacons stood in the water, beating back snakes and keeping at bay, the children hoped, the alligator they believed to live there.

One by one, the children entered the pond, the boys dressed only in their underpants, and were lowered backwards into the water. As they were released, they scrambled up the bank and were toweled dry and wrapped in white sheets by the church sisters. Then they made their way back up to the church to dress. On this all-important Sunday in Alvin's young life, the joyous prayers were interrupted by Miss Hattie's voice suddenly raised in the haunting, troubled spiritual "I Been 'Buked and I Been Scorned." Unforgettable intimations of pain as well as of mortality lay in the song's simple words. Pain and joy, Alvin learned early, usually accompanied each other.

Work often took Lula away from Alvin, and she sometimes screamed at him and hit him when he cried at her departures. At times the abuse was psychological. Cruelly, she once told him that his father was a dashing young man named Eddie Warfield, whom Alvin had observed from afar in a barroom brawl. Although she confessed soon after that she had been teasing, a lifelong doubt was planted in Alvin's mind.

His life was soon to change profoundly, with another move. Determined to make a home for herself and her son, Lula searched relentlessly for better and better jobs. She was driven to provide a good life for the two of them, no matter the cost. She hated "handouts," wanting no one "to give me something for nothing."

In the summer of 1936, Lula came across an advertisement in a local newspaper for work in Navasota, a larger town where help was needed preparing meals for a highway crew. She dropped Alvin off with an older sister and left for Navasota.

Three weeks passed and she returned. Her five-year-old son, pushed by his dislike for a pretty, slightly older little cousin, had left Rogers, hitchhiking the miles to Milano and another aunt. Alvin later intimated that the children had experimented sexually with each other. "Stars of mercy," Lula exclaimed many years after. "Oh, boy, maybe that's why they were mad at each other. You never can tell what children will do." She collected her son and the two traveled back to Navasota—to a time Alvin would remember as one of the happiest of his life.

two

A LIGHT AND
SHADOWED PARADISE

"My whole early life in Texas was a kind of rambling, rural life," Alvin once said. "We lived around with a lot of people. We were always on the go. I began to feel as if there were a lot of trains in my life. I also remember that I felt very alienated—never really having a father. I always felt like an outsider around kids who did. I was always very lonely—I knew that I was loved, but I never felt understood."

Navasota must not at first have seemed a promising place to Alvin. He and his mother moved into the boardinghouse where the road crew lived. Five months after they arrived in town, Lula became very ill and was hospitalized for an emergency appendectomy, followed by an eye operation. For the first time in his life, at the age of six, Alvin was left entirely alone to fend for himself.

At the hospital, Lula met the three doctors who operated a clinic in town, and they offered her work that would help pay her hospital bills. Then she was hired to work at the hospital, sterilizing surgical instruments and assisting elderly patients. It was an unusual job for a black woman, but it paid $12.50 a week, the highest wages she had ever earned.

Life grew even more promising when Lula met a man who would

become one of the most important people in her son's life. Amos Alexander, gangling and quiet with a pronounced limp, was one of Navasota's most successful black businessmen, known and respected by both blacks and whites. Fifteen years Lula's senior, he seemed much older to her from the first. She had gone one Saturday night with a group of other girls "dressed cute" to a café in Navasota, owned by a husband and wife who were known as Booby and Fanny, that had a jukebox and the best food in town. Although the women were asking the men to dance that night, Amos hobbled over and asked Lula's name.

He began to visit her regularly at the boardinghouse, and then informed her that he was going to take her to his home. Lula was intrigued but as always stubbornly cautious when fate threatened to smile unbidden on her. "His house had a guest room, a dining room, a kitchen and an outdoor toilet. He had all kinds of trees, pear, pecan, God knows what the other trees were. We had known each other for about a year. I told him I'd think about it." Eventually, she and Alvin moved in with Amos, whom Lula always considered a boyfriend although he was intent on marrying her. "We were all crazy about her," Ruby Alexander Phillips, Amos's sister, said.

Everyone had been the same in Rogers, one of Alvin's cousins later commented. In Navasota, however, whites lived in one area and blacks in another. An older, much bigger town with a larger population than Rogers, Navasota was cosmopolitan in comparison. Like Rogers it had grown up around an all-important railroad, but the more commercial Navasota had a reputation for rowdiness in its early history. Founded as a stagecoach stop known as Nolansville in 1831, it became Navasota in 1858, its name likely derived from the Indian word *nabatoto*, which means "muddy water."

The town was a rough-and-ready place. Its center was and is bisected by railroad tracks, over which a long, low, handsome brown depot once presided at the juncture of tracks traveled by the Missouri Pacific and Southern Pacific Railroads. A bronze statue of La Salle on a main street commemorates the death of the seventeenth-century explorer in Navasota, at the hands of his own men. The town was also notorious for its Marshal Frank Hames, the lawman who finally captured Bonnie Parker and Clyde Barrow.

Navasota had a reputation for culture as well as carousing. One of its earliest recorded theatrical performances consisted of a pet brown bear, fed with a bowl of honey, waltzing with slaves in the old Nolan Hotel in a floor show for hotel guests and townspeople. There was an opera house on Tenth and McAlpin, and in 1885 the Dramatic Club, a little-theater group, performed regularly in town. Stock companies included Navasota on their tours, performing there on Friday nights and Saturday afternoons. And Alvin would long remember the blues singers and minstrel shows that traveled through Texas during his young years.

Navasota grew as it became established as a railroad terminus. Newcomers flocked into town. Freight was received from around the country, and wagons brought flour, cotton, lumber, wool and meat to be shipped out. Wagon drivers learned to sleep near their loads. Bars had sprung up on South Railroad Street and around the depot, and robberies and brawls were commonplace.

The wagons are gone today, of course, but much of Navasota remains unchanged by time. Most of the buildings that lined East Washington Street in the late 1800s, running parallel and open to the tracks, are still standing a century later, as is the pool hall that was one of Amos's chief business ventures and the building that was once the Dixie Theater, the segregated movie house where Alvin and his young friends could see a cowboy movie on Saturday afternoon for nine cents.

The cotton gins and plantations have mostly disappeared, although at Tom Moore's spread the long fields and workers' low shacks remain much as they were when Amos shuttled day laborers to nearby cotton fields. Grimes County, where Navasota is located, has become primarily beef country, its pastures filled with grazing cows and dotted by small, insect-eating white egrets known locally as cow birds.

Of the twelve Alexander children, only Amos remained in the town where he was born. Jeff Alexander, a preacher and vegetable farmer, and Ellen Alexander, who ran a fish restaurant near the depot and later a boardinghouse, were busy, forward-looking parents who had emigrated to Texas from Louisiana, like many Navasota blacks. All the girls were sent to college by their mother. The boys were to be sent by their father, but he was able to put just one through school. The rest became cooks, with Amos the only child in the family to go into business.

Amos's stubborn streak became evident early on when he jumped from a corn crib, sprained his ankle and repeatedly refused to be taken to a doctor, choosing to limp through the rest of his life. As he grew up, he took on a variety of jobs, moving up from wrapping and delivering packages in a white grocery store and delivering laundry to the white families for whom Mrs. Alexander washed and sewed, to picking cotton with impressive speed on plantations in West Texas, where crops were large and good money could be made from the backbreaking work.

He invested much of the money he made. Formal and rather standoffish, Amos impressed people as a man of few words, "a very nice man who paid his bills well and didn't carry on with much foolishness," as Roy Elliot Goodwin, a white businessman and the unofficial town historian, put it.

Everyone seemed to know Amos in town, in the fields and at the Truevine Baptist Church, which he joined in 1925 after separating from his first wife. A fastidious man, he dressed with a quiet flair, and he enjoyed and was good at gambling. "In Navasota, they would have fish fries and Saturday night suppers," Lula recalled. "While they were having those suppers the men would get together down on the Brazos River and have their gambling games. Dice, cards, I don't know. Maybe poker. Amos would go with big money. And maybe later in the game he'd get broke. He would send somebody to the house with a note to send him some money. But he'd send the note in one of his shoes, so I'd know he really sent it."

That a young boy of none too comfortable means would be impressed by all this worldly expertise is not difficult to imagine. And Amos, devoted to his own mother, may have seen something of himself in Alvin. He was able to offer the young boy something Alvin had never had—security and a safe home.

Amos's white box house, inherited from his mother and then torn down and rebuilt with the same boards, sat on the corner of Roosevelt Avenue and South Malcolm Street in the swampy black section of town known as Mudville. The kitchen was the first large, well-appointed one Lula had known, and she soon filled it with the heady perfumes of southern home cooking. There was a grandfather clock, a Victrola and a piano on which Alvin worked out a couple of tunes by ear. "We had a ball," Lula remembered. "We sang at Christmas. The house was always full of music. Our favorite tune was 'Annie Laurie.' "

Behind the house were gardens, animals and an orchard that Alvin helped to plant. Tomatoes grew in the garden, along with peas, okra and corn that Alvin and his young cousin Lucious were responsible for picking, and then packing into small baskets and selling to neighbors. Amos gave Alvin his first dog, taught him to ride a horse and assigned him the job of feeding the pigs and chickens.

Alvin felt loved, but, as he later recalled, "when Mr. Alexander's sister came to visit him and brought along her small children, I always felt very alone and left out. Although they were extremely nice to me, I was always reminded at those times that he—this man—was not my real father and that I was existing in a make-believe situation."

Alvin was enrolled in the George Washington Carver School in a white section of Navasota. The trip to school and back was a potentially adventure-filled walk and run along field trails, across the Southern Pacific Railroad track and under its stopped trains, and through the less rough-hewn black neighborhood of Freedman Town. There was always a flock of children, although Alvin tended to tag along behind or walk ahead of his schoolmates.

He seems to have charmed the Carver principal, J. C. Madison, who had introduced a music program into the combined elementary and high school. Madison was sufficiently impressed with Alvin's fondness for music to find him an instrument when the child expressed a sudden and surprising desire in fourth grade to play the tuba.

"Head," as Alvin's nickname was now shortened to, was by most accounts a model and rather meek student, although he could be outspoken. "Alvin was not a person to start a discussion," Darcell Jackson, a classmate, recalled. "But he liked to lead. He had ideas. And he wanted to be successful. Amos was successful."

Alvin tended to get into trouble in school only when everyone else did, as in pranks like eraser fights for which the entire roomful of students was whipped. James Henley, who attended school with Alvin, remembers him as "an ordinary little fat-headed boy, short, a little on the chumpy side." But he was smart. "Alvin made good grades. We'd copy off his papers. Pass them under the desks. If he made a mistake, sometimes the whole class would make a mistake. He'd be getting his lesson while we'd be showing out. That's why we had to copy."

Henley was not surprised, he says, that Alvin became famous. But he did not show any special aptitude for music, at least in the stick and tambourine band in which class participation was required. "He never did any dancing in school. And I never saw him at Sugar White's, where we used to go dance on Friday, Saturday, maybe Sunday. He just didn't go out much."

Alvin was also mannerly with the girls. Evelyn Ashford, another classmate, remembered him affectionately: "He didn't pull our pigtails on the way to the pencil sharpener." He was nonetheless a popular candidate for their teasing.

Alvin's life outside school seems to have been a good deal more engrossing. He alternated between constant talking and scribbling in the large ruled pads he carried everywhere with him, even while doing chores. There he sketched insects and small animals and wrote incomprehensible notes to himself about the drawings or what he had seen or thought about that day. He was seldom satisfied with the results, incurring Lula's exasperation as he tore sheet after sheet off the pads and threw them away.

As he grew older, Alvin made occasional trips to the Dew Drop Inn. Every small southern town seemed to have a Dew Drop bar or café. The relatively circumspect one in Navasota, a shed on a grassy corner where two dirt roads intersected, was run by Iva "Sugar" White, a big, light-skinned black woman who made memorable hamburgers, chicken and ice cream. It was a place where students hung out on Sundays, black and white families ate meals and working men collected their lunches and, if they were unmarried, their dinners, too. At night, on weekends, the place was full of hot, pulsing music and fabulously dressed black bodies jammed tight together on the small dance floor.

Too young to venture into those late-night parties, Alvin would peer through the window with other children, learning almost subliminally to love what poured out of the jukebox. "I remember the music and the dancing—an atmosphere of sensuality always accompanied by fear or a sense of impending trouble," Alvin said. "There were always fights and talks about so-and-so's love affair—there were killings." He was sometimes troubled that the men and women he saw pulsating so sensuously at the Dew Drop Inn turned up at church on Sundays, although he loved the theatricality of the throbbing services at the Truevine Baptist Church. A solemn child, he had wondered anyway about God.

Christmas was a happy time for Lula and Alvin, even during their relatively poor days in Rogers, when Lula would cut down a pine tree and trim it with bits of saved ribbon and popcorn stuck on pins. But the holiday was also the occasion of a painful revelation for the child. "When Alvin was about seven or eight, he wrote a Christmas list from here to the end of the living room," Lula recalled. "That's when I told him there was no Santa Claus. I thought I might just as well come down to the point. I am the Santa Claus, I told him. He kind of said, 'Ooo-eee, you kidding?' No, I said. 'You had to do that?' That's right, I said."

"Unbelievable," Alvin responded at last. "Well, I'll tell you what to do. Give me ten dollars and I'll buy both of us presents."

A day or so later, still thinking over this news, he returned to Lula to continue the conversation. "Mom, you know that's a shame," he told Lula. "Just look at the parents who have lied to their children. Now I'm wondering if they lied about God." His mother was taken aback. Troubled, she watched him ponder it all for another few days and then decided to talk to him. "I told him, 'Honey, as far as I know there is a God. He is a spirit.' Something similar to that. I asked him who he thought made his body, gave him two arms and one heart. 'Who gave men knowledge to make false teeth and eyeglasses?' I asked him. 'The whole world would be blind. The whole world would be toothless.' I just kept pushing him after that. He worried about it for a while. Then he told me, 'Well, I believe it, Mother.' "

Around the same time, Alvin provided Lula with rather chilling evidence of her importance to him. Several kittens were living in the house, one of which mewed loudly and wound around Lula's feet in the kitchen. "You get on my nerves," Lula told the cat. "One of these days you're going to end up dead or I'm going to kill you." When the kitten relieved itself on the kitchen floor one morning, it was the last straw.

"That's it," Lula told the little cat. "You're going to end up dead before the day is gone." Around noon, Alvin came into the kitchen. "You don't need to worry anymore," he told Lula. "I just killed the cat." He had drowned the kitten in a stream near the house. Lula asked him why. "Mama," he explained, "the cat worried you and you said you was going to kill it so I did it for you."

In the way of children, Alvin kept a good deal of his life from his mother. Most of the boys in the neighborhood, including Alvin, played in the Brazos and Navasota Rivers even though they could not swim and had been forbidden by their parents to try. One of Alvin's best friends was a Mexican boy who lived down the street. The family taught Alvin Spanish and an appreciation for Mexican food and adventure. "Life was much less interesting after the Chicanos moved away," he later wrote. "There were no more romps through the moccasin snake-ridden countryside, no confrontations with the white folks' dogs on the other side of the tracks. Life seemed lonely."

Another best friend was Chancey, an older boy with a reputation for bad behavior who filled the gap left by the departure of the Mexican family. Chancey, who had never known his parents, was being raised by an old aunt in extreme poverty. Looking back from the perspective of adulthood, his schoolmates recalled that he always seemed to be in a hurry and would not allow himself to be picked on. Physically strong and tough, short but well muscled, he fought in the gangs of neighborhood boys who habitually drove one another across the tracks from Freedman Town to Mudville and back.

"He was kind of a hard-time fella," Henley recalled. "He was kind of old-looking. He looked as if he came into the world fighting. He liked to try to gamble. There was an older guy named Bounce who liked to cheat at dice. Me and Chancey and the others would play for fifteen cents. We liked to hang out with Bounce. We thought we were big."

Chancey and Alvin liked to play in a water tank just outside of town. Twenty feet deep, it was a dangerous and forbidden place. One day Alvin slipped into the water, began to flail about in panic and was drowning when Chancey pulled him out and onto the ground. He jumped on the younger boy's body and began to pump it, trying to push the swallowed water out. Gradually, Alvin's fear and panic subsided, to be replaced by new and frightening feelings of physical pleasure.

It must have been like most youthful sexual experimentation. Did sky and grass whirl together and breath grow short in that first encounter with the rough older boy? Were those somehow frightening sensations of pleasure followed by an instinctive guilt and terrible anticipation? However Alvin felt, wrestling sessions soon began to occur in which Chancey would climb onto Alvin's body and rub against it. The experience considerably quashed some tentative sexual exploration with a girl in his school. Many years later, Alvin described the sessions to a lover not just as an instance of youthful sexual exploration but as an experience of haunting purity and loss.

But the light and shadowed paradise of Navasota was soon to become a thing of the past. In the autumn of 1941, Lula decided to follow friends to Los Angeles, where, she had heard, there was lucrative war work and a chance at a better life for her and her son. She was tired of her life in Texas, and she was not interested in marrying Amos. "There was the age difference and everything. My girlfriend said to me, What do you want with that old ugly man? I had some cousins in California who were working and in good condition. I thought the best thing for me to do was to get my heels aclickin'."

Alvin was to stay behind to finish the school year. Angry, he begged his mother to reconsider, but Lula would not be persuaded. She left Navasota with $18 in her pocket, her only money, arriving in Los Angeles on January 2, 1942, three days before Alvin's eleventh birthday. Bidding her good-bye, Alvin shed few tears when she left, affected, perhaps, by Amos's stoical acceptance of her departure. But the months he lived alone with Amos were sad and filled with dread at the thought of his coming departure for a strange new city up north at the edge of a vast ocean.

Alvin wrote often to his mother with news of his life in Navasota. He sent her $15 he had earned picking and selling bones for fertilizer, a popular depression-era job among blacks and whites in the area. Then school and his life with Amos were over. The man everyone thought of as his uncle drove Alvin to Houston to board a train bound for Los Angeles, giving him a few dollars of pocket money and a bagged meal of a chicken sandwich and jelly cake to eat on the trip.

Such journeys were not uncommon for black children in those days. The experience was remembered clearly, although in reverse, by the writer Maya Angelou, who was to become Alvin's friend and dance partner in California. "When I was three and Bailey four," she wrote of herself and her brother in *I Know Why the Caged Bird Sings*, "we had arrived in the musty little town, wearing tags on our wrists which instructed—'To Whom It May Concern'—that we were Marguerite and Bailey Johnson Jr., from Long Beach, California, en route to Stamps, Arkansas, c/o Mrs. Annie Henderson.

"Years later I discovered that the United States had been crossed thousands of times by frightened Black children traveling alone to their newly-affluent parents in Northern cities, or back to grandmothers in Southern towns when the urban North reneged on its economic promises."

Did kindly fellow travelers take an interest in the small chubby boy from Navasota as the train traveled across Texas and through New Mexico and Arizona on into California? Did Alvin spend his time looking out the window, perhaps noticing small boys like himself, waving the train on as he once had as it sped through their dusty towns? No record of his thoughts on that thirty-hour trip exists. At its end, he alighted at Union Station, Los Angeles, and spotted his mother waiting beside the gate.

He ran toward her, and then slowed, handing her a small, stained paper bag. "What is this?" Lula asked, bending to greet her son. He reached out and crooked one arm around his mother's neck. "It's the lunch they fixed for me, Mama," Alvin murmured. "I thought maybe you was hungry."

three

LOVE AND NEED AND
GROWING UP

When Lula and Alvin walked across the sprawling, busy train station and out onto the streets of wartime Los Angeles, they entered a vibrant, chaotic world.

Manana had once ruled here, in a place where land and oil and gold were to be had, it seemed, only for the asking. But in 1942, Los Angeles was a city of the newly arrived, with residents of a mere dozen years or so counting themselves as longtime citizens. Formed by Spanish Catholic missionaries, the city was by the 1800s imbued with the Protestant work ethic of American adventurers and sterner Yankees. The arrival of the railroads and the construction of a harbor in nearby San Pedro, wild real estate booms and pitiless droughts, all had helped to transform a sleepy town into a major American urban center in the last quarter of the nineteenth century. World War I brought in a new wave of industrialization and agricultural production. Aircraft plants and shipyards sprang up during World War II, and Americans headed for the city from across the Midwest and South in search of wartime jobs.

Los Angeles was a sunny, easygoing mecca for crackpot religions and fantasies endorsed by the movie industry. Film played a major and intrinsic role in American lives by the time Alvin arrived there, thirty-two years after the construction of the city's first motion picture studio, a lean-to with canvas sets behind a Chinese laundry on Olive Street near Seventh Street.

But everyday life for Lula and Alvin revolved around the reality of black life in urban America in the 1940s, which was at least as harsh in its way as that of the rural small-town experiences they had left behind. Although there were cousins in Los Angeles, too, the warm and sometimes overbearing sense of family was gone. A new family had to be created, of friends, coworkers and schoolmates. A new life had to be carved out of long hours of mostly thankless work, days spent in crowded, hectic schools and nights in theaters and clubs where Lula and Alvin encountered a sophisticated black culture that hummed with unexpectedly familiar life.

Relatively little black migration to Los Angeles took place up to 1910, but it had increased dramatically by the 1930s, when the city boasted the largest black population of any urban area in the West. With the increase came growing racial discrimination and unrest between blacks and whites. But there were jobs and a black community established in—and confined to—the south-central section of the city, where Lula and Alvin eventually settled.

The greatest increase in black migration to Los Angeles took place during the war years of the 1940s, in part because of the promise of work in the wartime defense industry. By the spring of 1942, three to four hundred blacks were entering the city each day, reaching a peak in June 1943.

Lula had arrived in Los Angeles expecting to find a job in the aircraft industry, but when she applied for work, she was told that she must supply her birth certificate. She wrote back to Texas for it, and hunted for other work and a place to live, settling into a room in a boardinghouse on East Twenty-seventh Street in a bustling, predominantly black south-central neighborhood. The woman who owned the house, a fellow Texan, took the pretty young transplant under her wing, giving her a free room until she found a job and coaching her in how to speak and present herself in job interviews.

A month went by, during which Lula lived on a daily slice of bread and cabbage greens, cooked on a hot plate in her room. Unable to afford bus fares, she walked to interviews. Sundays meant a slight relaxation of economies. Across the street from the boardinghouse was a restaurant run by disciples of the black religious leader Father Divine, where Lula treated herself to sumptuous breakfasts. "Boy, they had scrambled eggs, grits, biscuits and jelly and jam, all for a dime!" she remembered with delight a half-century later.

Lula went to an employment agency and was shocked to learn that she would have to pay the firm to find her a job. Down to her last $2, she found work as a maid in a luxurious apartment building on Valencia Avenue in the Westlake section of Los Angeles. She was cleaning up after white folk as she had done in Texas, but it was a job. And once again fellow Texans extended unexpected kindness.

When the head housekeeper discovered that Lula was from her home state, she provided her with a four-room basement apartment on the premises for Lula and her son. It was to this dream home, better appointed and with more space than the two had ever known, that Lula took Alvin on his arrival.

Lula enrolled her son in the neighborhood public school, which happened to be white. "Alvin was the only little black boy there," she recalled. "He got disgusted because it was all white. I told him always hold your head up high, even if you don't have a quarter. Sometimes I think he did. But he wanted to go where some black kids were." No one had treated him badly, Alvin told her, but in just a few days he had begun to feel as if he were a curiosity to the other children and the teachers. And they were strange to him. He had never had a white friend. He wanted out.

Lula quickly found a new home—a three-room, second-floor apartment reached by an outside stairway in a small house on East Forty-third Place, only three blocks from a junior high school filled with black, Latin and Asian children. It was a long trek to her job on Valencia Avenue, and there was rent to pay. Lula was forced to take a second job cleaning offices in downtown Los Angeles, which meant a thirteen-hour workday and many solitary hours for Alvin, who performed some extra household chores.

Life there was a little like living in the suburbs, Lula recalled. "There was grass, and flowers. And lots of yard. We never did stay in the apartment. It was really lovely." Some five decades later, in a city and on a street worn and hardened by racial polarization, riots and ingrained poverty, the oddly stacked together–looking house at 912½ East Forty-third Place, now covered with pink stucco, still looked pretty and well kept.

Alvin felt comfortable at the nearby George Washington Carver Junior High School, which paid its students the compliment of high expectations and often loving attention. Enrollment had risen sharply during the war years, and school traditions reflected a country at war. Alvin was a "parachutist"-level reporter for the *Cross Roads*, the school newspaper, which boasted "turret gunners," "rear gunners," "navigators" and "pilots" on its staff. Graduation ceremonies for the class of 1945, known formally as "the Determinators," included a rendition by the school orchestra of "There's Something About a Soldier"—as well as the recitation of a poem called "The Negro Scientist," written and read by students with another student providing piano accompaniment.

At Carver, Alvin began the process of opening up and out to the world. He was not a consistent honor-roll student, although he was cited at graduation for three years of perfect attendance. He was recognized as having a gift for languages. Mathematics was a torment, and baseball frightened him. He generally avoided competitive sports after a little gratefully accepted discouragement from his mother, who feared that her boy, who had grown from a big baby into a hulking child, might hurt himself in the rough-and-tumble of games like football. "Oh, my God, you getting ready to get your leg broken?" Lula exclaimed when Alvin approached her with news of a school football game he was to play in. He had never considered that, he told her thoughtfully.

But the little boy who had written indecipherable poems for himself, then crumpled them and thrown them away, was now exposed to formal poetry in a creative writing class. He spent long hours reading in the school library. He wrote at home, in his time alone there, and began to feel consciously creative, largely because of the enthusiasm of several favorite teachers for their subjects. He also sang with gusto in the school glee club, directed by Mildred Cobbledick, one of those favorites.

Another was Lois Rabb, a teacher he would long remember. "She was a darling," Blanche Sutton, one of Alvin's schoolmates, said. "She lived in the neighborhood. She was a warm, loving teacher. More like a parent to us. You don't mind studying when a teacher is so personable."

The school staff believed in exposing its students to the larger world of the arts in field trips that were often partly subsidized by the teachers themselves to ensure that every child could take part. Alvin was to remember two trips most fondly. In one, Miss Cobbledick took the class to see a production of *The Mikado*. And when the children visited a radio station and met Lena Horne, already a ravishing young star, she gave them autographs.

During his years at Carver, Alvin had a brief—and expensive—fling with tap dance taught by Lauretta Butler, a neighborhood teacher who gave popular half-hour classes on Saturdays for fifty cents. "A bunch of kids were taking her classes," Lula recalled. "They wanted to be like Bill Robinson." Alvin lasted two months. Tap dance classes were not an enjoyable experience for a shy and introverted child. Lula was now making more money and managed to save much of what she earned, but she resented the $36 she paid for "those cotton-picking shoes."

But the most important part of Alvin's new life was his discovery of the teeming, seductive world of Central Avenue. Along that wide, long street, two blocks from school and four from home, were theaters, restaurants, nightclubs and bars—the Dew Drop Inn magnified and intensified—that formed the heart of black social and cultural life of the time. Even the names of the long-ago theaters and movie palaces—among them the Savoy, the Rosebud and the Florence Mills—have a magical glow. Cocktail lounges like the Last Word, the Down Beat and the Memo, or "Meemo" as it was pronounced by habitués, linger in the memories of those who drank there as sophisticated and fun.

Alvin spent many Saturdays in the Florence Mills and the Bill Robinson, both movie houses. At the Lincoln Theater, alone or with school friends, he watched top black vaudeville acts like Pearl Bailey, Billie Holiday and the raunchy comedian Pigmeat Markham, whose famous "Here Come De Judge" routine bemused him. He also saw Horne sing at the Lincoln and savored her dazzling beauty on the screen in *Cabin in the Sky* and *Stormy Weather*.

For children to frequent such places was not unusual then. "I did everything to try to keep him straight," Lula said many years later. "I would rather he go to a theater and watch than hang out around home or the avenue. That way he would maybe get with the right people, theater people who were trying to do something in the arts. Not someone shooting dice on the street."

Lula would question him about fights. No, Alvin told her, he never fought.

When Lula returned home from work on weeknights, Alvin would entertain her with wild stories of improbable adventures that day. "He'd make it exciting," Lula recalled. "He'd say, 'Guess what! I almost got hit by a car. I ran across the street and the brakes squealed.' I'd say, 'I told you to wait for the light.' He said, "It wasn't on there and I thought I could beat the car.'"

Alvin would occasionally help his mother out at her Saturday job. If not, he offered lively accounts of what he had seen in the theater that day. "He'd act it out, step by step," Lula said. "Oh, he was carried away by the dancers."

It was in a movie theater on Central Avenue that Alvin was first impressed by films with Gene Kelly and Fred Astaire, the Nicholas Brothers and Bill Robinson, and imitated them by himself in his back-yard. He was drawn to the dancing of Kelly, in particular, whom he would later in life remember as "a man who wore a shirt, pants and a tie and danced like a man."

With an allowance of twenty-five cents a week and pay for odd jobs that included the mowing of three or four lawns in the neighborhood, Alvin was able to spend a fair amount of time inside the theaters of Central Avenue. Sometimes he borrowed money from his mother, who had gotten a better-paying job at the Lockheed Aircraft Corporation the year after they moved to East Forty-third Place.

"I'd tell him no if I couldn't get something," Lula said. "If you had a fifty-dollar bill, you were rich. But if he ran out of money, I'd pay his way. We had a closet with a rug on the floor. Lots of times when I got paid, I'd throw money under it if I couldn't get to the post office. You could save money at the post office then. If he needed money, he'd put a note under the rug—'Mother, I took $5 today.'"

The now desolate Central Avenue at that time had the crowded, exuberant vitality of a Reginald Marsh urban nightlife painting. The Hotel Dunbar, a pink and chocolate-colored brick monolith on the avenue at Forty-second Street, was just a block from home, and Lula and Alvin ate dinner there and took in shows by top stars like Duke Ellington and his band. The hotel was also home to black performers appearing in the city, many of whom unwound late at night at the nearby Club Alabam, performing spontaneously as the fancy took them. Gone now, the nightclub, with its blazing neon lights, was one of Lula's and Alvin's favorites, a place where everyone went dressed up for Saturday night family dinner.

Between weekends there were long periods of solitude for Alvin while Lula was away at work on the 4 P.M. to midnight shift. But his first years at Carver were generally happy. He had fashioned a neatly ordered retreat for himself in his room upstairs, soft with filtered light from the street and fitted with a shelf lined with books, a record player given to him by Lula's godmother and a battered old typewriter Lula had bought for him secondhand. He put a few of his drawings up on the wall and made mobiles and hung them from the ceiling. The room, although not large, had enough space for a small bed, a table for his typewriter, a chair and a closet.

At one point Alvin also had a glass tank in which he kept a snake. "Mother, don't go in my room today," he told Lula the morning after the snake had arrived unannounced in the Ailey household. "I cleaned up real good. Now don't go in there." Lula asked him why and was told, "Just don't go. Promise?" His mother told him she would not promise, and as soon as Alvin left she slipped into his room.

"I thought, 'What doesn't that guy want me to see?' I couldn't wait until he got out of there to go to school. Then I walked in and he had this thing in a big fishbowl sitting up on the table beside his bed. A black little chicken snake. They had them at school or something. It scared the hell out of me." Alvin was not fooled. "Mother, I know you've been in my room," he said accusingly when she arrived home from work. "How?" she asked. "The snake was nervous," he told her.

During Lula's hours away from home, Alvin was looked in on by Ophelia Wilkes, who lived with a series of boyfriends in the adjacent upstairs apartment at the house on East Forty-third Place. Many years after, Alvin would scrawl her name in the penciled lists of subjects for ballets that he kept throughout his professional life. A caterer, Ophelia was very tall and thin with hair that never seemed to grow, which she wore natural. She was dark skinned and in her late fifties, although she looked much younger.

Alvin's already active theatrical imagination was sparked by Ophelia and by another of his mother's friends, a pretty woman named Margie with sophisticated hairdos and the highest of heels. He would never forget the day Wilkes shot her boyfriend, a railroading man, wounding him only superficially. Alvin was never told the details, but he was thrilled by the crowd of police and ambulances when he arrived home that day from school.

When Wilkes moved on, the Hurd family rented her apartment, providing Alvin with a grave and charming soulmate six years older. Ella Hurd, whom he eventually called "Sister," had a piano in her apartment. The two met daily after school to sing together, listen to Alvin's records and go over the music for Alvin's glee club assignments. He wrote a paper for her that enabled Hurd to skip her college freshman course in English composition. She tried to teach him how to play the piano, but he had no great talent for it. And his later attempts to teach her to dance reduced the soft-spoken matron, Ella Hurd Harris, to helpless giggles decades after as she tried to demonstrate a sinuous movement of the head and arms that had proved utterly impossible for that well-behaved young woman.

Hurd knew Alvin was smart, and given to thinking profound, often unspoken thoughts. They talked, for the most part, about religion and music, laughing together over the peculiarities and excesses of churchgoers at the gleaming white-painted McCoy Baptist Church nearby, where she had once played the organ and where the Aileys worshiped and sang in the choir. He read her things that he had written.

Hurd watched with amusement as two small neighborhood children, a brother and sister who had taken to this boy who loved babies, tailed Alvin to his home and back and through the streets like ducklings following in a mother's wake. She observed his growth into adulthood, capped by a senior prom date, complete with tux, with a good-looking schoolmate named Jean. She glowed with pride at a graduation honor he received.

There was little talk of a very personal nature, although Hurd sensed her friend was sometimes troubled. Alvin, she said years later, was "moody." "Sometimes he was very temperamental—really fiery— then again he would stand at the side of the house for hours and never speak. When this happened, one left him alone to commune with nature or whatever it was he wished to do. I think the yard offered a feeling of serenity—it was a peaceful place."

One event that may have brought on those moods was the arrival of an unwelcome third person in the Ailey family. On her own at last, Lula had become both more girlish and tougher after she landed the job at Lockheed. She and her son were financially better off, although she was still careful with her money. "All those girls that worked with me at Lockheed," Lula remembered. "They went crazy, making all that money. They bought fur coats and all that stuff. And they said, 'Girl, why don't you buy a fur coat?' I told them I didn't want one. I was always like that. I saved my money. Because I knew it wasn't going to last always. And boy, all of a sudden they started laying those people off. Terminating and all that type of stuff. And they were dead."

But Lula had her frivolous moments. Wilke's nephew was in the army, and his aunt enjoyed cooking for him and his friends. One of those friends was Fred Cooper, a quiet, polite sailor stationed at the naval base at Oxnard. Cooper soon gravitated toward the good-looking and vivacious Lula and asked her out.

Lula already had a devoted boyfriend, a married coworker at

Lockheed. She dated Cooper, however, even though his shyness exasperated her. She was not sorry when she learned that he was about to be shipped out to join the war effort. But he left money for Alvin, and then wrote from Hawaii asking for her ring size. He proposed in a telephone call and mailed her the ring.

"I said to myself that I had this beautiful diamond ring," she recalled. "He might go over and get killed. Isn't that awful? But Margie and I caught hands and did the floop-di-floop." Three months later he was back in Los Angeles.

"I heard these feet hit the steps and I said, 'That sounds like the eager man's feet.' And sure enough, I opened the door and he said, 'Surprise, I'm out of the navy.' He was out of the navy." The older men had been sent off ship. "I didn't care anything about it but I could see that he loved Alvin. I said now later, you know, later is a possibility there. You learn to love later."

Once more Lula allowed herself to care for a man who cared for her son. But unlike Amos Alexander, Fred Cooper pressed the issue of marriage. Alvin took it very hard. His closest friend, the most beautiful woman he knew, the adult who had been his sole protection against an unstable world, was about to desert him.

He locked himself in his room whenever Cooper visited, or went for long walks without telling his mother where he was headed, eventually to avoid the sounds of their lovemaking. Then came the shock of his mother's announcement that she and Cooper were to marry. He was already fourteen, he told Lula, and in another couple of years he would be able to support her. What did she need Fred Cooper for? "Look, I'm going to marry this man," his mother retorted. "I'm tired of getting up at four and going off to work." That, she felt, he understood.

At school, Miss Rabb drew Alvin out and tried to console him. And Cooper was patient. About three months after the wedding, he began taking Alvin with him to baseball and football games. By their first anniversary, the boy seemed to have accepted his stepfather, as well as his mother's involvement with him. But Alvin would always remember 1945 as the calamitous year that President Roosevelt died and his mother married.

The sorrow of losing his central place in his mother's life, exacerbated by the birth of his stepbrother, Calvin, in 1953, never completely left Alvin. Nor did his anger. Years after, there were times when he refused to go to the telephone when his mother called, telling friends to say he was out, and through much of his life he veered between a

cutting hatred of her and intense love and need. He swallowed his feelings, keeping them to himself for decades. But now he began to spend
more time away from the house, associating for a time with a set of
unsavory boys who were clearly headed for prison at an early age. In
brief notes Alvin made late in his life for an autobiography, one cryptic
memo suggests that Cooper may have had to intercede for his stepson
with the police, although no public record of an arrest exists.

Beneath the wariness and studied detachment that made for a
near-impenetrable protective shell, Alvin was lonelier than ever. And
because of that sense of loneliness and betrayal, those few in whom he
confided suggest, Alvin never quite trusted anyone, whether friend,
lover or colleague, for the rest of his life.

four

APPROACHING CENTER

Experiences and friends at a new school crowded in on Alvin's painful musings about his mother and her new husband, and eventually a new interest began to shape his life. In the fall of 1945, Alvin became a student at Thomas Jefferson High School on Hooper Avenue and East Forty-first Street, four blocks from his home. Many Carver pupils went on to Jefferson, which had a poor reputation and did not attract students from outside the neighborhood. But for Alvin and others, the school continued the work Carver had begun.

"Jefferson has always been mainly black," said Don Martin, a high school friend who became one of Alvin's earliest dance colleagues. "There were a lot of Mexicans, Chinese, Japanese then. Jeff was a school nobody wanted to go to. They thought it was a bad school. Blacks wanted to be as closely associated to white schools as possible." Like many, Martin had lied about his home address in order to get into a school in a better neighborhood. He was caught and transferred to Jefferson for his senior year. "I thought, 'Oh, God, this is the end of my world.' But it was the best thing that ever happened. When I got to Jefferson, I found out that it was totally different. The teachers were better. They were more interested in you. It was a better school."

As at Carver, it was school policy to take students on trips into worlds they might otherwise not experience. At Jefferson, a reluctant

Alvin got his first taste of downtown Los Angeles and concert dance when his class attended a performance by the Ballet Russe de Monte Carlo.

The Ballet Russe, formed by the Russian choreographer and dancer Léonide Massine in 1938, settled in the United States when war broke out. The troupe almost single-handedly introduced much of America to the exotic art of ballet, through exhaustive tours that took the dancers not only to big city opera houses but to the smallest and most improbable of cow-town auditoriums. When the company appeared in Los Angeles in the fall of 1945, it was at its artistic height, headed by the piquant Russian prima ballerina Alexandra Danilova and Frederic Franklin, her genial English partner.

The dancers that Alvin saw that Saturday matinee at the Los Angeles Philharmonic Auditorium included the American Indian ballerinas Maria Tallchief and Yvonne Chouteau, and a dancer named Karel Shook, an American who would teach ballet to Alvin in far-off New York City, improbably enough a scant ten years after this first boyhood glimpse of live dance.

Looking back, Alvin would remember best *Scheherazade*, the program's culminating ballet. Based on a tale from *The Thousand and One Nights* and danced to music of a thundering exoticism composed by Rimsky-Korsakov, the ballet told the story of the beautiful slave Zobeide, favorite concubine of Shah Shariar, and her lover the Favorite Slave. Michel Fokine, its choreographer, had included a protracted orgy and an even longer and more writhing death scene after Zobeide brings bloody vengeance on herself, the other concubines, a chorus of handsome male slaves and the eunuch who guards the harem.

The costumes were sensuously skimpy, and the ballet impressed some spectators as almost pornographic. All in all, it was entertainment one might have expected would appeal to a fourteen-year-old boy who had cut his artistic teeth on cowboy movie matinees back home in Texas. But Alvin, an astute critic even in his midteens, found *Scheherazade* disappointingly tame and unsexy. What seems to have impressed him most was the glimpse the trip gave him of the well-appointed world of downtown Los Angeles and its arts.

Emboldened by that first exposure, Alvin began to explore the area, dividing his Saturdays between Central Avenue and the Orpheum and Biltmore Theaters downtown. His trips were the sort of exciting private journeys that tend to occur in an unhappy, solitary adolescence, drawing the imaginative into some golden enclave of the heart and mind that is both goal and haven. Downtown Saturdays began and ended with the ritual of a bus ride, a time, one imagines, that must often have been filled with mute anticipation that was followed, on the way home, by dreamy satiation.

At the Orpheum, Alvin heard music by the best bands of the time and had his first conscious experience of the slyly seductive sound of Duke Ellington and his musicians. But it was at the Biltmore that his life was changed.

Alvin had never seen black performers at the Biltmore or even expected he might see them there. Then, on one of the many theater handbills he collected on his forays downtown, he found an advertisement for the black woman dancer Katherine Dunham and her "Tropical Revue." He bought his ticket and settled into a seat at the back of the house to watch a spectacle that had astonished theatergoers throughout the country.

Like a door opening out into a sensual world of heat, light, intense colors and pounding, driving rhythms, the show unabashedly ensnared its audiences with lush dance and music from the Caribbean, costumed with telling subtlety by John Pratt, Dunham's designer-husband. An anthropologist as well as a performer, choreographer and brilliant director, Dunham had taken vernacular ethnic and social dancing and made of it the stuff of lavish Broadway musicals.

In the process, much of the dances' simplicity and freshness were retained, giving them a powerful immediacy. And Dunham's highly trained, skillful performers danced as if their lives depended on it, which, given her iron perfectionism, might well have been the case. It was "as if the performers were dancing because they felt an overpowering urge for rhythmic movement and not merely because they were scheduled to give a show," the dance critic Walter Terry wrote of an earlier Dunham program.

The show must have had an incalculable effect on a smart but confused young teenager, a conscientious student and churchgoer whose carefully guarded interior life involved attractions to both tough and effeminate boys, to girls and to sexual behavior mocked at school and denounced in the larger world. Sitting by himself in the privacy of a dark theater, up in the balcony of the Biltmore, Alvin could lose himself in the uninhibited physicality and glamour of the moment.

He hurried out and followed people making their way to Dunham's dressing room after the show. A crowd of admirers gathered at the closed door, waiting for word from her dresser that Dunham was ready to receive them. And when the door opened at last, Alvin was greeted with a vision of opulent loveliness. Every surface in the room seemed covered with beautiful, foreign-looking fabric. The floor was carpeted, and on the walls hung tapestries and paintings, some of them Dunham's work. There were books to read, and fruit to eat. Flowers were everywhere. For Dunham, everything had to be real, everything had to be authentic, in this little home within the theater.

She liked to dress in exquisite clothes or silk dressing gowns in intense blues and other vivid colors as she signed autographs and greeted friends. Dazzling jewelry was sometimes spread out on her dressing table. There was a feeling of comfort and beauty to the room, a luxury beyond the norm for stars, although Alvin could not have known that. He was prepared for heaven. Backstage was satisfyingly mysterious and full of a tumultuous, different kind of life. The dancers he observed in passing were exotic creatures, their bodies dressed and faces painted in bright and glowing colors. And Dunham herself, light skinned and speaking in a slow, soft voice, exuded not just the gaiety and power so visible onstage but the bruisable and perfumed beauty of a gardenia.

He asked for her autograph. He would return, he knew—and he did, several times a week during the three-week engagement, recognized eventually by a kindly Dunham dancer who passed him through the stage door and into the theater without a ticket. He got more glimpses of backstage life, but it was what happened onstage that gripped his imagination. For there was theater that was both new and yet familiar, as hot and irresistible as the preachers and singers and moaners of Texas church Sundays. The women who danced were beautiful. The men were big and virile and unlike any other male dancers he had ever seen. And they were black. They were all black.

Alvin seems to have told few of his high school friends about his second life in the theater. He urged Don Martin, who became a friend in senior year, to go to see one of his favorite shows, Jack Cole's *Magdalena*, at the Philharmonic. Martin never did. But Alvin's appreciation of the relatively unacknowledged musical was a good deal more sophisticated than the simple enthusiasm of a starstruck adolescent.

Magdalena was a spectacularly beautiful and imaginative show that told the tale, with the help of an atmospheric score by Heitor Villa-Lobos, of a revolt in a Colombian emerald mine and a pious young peasant's attempts to convert her rowdy boyfriend. The show died quickly in New York, but it is now thought of as an unjustly neglected signature work by this early and influential master of jazz and musical theater dance.

Life outside the theater continued along its relatively even way at school. The school grouped each new class by names the students chose. Alvin was a member of the Prometheans, who with the Carthaginians formed a class of 405 boys and girls that was the largest that had ever graduated from Jefferson. The light-filled institutional hallways and open green courtyard of the school, considered a landmark of modern-movement architecture in Los Angeles, have not changed much over the years, although the students who pass through them today call themselves Untouchables, Majestics and Royal Knights.

Alvin was becoming known at school as a quiet, confident boy with a facility for languages. He had attempted to learn Chinese on his own from a neighborhood store owner, and at school he was sometimes called on to substitute for absent teachers in their Spanish classes. It was assumed that he would grow up to be a translator or a teacher. He looked studious, armed, as he would continue to be throughout his life, with portfolios of trailing papers. But he was already developing the lifelong habit of evasiveness that was to amuse and exasperate those with whom he later worked. "He'd be here one minute and then he'd be gone," Martin said.

Alvin had nearly grown into his large, solidly built body, looking now like a rugged, handsome quarterback, although he had managed largely to avoid playing football and other competitive sports for the school. He was otherwise "into everything," according to Blanche Sutton, the class historian, and is easily identifiable in several photographs in the yearbook for the class of 1948. He was chosen to take part in the graduation ceremony symposium, arguing the position of the statesman in a debate on "Building the Peace." "I was so proud of him," Ella Hurd Harris recalled. "He was just like my little brother."

Alvin's two lives began to merge well before graduation. The youngster who spent most of his free time in the school library and read and wrote for long hours in his room at home was beginning to learn firsthand about the art he had so far participated in only from a distance. He had become friendly with a neighborhood boy, Ted Crumb, a tall, thin, bright-eyed adolescent who was passionately in love with dance. Crumb became well known among young Los Angeles blacks interested in the art, eventually appearing in revues and with Joseph Rickard's pioneering Negro Ballet Company. But he was simply an eager amateur when his and Alvin's lives intersected.

Crumb wanted to perform. He had studied a variety of dance techniques, which he practiced in his backyard around the corner from Alvin's home. Alvin watched and asked question after question about what exactly Crumb was dancing. Occasionally, he would let Crumb try to teach him.

The two shared a love for Dunham's dances and her company. Crumb managed to find out where the dancers rehearsed when they were in town and sneaked in to watch them. When one of the dancers began to teach classes in Dunham technique during the day at a downtown nightclub, Crumb enrolled and talked Alvin into going with him.

Alvin lasted only one class. He had become an enthusiastic gymnast at Jefferson, impressing some of the girls with his strength and sleek fluidity in motion. He could not have had much trouble with the kind of physical control that Dunham's style demands. But the technique also makes use of the entire body and requires not only rhythmic coordination and lyricism but the ability to abandon oneself sensuously to movement. Alvin's repertory of behavior did not include abandonment, at least not in a public setting.

He did not enjoy the experience, and he was not impressed by the other students and the setting. He hated the sour smell and atmosphere of the club, where chairs had been pushed back to create a studio floor. Alvin was fastidious and even a bit of a prude. It was one thing to participate vicariously in Dunham's world, but the real thing was threatening and disappointingly tawdry.

He was more comfortable with the straightforward physicality of another kind of modern dance that Crumb showed him. It was the work, he told Alvin, of Lester Horton, with whom he studied in a studio in Hollywood, a ride of about an hour and a quarter from home. Why not go with him and take a class? Alvin was interested, but it took the school performances of a very pretty fellow student at Jefferson, Carmen de Lavallade, to finally draw him in.

De Lavallade lived in a somewhat different world from most of the other students at Jefferson. Her mother dead, she and her two sisters were raised by their strong-minded Aunt Adele, who owned a bookstore devoted to black writing—a rarity in that time and a profession that brought the woman a degree of notoriety even in the black community. Light skinned, de Lavallade looked as if she might be of Spanish or Indian descent. And her cousin Janet was a famous dancer.

Janet Collins became the leading ballerina of the Metropolitan Opera in the early 1950s. Many believe her to be a casualty of racism in this country, an artist talented enough to have danced with much more major ballet companies of the time. To her small cousin, however, she was the epitome of success. "Janet was always my idol," de Lavallade recalled. "She would blow into town like Auntie Mame. She had the most beautiful dresses. I always wanted to be like her.

"I was one for dancing on the front lawn, while my Auntie Annette played the piano. She was a very good pianist, but of course in those days one did not go into the theater. It was not a proper thing for a lady to do. But Auntie Annette would play Beethoven. My favorite was *Moonlight* Sonata, of course. And I just couldn't contain myself."

It was Aunt Adele who eventually looked into dance training for her niece and enrolled her in racially integrated classes, another rarity, taught by Melissa Blake. The child was in her element. "My dear, my head was somewhere else. I think probably everybody in school thought I was a little peculiar. I didn't go to any football games hardly. I didn't hang out with many of the kids. After school I was on the streetcar going to my lessons."

Later a noted modern dancer, actress and teacher, de Lavallade began early on to attract attention. She and a schoolmate, a free spirit named Ronald Gaffney who wanted to dance but was untrained, found each other and began to practice together.

Alvin was fascinated. Here was a boy his own age who didn't hesitate to put on a record and dance for anyone who happened to be passing by. Gaffney had no qualms about presenting his dances at school assemblies and in impromptu cafeteria performances. He did not seem fazed by the "sissy" label that attached itself to him.

It was at one of those performances that Alvin's eyes were opened by de Lavallade, who was to become for him a lifelong symbol of beauty and grace, always serenely present a little outside the circle of rushing life he drew around him. The auditorium theater curtain rose on someone who was barely recognizable. The quiet, studious-looking girl in short skirts and pigtails had been transformed into a sexily abandoned Scheherazade dressed in clinging crimson and flaunting her charms before a boisterously maddened Gaffney.

"Yes, yes, that was a famous performance," de Lavallade remembered, laughing, many years later. "They still talk about that. Poor little Ronald, the kids used to make fun of him all the time because he liked to dance. But anyway, we got this ballet together for assembly, and we had risers and we put these black curtains over them and made them all kinds of shapes.

"My costume was a shiny red Chinese silk tunic. My hair was up. I never wore my hair up. My legs were all bare. At one point Ronald was chasing me and I was pulling out all my modern dance technique. I would whup around and get up and run up the stairway. And at the very end I killed Ronald. He fell down the stairs. The kids were screaming. They had never seen anything like it."

De Lavallade also danced a quasi-ballet number with Gaffney, performing to Mozart and dressed in a pink tutu and pink point shoes. "I was working on point then," de Lavallade says. "My feet would never fit into toe shoes well but I tried, God knows I tried. I did something with my arabesque. Some dumb thing. Those things you do in school. Oh, God, that was one moment I would love to have forgotten."

For Alvin, however, she was a poetic vision, a creature of unparalleled loveliness and daring. His interest in dance intensified. In his last year at Jefferson, he began to spend less time in the library and more in the school auditorium. He continued to be a good student. He never performed. But at least one friend, a cousin who attended Jefferson, was shocked to see his growing interest in something as frivolous and even unmanly as the theater.

Alvin began to think more seriously about visiting the Horton studio, where both Crumb and de Lavallade studied. He would be going on to college and a major in Romance languages after high school. There could be no harm, however, in watching a few classes at the Horton school. Perhaps he could talk his friend Don Martin into going with him.

He ventured nervously out to Melrose Avenue in Hollywood, following Crumb into the squat, brown-painted little building, and stationed himself at the back of the tiny theater to watch the class taking place on the stage. Strange colors and objects filled the room. The dancers, some of them black, amazed him, diving, rising and twisting into turns with all the ease of gleaming fish. Horton, a big white man dressed in colorful, comfortable clothes, came back to say hello and welcome him.

Alvin returned, bringing Martin with him, and they watched in awe as Horton taught, his star dancer Bella Lewitzky demonstrating the steps to the students. "I had never seen anything like this in my life," Alvin recalled. He was stunned, not only by all that this dancer could do with her body but also, even more, by her fearlessness and absolute authority. This, he suddenly felt, was what he wanted to do.

Alvin watched for six months before he decided to take his first class. Although frightened, Martin took less time to make up his mind. And like a piper, Horton led the two little by little into the world of dance. At times, Alvin turned away. But he never turned back.

five

"HARD TIMES BUT THE BEST TIMES"

The small, unwieldy empire that Lester Horton created in Los Angeles was an outpost of sorts, little known in the busy modern dance scene back on the East Coast. Horton was considered an oddity by most eastern cognoscenti, and his school and company at best a noble experiment. But he offered the dancers a kind of freewheeling, encompassing artistic atmosphere that existed only in his studio and theater.

Horton was good at charming people. His dancers were his family, surrogate children whom he fed, educated and drove mercilessly as artists. He pushed dancers—goaded them, even—to step off the edge and plunge into artistic self-knowledge, equipped with newly pliant, daring bodies and a sense of themselves as living in a larger and more exciting world. And all were welcomed, whatever their race, so long as they worked hard and shed all preconceptions.

The world at the edge of which Alvin now found himself had had its beginnings in the heady, anything-goes early days of American modern dance and in its careering journey from abstraction to narrative and back again. Isadora Duncan had thrown off her corsets and her shoes, along with the confining technique of classical ballet, early in the

twentieth century. From then on, it was every woman—and an occasional man—for herself.

Ruth St. Denis, that other early matriarch of modern dance,
found inspiration in the serene exoticisms of Hindu dance as she imagined it. Her husband, Ted Shawn, told the world to forget about men
wearing tights and steadying ballerinas, in choreography that sought to
establish a central place for male dancers in this new American art.
Martha Graham taught audiences that a proper subject of choreography is the choreographer herself, and by the mid-1930s, Doris
Humphrey was weighing in with universalizing myth, in dances that
were Jung to Graham's Freud.

There were no rules to be made or broken. That atmosphere,
along with the exotic artifice of much of the dance that made its way to
the Midwest in the early 1920s, was oxygen to a rebellious adolescent
growing up in Indianapolis at the time. Increasingly drawn to dance
and theater, Horton quit high school over his mother's objections.
School was boring. He had been a good and popular student, but from
now on he would educate himself. And he did.

He found his way to dance as accidentally as Alvin would when, at
sixteen, he saw a performance by Denishawn, the pioneering company
formed by St. Denis and Shawn, which toured the country bringing a
new kind of movement, colorful and mysteriously foreign, to audiences
throughout the United States.

Their dances would later tend to look kitschy and insubstantial.
But the themes were compelling, whether the seductive Orientalia of
St. Denis's pieces or Shawn's unabashedly heroic evocations of American culture. And Denishawn's exhaustive American tours, from 1915
to 1931, encouraged visionary youngsters to dream of other worlds
and of an art that communicated not with plain words but through
unfettered physicality. One of those youngsters was Horton, and he
would later expose another crop of dreamers to that startling sense of
revelation.

Mesmerized by the larger-than-life, sometimes scantily costumed
Shawn, Horton began to study ballet and a kind of lyrical wafting,
based on Duncan movement and American notions of ancient Greek
dance, that was then popular studio fare. Like Duncan, Horton had
quickly rejected ballet as requiring too much discipline and technique.
Instead, he learned some Denishawn dances from a local teacher who
had appeared with the company and who gave the teenager his first
performing job.

Horton had a gift for being in the right place at the right time. The community- or little-theater movement sweeping the country in the mid-1920s was alive and healthy in Indianapolis. At nineteen, he found himself serving as choreographer, dramaturg and star of *The Song of Hiawatha*, a spectacular outdoor production complete with te-pees, a bonfire and carefully researched Indian music, dance and art. Its sponsor, a local arts patron named Clara Bates, befriended the teenager and installed him in her carriage house. Bates paid for art lessons for her protégé in Chicago, where Horton saw more dance and performed for small audiences for the avant-garde. She also sent him to Santa Fe to learn about American Indian dance and music. Fascinated by Indian culture as a child and now by the power of dance, Horton threw himself into these new experiences.

The Song of Hiawatha was Horton's ticket to golden California. He accompanied Bates there with the touring production and stayed, to her chagrin, establishing himself in this new land slowly but steadily as an expert teacher of the young and an imaginative director of theatrical pageants rooted in movement.

A solitary man who was inept at caring for himself, Horton moved those who attempted to fill that void—generally older women like Bates who were comfortably well off and interested in the arts—with his rash disregard for anything but his work. Money for food might be spent on fabrics he thought odd and beautiful. He dressed in Mexican and American Indian work clothes and expounded on Indian culture and any other topic of interest to him at the moment, with such pompous certainty at times that he seemed endearingly fraudulent.

California friends told him to settle in Los Angeles. San Francis-cans were too enamored of European culture. In Los Angeles, there was an appetite for the new and unfamiliar. Less cultivated and even more freewheeling than San Francisco, the city and its surrounding moun-tains and deserts were a place where Horton could live as casually as he wished. He moved there, living in a large chicken coop—cottage-sized, really, on a rich friend's estate—which he filled with feathers, shells and plants as well as costume and set pieces.

Horton performed with other modern dancers and toured for two years with Michio Ito, an innovative Japanese dancer and choreogra-pher whose simple, stylized and evocative dances profoundly influ-enced the young American. From Ito, Horton learned to move large groups of dancers around the stage in formal patterns. And props, he discovered, need not be simply an element in a set or a device to further a narrative; used organically, as a part of choreography, props could extend and color movement.

Horton's many-faceted career as a pioneering choreographer, director, performer, designer and composer started to take off in 1932 on a long and bumpy road of exuberant successes and soul-killing personal and professional failures. His staging of a high school pageant led to an invitation to direct a one-act play that won him a prestigious local award and new attention in the Los Angeles little-theater world, culminating in a performance at the Los Angeles Philharmonic Auditorium in conjunction with the 1932 Olympics. He began to meet and exchange ideas with modern dance choreographers and performers from the East Coast and from Germany. By the late 1930s, the Horton company was performing in dance series with eastern luminaries such as Martha Graham, Hanya Holm and Lincoln Kirstein's Ballet Caravan.

By 1947, when Alvin materialized at the back of the darkened theater one fall day to watch his first class, Horton had abandoned his explorations of American Indian and other ethnic dance forms and moved on to pieces that dealt with social issues. *The Mine*, a pared-down, stoic dance about women waiting for news of their men in a mine disaster, won Horton a prized review from John Martin, then the leading American dance critic, in the *New York Times*. Martin, who was visiting Los Angeles, found the rest of the program derivative, but *The Mine*, he wrote, had a strong theatrical impact.

Horton's views on racism, poverty and police brutality would draw dangerous attention to him during the communist witchhunts of the late 1940s and the 1950s. Unlike many of his dancers, Horton was a romantic rather than an ideologue. But he could doggedly stand his ground. When a friend suggested ways to clear his name as a suspected communist sympathizer in the late 1940s, Horton turned wordlessly and stormed out, slamming the door so hard that the room shook.

Loving the role of mentor, Horton had many lessons to teach. The world might seem an overwhelmingly large collection of alien peoples, but Horton believed that they were knowable through their art, their history and their music. Wonderful noises would spill out through the Horton studios, the sounds of drums, gongs and bells from all over the world that Horton had collected haphazardly, whenever there was money.

The "kidlets," as he called his dancers, learned about other cultures from the restaurants he took them to in the city's ethnic neighborhoods, the stores in Chinatown where he shopped for costume fabrics with them, the Mexican and black friends' homes he visited with them and places like the Club Alabam, where he and his dancers were invited to watch after-hours performing. Horton's appetite for information was huge and his delight in learning infectious.

His embrace of popular culture extended to the movie musicals of the time, which provided lucrative employment. Choreographic assignments flowed in from Universal-International Pictures after Horton's first film, the 1942 *Moonlight in Havana*. These meant a little money for the Horton dancers, who got paid only for teaching, as well as less worry about keeping up a succession of small studios around Los Angeles.

Horton choreographed nineteen films in all, putting as much spirit, care and attention to detail into movie choreography as his concert work, although his best efforts were often lost when the camera zoomed in on the stars. Ahead of his time, Horton saw the medium as particularly suited to dance, and he proposed a series of short dance feature films. He was turned down, but a surviving scenario suggests the quality of Horton's wit and imagination.

"The story of a lonely secretary to an art dealer who encounters Surrealism, unleashing a surge of urges, most libidinous, so wacky as to circumvent the need for censorship," Horton wrote in *Dilly Dali*, a scenario for one of the films. "Underlying this action are many jokes at Surrealists who are not mysterious to any ticket purchasers over the age of nine."

Nightclub engagements also helped financially, giving the dancers paid jobs and providing Horton with small surpluses to plow back into the school and theater. And he lived simply, often in the studios themselves.

But money was always in short supply. However popular the school might be at any moment, many of the students were needy and on scholarship. And there were many disappointments. Horton could not afford to send the company to New York to be seen by sophisticated dance audiences and appraised by the nation's leading critics. As promising new projects failed, Horton grew practiced at picking up and starting over again.

The happiest years of his life were probably those spent building the Lester Horton Dance Theater, the nation's first theater created for and devoted to the presentation of modern dance. Horton's dream of establishing a school and theater of his own had stretched like a strong, unbreakable thread through his checkered career. In 1946, he at last found the perfect site, a gutted building and a half formed by a machine shop and nightclub at 7566 Melrose Avenue in West Hollywood.

Providentially, one of Horton's former dancers, Newell Reynolds, knew something about construction and architecture, a field he later entered, and was able to carry out the ingenious plans of the building's designer, R. M. Schindler. Reynolds was also the husband of Bella Lewitzky, Horton's longtime lead dancer and cofounder of the new facility. A family affair to which the dancers, too, contributed their labor, the project proceeded little by little, over a seemingly endless two years, financed by whatever money was left over from the school budget.

The slow pace of construction gave Horton a chance to linger lovingly over every feature of his new headquarters. No inch of space went unused. The narrow building housed a small studio, dressing rooms, sewing and costume rooms, two very small offices and a theater. There was an open scene dock in the back, usually dappled with warm California light and shadow.

The stage doubled as a large classroom, with a floor laid over war-surplus airline hose that gave the surface a remarkable resiliency. Too small a stage for anything but the simplest sets, it was larger than the seating area and was so close to the first row of seats that audiences sitting there could put their feet on the stage apron. Sometimes they found themselves sprinkled with the sweat of whirling performers.

Black louvered panels were erected to mask the overhead lights and narrow wings. Horton's stage floor looked a little like a Jackson Pollock painting, its black surface flecked with yellow, pink, gray and green. The walls were dark gray and bare, but Horton spackled and painted the floors of the auditorium aisles with free-form designs. The 133 seats, molded plastic benches famous for their terrible uncomfortableness, were also painted different colors.

Horton felt that the new theater must be made as magical as anything that happened onstage, and he succeeded. "You knew that you were in some place different," Don Martin said. "Just this rundown dinky dance theater, but it was very special." As work drew near to completion, Horton wandered out onto the street and, scratching his head and smiling broadly, corralled passersby to tell them about what they would soon see in this curious-looking building. Inside, everyone pitched in, working day and night in the weeks before the opening. The last seats were installed early on the morning of the first performance, on May 22, 1948, not long after Alvin had crept into the unfinished theater for a first look at the man and his dance.

The outside was painted chocolate brown with the legend "dance theater" written in golden yellow script, with double doors painted a brilliant red and flanked by windows that displayed information about the dancers and productions. Soon it seemed as if there had never been a time when the building was not filled with eager, often exhausted young dancers.

Bare legged and typically dressed in leotards dyed in bright, rich hues, with colored yarn wound through the women's hair, company members and apprentices were there to study not just Horton dance but music, the history of the arts, choreography and the design and construction of sets and costumes. Classes in lighting, makeup, speech and even current events were also given. It was, as Alvin later said, an unparalleled education.

Dancers learned how to model clay, copy scores and perform in the company's percussion orchestra. They were also expected to work as crew or technicians even on nights they danced. One of Carmen de Lavallade's earliest assignments as a hardworking Horton scholarship student was to perform in the percussion ensemble that accompanied performances of *Salome*. Solemn and big-eyed, the teenager shook a pot of screws as she studied the wanton antiheroine from a distance, a role with which she would soon make her name as a glowing new young dance artist.

The family that Alvin joined was wide flung and spirited, with a hardworking inner group. Hollywood stars occasionally took class at the theater, Vera Ellen among them, but most movie dancers found the training unnecessarily difficult for the kind of hoofing that was expected of them. Children piled into the studio two afternoons a week and on Saturday mornings to study dance and improvisation. Their teachers were usually company members who also scrubbed floors, worked the primitive light and sound boards during performances, and helped Horton paint flats and tie-dye and piece together costumes.

The finishing of a costume could turn into a full-blown creative session. De Lavallade's costume for one dance began as a simple white muslin dress. As she stood in it, Horton filled his flit gun and applied layers of colored paint until she looked like an Orozco peasant. Pots of dye always seemed to be boiling in the back room. When Horton had finished streaking, bleaching, staining, splattering, tie-dying, painting and stenciling a costume, usually whistling through his teeth as he worked, he would sometimes pop it back into a pot for another application of color.

James Truitte, who later danced with Alvin and became a leading teacher of Horton technique, was so messy a painter that he was given the job of typing press releases. One of the few dancers with experience performing outside the company when he joined Horton in 1950, Truitte had taken an indirect route to the stage, winding through a minefield of racism familiar to most if not all of the black students and performers who benefited from Horton's unself-conscious lack of prejudice.

Forbidden by his mother to study dance as a child, Truitte met Archie Savage, a former star dancer with Katherine Dunham, while working as a bartender at the Club Alabam in his early twenties. He accepted Savage's invitation to train and perform with him, and then joined the cast of a touring production of *Carmen Jones*, a black musical based on the opera *Carmen*.

On his return to Los Angeles, Truitte decided it was time to get some concentrated, formal ballet training to strengthen him and polish his modern dance skills. Performers in the musical suggested he study with Eugene Loring, the show's choreographer. Loring had been a member of pioneering American ballet troupes, among them early companies formed by George Balanchine and Lincoln Kirstein as well as Ballet Theater, before settling in Hollywood and opening his American School of Dance. Truitte and two other black dancers went to see Loring, who invited them to watch a class and have coffee with him afterward.

Truitte vividly recalled the meeting. There might be objections to their presence in his regular classes, Loring told them. But if they could find enough students on "your side of town," he would come to teach there. Well, that's the end of you, Truitte and his friends thought as they left him. Another ballet teacher responded similarly, offering to teach Truitte and a friend privately "because I know you people work so hard." Years later, the mild-mannered Truitte would talk half-laughingly of wanting to slap her and give her two pirouettes to do as penance.

At times on tour in *Carmen Jones*, the performers had had to sleep on trains because no hotel would take them in. But this subtle prejudice was more difficult to accept.

"You'd say to yourself it's just not possible we're going through this cancerous, insidious excuse that they all gave us," Truitte said. "It was LA. But racial prejudice in LA was very insidious. And that's why all my life I've given the South credit. It was black and white. There was never a gray area. And that's honest. You knew what it was and you appreciated the honesty, whether or not you agreed with it."

Lester Horton and Carmelita Maracci, close friends who frequently exchanged and shared pupils, were known as good teachers who were not afraid to teach nonwhite students. Maracci, who died in 1988, was a peppery individualist who not only taught but choreographed and performed, all with a legendary electricity. She made it plain to her other students that they were not to enroll in her classes if they didn't like studying with black peers. Horton told Truitte and his friends that he didn't care if they were green with purple polka dots.

Horton's company was the first established multiracial troupe in the country, and he resisted all suggestions that he split his dancers into segregated units, even though that lost him much-needed nightclub jobs. A champion of all his dancers, he campaigned, tirelessly, angrily and successfully, to get charges dropped against a gentle young black student—one he knew to be incapable of violence—who had been wrongly accused of raping a white woman.

Truitte approached the Horton school warily, not knowing the extent of Horton's commitment to racial equality and justice. He found it hard at first to believe that black dancers were as welcome as they seemed. But he was almost immediately converted. Horton, standing at the desk when Truitte walked in, greeted him warmly. Feeling that "this was the place to be," Truitte enrolled in the school, although he had almost been scared away by the sight of Bella Lewitzky's extraordinary dancing.

After six months, Horton suggested that Truitte move up into the advanced class. "I said no. He said yes. I said no. And he said, 'Well, if you're going to keep saying no, don't come back.' "

Truitte stayed on, and five months later Horton asked him if he was interested in joining the company. Truitte refused. Horton said nothing at the time, but continued to talk to Truitte about dancing professionally. He knew, he said at last, that the decision to become a dancer was probably as traumatic for Truitte as it had been for him at the same age. "One of these days you're going to wake up and sit on the side of the bed and just laugh and it will all be over," Horton told him. "It will all be so."

Two weeks later, Truitte woke up and began to laugh. "And that evening I went in and said if the offer was still open I'd take it. And he told me to see him after class and he'd give me a rehearsal schedule. And he never asked me one question."

He and Horton had long talks, sitting in Horton's car outside Molly's, a restaurant near the studio where the dancers hung out and were allowed to run up tabs. Horton knew, he said, that Truitte had a gift for building walls around himself. Looking back, Truitte acknowledges those walls and wonders at the way Horton's patient intensity mysteriously cut through them. "Lester was never one to give up on someone or something that he earnestly believed in," Truitte remembered.

Work with Horton was an endless process of education. No assignment was ever quite what it seemed to be. Told to paint a flat for *The Park*, a dance based on newspaper accounts about police brutality against Mexicans in a local park, Martin found himself learning about letting go a little more when Horton insisted that the self-contained young dancer use bigger, broader brush strokes.

There were few lost moments, and there was little time off. Driving down a highway, Horton might talk intently to his dancers about history or a film he had seen. He would point excitedly to a snake track, so far ahead as to be invisible to everyone else in the car, and deduce the kind of snake it was and where it had been headed. A dancer who made a move to crush a spider wandering onto the theater loading dock was told in no uncertain terms to stop. Horton picked the spider up, held it in his palm and asked if the insect was bothering anyone. If not, he added, why bother it?

Horton could be petulant and undisciplined as well as controlling. He drove his dancers so hard and for such long hours, insisting they dance full out in rehearsal, that at times some thought they might collapse. But all had the sense that Horton was there for them in individual and very powerful ways, although he had no detectable favorites among his performers, preferring to encourage what he saw as a healthy competitive jealousy. He made it clear that for all the company's family feeling, they were expected to be independent and not to balk if a time arrived to leave the nest and go on to bigger things.

Horton's sense of humor, often bawdy, saved situations from becoming unbearable. A wicked mimic, he could reduce impromptu audiences to helpless laughter with imitations of Shawn and St. Denis. His most popular routine was "Miss Ruth Hanging Out the Wash," complete with her familiar sweetly curling lips, snaking arms and Indian hand gestures. St. Denis paid a visit to Horton's school and theater in 1952 and admitted to being impressed with the facility but not the performance she saw. Dance, she said, should be a matter of head, heart and pelvis. "Too much of here," she said of Horton's choreography, pointing to her pelvis. "You know what I mean?"

Horton seemed to understand instinctively how to deal with the youngest students, including one memorably fractious little girl who shattered everyone's nerves with her screams when she was delivered to the school every Saturday. Finally Horton had had enough. He dropped to his knees, eyeball to eyeball with the child, and let out a scream twice as loud as any of hers. She opened her eyes wide, startled. "Do you feel okay now?" Horton asked her. Yes, she replied, then trundled peaceably off to the studio. Truitte, one of the children's teachers, recalls that from then on she was "a pet" to deal with in class.

Horton sometimes approached his company similarly. One night, the dancers were so tired that they began to attack one another verbally. Horton walked into the room and summoned them onto the stage. "One, two, three," he called out in his huge voice. "Everybody kvetch. Oy, oy, oy." Laughter broke the tension. "Then back to work," de Lavallade remembered. "Hard times but the best times. What else would we be doing?"

Horton was for de Lavallade "like another daddy." He prodded his dancers along like a stubborn shepherd—big, straight spined and dressed in informal, sometimes shabby clothes in glorious mixes of warm colors that no one else would have dared to combine in those days. For many of those "children," there would never be another family like the Lester Horton Dance Theater, an experiment that was never quite equaled in American modern dance.

"The biggest thing was the simplicity of it all," Don Martin said. "It was hard work. If this was what you chose, then you had to give in to it. There was no halfway measure. But it was no big thing. Everybody and anybody could have been doing this."

Rehearsals could go on until the early hours of the morning before a season. Some of the dancers had daytime jobs. Others were still in high school. Lelia Goldoni, one of the youngest dancers in the company when she joined in 1951, remembers that somehow she managed to graduate, in spite of the demands of being a Horton "kidlet." If there had been a prize for the graduating student who had spent the least time in school, her high school principal told Goldoni dryly, she would have won it.

Historical and cultural research was required of the dancers, to give them stronger senses of their characters. De Lavallade and the other cast members read and discussed Garcia Lorca's *Yerma* before working on Horton's haunting danced version, *Prado de Pena*. For *The Park*, Horton sent the dancers into Pershing Square to do potentially dangerous interviews with park habitués tormented by police. Two properly raised young female members of the company were dispatched to study skid-row prostitutes at work for *The Bench of the Lamb*, a dance about a young whore. His dancers, Horton felt, must be open to all kinds of experiences in order to grow as artists.

The Beloved, one of the few Horton pieces to survive him and become a classic, depicted the relationship of a religious man and the wife whom he beats with his Bible and kills when he suspects her of infidelity. The dance was, as Horton wrote in program notes, "a kinetic projection of the social savagery of the double standard." But its performers were expected to know a good deal more than that about the duet and their roles.

The dancers analyzed newspaper stories on which *The Beloved* was based in order to understand the motivations of the characters. De Lavallade watched Horton and the first interpreters of *The Beloved*, Lewitzky and Herman Boden, talk about the relationship between the man and his wife. Had the woman committed adultery or not? they wondered. Was there a milkman hovering in the wings? Horton refused to speculate, and so his dancers were forced to follow their own hunches in interpreting the characters.

All the arts were there for the taking at the school and theater. For someone like Alvin, who wanted to write, paint and make music as much as to dance, the Horton experience was an exercise in living, taught by a man who embodied that life and was irresistible.

six

STUDIO DAYS

Lester Horton's intriguing new student must have presented immense challenges, even to a choreographer who specialized in developing raw talent and breaking through impenetrable-seeming emotional barriers. What lay beyond that tremendous, almost arrogant reserve? What might that body, with its reined football player's power, be capable of onstage?

Alvin was placed at first in the beginners' class, where he attracted attention immediately. "I could see that he had a special quality," Marjorie Berman Perces, Alvin's first teacher at Horton, recalled. "That quality had to do with his courage to extend the motion beyond the specific line that I was describing. He understood it and immediately created something of his own with it." Soon Horton was told that Alvin was attending classes at last and that the boy might even be gifted.

Alvin's charm and outstanding coordination also impressed his first teacher. "He was a very good-looking person," Perces said. "And he had a wonderful smile. He was really more than bright. Really brilliant, I thought, in the way he articulated things. And he was so attentive, so interested in everything presented. You knew immediately that this young man really found something that he adored. That made him feel good. When he went across the floor in class, it was with special pleasure.

"He was scared. In Horton technique, you would have had to study with Bella at least five years to really get the proper training. But Alvin was scared and very courageous simultaneously. He had ego and no ego, both at once. Those kinds of people can just plunge in, and they do things."

Alvin had gone to work to earn money for college after graduating from high school in June 1948. Intensive study had to wait until January 1949, when he had a month free between the start of college and the end of his full-time job as an office clerk at the Atomic Energy Commission in downtown Los Angeles. He daringly treated himself to eight classes, taking care to stand at the back of the room, dressed in his high school physical education uniform and feeling distinctly strange. But all too soon it was time to begin his studies at the University of California in Los Angeles, where he planned to earn the Ailey family's first college degree and join one of the two professions that Lula thought suitable for a smart, ambitious young southern man. Preaching was out of the question, but he could imagine himself as a teacher.

College was time consuming. Alvin caught the bus to school at six in the morning and made it home by seven at night. There was no extra money for amenities, even such necessary-seeming ones as dance classes. Concerned when Alvin disappeared, Horton visited Lula to ask after her son and then called him to find out what had happened. Alvin explained that he had no time or money to continue classes, although he had enjoyed the experience. Horton told him that he had a chance of becoming a good dancer. Was he interested in that? When Alvin said yes, Horton offered him a scholarship that provided for classes on Saturdays in exchange for jobs like helping with lighting and working as a handyman in the theater during the season.

Alvin found a night job at Molly's and, unhappy at home, moved into a room at a boardinghouse where other Horton dancers lived. He was not at all sure he wanted to perform, although he was beginning to sense that he might one day want to be a part of Horton's theater.

But dance is a jealous mistress, exacting its fullest devotion from those who come to it late in adolescence or in early adulthood, as Alvin had, with a conscious sense of hungry yearning for some ideal. School required more wide-awake attention than he could muster while leading this triple life of study, dance and work, and Alvin's grades for his first semester at UCLA were mediocre. Service loomed in the Reserve Officers' Training Corps. Most of all, he was tired.

He did not return to UCLA, but took one course during the fall at

Los Angeles City College, where he enrolled full-time in the spring of 1950 and did considerably better. He moved back home and continued to work at Molly's and take classes on scholarship at the Horton studio. Watching Alvin and consulting with his teacher, Horton decided to let him skip the requisite intermediate classes and go right into the advanced level, where he could keep an eye on the boy and give him extra attention, building up both his confidence and his unresilient feet.

Horton put Alvin and his friend Don Martin on the theater stage crew—pushing them at times to be more responsible about the job—and gave Alvin the job of stage manager for the children's workshop performances that June.

The workshop suggests something of the free-spirited, slightly precocious atmosphere of the Horton school. Organized by the children themselves, the event began with class demonstrations by students in the three- to five-year-olds' and six- to seven-year-olds' divisions. The older children created six pieces, among them a piece set to Stravinsky, a dance called *The Bride That Flew the Coop*, and the program's most ambitious work, *A June Trip*, which progressed from "Monica's Party and Plans to Take Guests on Trip" through "Patsy's Desert Dance" to the culminating "Michelle's Dance with Flowers into Celebration and Exhaustion from Trip."

"Lester's method of involving people was to put them immediately into everything," Perces observed. Making Alvin the stage manager was the first step, she believed, in involving him in something outside of class work.

By the end of the summer, however, Alvin was ready to disappear again. He felt restless living at home after his first taste of freedom, and he was still a little uncomfortable with his stepfather. At the studio, there was growing friction between Horton and Bella Lewitzky, the dancers' artistic parents.

Horton had gone through a devastatingly painful and chaotic year in 1949, when William Bowne, his lover of seventeen years, left Horton to marry a former member of the Horton company. Bowne and he had worked together closely, sharing the dreams that culminated in the opening of the theater, and Bowne's emotional support was crucial to Horton's functioning. And now Lewitzky, the most important person in Horton's professional life, was leaving.

Lewitzky to a large extent had formalized Horton's teaching during her fourteen years with the company, helping to codify his instinctual experiments and discoveries into a body of steps, gestures, phrases and principles that were generally recognizable as a technique. She and her husband, Newell Reynolds, had been partners with Horton and Bowne in the founding of the theater and school on Melrose Avenue, and the two participated in their institutionalization.

By the time Alvin enrolled at the school, Lewitzky had begun to pull away from Horton, dismayed by his growing interest in creating lighter dances and by his refusal to espouse publicly the progressive politics of the time as the excesses of right-wing demagogues like Senator Joseph McCarthy seeped into every area of national life. A new man had entered Horton's life, too, a natty young film and theater writer named Frank Eng.

Eng, a champion of little-theater companies, had gone out to look at Horton's work during the company's opening season after a reader suggested he write about "this group that performed on Melrose on Sundays." He had never written about modern dance, but he was impressed by what he saw at the theater, particularly by the dancing of the "astounding" Lewitzky. When the prickly young idealist lost his job at the *Los Angeles Daily News*, he found work as a press agent and eventually, at the suggestion of a mutual friend, offered his services as a publicist for free to Horton.

Their relationship was beginning around the time Alvin finally committed himself to the Horton school. Eng became general director of the theater and eventually moved in with Horton, accustoming himself to a life of coffee-shop dinners at 3 A.M. and time together snatched out of very long workdays shared with a crowd of dancers to whom he was inevitably an outsider. Some nights he and Horton slept in the studio on a bed made of a board stretched between two sawhorses. He worked for the company for free, taking on a succession of full-time jobs. His wages, with the exception of money he sent each month to his mother, went into keeping the theater and school afloat.

Eng was in love. "I think it became immediately obvious to the kids at the theater. How could it not?"

There was an atmosphere of casual acceptance of sex and sexuality at the Horton studio. Homosexuality was not discussed, it was simply a fact of life. Lelia Goldoni looked back, laughing, on an inexperienced adolescent self constantly exposed to the heightened sensuality of much of Horton's choreography. Her colleagues, almost as young as she, portrayed repressed murderers, prostitutes and the lethal Salome, a theme that obsessed Horton. They lilted sinuously through Caribbean-style dance with no one seeming disturbed, in those vigilant days, that the sultry lovers leading the dance were a black man and a white woman. And almost before she knew what homosexuality was, Goldoni was taken to her first gay bar by one of the dancers and found the experience interesting and not at all perplexing.

What must that relaxed, freewheeling environment have meant to Alvin? At eighteen, he seems to have decided that he was gay, although he told a college friend that he had had fleeting involvements with women. Alvin had become friendly with a fellow student at UCLA, David McReynolds, and helped McReynolds to accept his feelings of attraction to men. The two teenagers had long talks about what makes men "queer or not," as McReynolds put it.

"Alvin told me that in dance you hold men so much it's very difficult not to get physically involved. But he said he could have gone either way. I don't think he was clear in his own mind what he was. That's a rough time. A very rough choice. I think he tried to dissuade me. He took me to visit friends who were very effeminate."

The two shared a love of poetry, reading their poems to each other and commenting on them, although McReynolds was so in love that he dared not be as tough a critic as the cooler-headed and unreciprocating Alvin.

Alvin introduced McReynolds to the writing of Kenneth Patchen and William Carlos Williams. He told McReynolds about having read Williams's "This is just to say," a simple, plainspoken little poem about eating the plums from the icebox. It was just everyday speech, he said, and terrible. How could Williams call himself a poet? A week or two later, he called McReynolds to say he had been thinking about the poem. "I realize it's one of the best poems I ever read," Alvin said.

Sexual and poetic fantasy converge in a haunting prose poem Alvin wrote soon after, a piece that has something of the inextricably bound pain and pleasure, the terror and excitement, that were so much a part of the forbidden gay life and imagination of the early 1950s.

"You know the type—you've seen them," Alvin begins, writing on ruled school notebook paper in neat print that becomes more cramped and larger as the fantasy builds:

He had been afraid a long time now—and this he did not like. He had always clung to the thought that the thin boy would someday return to him, and that they together would find something more beautiful and real. He would create things more beautiful than ever before—especially for the boy—the serpent dances from those brief summer days in Mexico—the role of the passionate stranger in the long work: nothing would deny him now. If only the boy would return from wherever he was. See you soon—the last postcard had said—this was from Miami, and for a few days after he waited and waited and could barely take an hour's sleep lest the boy come and ring the bell or knock and not be heard, . . . or perhaps he would come one day suddenly out of nowhere—sweeping up off La Brea in a shiny dark car that of course didn't belong to him and with airline baggage tickets on his luggage and the long broad smile showing the small teeth, the eyes, too, of course, smiling—but the shoes would be scuffed and dirty and unshined like always. This is what he was thinking about when the pain came. And this one was the most severe of all since the pains started three years ago. He dropped his pencil and it rolled along the floor for a long long time—he could hear it in his mind still rolling along the floor while the pains darted across his chest and made him gasp for breath in little short snaps of spasmodic lurch. He was in a daze of pain and in the sharp strike after strike at his insides the room swirled inside his head and his eyes seemed pressed down into his mouth with their throbbing, bringing streams of blood through his brain—

Suddenly, toward the end, the fantasy seems to burst out into a vision of a dance.

> He could see it all clearly now—the whole thing: Ted in the old costume standing at the head of the group—all men—their legs vibrating, trembling underneath the sweatbare torsos and the heels essaying a barrage of staccato into the floor until the room itself would seem to tremble—then the girls running in swiftly, faster than a six-eight, circling the trembling men—yes, that is how it would be and the end with the men tearing space with their arms and legs

There the writing stops, without punctuation.

This was a self Alvin hid at home. At the Horton studio, hiding was less necessary. In any case, it was not possible to escape the intensity of Horton's attention, which could be as overpowering as his unqualified-seeming belief in untried talent. And Horton was in many ways like Alvin.

Alvin applied himself seriously at first to the difficult Horton technique, growing more and more involved in the daily life of the studio. Although a secretive loner who was all too aware of his poorly shaped dancer's body, his unsupple feet, and his lack of training, he found himself drawn by Horton's demanding, all-encompassing dance.

In a Horton class or rehearsal, to move was to explore. Gravity meant nothing. Balance existed to tilt off, floors to leap up from and air to fall or cantilever through. But Horton dancers also had to be able to express themselves powerfully through stillness. They had to have an eastern dance expert's complex coordination and ability to isolate and make plain the action of every body part in motion, all the while maintaining an experienced actor's hypersensitivity to emotion and atmosphere and a big, open, lyrical flow.

To achieve all that was not easy. Truitte woke up the morning after his first Horton class to discover that the only part of his body he could move without pain was his head. He rolled over the edge of the bed and put first one knee, then the other, on the floor. He grabbed the side of the bed, pulled himself up very slowly to a standing position and began an even slower journey to the bathroom and eventually made it to work. The torture continued. As soon as Truitte thought he had settled into the crippling technique, Horton would go off on a new tangent, and the morning-after process would begin all over again.

Truitte at least had had some previous training. Alvin had none. "He was not a good technician," Truitte recalled. "And he couldn't remember things. He was rather shy, and pulled back. But when he moved it was absolutely magnetic. He had this wonderful kind of cat-like quality, with all this masculine strength."

Alvin was also innately seductive, even then. "He had a wonderful way of making people feel a part of him, until they actually fell in love and then he was ready to leave them," Cristyne Lawson, who studied briefly at the Horton studio when Alvin was there, remembered. She herself was soon in love with him. "He was a lot older than I was and I thought he was really Someone. Because he was older, and he also cared about what I thought. Most people didn't really ask you questions, ask you what you thought about dancing. Not at that age, anyway. No one asked me anything. And Alvin really did care. We always talked about dancing. He was all excited about it."

Alvin felt that Horton's choreography suited him, but he worried that he didn't dance it very well. "He was never secure, about anything," Lawson said. "You know, Alvin never really had a chance to study dance, did he? He wasn't with Lester long enough. He never got that sort of security underneath him."

Horton dancers and friends of the time describe Alvin as an up-roariously funny mimic and storyteller who was forever launching into sudden impromptu comic exchanges with friends. Truitte was a frequent partner in this sort of bantering.

"Alvin and I dreamed that someday we would each own a Jaguar," Truitte said. "One day out of the blue I said to Alvin, 'By the way, what happened to your Jaguar?' And he replied, 'I was forced to sell it because the ashtray got full.' Out of this came our little poem: 'They'll never know what a hag you are, when you're riding in your Jag-u-ar.' "

Alvin tempered his humor with more delicate play on long bus trips with Carmen de Lavallade from their neighborhood to the theater and back again. Waiting for the bus home, the two would gaze into the windows of the furniture stores on North Vermont Avenue and Melrose Avenue and contort their faces and bodies to match the masks and sculptures in the showrooms, adding appropriately silly voices and laughing hysterically.

Yet his antics hid a continuing self-doubt. Alvin exasperated the other dancers by fleeing the theater when his nerves got the best of him just before one of his first performances, in 1951. That there was no point in participating in the life of the studio if you were not ready to capitulate wholeheartedly was commonly understood. But Horton said and did nothing, allowing Alvin to try again at his own pace.

That did not prevent Alvin from coming and going frequently—and abruptly—during his five years as a Horton student and performer. His need to hide, his ability to slip away or disappear almost before one's eyes, would persist throughout his life. Like Lula, like Horton, Alvin was an outsider equipped with an outsider's acute sensitivity to situations and expectations. "Just when we really sort of started getting settled in there and taking classes and being in the group, he would leave," Don Martin said. "And then all of a sudden we'd find out that he was in the hospital with a kidney operation. I think Alvin's running away was probably in search."

Pressed for money, Alvin had returned home to live but continued to feel uncomfortable with his mother and "Mr. Cooper," as he sometimes referred to his stepfather in private. In late summer of 1951, Alvin left Los Angeles for San Francisco to work and go to school. It was only a matter of time before he found himself back in a dance studio.

In his first weeks in San Francisco, it seemed possible to make a new life. The air was seductively fresh and cool and filled with an adrenaline-raising sense of freedom and energy. Alvin stayed at the YMCA and in the cheapest hotels he could find while he looked for work, as hungry at times as his mother had been in her first months of job-hunting in Los Angeles. Finally he found soul-numbing work as a file clerk at the state tax bureau, then switched to a more bearable, more physical job as a baggage handler and sometime translator at the city's Greyhound Bus station.

His shift, from 4 P.M. to midnight, meant that Alvin could make it to morning college classes. He had contemplated transferring to the University of California at Berkeley, but, possibly because he had pulled himself up to only a B average at Los Angeles City College, Alvin enrolled instead at San Francisco State College as a language major early in 1952.

He lasted just one semester. At the start of the fall term, Alvin became ill and was hospitalized for removal of a kidney. Again, he was tired. His life in San Francisco felt rootless. As he convalesced, Alvin began to slip back into dance.

He became friendly with a young singer and dancer named Marguerite Angelos, later known as the writer Maya Angelou. The two met in the studio of Walland Lathrop and Ann Halprin, the best-known modern dance teachers in San Francisco. Lathrop offered a more traditional form of dance than Halprin, who gave her students lyrical, funny dance exercises with a good deal of improvisation, and soon after became a pioneering avant-gardist in dance.

The long, light-filled studio was enticing, and there was another black dancer, a woman named Ruth Beckford, at the school. "It was a shock to see a black man in class," Beckford recalled. "Alvin and I just sort of hooked up. He had a gorgeous body and he was very friendly and funny and just good to be with." Alvin talked a lot about Horton to Beckford but made no move to return to Los Angeles.

He did not stay at the studio for long. Neither he nor Angelou could afford to take many classes. The two kept busy, though, working up a fledgling nightclub act called "Al and Rita" in her living room, and they performed occasional gigs at events held by black organizations like the Elks and the Eastern Star. Alvin found work as a waiter and then danced at the New Orleans Champagne Supper Club.

He had found the job through a chance meeting on Fillmore Street in the spring of 1953 with a Los Angeles dancer, Lon Fontaine, who was looking for male dancers for an act he had choreographed for the club, the biggest and classiest black-owned nightclub in the city. Alvin stayed on, and even began to choreograph acts himself. Not so long ago he had been uncomfortable in the atmosphere of the seemingly unbridled physicality of Dunham dancing. Now he was studying the club's ravishingly pretty stripper, Laurena Hardaway, for makeup and costuming tips. He learned a little about jazz dance, stage projection and his own power to attract, but his time at the club was also an intensive crash course in the customs of a sensuous new world. Alvin's college days were over.

Fontaine's act moved on to Los Angeles to a place owned by the proprietor of the Champagne Supper Club. Alvin found himself drawn back to Melrose Avenue, although he was still undecided about becoming a professional dancer. But he was comfortable in the sinuous Latin numbers that Horton was now choreographing, and he felt ready, at least for the moment, to settle down and become a Horton dancer.

It wasn't otherwise an easy time, for he had a new baby brother at home, born in January. The studio offered something Alvin could pour himself into, however, and he started taking two or three dance classes a day. Soon he began to learn Horton dances as a member of the choreographer's workshop group, a sort of junior or apprentice company. He also created his own first formal concert dance, *Afternoon Blues*, to music from the Broadway show *On the Town*. Choreographed as part of his dance training, the three-minute solo was inspired by Vaslav Nijinsky's hedonistic *Afternoon of a Faun*, a knowing choice of influences given Alvin's distinctively sensual animal-like stage presence and prowl.

It was a sad but exciting time at the Horton studio. Lewitzky was gone, Horton was bankrupt after paying her and Reynolds a small settlement, and there was a terrible tension in the air. Horton seemed to be in extraordinary emotional pain. His hair had turned gray, and although he had retained his impressively erect, dignified posture, his eyes were sunken and he often looked as if he were about to cry. Yet it was also a richly productive period for Horton. Imaginative dance seemed to flow out from him, informed by a new playfulness and a lush, easy physicality. Alvin's role as a performer was limited to the chorus, and his presence at the studio was intermittent. But he drank in every detail of Horton's work process, of the performing of star dancers like de Lavallade and Truitte, and of Horton's impressive range of styles and themes.

Horton had choreographed the last of his social protest pieces in July 1950. *Brown County, Indiana* took a look at the evils of slavery in a somewhat stereotypical tale, with a thought-provoking psychological twist in which a Quaker woman is driven to violence to protect a runaway slave. The following March, Horton produced *Tropic Trio* and *Another Touch of Klee*, two of his most popular dances.

Another Touch of Klee, a suite of four dances set to jazz by Stan Kenton, opened with a dreaming, witty trio featuring a masked woman wearing one toe shoe and holding a blue rope that divided the stage. On a note of delicate theatricality, there was a moment in the last section when a ball was tossed high and disappeared, followed by a wash of slowly descending bubbles that at one point was blown down by Alvin, perched precariously above the stage. *Tropic Trio*, the work during which Alvin suffered his crisis of nerve and ran away, was a suite of group pieces drawn from Brazilian and Panamanian dance.

In a filmed excerpt of *Cumbia*, the popular middle section of *Tropic Trio*, the dancers exude a hypnotic sensuousness as the lead man, holding a lighted candle and moving backward, coaxes his lilting woman toward him through a sea of undulating bodies. In *Frevo*, the closing section, the dancers startled the audience by bursting down the aisles and onto the stage for a carnival finale in which hard-dancing men and women hefted umbrellas as they moved.

Other signature works followed, among them *Prado de Pena*, inspired by Garcia Lorca's *Yerma*, and *Liberian Suite* and *To José Clemente Orozco*, one of five tributes that made up the 1953 *Dedications in Our Time* and a dance that Alvin later described as a killer to perform.

Liberian Suite was set to Duke Ellington's score of the same name, commissioned in 1947 to celebrate the centennial of Liberia, the country founded by black Americans eager to return to their ancestral home of Africa. Ellington's visit to the Horton studio provided a much-needed boost to the choreographer's tired spirits and a bit of excitement for the dancers, who clustered around him, smiling, for publicity photographs.

One of the most vivid evocations of Horton's work is a description by his biographer, Larry Warren, of *Liberian Suite*. "Working with great enthusiasm, Horton designed some of his finest costumes and accessories for 'Liberian Suite,' " Warren writes in *Lester Horton: Modern Dance Pioneer*. "He chose deep brown and red as his basic colors and created belts and hair ornaments of brass for the girls' costumes. For one section he constructed an ingenious skirt, mini-length, with broad raffia-trimmed panels attached to the hemline. One shoulder was left bare, creating a stunning, lush, asymmetrical line, which would look contemporary today. Weighted scarves were used both for their line and for the sound produced when they were beaten against the floor. The sets, too, revealed the gusto with which he was working. Large flats painted with free form human figures dressed the stage, and for the second section the rear studio was used as part of the dance space. Horton had stretched lengths of fabric, also figured, over the doors, creating a deep, cave-like illusion. In one section, two figures appeared at the most distant visible point in a spotlight and inter-twined slowly in a series of breathtaking lifts and balances, somehow giving the impression of an approach from a great distance. His chore-ography had an understated primitive elegance with bursts of joyous playfulness. The characteristic bearing of the upper body was the lifted open chest of the proud African tribesman, the head held with an elo-quent sense of purpose. The movement phrases were long and rhyth-mically complex with an underlying sense of childlike naivete about them. Modern, ethnic and jazz motifs flowed together unselfcon-sciously. It was pure Horton and, as such, it was ahead of its time: too bold, too colorful, too physical for 1952. The music was purposely played very loudly to heighten the experience."

All of this took place on a small stage, only thirty by thirty feet, in an even smaller theater, on the most meager of budgets.

Horton's faith in Alvin was confirmed when Jack Cole, then a leading Hollywood choreographer, chose him as well as de Lavallade to dance in the film *Lydia Bailey*, which was to be released in the late spring of 1953. But Alvin was not up to Cole's depersonalized, demand-ing combination of ethnic and jazz dancing, a style that John Martin described as "nervous, gaunt, flagellant, yet with an opulent sensuous beauty that sets up a violent cross-current of conflict at its very source." In the end, Cole was forced to partner de Lavallade himself, coating his white skin with dark makeup in the film's Haitian voodoo duet. He cast Alvin as a sacrificial fowl-carrier instead, but Alvin pulled out al-together when he became sick with mononucleosis.

Still, Alvin was able to scrutinize the man Horton had said was the world's greatest living male dancer, a choreographer whom Alvin had admired and was greatly influenced by. It was Cole who had choreo-graphed *Magdalena*, the show that had so mesmerized Alvin in high school. And Cole was intrigued by the youngster.

"I had to dance with Carmen because Alvin at that time was very unmusical," he told an interviewer. "He got turned on to movement and didn't hear a thing but he danced marvelously—he was one of the

most beautiful men that one ever wanted to see. He had black curly
hair and reminded me of a Renaissance cherub or a 19th century
Othello with this very beautiful, muscular, round body. Even if he was
dancing the steps incorrectly, he was just so marvelous looking that it
was a pleasure to watch him."

Around the same time, the studio was filled with the exciting
news of a New York engagement for a group of Horton dancers. Colleagues and fans had been telling Horton for many years that it was
time to take his dances to Europe, or Latin America, or New York City.
There was never enough money. Finally, at this peak of creativity, two
dates were set early in 1953 for performances by the company at the
historic, reputation-making theater of the Young Men's and Young
Women's Hebrew Association on East Ninety-second Street, familiarly
known as the Ninety-second Street Y.

Money had to be raised to finance the trip and the performances.
Horton was ragged with exhaustion, creating dances not just for the
upcoming season but for the company's Bal Caribe, a costume party
that had become one of Los Angeles's most glamorous annual fund-
raising events. He also took on extra film work to earn enough for the
trip to New York and room and board there. He and Eng reasoned that
box office receipts would help pay the way back to Los Angeles. And so
six members of the company set off for New York on March 18, 1953,
stuffed into two station wagons with Horton, Eng, sets and costumes,
and Goldoni's mother, Sara Leghorness, who went along as a chaperone
for her daughter and the two other young women in the group. Alvin,
who had broken a toe, was left behind.

A terrible disappointment awaited the little group when it pulled
into New York six days later. The Y did not provide publicity, as Eng
had assumed, and no one in New York seemed to know of the engagement. Eng scrambled to spread the word about the performances, on
which Horton had pinned hopes for major recognition from his peers
in the East. But he had few contacts in New York. Only 300 people
attended the Saturday night performance in the 920-seat house. Two
hundred tickets were sold for Sunday afternoon, netting the troupe a
total of $100.

All but one of the reviews were good, with P. W. Manchester singling out the performers in *Dance News* for their complete unselfish-
ness in "subordination to the discipline of the group." John Martin, the
critic whose response Horton had hoped for most eagerly, attended the
performance but did not write about it.

Humiliatingly, there was not enough money to return home or to accept Ted Shawn's invitation to perform that summer at his Jacob's Pillow summer dance festival in the Berkshires in Massachusetts. Horton's agent wired him emergency money to tide the company over on the way home.

Horton drank a great deal as they traveled back across the country. Discouragement and the pressures of keeping his company and his work going had pushed him to drink too much in the past, but now the hopes of many years had been dashed in a humiliating rout. Eng, who had nursed him through a heart attack, realized how sick Horton was both physically and emotionally. He found a small, comfortable house on Mulholland Drive, and Horton's parents moved in and helped take care of him. There Horton and Eng cooked large dinners for the dancers, who noted a new gentleness in Horton. And there were happy surprises.

The group was able after all to perform at the Pillow, traveling back once more by car from Los Angeles. The season was a success, although Horton and Eng could not afford to accompany the group to Massachusetts for the festival. And Horton was immensely pleased when the 1953 edition of the Bal Caribe brought an invitation to the company to appear, as a single, multiracial group, at the surpassingly chic Ciro's Nightclub in Hollywood.

Opening for the singer Johnny Desmond, the dancers were so big a hit that they were invited back for another two-week engagement. Horton was overjoyed when he heard the news. But the following morning he was dead, struck down at his home by a massive heart attack on November 2, 1953.

seven

FILLING LESTER
HORTON'S SHOES

No one could believe, as sick as Horton clearly had been, that he was gone. "It took me a year to get over Lester's death," Frank Eng would recall many years after, the pain still fresh in his voice. "I felt like an animal torn in half. I lay very still so I wouldn't bleed to death."

Eng dealt almost blindly with the pressing duties of survival, pushing himself, in a show of solidarity, to go to the company performance that night at Ciro's. Someone had volunteered to call the dancers. Not all received the message. Looking back, Lelia Goldoni still sounded numb when she recalled the shock of learning why Horton had stood her up at a luncheon meeting that day.

Eng moved into the theater on Melrose Avenue, leaving the house for the next few weeks to Horton's stunned parents. Recognizing that the directorship and future of the impoverished company might be called into question, Eng quickly transferred the costumes to a friend's garage. He and the dancers put up a good front, swinging into action almost immediately after Horton's sudden death. The most important thing, they all knew, was to keep the Lester Horton Dance Theater going.

Eng quickly called a meeting at the house, the first of many over the following month, to delegate duties during this transitional period.

Alvin had disappeared again, apparently on one of his many trips to San Francisco. No one knew where he was or even wondered that much. As secretive as ever, he had managed simply to drop from the edge of the earth. But news of Horton's death reached him, and he reappeared a few weeks later at a company meeting. Suddenly Alvin was once more a part of the group, and an unlikely major player in the preservation of the Horton company.

The group did have its repertory of Horton pieces, as Eng pointed out to the dancers. But there would be no more, and every season needed a new attraction. Surely among the performers seated around him in the little living room, nervously erect or straddling their chairs or stretching dancer-fashion on the floor, there must be one or two budding choreographers who would help to extend the Horton repertory.

Eng, inviting the dancers to submit ideas, was met with a fearful near-silence until Alvin spoke up. "He wasn't afraid," Eng recalled. "I was kind of astounded. I always remembered him as being standoffish."

Not only was Alvin interested, but he returned to the next meeting with eight ideas for dances. Eng believed that two of them might work. One was an homage to Horton called *According to St. Francis*, a piece for James Truitte, whose elegance and dramatic eloquence Alvin knew instinctively were to be celebrated. The second, *Morning Mourning*, was a dance for himself, Truitte and Carmen de Lavallade that drew its atmosphere and characters from the plays of Tennessee Williams. But first there was a commission from the San Diego Symphony Orchestra for a group work to be set to Darius Milhaud's *Creation of the World* and performed by the Horton dancers during the orchestra's 1954 winter season. All agreed that Alvin should be the choreographer.

He was now immersed in dance. Eng had pressed him into teaching at the Horton school, although it was something he was neither good at nor enjoyed. A choreographer in spite of himself, when Alvin faced the students he found himself giving them flowing passages of his own movement rather than the sequences of Horton technique they needed for their training as dancers. "Alvin couldn't teach his way out of a paper bag," Truitte said with wry affection. "He couldn't remember the technique. He would take an element of it and then devise something. His creative processes were working all the time, even with technique. It would almost get to the point where he was doing choreography in class, which was wonderful because you had the sense of moving."

Alvin did try to be a model academic. He studied the ways Truitte and de Lavallade passed on the Horton technique in the studio, taking careful notes on the material they taught and the structure of their classes. He contemplated the effect of class-taking on himself, analyzing his own instincts in the studio. He was now, as dancers are for all their lives, a full-time student.

More earnest than ever at twenty-three, Alvin filled page after page with notes on teaching in a neat script that changed very little over the years, spreading to a wild scrawl or contracting to cramped, childlike curlicues in moments of pressure or distress. "Take notebook to all dance classes taken and note all material given as to what it accomplishes and how it fits into the given structure of the whole technique," one memo read. "Notes from Carmen and discussion of exercises. Clarify for self ability to communicate this to others verbally and by physical demon-stration."

He carefully listed six years' worth of issues and page numbers of *Dance Magazine* in which references to Horton and his technique were made. He reminded himself to pay attention to each student's psychol-ogy and development in class. "Overt enthusiasm on part of instructor without patronization of student—should seem more creative than pa-tronizing," Alvin wrote. "Long line of body and importance of weight distribution. Strengthening of extremities: feet, foot alignment, hands."

No amount of self-tutoring seemed to help Alvin in his occasional teaching of the children. He dreaded the sessions, although years later he remembered the name of at least one of the most gifted little girls. He could not relate to the young students, who had a terrible habit of asking too many questions and expecting orderly and unimpulsive teaching.

Alvin was saved for a time when he answered an audition call for dancers for the film version of *Carmen Jones*, to be choreographed by Herbert Ross. The Broadway musical, a hit in 1943, transposed the Bi-zet opera to the black American South during World War II. Released by Twentieth Century–Fox in October 1954, the movie had all the heat of refried beans, with clattering lyrics that neutralized the effect of the opera's familiar arias. Dorothy Dandridge played Carmen, here a seduc-tress who works in a parachute factory. Harry Belafonte was Joe, an innocent young soldier. Escamillo became a swaggering prize fighter named Husky Miller. And Pearl Bailey nearly stole the show as Car-men's sidekick, the ruefully high-living Frankie.

With the exception of a glimpse of de Lavallade in a long shot, her hair tied in a ponytail that cascaded down the back of her summer dress, only Truitte can be easily spotted in the film's one dance number. But Alvin is there among the dancing soldiers and their girlfriends in the scene, a roadhouse party performed to Bailey's singing of the Gypsy Song as a tongue-twisting number called *Beat Out the Rhythm of That Drum*. Elbows pumping and face radiant with the biggest grin in the crowd, Alvin seems to be hurrying a little to keep up with the group and with the hectic rhythm of the dance.

At work in the Horton studio in the first half of 1954, Alvin scribbled as intently as ever, the lifelong habit vindicated now by his elevation to the job of choreographer. Notes poured out of him on ideas for dances, complete with costuming and accessory details and often accompanied by a doodle of a featureless upper torso, arms stretched out and up in one long horizontal curve, that he would draw in margins for most of the rest of his life. Then and later, any piece of paper torn or whole would do, from school notebooks, envelopes and the backs of concert programs to both sides of an airline air-sickness bag.

In that crowded, exciting, demanding year, Alvin thought of choreography inspired by the writings of Truman Capote and Garcia Lorca and the life of Ernest Hemingway. What about an impudent nod to "Ted, Izzy and Ruthie," the modern dance icons Shawn, Duncan and St. Denis, or a satirical, slightly scatological look at Martha Graham? Or a stylized "nite club revue" that incorporated a ragged razz of his own creation? The latter was preserved for dubious posterity in these eager jottings:

> We've Something to please everybody
> Something great—Something grand
> for the Sophisticate
>   you who read the New Yorker—
>   we're M. J. Jasmine Adams
>   (she's a corker)
> Then we've some sexy dances
> To keep the temperature up
> Something to please Everybody
> Even you

There are lists upon lists of scores to be listened to, ranging from jazz and folk to classical music and contemporary experimentation, along with the recordings on which they might be found. Haitian legend appealed to him as subject matter, as did reworkings of Horton's ethnic dances. Shrewdly, Alvin comments on the commercial appeal of Jack Cole's exciting use of arms and hands as "movement motivators." Hired to choreograph a segment of Jack Benny's television show, he briskly reminds himself to make work dances—Horton's term for popular numbers that would attract outside jobs for his performers—"based on materials already investigated and on hand—designed with television angle and spacing in mind—negligible time, energy, financial expenditure." Overall, Alvin revealed himself as a poignantly wise young visionary. "In one's programs one should always promise for the future," Alvin wrote in a notebook of the mid-1950s. "The beautifully unstated is an integral and irrevocable part of the action."

Each artist must create "his own unity according to his own experience and belief," he continued:

> i.e.: do not adhere to heretofore set pattern. Let own creativity be guide. Avoid too much influence from anyone. Exact an extremely personal and choreographic discipline. Demand much more of self than others both choreographically and technically. Study constantly to increase scope—both dancewise and worldwise. Establish a principle and adhere to it even if it is vague to others. Believe in oneself and own fulfillment.

He described carefully worked out ideas for dances to blues music. "The Big City Blues," he wrote about one possible piece, would be "a ballet for moderns—a city anywhere, as big but as small, as crowded but as lonely as the most insignificant spot on earth. Everywhere. Everytime. To include modern sounds, rhythms, tempos, frustrations, hopes, losses, gains, sorrows. Poems about the problems of little people—love and death in the city."

Hauntingly, Alvin made notes for a blues piece to be called *Cycle on History of Negro*. Across the continent in New York City, Talley Beatty and Donald McKayle had begun to explore black themes in American history and culture. Many years before, starting in 1929 and continuing through 1942, Helen Tamiris had set dances to Negro spirituals. On the West Coast, breathing the same air, Alvin found his way into the black experience as a choreographer through the blues.

"The stage is dark," he wrote in a deliberate hand on a page in one school notebook. "A lovely solo voice sings suddenly out—a plaintive, moaning, almost wailing song; his voice vibrates and rolls and the rhythm of the guitar accompaniment is vital and low and steady like a heartbeat":

> Bright stars falling
> won't be long 'fore day . . .

"The stage is suddenly dim with blue light and dark figures are noticed there. . . . The song continues as the stage and the figures become more and more clearly defined":

> . . . Bright stars falling
> and my baby's gone away . . .

"The singer moans his song to a finish and stops abruptly. The dancers, placid all the while, come suddenly to action, and their movements are hard and angry, beaten into the floor, and their faces are strong and their teeth gritted. . . .

"The men move down stage flailing their hats from side to side, beating their feet into the floor, their faces always forward, staring and angry. They fall into the floor, their hats trembling frantically as the women repeat the pattern. . . ."

The potency of the writing itself is not accidental. Alvin still read as much as he wrote, and his jottings include bits of his own poetry and prose, well shaped and rambling, overwrought and elegantly urgent, that suggest a strong sense of literary style. "I bring you dusty flowers," the young nonsoldier writes in "War Poem I,"

> wrapped in newspapers
> withered,
>> veined like the wrists
> of the world

The last two lines are circled and in the margin Alvin, still an admirer of the poetry of Kenneth Patchen, has noted "take another image—too Patch." Next to another line of equally purple poetry, he writes "out!"

His notes for the blues cycle contain prophetic glimpses of the pieces that were, within the decade, to make Alvin's name as a choreographer in New York. The writing has as great a richness as the imagery of the dances to come, incorporating not only the soul of the music but also hope and biting anger, rendered with the theatricality that he had learned from Horton and for which he himself became famous. Even then, too, Alvin was intent on displaying the male dancer in all his vitality.

Ideas tended to grow in Alvin for many years before they saw the light onstage as full-fledged work. But time was compressed in these notations by a young choreographer in a hurry and already pushed by circumstance. And so the handy writing of Tennessee Williams soon become choreography, along with Alvin's musings on Horton and his work.

According to St. Francis and *Morning Mourning* were Alvin's first major pieces, created for a program to be performed early that June at the Wilshire-Ebell Theater, where Horton had presented his last premieres. And on those dances Alvin lavished all his young heart and energy, putting to work the jumbled observations of the fragmented time he had spent soaking up the atmosphere of Horton at work and watching Cole and Horton's dancers engaged in the profession of dancing.

Alvin poured everything he knew about Horton's technique and style—and modern dance in general—into *According to St. Francis*, which he described as "a dance play in five continuous scenes after the life and spirit of St. Francis of Assisi." He saw it as a play-within-a-play in which the saint moves from youthful revelry through the rejection of the flesh to faith and redemption. Truitte's St. Francis shared the stage with Misaye Kawasumi as a figure of poverty, vision and rebirth, and with a chorus of six wandering players.

At times, Alvin clung slavishly to what little he had observed first-hand of the process of making dances. Horton had shopped for the perfect costume fabrics, and so did Alvin. If Horton had painted those costumes himself, then so would Alvin. And if those costumes ended up being dyed a final time, then the costumes for Alvin's dances would, too. Imitating Horton was the only way he knew how to create choreography.

He put all of Horton's hardest steps into the piece. The long-suffering Truitte, dressed in a woolen undergarment and with two fast costume changes in the dark in his few moments off the stage, lost about fourteen pounds from his tall, rail-thin frame. "We rehearsed until he got tired, or until one of us gave out," Truitte said. "Every day for about three or four weeks."

Alvin worked with an authority that no one questioned. There was almost no jealousy, because one of the group was succeeding and that meant all would have work. But underneath his assured manner, Alvin was so frightened that he slept in the theater, unwilling to let go of the surroundings in which he was creating dances. Occasionally he slowed to a near halt, provoking Eng to push him to keep choreographing and to perform adequately.

He was blocked, Alvin told an angry Eng one Saturday morning before the children's classes. Eng was not impressed. " 'Well, get around that damned block,' I told him. 'You aren't Lester Horton yet.' He was dillydallying. But we were professional. We had announced an opening date. At the rate he was going we were going to miss it by a mile. I think it didn't sit well with him. He didn't say a word." It worked, however, as it had worked when Eng lost his temper about some performing he thought listless.

Preparing for a performance at the theater one night, Alvin had dug in his heels over something Eng wanted him to do. As the two screamed at each other, Eng challenged Alvin to go out onstage and do better that night. The result was performing of such intensity that the other dancers' mouths dropped open as they watched. "God damn it," Eng yelled at him. "You can dance like that. You've been giving us shit."

Alvin's wavering self-confidence was strengthened by each day that he survived. "Alvin was a tremendously bright person," Truitte said. "He was terribly intelligent. He was intuitive. He was sharp. He also had a terrific ego. He was probably one of the better dancers that I've seen in a lifetime, but he had a kind of reverse ego thing about it. He knew he could do pretty much anything that he wanted to do."

There was another explosion when, having just finished *According to St. Francis*, Alvin was told by Eng and the dancers that at forty-five minutes the piece was just too long. He cut eight minutes, leaving Truitte to dance what was in effect a thirty-four-minute solo.

Rehearsals went more smoothly for *Morning Mourning*, which Alvin later described as "fantastically strange—but it worked." He knew his Tennessee Williams, but adapting his stories to dance was a project that might have stymied a much more experienced choreographer. Over the same three weeks that he choreographed *According to St. Francis*, however, Alvin eventually put together a suite of three scenes in which three performers changed characters, disappearing to put on new costumes behind shutters and a rocking chair that were meant to suggest a torpid southern setting.

Alvin had paid tribute to Truitte in the St. Francis piece. Now it was his beautiful, dreaming Carmen's turn to be celebrated as a Blanche

Dubois–style southern woman. Such literary characters obsessed him at the time. In earlier notes for a dance he called *Sweet Summer Blues,* also inspired by Williams's writing, Alvin wrote of a "dried-up Southern belle the morning after the rent's due": "A bottle. A whore. Magnolia on stage too. Woman figure, preferably red or blonde hair, sprawled in a mousey, tattered robe, feathered boa type satin over a chair—the symbol of everything. Slow lament-type movement. With starts and surprises." Getting into the mood without much difficulty, he observed "profligacy—ineffably beautiful."

A Bessie Smith recording seemed like the right music for such a dance. In the end, however, both new works were set to scores by contemporary composers. And the Williams piece underwent some significant changes. A program quote from *The Glass Menagerie* planted the idea of "truth in the pleasant guise of illusion" rather than a cry in the night from a broken-down belle. De Lavallade played first a young woman returning from "a night in the world," troubled by family problems, and then a series of women remembering lost love and anguish. Truitte was the father, a young suitor and a stranger, and Alvin made a late entrance as a Stanley Kowalski type.

As with *According to St. Francis,* Alvin arrived at the studio each day with specific choreographic ideas for the dancers. First he would demonstrate, then ask the dancers to try the steps and gestures. Then he and they would try again. "He worked with you," Truitte said of Alvin's remarkably consistent work habits over the years. "He wasn't Agnes de Mille, who'd say 'Everybody, now take four of those and three of those.' He had an outline."

Alvin later confessed laughingly that he had not been at all sure of what *Morning Mourning* was about. In addition, he had trouble remembering the choreography he had given himself. The results of his hasty improvisation, Truitte recalled, could be fascinating. "A lot of times I'd be standing in the wings, with Carmen with her hair down looking all gorgeous, and we'd say, 'What is he doing?' He had the greatest talent for improvisation of anybody I've ever known."

Morning Mourning was a success with one of Alvin's harshest critics, his mother. Lula Cooper visited the theater very infrequently, although Eng did observe her enough to note a hauteur from which he felt Alvin might have gotten his chilly pride. Lula must have had at least an inkling by now that her son might be homosexual, but she was never able to face the subject openly. Worried and suspicious about the life that he had so carefully kept secret from her, she had been horrified when she saw him backstage for the first time in makeup. Without warning, she had slapped him hard. But *Morning Mourning* won her over to this latest preoccupation.

Other critics were positive but not entirely convinced. The June program opened with four of Horton's Bal Caribe dances, including *Cumbia* and the shimmering *Sarong Paramaribo*, which Alvin's own company would one day dance, followed by *Morning Mourning* and Horton's *Dedications in Our Time. According to St. Francis* was not only long but last on the Wilshire-Ebell program. Filing their reviews for the next day's paper, most of the critics concentrated on the Williams piece.

Alvin's first notices were not what a new young artist might have hoped for, perhaps, but they were not at all bad for a first-time chore-ographer, particularly in view of the drubbing Horton had sometimes received at the hands of local critics. Patterson Greene, writing in the *Examiner*, described the program as "a stimulating and heartening event" and felt that Alvin "evidenced a strong creative talent."

Morning Mourning, "an interpretation of the amalgamated frustra-tions of Tennessee Williams's heroines," had "not yet achieved the clar-ity of meaning that is inherent in it, but the brilliant performance of Carmen de Lavallade is already one of the more incandescent offerings of the dance stage." Reporting on a rehearsal he had seen the week be-fore of *According to St. Francis*, Greene wrote that it "asserted itself as a reverent evocation of the spirit of the Saint of Assisi," with Truitte com-bining "phenomenal technical control with poetry and sensitiveness."

The critic for the *Los Angeles Times*, Albert Goldberg, found the dancing of the Horton company more professional but the dances less lucid than in the past. Alvin, he observed, was "a promising young dancer of lithe movement and definite stage personality." Of *Morning Mourning* he wrote that "the general idea seemed to be a sequence of conflicting triangular situations, though nothing like a clear story line was apparent to this observer. But in spite of that there was a rather vivid theatrical quality to the conception, and the impression was that once Mr. Ailey is past the arty stage he might have something of real value to bring to ballet."

Russ Burton of the *Daily News*, Eng's old newspaper, was support-ive and singled out Alvin's costuming and decor for the Williams work. But he criticized the young choreographer for "a tendency to prolong moods on a static level without instilling them with development or shading."

The harshest review came from David Bongard of the *Herald*, never much of a Horton admirer and now sharpening his wit on a new generation. "The frustrated world of Tennessee Williams is conceived in the most abstract terms in 'Morning, Mourning' so that if program notes weren't available for proper advice, the net effect could easily have been 'According to St. Francis,' which was the second Ailey premiere for the evening," Bongard wrote. He went on to add, in rather thoughtless language, given the race of the choreographer, that the second piece was "tarred with the same brush."

The ballet dancer Frederic Franklin had managed to transfer Williams's *Streetcar Named Desire* to the dance stage successfully, Mr. Bongard observed. "It's about time the young exponents of 'modern dance' realize that a reasonable, realistic impression can never be told in an undisciplined subjective orgy."

Alvin tried at first to hide the reviews from the others, but he was unable to conceal his hurt. And much worse was to come, from the usually genial Walter Terry and Ted "Papa" Shawn, when the Horton company performed in a return engagement at Jacob's Pillow the week of July 22. The invitation from Shawn to dance at his summer festival had arrived before Horton's death. Once more, the dancers piled into cars loaded with scenery and costumes for the long drive across the United States to Becket, Massachusetts, a tiny enclave that was almost unnoticeable from the road that wound past it through the lush Berkshires.

Rustic and chummy, the Pillow had been established in 1930 by Shawn as a retreat where he later formed a company of male dancers. Shawn was not fond of jazz or tap, but just about every other form of dance was represented, programmed for the most part in a sometimes dizzying variety of styles represented on the same evening.

The performers changed from summer to summer, but the scene remained the same over many decades. Dancers lived together in exuberant, bickering camaraderie in nearby rooming houses or in the small, slightly musty cabins scattered through the woods, their walls decorated with posters, newspaper clippings and photographs of famous dancers. Rehearsals were held in cabin studios. Performances were presented in a functional but cozy little theater with plain wooden walls and rafters where two legendary squatters, a pair of bats nicknamed "Ted" and "Miss Ruth," later took up residence.

The twelve Horton dancers had driven east from Los Angeles in two station wagons to perform on a program that included the famed British ballerina Alicia Markova, a model of classical decorum. The fervent Horton dancers were not a success, garnering some blandly kind remarks about *According to St. Francis* from one local reviewer and a scorching appraisal from Walter Terry, who found the piece "sincere, dedicated and interminable."

"The choreographer treated the story of St. Francis as if it were being told by players, presumably naive," Terry wrote. "And it was naive choreographically, for there were great expanses of seemingly meaning-less movement, unrelated motion and subdynamic activities, all set to lugubrious music by Gershon Kingsley. Everyone danced hard and well and Mr. Truitte had some impressive moments as the Saint, but the total effect was more sleep-inducing than stirring."

His comments made for painful reading, but Shawn was even more critical. Enraged by Alvin's dances, he dashed off a letter to Eng berating him for having sent such "unfinished, unformed, unstruc-tured" dances to the festival. Not only did Alvin know nothing about choreography, Shawn wrote, but he was not even a good dancer. Why had he been chosen to head the company? What about Truitte or de Lavallade?

"Carmelita Maracci was on the bill with us, which didn't help any," Truitte recalled. "She was 'viva tu madre' and castenets, cleaning up. And there we were. Shawn was fit to be tied."

Eng defended his new young choreographer, with whom Shawn later became friendly. Still, the humiliation was crushing.

Fortunately, something of much greater importance to Alvin's ca-reer was about to happen. An East Coast promoter named Monty King, who admired the Horton company, had invited the dancers to audition for television work in New York on their way up to the Pillow. The group performed one of Horton's sexy Latin work dances for an audi-ence that included producers and choreographers gathered for the next audition. One of those who watched was Arnold Saint Subber, a gaunt young man who had produced the Broadway musical *Kiss Me Kate* and would become known for his work with Neil Simon.

Known to the Broadway musical theater world simply as Saint, he was casting a Broadway show called *House of Flowers* that was due to open on Broadway in the winter. Adapted by Truman Capote from one of his short stories, the show required a large cast of black dancers and singers to tell its tale of two rival bordellos on a lush West Indian island.

The musical was to be directed by Peter Brook and choreo-graphed by George Balanchine, who had done some Broadway shows but who was known best as the raison d'être of the New York City

Ballet. Saint Subber expressed interest in Alvin and de Lavallade, who had danced the leads at the audition. Pure-minded modern dancer that he was, Alvin politely declined. They must return to California, he said, to keep the Horton company going.

Back home, Alvin felt worn out and hungry for the solitude that had once fed him. But he and Don Martin moved into the house Eng had shared with Horton, at Eng's invitation. It was a spartan existence, but it was free. "On good days we ate hot dogs and beans," Eng recalled. "On bad days, bread and jam. We improvised, in true Horton fashion."

The atmosphere at the house and studio was as tense as ever. Pressed into action, Alvin found it difficult to conceive of himself as a mere resident choreographer. To create dances, he had had to imagine himself as Horton, and Horton had also been the company's director. But Eng was now the director, and he was careful not to let Alvin's achievements go to his head.

Then, on December 11, Saint Subber called the house from Philadelphia, where *House of Flowers* was in tryouts before opening on Broadway. Balanchine had been fired. Herbert Ross, who had replaced him, wanted Alvin and de Lavallade to join the show as featured dancers. Would they reconsider? Both decided to accept Saint Subber's invitation.

Eng felt betrayed, particularly by de Lavallade, on whom Horton had lavished so much attention. Horton had always encouraged his dancers to leave when they were ready, however, and de Lavallade was hungry to try her wings in the larger and more glamorous world of New York theater and dance.

Alvin promised he would return in five months, newly educated and experienced in American modern dance, to help Eng keep the Horton company going. He meant it, but he did not keep the promise. On December 14, Alvin and de Lavallade flew out of Los Angeles bound for Philadelphia. The Lester Horton Dance Theater struggled on for six more years, and then closed its doors.

eight

COMING OF AGE
IN NEW YORK

Beautiful, young and seemingly destined for stardom on Broadway, a continent away from their homes and families, Alvin and Carmen de Lavallade were poised at the edge of important careers in theater and dance. *House of Flowers* would one day be seen as a one-of-a-kind musical, a show that rode in on a wave of enthusiasm in the United States for things Caribbean and established itself as a magically evocative and lavish work of art. Its songs are among Harold Arlen's most wrenchingly poetic and ebullient, and it boasted at least two matchless performances.

Pearl Bailey, the show's star, played Fleur, a conniving madam who will do almost anything to defeat her rival, Madame Tango, and reestablish the reputation of her House of Flowers after a disastrous plague of mumps. Madame Fleur's protégée was played by the teenaged Diahann Carroll, a hit as the luminous young prostitute Ottilie, who has ill-advisedly given her heart to a handsome, earnest boy-next-door.

The musical had just acquired a new choreographer, however, and friction had arisen between Bailey and Peter Brook, the director, who felt that Bailey was hard to work with and who sensed, in retrospect, that the performers had found his English reserve difficult to deal with.

With three weeks of performances behind it and a Broadway opening in another two weeks, *House of Flowers* was undergoing daily revisions by Truman Capote, locked in his hotel room and rewriting furiously. Herbert Ross, the show's new choreographer, was committed to a television project in New York City and could rehearse only from midnight to 5 A.M. And Alvin and de Lavallade were arriving late as featured performers in an already superior dance cast.

A who's who of noted black ballet, modern and musical dancers of that time in New York, the cast included Louis Johnson, a choreographer and gifted ballet dancer, and Arthur Mitchell, who became a New York City Ballet star and cofounder of the Dance Theatre of Harlem. The cast ranged in experience from Albert Popwell, a veteran Broadway dancer, to Cristyne Lawson, who had come east to study modern dance at the Juilliard School, and another youngster named Glory Van Scott, then at the start of a long career on Broadway and with Katherine Dunham. Most knew each other as part of the small but growing group of black professional dancers in New York. All were thrilled to have been chosen to work with Balanchine—and were not happy to be working with these gorgeous young upstarts from California.

Geoffrey Holder, an expert on Caribbean dance and music and a lead performer in the show, recalled his first encounter with de Lavallade, whom he had heard about and glimpsed, longingly, from a distance. "One day, it was a Saturday between matinee and evening, I got dressed to go for dinner. And somebody knocked on the door. I opened it and there was Carmen de Lavallade." His voice softened and grew higher pitched in imitation of the tired new arrival, whom he would one day marry. " 'Excuse me,' she said, 'I'm supposed to meet Herbie Ross.' " It was love at first sight.

"Then I met Alvin. He was the most striking young man. A face to die over. It was his Indonesian eyes. And the way he moved like an animal. There was a rawness about him. And something noble in the face and a bigness that José Limón projected. When you saw it you knew that was a man dancing."

Ross took care to rehearse the newcomers separately for a time. The others watched and waited. Sensing their animosity, Saint Subber asked Holder to keep an eye on Alvin and de Lavallade. And Louis Johnson eventually took the two under his wing.

"There was a little grumble among ourselves," Glory Van Scott admitted. "Then that quieted down because we got to know Alvin and Carmen. They had come in innocently, and they didn't have difficult personalities." She was drawn to Alvin when he teasingly renamed the wide-eyed and impressionable newcomer from Chicago "Sugar Lover"—a nickname, inspired by a line in the show, that stuck through the next three decades.

The amount of work to be done did not allow for energetic grudge-holding, and Alvin and de Lavallade were even busier than the others. Keeping up with all the changes was hard, and the two recruits also had to learn the show itself. The performers were given notes after the show and then expected to come in early the next day and rehearse the changes for that evening. They were also adjusting to Ross and what he wanted, which was quite different from what Balanchine had asked of them.

The customary schedule for a Broadway-bound musical was six weeks of rehearsal, three weeks in Philadelphia, three weeks in Boston and then on to New York City. The producers of *House of Flowers* kept adding towns for what eventually amounted to a twenty-week tryout period. So arduous were the demands of the show that, together with two other musicals of the time, *Silk Stockings* and *Fanny*, it prompted changes in the standard contract of the Actors' Equity Association, the performers' union.

Balanchine had gotten off to a rocky start by creating a theatrical-ized version of the mambo for performers who were already adroit practitioners of that dance, but much of his work was left intact. Ross added a number that featured de Lavallade and redid the Mardi Gras scene that closed the first act, adding a languid, sensuous, showstop-ping little duet for Alvin and de Lavallade, their bodies entwined as they crawled along the floor.

Ross then added an even more spectacular solo for Alvin, appro-priately called *Slide "Boy" Slide*. Dancers sharing the stage with Alvin learned to clear a path during it, so fast did he skim the floor on his knees and just about every other part of his body. They quickly discov-ered that it hurt if he hit them.

Alvin's pants split one night in the fervor of the solo, the first of many times that was to happen to him. Van Scott and the four other women on the stage at the time, one of them the magisterial Juanita Hall, tried hard not to laugh as he danced faster and faster, doggedly turned toward the audience as his pants opened up around his but-tocks. On another night, having forgotten to put on his kneepads, Alvin hit the scenery-moving tracks on the stage floor and ripped open his knee. But the solo was an audience favorite, as was de Lavallade's.

House of Flowers opened in New York to mixed reviews and lasted only five months. Some felt that the show had been irreparably undermined from the start by the continuing battles between Bailey and Brook. The singer, who was playing her first star role on Broadway, was determined to be the star. A vaudevillian, Bailey had a different, more comfortable sense of her relationship with the audience than did the director. She also had a trying habit of fainting during rehearsal—most often when performing with a large black crow, subsequently written out of the show, that frightened her and tended to forget its cues.

The dancers' sympathies were with her. "Peter Brook was very rude," Holder said. "He was condescending to the dancers. He'd address us as 'you people.' It was bad manners. It was very racist. And everybody just froze. Pearl did not like the way she was directed. She'd get up and say, 'He wants to create a new Pearl Bailey? Well, honey, I'm not through with the old one yet.' He wanted her to be *this* kind of madam. She wanted to be *that* kind of madam. Everybody said Pearl was impossible. But Pearl knew Pearl."

The musical was ahead of its time in several ways. It dealt unself-consciously with interracial relationships. And Oliver Messel's sets and exquisite costumes were extraordinarily lush. "The costumes were absolutely phenomenal," Van Scott said. "I'd have on a $500 bikini, incredible silk. Everything was so glorious, so grand." The show was also an occasion for pride, as cast members eventually took to counting the number of black audience members, feeling excited and pleased that they were there to see them.

Disappointingly, none of the reviews mentioned Alvin by name. But New York seemed to be opening up to this handsome, articulate newcomer.

It was a short walk from the Woodward Hotel on Broadway and Fifty-fifth Street, where Alvin lived in the show's early days, to the theater where he was performing, which was rather suitably named, he thought, the Alvin. To his young California eyes, the walk was filled with other kinds of magic: an undiluted dose of the theater district at its most tawdry yet magnificent. Strip houses jostled Broadway theaters with enticing marquees. Looking south on Broadway, he could see the huge billboards of Times Square, from which spewed fantastic steam and even a waterfall, their brilliant colors and lights adding to the sense of crowded sidewalks overflowing with men and women restlessly searching for something and eager to buy.

Alvin was now a part of it all. Only twenty-four, he was going places. He was in a Broadway show. Before each performance, he slid casually through an unnoticeable stage door into a world unknown to most. Leaving each night, he knew someone just outside that door might stop him to ask for an autograph as he made his way through waiting fans.

He had moved on from a company in which black dancers were featured to an all-black cast that was filled with stars, in a show whose splendor was dazzling after the impoverished ingenuity of the Horton productions. He began to meet people he had heard about but never dreamed of knowing.

Could the small, fey man who sat at the back of the theater during rehearsals, wrapped in large shawls with his little feet encased in run-down moccasins, be the Truman Capote who had written such intensely poetic evocations of the South? Could the haunting sweetness of life in the House of Flowers really have been conjured up by the possessor of this frail voice, who had refused to sit through script meetings in Philadelphia unless he was cozily ensconced in Arlen's lap and who had tried unsuccessfully on rides into New York to give his old Rolls Royce to Alvin?

Arnold Saint Subber was another intriguing character, and later became a friend. Chain-smoking, nervous and shy, Saint Subber was known as a producer who took an active creative hand in his shows, but he spoke in a voice so quiet that it could hardly be heard at times. "He was the strangest-looking and most enigmatic man," Michael Shurtleff, a casting director of the time, recalled. "He looked as if he were embalmed. He'd get out of his limousine and I'd think he couldn't make it across the street. I used to sit and watch him at auditions. I could never guess what he was thinking."

The most impressive member of the extended *House of Flowers* family was an elegant woman with long, tapering legs and a familiar face who haunted the show. She sewed and chatted with the wardrobe staff in the theater basement and tirelessly ran errands for the performers. They would not soon forget her arrival at Brooks Costumes at a rainy day fitting session when, dressed in a sleek black raincoat, she made the rounds of chorus dancers and principals taking orders for coffee and danish.

"It was Marlene Dietrich," Holder recalled, still stunned. "Taking orders from dancers!" Arlen's lover at the time, Dietrich wanted the show to be a success. She also seemed to enjoy being with the performers and had a special affinity for the dancers, drawing them out and listening to them talk about their lives.

Alvin met the genial master poet Langston Hughes, who became a lifelong friend and confidant. Saint Subber introduced him to the finicky and obsessive novelist Carson McCullers, whose work Alvin had analyzed for hints on writing styles not long before in California. The photographer and writer Carl Van Vechten, a champion of black artists both famed and fledgling, let it be known that he wanted to meet the dancer and was soon writing Alvin effusive notes signed "Carlo Patriarch." There were photo sessions and visits to Van Vechten's apartment on Central Park West, a salon for the New York art and literary world. His fascination with Alvin is clear from the photographs and from a review of the time.

"Alvin Ailey has all the attributes of a great dancer," Van Vechten wrote in one starry-eyed essay, singling out Alvin and de Lavallade for the "happy explosion" and "desperate energy" of their dancing in *House of Flowers.* "He is young, beautiful, strong, with a perfect body and with the technique of dance well welded into his system. He knows how to approach practically all the dance problems, except perhaps those of classical ballet, and I dare say he could easily learn to perform these—given desire, time, and a period of study with the professional experience of George Balanchine."

There was also the busy social life of a Broadway gypsy. Many nights, the dancers would pour out from the theater and over to the nearby Palladium. "We'd get on that floor and dance!" Van Scott exclaimed. "We'd all get down there and go for broke. And they'd say, 'Here come those dancers, those pro dancers.' Alvin, too. He fell into real life and activity.

"We were all buzzing and doing this and doing that, getting in there and dancing half the night. Doing everything. Spanish dance. Cuban dance. Fast and furious. We were crazed with the beauty of the movement, crazed with the rhythms. We'd get high off each other. Tito Puente. Celia Cruz. You'd hit the place in these little tight outfits. In those days dancers really dressed." One night they might spot Marlon Brando sitting on the floor and watching. Another night, someone would point out Darryl Zanuck in the crowd.

Juanita Hall held dinners at her home for everyone in the cast. Meals filled with gossip and talk of the night's show took place at theater-district hangouts like the dingy Downey's pub on Eighth Avenue, known to all as "the poor man's Sardi's." A Chinese restaurant across Fifty-second Street from the theater was another favorite place to eat. On less affluent days, the cast ate at greasy spoons like Sid and Al's or Francine's.

The gypsy bar scene was new to Alvin, but he soon learned to be a sophisticated social drinker and discovered that a drink was useful for summoning quick courage. "Drinking made him very expansive and very happy and larger than life," Michael Shurtleff said. "It released him to be this exuberant person that was under this shy person."

He still carried a book or notebook with him everywhere. "I used to tease Alvin," Arthur Mitchell said. "He was always trying to learn something. That catch-up thing! Whether it was going to be about dance, or drama, or acting, or speech, I always remember him carrying those books." And he was as irresistibly handsome as ever. Older white men, some of them powerfully connected in the arts, succumbed with particular irrevocability to the charm of this big, sensuous, graceful man who wore his dignity like a casually donned cloak.

Alvin shared a dressing room with Holder, with whom he also boarded briefly, and the two talked of literature and painting. The subject of dance tended to arise for the most part only in Alvin's continual worrying over his deficiencies as a dancer. They talked, too, of favorite composers and scores—for Alvin, Samuel Barber and *The Songs of the Auvergne*. Holder remembers Alvin singing out "Soon, soon, beni, beni, beni," a refrain in one lullaby-like French folk melody from the suite of songs, as he sat at his dressing table.

In Los Angeles, there had been one center of dance activity. In New York there were many, and Alvin began to sample them all, skipping impatiently through trial classes with Hanya Holm and Martha Graham, studying choreography with Doris Humphrey and dipping a toe into the churning, pounding waters of Katherine Dunham's popular school on an upstairs floor at the back of the Lyric Theater on West Forty-third Street between Seventh and Eighth Avenues.

Back in Los Angeles he had read of their schools and taken laborious notes on their teaching. Now he was present in their studios, breathing in the air of their august presences from the back of the class or from the sidelines as an observer. The easy camaraderie of the students must have reminded him of Horton days, although nowhere did he find the range and stimulation of the little theater on Melrose Avenue. But with nearly every visit to a new studio he learned of new places to study and new dancers to watch, on the stage and in the classroom. And he silently absorbed it all, curious about everything.

"Here he was in New York with all the great demons, being exposed to them all," Holder said of the modern dance greats whose classes Alvin sampled. "Demons and divas, and only a subway ride away."

It was an extraordinary time for a young person like Alvin, black and a dancer, to arrive in New York. The New York City Ballet was thriving artistically, looming always as an omnipresent if distant giant. Many of the founding choreographers of American modern dance were still at work in their own studios, where their techniques were the living material of daily dance classes. Merce Cunningham, Paul Taylor and other younger choreographers were beginning to make names for themselves with new ways of approaching dance, and black choreographers and dancers were becoming a part of the tumultuous scene. As the dance critic John Martin was soon to write in the *New York Times,* "All these passionate convictions, generally at variance with one another and frequently violently so, serve to unite the scene rather than to divide." The coming years should be, Martin added, "a provocative and illuminating period."

To be a part of such an era was an exhilarating experience. "Everything was going on," de Lavallade recalled. "Like a great big candy store. Everyone had companies. Everyone shared the people. Good people were dancing. Creativity was coming out of the woodwork. We didn't even think about it." The world seemed full of promise.

Alvin had a hard time finding work after *House of Flowers* closed, however, though he was becoming known about town. He lived on unemployment and the money he could make by teaching modern dance classes in studios and a church, meager pickings after the security of performing in a Broadway show. He moved into a rented room in a dingy five-floor walk-up at 109 East Ninth Street, where he lived for about a year after the show closed. It was at the edge of the fabled Greenwich Village, a place where the rebellion and freedoms of the 1960s were already beginning to be felt in the late 1950s. The gay rights movement had begun in Los Angeles and spread east, and the avant-garde arts were flourishing, arts in which black artists played an increasing role.

Although broke and often hungry, Alvin managed to take advantage of his new surroundings. There were films to see and poetry readings to attend in small, smoky bars, all affordable for impoverished artists. There was new music, and dance, and most of all new drama, in Off-Broadway theaters that bristled with work by Beckett, Ionesco and

Genet, an unsettling youngster named Edward Albee and tough-voiced black playwrights like LeRoi Jones and Charles Gordone. The work and much-publicized lives of gay Beat poets and artists had contributed to a growing atmosphere of sexual freedom in Manhattan and other urban areas. A new generation of Off-Off-Broadway playwrights dealt with homosexuality and lived openly homosexual lives, at least when south of Fourteenth Street.

Another kind of social turmoil was in the air, too, for the civil rights movement was beginning to push up through the unyielding surface of segregated daily life in America. The opening public salvo had occurred in 1954, the year that Alvin and de Lavallade went east, when the Supreme Court ruled unanimously that segregated education, no matter how "equal" it might be said to be, was a violation of the U.S. Constitution. The following year the Court ordered the desegregation of schools with "all deliberate speed," opening the door to the desegregation of all public facilities across the land.

What Alvin had lived as a black American, consciously and subliminally, was now the material of front-page headlines throughout the nation. In 1955, a spirited fourteen-year-old black boy from Chicago named Emmett Till was brutally murdered while visiting relatives in a small Mississippi town, killed in retaliation for a cheeky greeting, made on a dare, to a white woman working in a convenience store. The law can seem a distant, musty reality, no matter how shocking the changes it effects in national custom. A photograph of Till's waterlogged, tortured body published in the black weekly *Jet* worked its way irrevocably into the consciousness of black and white Americans with a terrible vividness that no legal decision could match.

More images followed, year after year, over the next two decades: bombed homes and churches; other murder victims, both celebrated and unknown; brave, set-faced young activists waiting to be served at segregated luncheonette counters, picketing segregated businesses and facing down politicians barring their way through the doors of august state academic institutions; grizzled old black citizens resolutely lining up to vote for the first time in their lives; and younger black children, nearly as resolute, making their way through violent crowds of white adults intent on preventing them from the simple act of learning how to spell or multiply with other children, just like them, who happened to be white. Crowds of marchers, black and white, began to move across the landscapes of America to protest the inequities of living life as an alien in one's own country.

Change was possible. One had only to speak out, it seemed, at last. Alvin occasionally attended meetings in crowded living rooms of apartments west of the theater district, listening to talk of breaking down racial barriers in the performing arts. Held by members of the Committee for the Negro in the Arts, a group founded by Harlem-based writers and performers, the meetings occurred at a time when black performers were becoming more visible on the Broadway and concert dance stage.

Black musicals had been performed before on New York stages, starting in 1891 and continuing in fitful cycles through the years. *House of Flowers* set off a new burst of shows, written by whites, that gave audiences a taste of homegrown exotica and were a gold mine for black dancers. From time to time, some semblance of ordinary life broke through, as in the 1974 musical *Raisin*, directed and choreographed by Donald McKayle. But blacks did not exist at all in the worlds of most other musicals, no matter how everyday these worlds might be. Several white choreographers, among them Helen Tamiris, Michael Kidd and Hanya Holm, pushed for the hiring of black performers. But the Broadway stage in general and in particular straight plays had been effectively segregated for a long time.

The rationale was that most shows were about whites and so blacks did not bother to audition. But the strongest and angriest did— or tried to. "When we went, it would be something else," Charles Blackwell, a dancer who became one of the first black Broadway stage managers, said of the auditioners' excuses.

Black performers were told that no blacks were being used. "It was very open," Louis Johnson said. "You'd sort of feel around, asking around if they were going to use a black. There was a grapevine. We'd know about black shows, which came about every five years. There were a lot of auditions you'd go to and you knew they weren't going to take any blacks, but sometimes you'd stimulate their interest."

Then, as now, subterfuges were sometimes practiced, although subtlety was not necessary in the 1950s. "In order to get past you they had a couple, a black couple, in shows," McKayle said. "Then they could say, 'Well, we have somebody,' though they weren't really that worried about complaints." The token black male was often the long, lean, handsome Albert Popwell. "Poppy was a dancer, but basically they used him for an actor. He was in *South Pacific* after Archie Savage. You could be one of the islanders, although they usually made up white people to be islanders."

A psychic point of no return was reached in 1961 with *Subways Are for Sleeping*, which McKayle described as "the big push." "I went to the audition. They told me they were not hiring. I said 'Is there anything wrong with my Equity card?' They said no. I said 'Then I'm auditioning.' The Equity lady tried to save me from embarrassment. But I auditioned and I got applause from all the fellow dancers. And the choreographer stopped me and said, 'You're wonderful. I can't use you.' "

James Truitte was in New York now and also auditioned for the show. "I went across the stage. I did my little bit. And it was 'thank you.' I said, 'But we do ride on the subway, don't we?' " The show opened at the St. James Theater with an all-white chorus. A small group of black dancers picketed the theater for two days, carrying placards and occasionally shouting slogans.

Some dancers fought back in small but often highly satisfying ways. Charles Queenan, a Pearl Primus dancer who moved on to Broadway, turned up for an audition for *Flower Drum Song* in full Oriental makeup. Geoffrey Holder went further. He had a featured spot in a production of *Aida*, choreographed by Zachary Solov, at the Metropolitan Opera House. Escorted onto the stage by two "blackamoors" who were white dancers painted black, Holder appeared in one scene with his body oiled, dressed in a costume he describes as "three white feathers out of my rear end and one sticking in the center of my head."

Solov had given Holder sixteen bars of music to improvise to, and the dancer grabbed at the opportunity. But backstage one night, the old black elevator man told Holder that chorus singers had been talking about the number, wondering aloud what "that nigger" thought he was doing on the stage. "I told him thank you very much," Holder recalled. "Little old me got back onstage for my triumphal ballet and the sixteen bars come and I turn the dance around and go right to them and begin dancing to them. All of a sudden they were in my travel spot. They couldn't chew the gum they usually chewed. All of a sudden they felt a part of my dance. And all my frustration was flying in their faces. They never said that again."

Black dancers fared even worse in classical ballet. There had been fleeting, ill-fated attempts to establish black ballet companies in New York in the 1930s, but many black dancers gave up and went off to perform in Europe after finishing their training. Dance based on ethnic themes fared better. Critics tended to be reluctant to accept black dancers in "nontraditional" roles, although in 1932, the *New York Times* critic John Martin cautioned black artists not only against "copying the white man's art" but against creating the more traditional work that whites "choose to believe is Negro art."

The most frequent argument was that black dancers did not have the proper physique for ballet. Sometimes they were criticized for looking out of place, a theory that was extended to modern dance. "I used to have lots of arguments with John Martin," McKayle said. "I wrote him letters. He'd answer me back." Martin once described McKayle and the even lighter-skinned Ronnie Aul as miscast in *The Village I Knew*, a dance by Sophie Maslow about Russian Jews.

McKayle wrote to Martin suggesting that if he was so concerned about authenticity, why had he not questioned the white choreographer Helen Tamiris's involvement in dance to black spirituals and the casting of José Limón as the Moor in *Othello*? "Martin didn't answer the point about Tamiris, but he wrote back saying that casting us in *Village* lacked theatrical verisimilitude and was as inconceivable as Shirley Temple playing Hamlet or John Barrymore playing Juliet." McKayle responded by telling Martin that if he was really interested in verisimilitude, he should know that there wasn't a Russian Jew on the stage.

Yet change was in the air. By the mid-1950s, black choreographers, drawn into modern dance by pioneers like Katherine Dunham and Pearl Primus, were becoming as much their own masters as whites were on the New York concert dance stage. McKayle, considered the leading black modern dance choreographer of the day, was carving a niche for himself with dances on social themes, performed by racially mixed casts. Louis Johnson and Geoffrey Holder were becoming names that the next generation of black choreographers and dancers could look up to. It was a new world. Talley Beatty, who had helped pave the way for McKayle's generation, was startled to hear some youngsters talking of the Dunham dancers of his own youth as outmoded "jungle bunnies." "I saw my whole life passing before me," Beatty said with wry laughter.

All this was taking place in the larger context of a city that was well on its way to becoming the bustling dance capital of the world. Johnson took Alvin with him to class at Karel Shook's studio, one of the few places in New York where black dancers were encouraged to study ballet and where just about every black dancer in New York seemed to congregate or pass through. Small, neatly attired and seldom without a cigarette in his hand or mouth, Shook had danced with the Ballet Russe de Monte Carlo the year Alvin had his first and fateful encounter with dance in Los Angeles. He had also performed with City Ballet and in Broadway musicals before retiring to teach at the Dunham school and in his own tiny studio on Eighth Avenue.

Shook, who later founded the Dance Theatre of Harlem with Mitchell, was a white man who believed wholeheartedly that ballet was not the exclusive province of whites. A pragmatic visionary, he was seldom gentle in his work, and for a time was considered a cult teacher, one dancer tartly observed, because of the way he screamed at students. But Shook offered scholarships to all who needed them.

He did not push Alvin to join his students at the barre. Ballet was important knowledge for anyone who wanted to choreograph, but Shook understood that the self-doubting young Californian might need to study it from a distance. Alvin often simply sat and watched. He also visited the home that Shook shared with Mitchell in a building on West Twenty-third Street where Mary Hinkson and Matt Turney, black women who were two of Graham's most resonant lead dancers and who studied with Shook, also lived.

A big pot of rice and beans always seemed to be cooking on the stove in Shook's kitchen in the evening, and word would go out up and down the fire escape lacing the back of the building that dinner was on. Black dancers flocked to the apartment, bringing with them supplies for the communal meals. Alvin would go off to a quiet corner with Shook and talk endlessly about art, literature and his current projects. He must educate himself about the larger world and other arts, Shook told Alvin impatiently. Otherwise he would never become a choreographer.

Alvin's other dance home, the New Dance Group, was a decidedly down-to-earth center for modern dance that had been founded during the Depression by a confederation of leftist dance groups. Consisting of its three small studios on West Forty-seventh Street, tucked neatly one to a floor and sharing the space with offices and dressing rooms, the school offered low-cost classes in everything from Jewish ritual dance to jazz, as well as in most of the major modern dance techniques, many taught by teachers who were choreographers and performers themselves. The atmosphere held little of the sense of near-religiosity about teachers and the dance itself that characterized some other studios of the time, possibly because of the New Dance Group's populist origins and because so many different kinds of dance were taught there.

A popular meeting place for black dancers in the mid-1950s, the New Dance Group studio was also a good spot to learn the latest news about jobs and classes. Alvin's connections there helped him find work after *House of Flowers* closed, chiefly with McKayle and two other New Dance Group teachers, Anna Sokolow and Sophie Maslow. Maslow choreographed the annual Chanukah Festival at Madison Square Garden, which helped uncounted dancers pay their bills, and Alvin appeared in the 1955 edition playing an Israeli soldier.

"We all ended up using the same people over and over in all these different groups," Mitchell said. "I'd say, 'I'm going to have a concert. Are you free?' 'Well, I'm dancing with Donny now, but . . .' "

Somehow, it seemed, the dancers always had money for class, no matter how impoverished they were at the time. They supported themselves with jobs as mundane as sales, restaurant and office work and as odd as carnival fire-dancing, painting baby rattles and putting caps on bottles in a hair tonic factory. Alvin's chief support was his work teaching dance, in rented studios, churches, hotels and even a small school in Mamaroneck, where he and Paul Taylor made a roomful of preteenaged girls feel like grown-up dancers on Saturday mornings.

It took Alvin time to establish himself as a teacher and he was always searching for work, but he wrote to his mother and emphatically reassured her that he did not need the $5 or $10 she had been sending him every week. By the late 1950s, he was teaching quite frequently at the notorious Michael's Studio on Eighth Avenue near Forty-seventh Street, the inspiration for the 1989 movie *Tap*, which rented rehearsal space to everyone from lowly anonymous hoofers to stars like James Cagney and Eleanor Powell. A dingy, seedy place with unisex dressing rooms, its floors were rutted from years of flamenco, tap and modern dance and ballet classes, as well as Broadway show rehearsals. In one large room, dancers could reserve a small spot on the floor to work on solo numbers. The place was so filthy that the fastidious Truitte dropped his newspaper ahead of him in a trail from the dressing room to the studio so his feet wouldn't have to touch the floor directly.

It was through his teaching that Alvin came into contact with the first of the improbable muses who were to figure importantly in his life. Marilyn Bord, known to everyone as Mickey, was a widow in her twenties who lived with her parents in Brooklyn and worked as a teacher with severely retarded children. Approached at a party one night by a man intent on rounding up potential students to study dance with his friend Alvin Ailey from Los Angeles, she soon found herself in Alvin's classes at the Broadway Congregational Church in mid-Manhattan.

"I was a nice Jewish girl from Boro Park," Bord said. "I lived in the same house practically where I was born. My mother was a teacher. My father had his own manufacturing business. Men's shirts and shorts. I grew up in an all-Jewish neighborhood, though I went to college out of town and had non-Jewish friends and a Negro girl as a roommate." Now she found herself falling in love with her handsome, likable teacher.

At times her affection had the intensity of a crush, which Alvin seemed to note with the quiet amusement he reserved for those who loved him from afar, whether man or woman. Bord was one of his greatest fans when he returned to Broadway for a featured dance role in *Jamaica*. She saw the musical many times, sometimes going backstage to bring him chopped liver in the shape of a star that her mother, who also adored Alvin, had made for him. Mostly, though, she would hide behind parked cars outside the theater with a starstruck friend, waiting for a glimpse of Alvin as he emerged from the stage door in all his glory. One day he saw her hiding and started to call out to her. The embarrassed Bord ducked. Then, realizing it was too late, she took off across the street into a dingy restaurant where she pretended to be eating.

Before long she was helping Alvin by registering students as they arrived to take class. Slowly, inexorably, she was drawn into his world, a small, sensible, comfortably rounded white woman who became his "Gina Lola Brigadigadoo," "Mickaela" and, eventually, company chauffeur, prop and costume hunter, wardrobe laundress, foot masseuse and the undemanding friend of a lifetime. "I did everything but perform."

Couldn't she learn to use a sewing machine? he asked her once. "If I ever did that, Alvin, I would probably have to go work for you," Bord told him. "And that would change our relationship entirely. I want to do this because I love you, not because I'm getting paid to do it."

One of Bord's duties was to help the less advanced students in Alvin's classes, with whom he was not always patient. "He was terrible," Bord exclaimed, brimming over with laughter. "I remember one time a little short, chunky white girl. She was so cute. And Alvin was teaching a triplet—down up up, down up up. This poor kid was going up when everyone else was going down. So he said to me, 'Do me a favor. Take her out in the hall and teach her to count one, two, three, one, two, three.' But his classes for the dancers were fabulous."

One of Alvin's professional pupils was Lelia Goldoni. A friend from Horton days, she had moved to New York to play a lead role in *Shadows*, the underground classic that established John Cassavetes as one of the most gifted American independent film directors. "Alvin's dancing was very inconsistent," Goldoni said. "But amazingly enough, when he taught class he was able to get people to do things they never thought they could do. If he hated teaching, it was astonishing, because he was building a school at that point. He suddenly had an adult Saturday class with fifty people. He had an amazing ability to critique so it wouldn't hurt and would enable students to get along."

Alvin was beginning to get television and acting jobs. In its early days, television provided new opportunities for dancers and choreographers in popular musical variety shows, although they tended to be as segregated as stage musicals. Dancers held hands as they bowed at the end of one weekly television revue. How would southern advertisers respond, the producer worried, if some of those dancers were black? But several television stars did attempt to employ black performers, and other kinds of jobs opened up, like the dance version of *Porgy and Bess* in which Alvin played Crown, in a television special called "The Gershwin Years."

Alvin returned to Los Angeles in the late spring of 1955 with a group of thirteen dancers assembled by Holder to film a pilot for a television show, *The Amos and Andy Music Hall*, that Holder was to choreograph. That fall he landed a small part as a Chinese bandit in the Off-Broadway play *The Carefree Tree*. And he joined the casts of two touring productions in 1956, *Sing, Man, Sing*, a road show starring Harry Belafonte that traveled through the Midwest for ten weeks, and *Caribbean Calypso Carnival*, a revue produced and directed by Holder that played four shows a day for two weeks at Loew's Metropolitan in Brooklyn before moving on to a week each in Philadelphia and Washington, D.C.

Alvin did not take the shows very seriously. Both were jobs. In *Sing, Man, Sing*, he exasperated Mary Hinkson, his partner and, like him, a featured dancer, with his lack of formal dance training and the unpredictability of his onstage behavior. In part, the problem was his old one of forgetting choreography. Sometimes he was so distant that he seemed to be in another world. And he would occasionally seize on an idea for ornamenting his performance but neglect to tell Hinkson, who once found her grip slipping in one moment of partnering because Alvin had experimented with oiling his body a little to give it an extra gleam onstage.

He was not much closer to Belafonte, whose alter ego he played in the show. The two had gotten to know each other in California when

both appeared in the movie *Carmen Jones*. Belafonte had seen the
dances Alvin made for the Horton company and talked to him about
choreographing this show. But Alvin, now a New York dancer and
more cautious than he had been in his innocent Horton days, was too
worried about his lack of experience to accept the job. At the same
time, he had a surer sense of his own potential, and that growing sense
of power may have contributed to an arrogance he talked ruefully of in
later years, after the two became friends. Already a star at the time of
Sing, Man, Sing, Belafonte was the unwilling recipient of Alvin's views
on the singer's commercialization of the calypso.

The two were as different offstage as on. Belafonte favored elegant
suits. Alvin dressed in blue jeans, T-shirts and boots and looked like the
renegade that he felt he was. And he didn't take the dancing, created by
the black choreographer Walter Nicks, very seriously.

Holder's *Caribbean Calypso Carnival*, whose cast also included
McKayle and Maya Angelou, had fewer pretensions to high art. Its
theme was simply the current battle for supremacy between calypso and
the Twist. McKayle recalls one performance with extra clarity: "Alvin,
myself and Harold Pierson were what Geoffrey called the three kings. I
remember we had purple capes, little brown G-strings and crowns with
feathers. We came out onstage with a little hobbling step, with the
cloaks around us, then did attitude turns and threw a kick, pom pom!"
At one point McKayle looked out into the audience and to his horror
spotted a white-faced Doris Humphrey, a matriarch of American modern dance, sitting in the front row.

House of Flowers had made Alvin something of a New York dance
personality. Shows like *Sing, Man, Sing* and Holder's *Carnival*, and a job
McKayle got him as a chorus dancer and assistant choreographer in a
Jones Beach summer stock production of *Show Boat*, were a relative
comedown, but he needed the money. He was also at loose ends emotionally. Holder had married de Lavallade the summer before, and although Alvin knew that he would never have married her himself, he
had a proprietary feeling about her. Now he had lost her to the larger-
than-life Holder, a dancer and choreographer like him but in every
other way very different. It was hard, as was often the case, to read
Alvin's true emotions. "I'm mad at you, Geoffrey Holder," he told his
friend teasingly, but he said nothing to Holder at the wedding reception.

At any rate, Alvin found himself drawn to another woman,
whom he never named. It was probably Cristyne Lawson, with whom
he had been working on a nightclub act for many months. "I guess it

has really happened to me—like a light out of darkness—and in the form of a wonderful girl whom I have known for a long, long time," Alvin wrote his mother in the spring of 1957. "She is from Los Angeles, too, and was in 'Carmen Jones'—she's a dancer, she's younger than I am—and she's twenty-one (I'm an ancient twenty-six) and she's very dark and beautiful. We have a great deal in common—we understand each other even though we fight sometimes—she is very arrogant and would require some taming but I am really very fond of her and I think she is of me—I think I would like to marry her if she would have me—I really love her very much and I think she loves me but we have never discussed it."

Lawson was unaware of any attraction Alvin might have felt toward her even after living with him for a brief period when Alvin carried her off to his apartment following a fire in her building. Eventually they drifted apart.

During the nearly three years that he had been in New York City, Alvin had acquired a huge circle of acquaintances who were charmed by his intelligence, good looks and irresistibly goofy sense of humor, although he had few close friends. He was free of his family and living a busy, eventful life. And he had his own place, at last. After renting rooms and living with friends like Holder, Alvin had moved into a typical city railroad flat, far east on Thirty-fourth Street in a neighborhood filled with performers and hangers-on from *House of Flowers* days. Life was hard at times, but he had found that he could swim very well in New York's harsh, invigorating waters.

nine

THE FIRST CONCERT

Word was out that another black musical *Jamaica* was being planned for the fall of 1957, with choreography by Alvin's idol Jack Cole. Alvin began to work up a duet with Cristyne Lawson that Alvin created in a style he was later to describe as "very Cole-ish." Donald McKayle, a skilled designer as well as a choreographer, made costumes for them and off they went to audition.

Not only were they successful, but Cole chose the two to "head the dance brigade" in the new Broadway musical, as an item in the *New York Mirror* put it. Rehearsals began on August 7, and Cole proved to be as fierce and cuttingly sarcastic as ever, driving the dancers through what they considered impossible choreography, and then executing it himself with the calm expertise of a bridge builder walking his twentieth sky-high girder of the morning. There was little out-and-out dancing and no big solos in the show. But Cole's choreography was so hard technically and so fast, with the dancers often moving on every quarter beat, that rehearsals were grueling. "If you ever did it full-out you needed an ambulance to carry you out," Lawson said.

Jamaica was a beautifully produced spectacle and yet another show that capitalized on the craze for the calypso. The musical had a score by Harold Arlen, lyrics by E. Y. Harburg and, like *House of Flowers*, some of the best black dancers of the day in its chorus. It opened

97

on October 31 at the Imperial Theater to generally favorable notices and played for a year and a half.

The show's chief attraction, aside from its extravagant production values and the heat generated by the calypso, was an electric cast headed by Lena Horne, with Ricardo Montalban as her consort. They were one of the Broadway season's most gorgeous looking duos. The dancers discovered that Horne had a good deal more to her, however, than the glossy allure of a famous club singer and the film star she had proven herself to be in *Cabin in the Sky* and *Stormy Weather.*

Beneath her radiance and honeyed reserve was a woman who had sidestepped racial stereotyping by playing femmes fatales instead of mammies. Her film career languished and her friendship with the outspokenly leftist Paul Robeson put Horne in further jeopardy. But she had continued to push for integration in the world in which she worked. "I fought for a black stage manager, for mixing minority musicians from the union and for a multiracial show, with Asians, blacks, whites, Mexicans, Puerto Ricans," Horne said of *Jamaica.* "You broke down the wall and opened another door." One of the doors opened onto a new life for Alvin.

The dancers soon found out the degree to which Horne was on their side. Nat Horne was one of the first to discover that. "I think I got *Jamaica* because people thought I was related to Miss Horne. It was my first show and I got such special treatment." He was stunned at the size of his first paycheck. It turned out that he had received the star's pay envelope by mistake. "They said, 'Miss Horne is looking for you.' But she was so charming. I walked into her dressing room and she said, 'Hi! You're Nat. I'm Lena.' I said, 'Pleased to meet you. I think I have something of yours.' We started laughing and it was wonderful. I tried to find out where she came from, but we were not related. But we continued to call ourselves kissing cousins."

The singer tried to make the partitioned chorus dressing room more comfortable for the singers, dancers and wardrobe staff who shared the submarinelike basement space. She brought visiting stars down to meet the chorus and spent time onstage talking with her fellow performers well before performances began. It was not lost on the chorus singers and dancers that while most stars waited until the overture began to arrive onstage each night, Horne would show up a good ten minutes earlier to mingle with them.

The cast also included Adelaide Hall, the famed club singer of the 1920s and 1930s; Ossie Davis; an unknown youngster named Melba

Moore; and Josephine Premice, a razzle-dazzle lead performer and a favorite of some of the dancers. Premice was hot flame to Horne's cool fire, and camps formed, with the hard-core Broadway gypsies in the show attaching themselves to Premice and the modern dance contingent favoring the less extroverted Horne. Although Alvin sometimes seemed a little apart from the others—a singer in the show recalled that he was one of the few dancers with whom one could carry on an interesting conversation—he dove with gusto into the fray, aligning himself solidly with the Horneites. He had good reason, apart from the appeal of her look and manner. Horne encouraged them all to think beyond the Broadway stage, pushing the modern dancers to plan on doing their own choreography and concert performing. When they did, they were almost sure to see her in the audience and to receive congratulatory notes from her.

On Saturday nights, the cast partied at Horne's spacious apartment on West End Avenue. Pearl Reynolds, one of the dancers, often cooked up chickpeas for the guests. "We had big spreads," Horne remembered. "We danced all night. We didn't have to work on Sundays."

"I didn't get to be with dancers until *Jamaica.* They became a family to me. I had always felt very lonely." She felt closer to other dancers than to Alvin, but she was intrigued by the Earth Man as she called him. "He was very intense and very quiet at that time. But he was very earthy. Solid, earthy like a tree. He'd tease me and say I was grounded." There was always plenty to drink, and eventually the two would gravitate toward each other and dance very close.

Alvin was moving inexorably, it seemed, away from the kind of sturdy little modern dance world he had known in California and into the fantastic, much more glamorous world of the Broadway musical. Musicals were hard work, particularly as choreographed by Cole, but they paid better and were, for the run of the show at least, much steadier employment. The perquisites were attractive, too. How else would Alvin have found himself in the arms of the great Lena Horne? Where else were there such extravagant costumes, sets and lights as on the Broadway stage, in shows in which Alvin had absolutely nothing to do but remember the steps and dance them as explosively as possible? Modern dance was a tightly closed circle in comparison with Broadway, where the theater was packed each night with new faces intent on drinking in the spectacular, sensuous allure of show-stopping dancers like Alvin Ailey, playing "natives" and dressed in revealing costumes. "Made by Johnson and Johnson" was how Alvin described his abbreviated costume to Mickey Bord, laughing over his Band-Aid–sized loincloth.

He still put in fairly regular appearances in the studio, but it was time increasingly focused on a new project rather than keeping in shape or teaching. Horne had suggested the dancers use the stage on matinee days to rehearse any acts and choreography they were working on in their spare time. "Everybody cooperated," Charles Blackwell, the stage manager for the show, recalled. "What was nice for the company was allowed. Nobody got into an ego thing." And Alvin seized the opportunity to work on what was to be his first concert in New York.

For some time now, he had been circling around the awesome notion of presenting his own choreography, performed by blacks, in the hometown of the great pioneering modern dancers. He had made a point of going to other choreographers' concerts since he had arrived in New York. Many took place at the Ninety-second Street Y in its Kaufmann Concert Hall, the small, relatively affordable theater where the Horton dancers had performed five years before. The Ninety-second Street Y was the most popular and formal of the small theaters in the city that welcomed new modern dance and ballet, the others being college and high school auditoriums. If you danced at the Y, you were on your way. It had taken Alvin time to get over the reviews of his earliest pieces and Ted Shawn's angry reaction to them. But a familiar itch was making itself felt.

He was giving his professional students dance combinations in class that were more the fleshings-out of choreographic ideas than academic sets of steps. He knew what he wanted in his performers. Earning $150 each week now from his dancing in *Jamaica,* he had, at last, dependable wages and even a little extra money.

He and Ernest Parham, a friend who was dancing on Broadway in *Bells Are Ringing,* decided to split the program and the $100 rental fee for the theater, a common arrangement among impoverished fledgling choreographers. Talley Beatty was recruited by Parham as a guest artist to lend the extra panache of a star to the event. The date was set for March 30, 1958, at 2:40 that Sunday afternoon. Now it was time to begin rounding up dancers.

Word of the impending performance traveled quickly along the grapevine. "There weren't a lot of black dancers in those days," Louis Johnson said. "You could name twenty-five you knew." Alvin had had his eye on several *Jamaica* dancers. Others he had seen in classes and performances, and more dancers approached him at the suggestion of other choreographers. Liz Williamson learned of the concert from McKayle, who told her that "a young man named Alvin Ailey" was putting on a performance. Would she like to dance with him? "Of course," she said unhesitatingly.

Although they were billed on the Y program as Alvin Ailey and Company and Ernest Parham and Company, the performers were simply groups of dancers who knew and liked one another and were eager for opportunities to perform. The Y engagement was just a concert. "In those days, nobody really had a company," Dorene Richardson, a recruit from the Juilliard School and the New Dance Group, said. "It wasn't 'I'm forming a company and I'd like you in it and we're going to get as many performances as we can all over the city, state and country.' Nobody even thought that way because there was no money. People who enjoyed choreographing decided that they'd give a concert the next year and asked if you wanted to rehearse now."

Thirteen performers began to meet with Alvin in September 1957 in an unusually harmonious mix of extroverted show dancers and "serious" modern dancers. Like true gypsies, they wandered from studio to studio throughout the theater district and beyond for rehearsals, many of which were held in snatched moments on the stage of the Imperial. "It was 'eat fast and come back' on matinee days," Ella Thompson, a *Jamaica* recruit, recalled. Not only did teaching, show-dancing, assorted jobs and other rehearsal schedules have to be juggled, but studio availability and budget had to be taken into account as well.

Alvin and his dancers did manage to rehearse at least three or four days a week for about three hours each session, an unusual amount of preparation then and now for a concert six months away. The sessions started with a modern dance class as a warm-up. Then, at the point late in a class when students dance in combinations of steps on diagonals across the floor, Alvin substituted walks forward, the dancers' arms up and undulating, later a signature Ailey dance image.

Only then did he begin to choreograph, half prepared and half letting dance flow out from the dancers. "He was totally opposite to Donny," Richardson, who had danced with McKayle, remembered. "Donny was organized. He'd have his notes. 'Do this, bap pa pa.' While Alvin was sort of like—'Well, remember when we did this? Well, do something over here. And this and that. Come through, just walk through, we'll figure that out later. Just cross.' He sort of maneuvered everybody like a painting. Sketched everything in, more or less, without anything finalized or set, sometimes until the day of performance."

Those work habits stayed with him through the rest of his career, but he suffered from procrastination that escalated with time and increasing experience. Dan Butt, the Y's stage manager in 1958, remembers that at the final technical or dress rehearsal for another program Alvin ran out of time and could not finish a new dance. With five minutes to go in the piece, he was forced, he teasingly told his dancers, to make "a cheap theatrical ending." "He threw something together and it was great," Butt said.

The rehearsals for the first concert were fun. Alvin never seemed to get angry or temperamental. As in the Horton days, the dancers were eager to work with him. He was one of them, but also filled with the drive to create.

Affection and good humor prevailed, but there was also a sense of mission for his determined dancers who understood that Alvin was concerned about the lack of opportunities for black dancers and wanted to do something about the problem. He was ambitious—although Richardson recalled that his was a strangely unegotistical ambitiousness—and one goal was to create a home for black performers. Martha Graham had an integrated company, but to spot black dancers in the major white choreographers' companies was otherwise nearly impossible, even though there was a strong sense of camaraderie and unselfconscious socializing offstage among black and white performers.

Most of all, Alvin was once again doing what he loved.

The dancers who worked with him on his first New York concerts remember that Alvin seemed filled with the pleasure of making dances. That his happiness was infectious is obvious from their memories of a time that pulsed with the pure joy of dancing and the excitement of watching and participating in his search for a path through to each blocked idea or for the key to the just-right phrase of movement. Caught up in the moment, he was clearly and completely immersed in his work.

It was not that he didn't enjoy performing. At times, the heightened physical control and abandon of dancing took hold of Alvin's self-doubt and banished it. He was often radiant with exhilaration as he surged off the stage and into the wings. But then his ever-vigilant sense of critical appraisal swung into action, dredging up every flaw, misfire or insufficiency, real or imagined, in his performance and in the choreography he had created. For those moments in the light, however, Alvin could forget not only the pressures of being a good enough dancer and choreographer but also, perhaps, the stored-away memories of what he had come from and the difficult family relationships from which New York had to some extent freed him.

Rehearsals over, a certain degree of moodiness or silly humor would overtake him. He hung out in the studio with the dancers, trading jokes exuberantly in the cooldown after a session of hard but productive work. Most of the time, however, he refused to leave with them for coffee or a drink at the end of the rehearsal. To breeze through such a get-together was harder with this smaller and closer extended family than with the pals he performed with each day at the Imperial and earlier in *House of Flowers*.

The studio was Alvin's home. There would be times in later years when he would forget that or when despair or the pressures of running the big, important company he had dreamed of robbed him of that simple sense of connectedness and purpose. He found it hard at times to push himself into the oddly impersonal, mirrored rooms of his career where work waited to be done and there was always something to prove, for yet another time, as the world outside bustled at the perimeter. But this was where he belonged, most comfortably. No, he'd tell one dancer or another as the performers left, he had to stay a little longer and work on the music, or some part of the choreography, or something.

Alvin had a dismaying habit of tinkering, then and throughout his career. An unadorned movement phrase of breathtaking loveliness and simplicity would spin out of him, and just as the dancers were admiring it, he would add an ornamental fillip here or there and the spell would be broken. His dancers learned to be ready for last-minute changes, sometimes just before the performance.

"Why did you remember that?" he would ask them half teasingly. "You know you're not supposed to remember that." At the same time, Alvin had an intensity of focus that seemed unusual to most of his dancers. He had a stronger idea of what he was after than most of the other choreographers they had worked with, in terms of steps, ideas and, particularly, the overall look of a dance. And movement was beginning to pour from him more organically than it had in Los Angeles.

He would tell the dancers to "try this" or "try that" in rehearsal. But it was clear that for him dance was, almost unconsciously, a way to communicate with whoever turned up to see his work, whether he was speaking about the power of the blues in black lives, the beauty of those lives or, indirectly, about how it might feel to be an ugly duckling, an uncertain authority or even, perhaps, a man considered not quite a man by virtue of his race and sexuality. Alvin understood more than most how universal specifics tend to be.

He wanted to communicate something about black dancers, he would later tell an interviewer. He wanted to show people, both black and white, how beautiful—and how open—they could be.

Part of that first small group, Dorene Richardson seldom missed a chance to argue with Alvin or question him in rehearsal. But for all her driving curiosity and intelligence, she sensed the depth of his feelings about the work. "I think he poured his heart and soul into dance. Whatever he couldn't express as a person he was able to express in dance. I think, at the time I was with him, that's what made him the happiest. All these pent-up emotions that he had, I think he felt the best way he could express them was through his choreography."

Now, for this first New York program, Alvin concentrated on putting the assimilative skills he had learned at Horton to work in the dances he was contributing to *Redonda (Five Dances on Latin Themes)*. He paid tribute to Lester Horton in *Ode and Homage*, a solo he created for himself that was, as his program notes put it, a "dance of faith." He summoned up childhood memories and a long love for a part of his musical heritage in a piece called *Blues Suite*.

The dance is set in a "sporting house." The characters are the men and women who frequent the place, drinking, dancing and flirting to the music of the blues over the course of a night that ends with the early morning sounds of a train and church bells.

Here were neighbors that Alvin had observed covertly from the windows of the Dew Drop Inns of his childhood, understanding the tumultuous scene through the music that poured out of the shabby little jukebox joints and into the silent, watchful boy. In the process of capturing and reanimating those memories, Alvin made something more of them than just the vehicle for a dance. *Blues Suite* became an expression of Alvin's vision of the strength, importance and universality of black culture, expressed in a note in the program: "The musical heritage of the southern Negro remains a profound influence on the music of the world . . . during the dark days the blues sprang fullborn from the docks and the fields, saloons and bawdy houses . . . from the very souls of their creators. . . ."

Blues Suite has changed over the years in structure, content and the ways succeeding generations of dancers perform it. At its first performance, the piece was a group of seven dances set to songs composed and arranged by Paquita Anderson and José Ricci, who were there to play the score on piano, flute and drums. Alvin had decided to stage the dance like a musical, with choreographed set and prop changes to be made during blackouts by the dancers, since there was no crew. That way, each section would flow into the next.

The men and women of *Blues Suite*, played by singers as well as dancers, are introduced as they slowly come to life at the start in *Good Morning Blues*. From their midst comes a man who dances alone, then three sad and lonely women and a cheerfully embattled couple, before the crowd takes over once again. The men might be gamblers, railroaders or field hands; the women, flirts and lovers. Together they have lived out a day, from quiet morning to rowdy late evening.

The first section of the piece initially called for little formal dance movement. Instead, the cast simply walked about, making the walking dramatic without being stagy. Each woman had a prop that identified her—a fan, or flowers, or a shawl. "I think it was to give you a character," Ella Thompson, who danced in *Blues Suite* later that year, said. "Alvin was very into that. More than the dance. You had to give him something. That was hard for me. I was used to being in a group on the Broadway stage."

Alvin had been amused to discover that Thompson's father was an Episcopalian minister. Calling her "Ellabelle," a name the sweet-faced dancer detested, Alvin told her not to be so "Episcopalian" in *Blues Suite*. "I was afraid a lot," she admitted. "But he made me do things. You trusted him."

In these early years, Alvin was unfailingly kind to the dancers, quick with praise that was delivered in a tone of near awe at times, although he shied away from the dancers' compliments to him. His generosity might have been prompted, at least in part, by their fear of performing *Blues Suite*. His dancers were prepared to work hard. They were even prepared to sing onstage, as the women did in the *Careless Love* section. But Alvin also wanted them to feel, to be alive to each moment they were on the stage as dancers and as human beings.

He had urged the dancers to tell him if they had problems with anything in his choreography. He did not need to say that he envisioned this as a cooperative effort. That was understood without being put into words. But some things were nonnegotiable. Richardson laughed as she remembered the quiet way he got what he wanted. "I don't think anybody really felt close to him, but somehow he had the knack of making you tear your guts out onstage. And you didn't feel embarrassed. It was the way he'd talk to you about the piece. You really wanted to give it all you had."

In what time he had left in his daily life, Alvin busily worked out the rest of the concert details. He asked Holder, who had a gift for eye-catching costume design, to create theatricalized everyday clothes for *Blues Suite.* "He gave me fifty dollars," Holder said. "I watched rehearsal. What was I going to get with fifty bucks?" One section, now called *House of the Rising Sun,* is a trio for sad young prostitutes. "What do women wear when they have the blues? I thought Anna Magnani, slip. So I went out and bought slips for the girls, and little negligees."

Normand Maxon, a white decorator and photographer who had befriended Alvin, offered to create costumes for *Ode and Homage* and for Alvin's four dances in *Redonda.* "A nice little Jewish boy who was trying to escape," as Herbert Ross described him, Maxon was drawn to black artists and to the dancers he met at New Dance Group, and he was generous to them all.

Maxon had begun to make a name for himself in his own field and had a good deal more money, both earned and from his family, than the dancers with whom he studied and occasionally performed. He also had imagination and a flair for design that resulted in such inspired bits of stagecraft as a curtain made entirely of spools of colored thread that he had coaxed from a manufacturer and strung together for McKayle's *District Storyville.* And he was intensely in love with Alvin, as he would be for the rest of his life, although without much encouragement.

Other friends rallied, too, including Bord. "When he told me he wanted to give a dance concert I foolishly said, 'Oh, gee, Alvin, please let me know if there's anything I can do to help you.' " She soon found herself scurrying to thrift shops and discount stores all over town in search of fedoras, men's pants and lace curtains for *Blues Suite* dresses, with $300 she withdrew from the joint bank account she and Alvin had established for such expenses.

Louise Roberts, a friend of McKayle who had proved astonishingly adept at promoting dance, supplied Alvin with a diagram for putting together a concert from beginning to end, based on the kind of production chart she had learned as a magazine caption writer. And everyone, including the dancers, pitched in to help in other small and large ways. "I felt so elegant," Liz Williamson remembered. "Alvin said

'Do you have any high-heeled suede shoes to go up and down the ladder?' Of course I didn't have any. But I got some."

No one minded—and few waited to be asked by Alvin to help. The dancers who were making money in Broadway shows did not hesitate to chip in to meet emergency expenses. Some turned up routinely for costume-sewing sessions as well as fittings, which often had to be held in early morning hours at Alvin's apartment or the homes of friends where costumes and props were stored. At times Alvin must have been reminded of the Horton workshop, with bodies scattered about the floor or tucked into available chairs, working and chattering. But there was no Lester this time.

Then, finally, the Sunday of the concert arrived. It was chilly and gray outside, but by 2:30 most of the seats were filled with friends and the Y's dependably knowledgeable, shrewd dance audience. Van Vechten was there, and Lena Horne, whose presence added an extra edge of glamour and expectancy to the atmosphere. If she was in the theater, it must be an event. Clark Cosgrove, one of Alvin's English teachers from Jefferson High School, had also turned up to see the concert.

The program opened with Parham's *Trajectories*, followed by Alvin's *Ode and Homage*. Both were received with appreciative applause. With *Blues Suite*, however, the excitement broke. Curtain call followed curtain call, to the surprise of some of the dancers. There had been warm and even excited applause for other concerts they had been in, but this was frenetic.

Alvin presented each of the women with a rose. Suddenly everyone felt like part of a company. "It was the first time I felt that way after working with other people on these one-night extravaganzas," Richardson remembered. Looking back, she wonders if the dancers knew sooner or more consciously than Alvin what a success the concert had been. For Claude Thompson, who was to be singled out for his dancing in the *Smokedream* solo in *Blues Suite*, the performance was almost a religious experience. He could not leave his dressing room for a long time afterward, although he knew that friends and family were waiting for him. "Everything had connected so beautifully, like a well-fit glove," Thompson said. "I knew then that I was an artist. That I had a responsibility, and had to be very selective." The next day, people reached out from a shop to pat Thompson as he passed on his way to the Imperial Theater, where he was dancing in *Jamaica*, and other performers in the show made much of him.

An elegant party took place after that first program. One dancer remembers it was the first time they had "really eaten" after six months of preparing for the concert. The reviews for Alvin's first New York program, which were not to appear until a few months later, were for the most part heartening. John Martin of the *New York Times* described the concert as a whole as "an impressive debut," finding *Blues Suite* the program's most substantial dance and an admirable work "overflowing with variety."

No review was published in the *New York Herald Tribune*, and the critic for the *Dance Observer* was unimpressed. But the reviewer for the major dance journal of the time, *Dance Magazine*, was delighted. "As a dancer, Mr. Ailey is exceptional," Doris Hering wrote. "He reminds one of a caged lion full of lashing power that he can contain or release at will. And perhaps because he is so unusual, he knows instinctively how to compose for other unusual dancers. . . . There was strutting, too, in 'Blues Suite,' but the dance went far deeper than that. Atavistically, it caught the murky, hopeless world from which came the blues."

In late April, about a month after the performance, each dancer received a thank-you note from Alvin with $5 inside. His note to Richardson was written on a Fravessi card with a bright, flyaway sketch of a bouquet of violets—in a very Alvin mix of breezy pride and self-criticism.

"Dorene sweetheart—," he wrote. "Would you do the favor of accepting the enclosed as a small small token of my great appreciation for the time and energy to [*sic*] so willingly devoted to my dances for the concert—needless to say, I learned a great great deal—only hope I can apply it well enough to make a noticeable difference in the next one—I think you know what I mean—anyway, thank you more than I can say + I'll talk to you or see you soon—love, Al."

The brash young "Al"—a name he never used—had been very much the self-doubting Alvin as the curtain fell at the Y that Sunday afternoon.

Charles Blackwell, who had agreed to work as Alvin's stage manager for the concert, never forgot what happened in a moment seen by no one else. "He was the rock in rehearsals," Blackwell said. "He was always there. Everybody would get nervous. They'd get frightened. And Alvin would be all right. He was there all the time. And when the curtain came down on the first concert, he came over to the side and he kind of fell into my arms and cried."

ten

SONGS OF TROUBLE,

SONGS OF LOVE

The Y concert had succeeded beyond anyone's expectations. Sensing that he had to keep the momentum going, Alvin booked another date nine months away at the Ninety-second Street Y, this time for his group alone. One New York season or performance a year tended to be the rule for modern dance in the 1950s. Veterans of that time talk wryly of working all year to pay for a single showing of their work. But for black dancers and choreographers, this was a time to push ahead. It was now or never, and if they didn't, who would? The concert date was set for December 21.

Alvin had been rethinking *Blues Suite.* He decided to present that hit again as well as *Redonda,* reworked and named *Cinco Latinos* for the second program but still drawn for the most part from Lester Horton's Bal Caribe dances. Carmen de Lavallade, who had been performing with the ballet choreographer John Butler and his company, would dance with Alvin in a new piece, set to a Debussy song.

He continued to perform in *Jamaica* until it closed in mid-April 1959. His own rehearsals resumed soon after the first Y concert, at most of the old haunts. Alvin loved to rehearse, the dancers observed rue-fully. Four of them had gone on to other jobs. Two of his five new dancers—Minnie Marshall and Ella Thompson—were to figure prominently in the next stage of Alvin's career. Marshall, a long-limbed, pretty "ur-Judith Jamison," as Charles Blackwell later described her, had an extra warmth and sweetness that quickly made her a favorite in the group.

Alvin had learned from the last concert. Herbert Ross had not been impressed with *Rite*, one of the Ailey sections in *Redonda*, remembering the duet danced by Alvin and Cristyne Lawson as "some ritual sort of African thing. . . . It was a little bit Vegasy, a little bit glitzy—oddly show biz." Part of the reason may have been that Alvin had put off rehearsing the duet until the last moment. He then forgot his steps and had to improvise during the performance, leaving Lawson adrift for a few moments at the opposite corner of the stage.

Possibly to forestall criticism like Ross's, Alvin had added a program note to this second performance, explaining that the dances were "not intended as exact duplications of any ethnic form but creative interpretations of the mood, style and rich variety of the Afro-Brazilian-Caribbean heritage."

There was an Ailey buzz in the air. Word was out that, in a time when solemn choreography performed by blank-faced dancers was largely the fashion in modern dance, this young black choreographer did not hesitate to make excitingly theatrical dances about real-seeming people whose stories were suggested not only through movement and music but with comparatively lush costumes, set elements and lighting. And in a sense, they were "real." The dancers in *Blues Suite* had been all sizes, with differing levels of dance technique, "which made it work," Claude Thompson said, looking back. "There were people up there. Real people."

El Cigaro, part of *Cinco Latinos* and a version of Lester Horton's *Rumba*, was to be a good example. Its battling lovers have become as much a staple of romantic narrative in black dance as princes and their reluctant bird-women and sylphs have been in classical ballet. But the duet and its jazz-dance sexual teasing were still a pleasant surprise in 1958.

The critic P. W. Manchester described *El Cigaro* as a "wonderful piece of fun demonstrating the subjugation of the confident male by the even more confident female, which Charles Moore and Jacqueline Walcott did hilariously." Walcott had "only to clatter across the stage in backless shoes," Manchester added, "and her audience is rolling in the aisles.

Next on the program came *Ariette Oubliée*, danced to Debussy's setting of Paul Verlaine's melancholic *L'Ombre des Arbres*. In its quiet lyricism, the dance expressed something of the ethereal delicacy that Alvin saw in de Lavallade, and one chorus woman remembered years later that dancing it made her feel extremely pretty. Alvin was The Man, a white dancer named Don Price played The Clown, and Carmen, draped in white by Normand Maxon, was The Moon, growing in one adroit bit of staging out of a crescent moon The Clown wears in his belt and trades to The Man for a flower.

The program's finale was, of course, the hit *Blues Suite*. Alvin had changed one section and slightly rewritten the program notes so that they read more crisply and authoritatively. "The Ballet" took place "in a barrelhouse," the audience was informed. And each dancer was assigned a specific character. Clarence Cooper, the singer, played a blind man, and Nancy Redi, the other singer, was a "woman 'upstairs,'" poised high up on a ladder, who bore a resemblance to Alvin's upstairs neighbor in Los Angeles, Ophelia Wilkes. Thompson was her lover, and Tommy Johnson, another upcoming young choreographer of the time, was The Other Man.

The house was sold out—uncharacteristically, for a relative unknown, with an encouraging complement of celebrities that included Duke Ellington this time. Once again, the audience responded with noisy ovations. Several of the performers later found they were regarded with new esteem by other choreographers who were impressed, after seeing them with Alvin, that they could "dance like that."

It was a happy time for Alvin. He had invited lively, pretty Lelia Goldoni to stay with him in his East Thirty-fourth Street apartment while she filmed *Shadows*. Goldoni had no money to rent a place in New York during the shooting of *Shadows* and would otherwise not have been able to make the film. And the two had fun together. Goldoni remembers those days lovingly: "We lived together for almost a year. He was very kind to me. I was in New York and finding the city so different from California." This very private man, who in subsequent years would allow almost no one into his home, was the soul of patience with Goldoni, watching calmly as her dog chased his kittens up and down the burlap that covered one wall of the living room.

Alvin gave her the middle room of the long narrow apartment, and he slept on a studio couch in the living room at the front. "For a person with no money, he had a lot of books, on bookcases he'd tossed together with bricks and boards. He was very busy doing things for all of us. He bought me a big chest of drawers for my clothes, as a welcoming gesture. Nothing in the house was even remotely indicative of any style. I think he was trying to get that. We'd go out together frequently. He knew all the really cheap places. . . . He made me so welcome in his strange little apartment."

One of Goldoni's favorite memories of the time is Alvin's delight in tossing around French phrases. "Je t'aime, je t'adore, Que voulez-vous de plus encore," he teasingly told her.

Always generous about passing the word along to other dancers when he heard of jobs, Alvin was growing too busy to think much of taking the jobs himself now. Invitations to choreograph and present his work were starting to come in more regularly now, enabling him not only to provide his dancers with work but to bring his dances to a wider public.

He began, in 1959 and 1960, to have the confidence to branch out and try his hand at a variety of projects. Shirley Broughton, a teacher and choreographer known for her brainy and voluptuously big-moving approach to movement, wanted a piece for her modern dance group. Alvin returned to the dramatic roots of his Horton days and created *Mistress and Manservant*, an eerie but psychologically astute version of Strindberg's *Miss Julie* set to the urgent Ravel String Quartet, which one reviewer found to be powerful and vivid. Soon after, he directed and choreographed a touring revue called *African Holiday*, starring Brock Peters, at the Apollo. There were jobs choreographing summer touring productions of *Jamaica* and *Carmen Jones*, and he entered a new piece called *Sonera* into a competition sponsored by Lincoln Kirstein and George Balanchine, although it was not chosen.

Ted Shawn invited the newly conquering dance hero back to the Pillow for a week in late June and July, on a shared program with Pearl Lang, a former Graham dancer. The Ailey dancers performed *Rite* and *El Cigaro* as well as *Blues Suite*, which one local critic interpreted rather surprisingly as a stylized account of the birth of the blues.

At the Pillow, the Ailey dancers felt more like a company than ever before. They were perceived as one. And they were working side by side with famous ballet and modern dancers such as the legendary Ruth St. Denis, then seventy-nine, who performed a properly mystical solo called *The Blue Madonna of St. Mark* on the same program.

Further bonds were formed when Alvin and his dancers stayed at a local landmark called the Here-U-R, a restaurant on a winding country road near the festival where the troupe rented a single, leaning cabin out back with peeling wallpaper and paint. It was a tradition at the Pillow for dancers to gather at the Here-U-R after performances to eat and relax, pouring into the kitchen to help Tessie Morawiec wash up the dishes while her husband, John, tended bar and performed magic tricks. Established stars of the American Ballet Theatre and newcomers like the Ailey performers mingled in the easy camaraderie of dancers. Alvin felt thoroughly at home.

"He would tell these jokes," Ella Thompson recalled. "He'd get everyone telling jokes. Crazy jokes. He had the best." Long after, Tessie Morawiec remembered Alvin and his dancers with special fondness. "He was just getting started then and they started poor," Morawiec recalled. "They paid us $15 a week for the cabin and everything they ate was on credit until Saturday night, when they got paid. We'd give them a buffet and they'd line up to pay us, one at a time. Then they'd be broke again.

"They'd go up on a truck to the Pillow each night and after the performance they'd come back for sandwiches and drinks and jump around. The dancers love to dance." During the day, they rehearsed on the smooth lawn in back of the restaurant. "That Charlie Moore, how he could pose," Morawiec said. Mickey Bord caught the fancy of John Morawiec, who remembered her as "that New Jersey schoolteacher" who drove by in a big convertible looking for Alvin.

The dancers returned to New York in time to rehearse for another performance a month later at the new Delacorte Theater in Central Park, where they were to represent the United States in a program called the World Dance Festival, on a bill with Cambodian and Spanish performers.

It was becoming increasingly clear that Alvin and his dancers were not merely a pickup company of friends devoted to performing the charismatic work of a new choreographer. Alvin himself had begun to sense that. Soon after his return to New York he was approached by Susan Pimsleur, who ran a concert management firm called Musical Artists. Pimsleur, plump, sweet faced and disorganized, had represented the companies of José Limón and Jean-Léon Destiné and wanted to add the Ailey dancers to her roster of artists. She sketched out a plan of tours and concerts and began work on a brochure for what she called the Alvin Ailey American Dance Theater, although the company did not formally adopt that name for several years.

There was a third concert to prepare for at the Y, on January 31, 1960. Blackwell, now a wise older friend to Alvin and his stage manager again, watched with concern as the search began once more for decent, affordable places in which to rehearse. Planning for rehearsals had come to seem like a dance version of the storming of Normandy Beach. The solution that he found, by perseverance, charm and luck, was to provide Alvin with a degree of stability unknown to most dancers and choreographers of the time during the trying early years of establishing his company.

In search of clean, affordable rehearsal space in the neighborhood, Blackwell walked down block after block of the theater district, investigating churches, empty storefronts and even the local offices of the national union for hospital workers, which he knew to be receptive to the needs of dance and theater folk.

"Then there it was, the Capitol Hotel, which was being turned into a YWCA," Blackwell remembered. "I went in and said 'Hello. Hi. You're the Y, aren't you? You folks say you're Christians. Show me some Christian responsibility.' That was the thought, not the dialogue." He was introduced to an elegant, delicate-featured woman named Edele Holtz, the no-nonsense director of activities at the new YWCA at Eighth Avenue and Fifty-third Street, and explained his mission. "You're looking for community stuff and I have this community project here," he told her. "They are wonderful people. And they just need rehearsal space."

Blackwell found Holtz to be "a person who embodied all those Christian ideals that others are phony about. My memory is that she immediately said that the Y was very interested in doing things with community groups. And I said that we were neighbors, at the Imperial. Did we qualify? She was wonderful and sympathetic. And she gave us— I think it was some dumb price, maybe $15 a month." It was a very good deal, for studio rentals started then at about $2 an hour.

Holtz, a Danish-American social worker, remembered that visit vividly: "One day I'm working away in my office and in comes this very very tall man, a black man, who obviously was very indignant. He said, 'I need your help. I've just come from an absolutely dreadful situation where a lot of young black people are being exploited. Everybody is having to rent space in this dangerous studio. A group of young people from musicals want to start their own group. They really need help.'"

Blackwell's arrival was providential. Holtz and her staff had gone out into the neighborhood seeking a population to serve in the sullen tenements that were as much a feature of the area as the glittering theaters surrounding the hotel. Here was a way to serve the two very different communities, families and theater workers, of the theater district. Holtz took him upstairs to see one of the large second-floor spaces that had once been used for wedding receptions. It looked like a palace compared with the dispiriting Michael's, and the dancers moved in. To Holtz, they were just another group of attractive and deserving young people. Her mind changed when she attended the January concert.

For his return, Alvin envisioned a concert that would suggest the richness of black culture, a panoramic program that would include dances set to the blues and to spirituals, in the Katherine Dunham mode, with interludes of Kansas City jazz and contemporary music. He soon abandoned the concept, however, in favor of the more manageable form the first Y performances had taken.

The composition of Alvin's company had changed as dancers moved on to lucrative work in musicals or into dependable teaching jobs. Only Dorene Richardson and the singer Nancy Redi remained from the first Y performance. The new dancers included Nat Horne, from *Jamaica*, and two sisters, strong performers named Merle and Joan Derby. Alvin recruited a chorus of six fledgling dancers—one of them a youngster named Dudley Williams, who would become an Ailey star and one of the great dance artists of his time—for *Sonera*, a suite of three plotless dances inspired by Cuban dance forms.

Alvin also invited Matt Turney, a dancer of hypnotically radiant serenity, to perform as a guest star. Although she was a leading member of Martha Graham's company, Turney was flattered by the invitation to perform with this much-talked-about young choreographer. Late into the rehearsal period, Alvin began work with her on a new duet called *Creation of the World*.

He had continued to rework *Blues Suite*, whose musical subject he now described with succinct poetry in the program notes as "hymns to the secular regions of [the southern Negro's] soul." Gone were the individual song listings, although the characters remained the same. Alvin took on the role of Her Lover, with Horne playing The Other Man. He had reworked a bit of his ever-green Latin suite, giving the old *Rite* a new name, *Canto al Diable*, clearer program notes and a new score. Next on the program would be the *Creation of the World* duet and a premiere called, simply, *Revelations*.

In the duet, Alvin and Turney, dressed in flesh-colored leotards with leaves over their genitals and her breasts, replayed what the program sagely described as "the world's oldest story." The piece reflected Alvin's growing and increasingly secure sense of theater, with an opening that Gary Harris, the Y's stage manager, recalled with wonder nearly four decades after the premiere.

Harris knew it was a good idea to try to hire an extra technician to meet the challenge of Alvin's theatricality and professionalism. He had been impressed with how prepared Alvin and the dancers were. He was used to disorganization, given the lack of sophistication and experience of many of the dance companies performing at the Y and the mere three hours of onstage rehearsal time the Y could offer each group. "The horrible times you have in one of those halls is when something is being put together right on stage and nobody knows what it is," Harris said. "When Alvin—and Donny [McKayle]—came in it was a big day."

By the time the troupe got to the Y, Alvin's instructions to the dancers, Harris recalled, were mostly a matter of warnings not to hit one another with a stepladder or umbrella. Nicholas Cernovitch, whose imaginative lighting designs helped early on to create the Ailey reputation for tasteful theatricality, knew exactly what Alvin wanted.

Interesting things, as Harris wryly put it, tended to happen during Alvin's rehearsals and performances, for all his preparedness, although they were seldom his fault and were usually fixed before they disrupted the work in progress. A self-splicing music tape wreaked havoc one time; a flood from the swimming pool above the theater caused trouble another time. "But Nicholas was so precise. Alvin was so clear. And he never presumed in the sense that he told us to do anything impossible. If we made a mistake we'd say, 'That's a mistake and we won't do it again.' And he'd say, 'Yup.' Every time they came in I knew it would be fun. He was so happy to be at the Y. We were happy back."

Harris remembered most fondly those first moments of *Creation of the World*. "It started off with a tan scrim in front. Luckily we had one lying around. There was this pink wash coming in on the scrim. In the middle was this bright red sun. The curtain went up, essentially in darkness. The scrim became very flat. The sun grew in the center of it. In the center of the sun, being lit from behind, was Alvin in a standing pose, symmetrical in the sun.

"You saw nothing when the curtain went up. It was all a progression. You saw a perfectly flat, formless nothing. In the center of that nothing grew a red sun. And just lagging it slightly was the image of the posed dancer. The world was created and the dancer was created in the same image. It was really, really wonderful."

Another memorable moment of theater occurred when Turney

Alvin Ailey in the early 1950s, in a portrait taken for a portfolio he was assembling. *Source: David McReynolds*

Lester Horton, the visionary modern dance
choreographer who gave Alvin a new sense of art and the
world around him. *Source: Marjorie Berman Perces*

A work session at the Horton Dance Theater school in the early 1950s. Leila
Goldoni fourth from the left; Don Martin at the right. *Source: Frank Eng and the
Lester Horton Dance Theater*

Alvin as a young choreographer, at work on "Le Création du Monde" in Los Angeles in the early 1950s. Joyce Trisler and Roland Goldwater in the background. *Source: Frank Eng and the Lester Horton Dance Theater; photo by Bob Willoughby*

"Le Création du Monde." From left: Don Martin, Larry Maldonado, Roland Goldwater, Yvonne de Lavallade, Joyce Trisler. *Source: Frank Eng and the Lester Horton Dance Theater; photo by Bob Willoughby*

Alvin with Carmen de Lavallade in "House of Flowers." *Source: Edele and Al Holtz*

Alvin with Lena Horne, star of "Jamaica,"
backstage at the Imperial Theatre. *Source:*
Schomburg Center for Research in Black Culture;
photo by Gus Dinizulu

Alvin with Mickey Bord in "the buns shot."
Source: Mickey Bord

Alvin, Joan Hackett and Robert Duvall in a poster for "Call Me By My Rightful Name," in which Alvin played his first major acting role. *Source: Edele and Al Holtz*

HOWARD TAUBMAN in **The New York Times** Says:

"LET US BE GRATEFUL FOR 'TIGER TIGER BURNING BRIGHT.' ..BRINGS DISTINCTION TO THE SEASON..ENORMOUSLY MOVING."

(Mr. Taubman's Review in Full on Reverse Side)

TIGER TIGER BURNING BRIGHT

Critics Acclaim a New Hit!

JOHN CHAPMAN in **DAILY NEWS** Says:
NEW YORK'S PICTURE NEWSPAPER

"TAUT ARRESTING DRAMA WITH A WALLOP. CLAUDIA McNEIL IS MAGNIFICENT."

(Mr. Chapman's Review in Full on Reverse Side)

■ BOOTH THEATRE, 222 West 45th St., New York 36, N.Y. ■

Alvin with Claudia McNeil in a poster for "Tiger Tiger Burning Bright," the play that convinced him to give up acting. *Source: Edele and Al Holtz* seemed to rise right out of Alvin's rib—a piece of magical stagecraft that underscored how superbly paired these two good-looking, almost stealthily compelling dancers were. The effect was received in a total silence of held breaths, but the moment the dance was over, the theater exploded with applause and cheers.

Already excited, the audience returned from intermission for the second half of the concert—and the premiere of what is perhaps the most beloved and popular of all American modern dance classics. Those who had read the program beforehand knew that they were about to see a work that explored "motivations and emotions of Negro religious music which, like its heir the Blues, takes many forms, true spirituals with their sustained melodies, ring-shouts, song-sermons, gospel songs, and holy blues—songs of trouble, of Love of deliverance." It was music, Alvin said many years later, that as a child he felt he could almost see.

The new piece was divided into three sections of song and dance based in and illustrating traditional music and rituals of black religious devotion. Those who had seen Alvin's first New York concert might have been forgiven for wondering if *Revelations* was simply *Blues Suite* on a somewhat grander level. Friends understood that the new piece came from a very deep part of his life.

Alvin had been nourished as much by his childhood church experiences, permeated with fervent song, as by the hot secular music that had poured from the Dew Drop Inn on Saturday nights and found a voice in *Blues Suite*. A bittersweet defining moment of his life, remembered keenly long after Alvin had become a man of the world, had been Sister Hattie Taplin's sudden singing of "I Been 'Buked" at his baptism, the song materializing and cracking through the joy of that communal celebration.

The first *Revelations* was as much song as dance. Six spirituals were grouped under the heading *Pilgrim of Sorrow*, six under the title *That Love That Jesus Gives Me* and four in the finale, *Move, Members, Move*. Interspersed throughout were ten dances. There were no characters or narrative. Instead, the singers and dancers performed alone, in ensembles or, at last, together as a group. What they performed was as intense an expression of heavenly faith, earthly despair and unquenchable humanity as has ever been created in dance.

Revelations underwent many small and substantial changes over the next three years, until Alvin made a kind of peace with the work in 1964. The musical interludes were dropped. Some dances were eliminated and some were moved to other sections of the piece. In all, five of the original dances survived without major changes.

Alvin kept the opening group dance, *I Been Buked*. Its first pose is the subject of a famous photograph by Jack Mitchell, the dance photographer who, with Normand Maxon, created the kind of powerful images that helped sell the company early on. The pose and photograph are so well known they seldom need identification.

Six dancers are grouped center stage, arms reaching high, fingers spread, heads tilting back. The men are bare-chested, wearing only body-hugging pants. The women's long, sleeveless dresses are plain but drape loosely around their thin bodies to reveal breasts and hips with a similarly plain, unsensual beauty. Warm light pours down from above, fixing the dancers in a moment of exaltation and yearning. "It looks so simple, and it is," Dorene Richardson said. The dancers move very little in what follows, and when they separate as a group they return and pull together.

One can see the influences on Alvin of Lester Horton and Martha Graham in *I Been Buked* and throughout *Revelations*. But those elements—bodies that contract and hinge, sudden sinkings and almost instantaneous rises, sashays across a crowded stage—are used not so much to narrate or to suggest but as direct expressions of emotion, with a flow and ease that are Alvin's own. And his sense of theatrical effect and pacing served him well in the steadily building *Revelations*.

Today, *Revelations* progresses gradually from an expression of sin and the hope of redemption, through a joyous baptismal scene and a solo communicating a readiness to be saved and sanctified, to heightened portrayals of the wages of sin and the joys of salvation. The three-part opening "brown" section, *Pilgrim of Sorrow*, is darkly lit and filled with sculpted bodies and simple patterns. In the solid expressive shapes assumed by those bodies was the clearest suggestion of Alvin's admiration for the work of Henry Moore. And here, too, were men and women pushing up from and going back into the earth.

Wading in the Water, the two-part "white" middle section, is essentially a baptismal ceremony, celestial in its interplay of white fabrics and props. The predominant color of the two-part finale, *Move, Members, Move* is yellow. The "yellow" section opens with an explosive trio for sinners, men desperate to escape the fires of hell, familiar characters who might have hurtled out from the blood-and-thunder sermons at Sunday church services Alvin attended as a child. The section closes with a gathering of gossiping women and their natty men—the faithful in all their exuberant human frailty—for one of those services. Mortal pain and toil have yielded before the promise of redemption in *Revelations*. That promise yields in turn to the realization of heaven and eternal happiness, for a short time each week at least, in a worshipful community's unrestrained embrace of the Lord of a far-off, untroubled kingdom.

Alvin was not averse to vivid theatrical touches in costuming and set designs. "Like Graham used to say, a little bit of red at the proper moment is a good thing," Ves Harper, one of Alvin's early costume and set designers, observed. "A little feather here or some kind of detail livens the moment. And I think Alvin knew innately how to use the elements that he was working with, in a manner which seemed theatrically interesting for the audience, to shorten the distance between the stage and the immediate public that he wanted to be involved in what he was doing. But I don't think theatricality per se was the important moment for him."

The costumes for *Revelations* were theatrical in their plainness. Truth, for Alvin, was plain. But that simplicity was meant to be expressive. For Alvin, the brown section was essentially a birth scene. And he and Harper dressed the performers in jersey dyed to match each dancer's skin tone, to create a look of nudity.

Other costume elements were a little more improvisational, as Bord was sent about town to search for fans for the church women, which she found at a Japanese tchotchke shop, and for nets for men's tops, which she discovered at the Fulton Fish Market. Harper found lace perambulator covers that made perfect tops for the women, and printed silk jersey for church dresses. Distracting in their relative fanciness, the dresses were later jettisoned. The one other extravagance was the women's straw hats in the church scene. "They cost a great deal of money," Harper recalled ruefully. "We gave them to the dancers, and they immediately began to stamp on them and to do things to them so that they became personal." Everyone contributed to the construction of the costumes. Whoever was passing by a rehearsal, Harper adds, might be called on to "put up a hem."

Alvin had talked to a few of his dancers about his idea of creating something drawn from Negro spirituals and his memories of drowsy Sundays spent singing and praying with his mother and observing churchgoers at the Truevine and the other churches of his youth. He had had a half-formed idea at the back of his mind for several years, thinking seriously about it as he listened to black religious music and worked out imagery as he rehearsed his other dances. Later, he gathered the group around him at the first formal group rehearsals, as he always did, to talk about his ideas for a new piece.

"Come dancers," he would often say, in a command one company member assumed was borrowed from Lester Horton since it seemed so uncharacteristically peremptory. Everyone rose and followed Alvin through sequences of steps, guided at first by his voice as he talked of what they were doing and why. Then they moved to music.

The group rehearsals began with the *I Been Buked* and *Wading in the Water* sections. The latter dance was at first performed without its now-famous white umbrella, which became an even more astonishing prop when Alvin moved Judith Jamison from the *Fix Me Jesus* duet to the chorus of *Wading in the Water* so she could hoist the umbrella high over her towering body in a stroke of genius not at first appreciated by Jamison, who felt demoted. In that dance, whose detail, attack and overall look suggested the influence of Jack Cole, Alvin re-created on-stage the gestures and ceremony he remembered from his own baptism, exaltation rising up from the stirred waters of the snake-ridden pond back of the church in Rogers, Texas.

It took Ella Thompson a little time to adjust to the fact that Alvin's rehearsals were as much about acting as moving, which meant she had to dredge up memories and even to sing. "It was like going to acting class, but you had to dance," she said. "Some of the movements he gave us were really alien. Alvin had another way of moving, and it meant something." He was clear about what he wanted, but gave the dancers evocative images to help them understand and deepen their interpretations. He was not happy, for instance, with the way the women lowered themselves onto their stools in the closing scene in *Revelations*. They were performing the choreography right, but something was missing. In his mother's church, he told the dancers, there had been several "Sister Full-Bosoms," top-heavy women whose breasts dictated the way they eased into their seats.

"Think," he told them, "that it's a real hot day and you're sitting on this stool, so you've got to open your legs. You've got to get some air down in here"—pointing to the bottom curve of those heavy breasts—"so you have to lean forward." And so the slender, ready-moving women in the company learned to evoke the heavy slowness of the Full-Bosoms without caricature. To suggest the wild exultation of the last dance, *Elijah Rock!*, Alvin told the women about little Miss Choo Choo, a friend of his mother who rose up from her seat at services and traveled through the congregation, arms churning like train wheels, every time she felt the spirit. Unlike her, however, the dancers had to devote a good deal of concentration to jumping up or getting down onto the floor on the exact musical beat to achieve a look of seamless group symmetry.

By the time of the Y performance, after about four months of intensive rehearsals, the dancers had come to know and feel comfortable with the Sister Full-Bosoms, Miss Choo Choo, and the gossipers and high-stepping men of the closing scene. They were even enjoying playing the roles, and did not expect any particular response from the audience to these homey eccentrics or this religious imagery. But something strange occurred after the curtain fell. There was dead silence in the theater. The dancers looked at each other, shaken. What had happened? None of them had thought that *Revelations* might be great art. The experience of learning it had been too much fun. But it hadn't seemed a disaster, either. They bravely stepped forward to take their bows as the curtain rose and were greeted by the sight of the audience rising to its feet, cheers mixed with applause. "We looked at each other again," Richardson recalls. " 'Guess they liked it.' We were totally naive about the reaction."

The ovation continued until William Kolodney, who oversaw the dance programming at the Y, stepped onto the stage and signaled for silence. A small, balding academic sort not given to flights of fancy, Kolodney wasted no words as he made his announcement. Because of the audience response, he said, he had decided that the company would return for a repeat performance on February 28. It was an announcement unprecedented in the history of that little hub of American modern dance.

eleven

REVELATIONS

The first reviews of *Revelations* were generally positive, but the audience's rapt silence said most about what the new dance was and the classic it would become. *Revelations* would one day be performed in theaters around the world. Night after night after night it would draw tumultuous applause, cheers, foot stamping and general mayhem in even the most circumspect of cultures. Audiences would demand to see it, over and over. By the late 1980s, it was estimated that *Revelations* had been performed more often than the nearly century-old *Swan Lake.*

What is the magic of *Revelations?* It is simple and direct, but so is Doris Humphrey's *Day on Earth,* a modern dance classic in which a man and woman and their child move with gentle inexorability through the life cycle. It is theatrical, but so, certainly, is Alvin's *Blues Suite.* It addresses the life of the spirit, in hope and in despair—like José Limón's powerful *Missa Brevis.* It is enjoyable fun, but so are any number of dances by Paul Taylor.

The spirituals to which *Revelations* is danced have a powerful, primal appeal. There is in the songs—and in the dance's choreography and scenic and costume designs—a subtle interplay and juxtaposition of complexity and simplicity. Most of all, however, *Revelations* was and remains the work of a community, from the larger worlds of black

122

Americans to the worlds of the individual dancers who helped create *Revelations* and passed it on to later generations.

Revelations was created for and by a devoted band of friends, men and women whose professional lives were, in effect, a work of hopeful activism. "The dancers were 100 percent behind Alvin," Nat Horne said. "We loved what he was doing. And that love—I think we portrayed it without realizing." Art and artists have undergone profound changes since then. Yet *Revelations* lives on, exerting its hold on audiences and the dancers who perform it.

Nothing in dance is foreign to human experience. The art of dance springs from the simplest, most universal human acts. Separate the movement from the music, costumes and sets, slow it down in the mind's eye, and dance can be clearly seen as first cousin to a walk. To dance is to stretch up into the warm sun or jump clear across a dauntingly large puddle. It is to measure balance and the immutability of the world around one by whizzing fast. Dance is wrapping one's arms around and steadying someone loved or pushing someone away. It is curling up, even for a moment, into a still, dark, private place.

Yet dance is also an art whose performers—athletes of God, as Martha Graham called them—must be superhuman in strength, coordination and training. It is an art that condenses experience, as Alvin observed in an interview a few years after he created *Revelations*. "Everything in dancing is style, allusion, the essence of many thoughts and feelings, the abstraction of many moments," he said. "Each movement is the sum total of moments and experiences."

Neophytes worry frequently that they don't "understand dance," a complaint not heard about spoken theater or music. The simplicity and distillation of the art can be frightening, throwing one back, without the safety of mediating words, on the most basic of physical impulses and memories. One great achievement of *Revelations* is that it straddles the worlds of the simple declarative sentence and the poetic metaphor, reaching both the naive and the sophisticated on their own terms as it plunges them into the most common of experiences.

Dance is, like the other arts, assimilative. Nothing is ever really very new in it. The freshness of a dance lies not only in what the choreographer brings to it, with honesty and expertise, but in how the elements are combined. Alvin borrowed from the world, a habit he cheerfully acknowledged, making a virtue of eclecticism and in the process creating something that was more a dance style or way of moving than a technique. What he wanted in a dancer, he once said, was the long, unbroken leg line and deftly articulated legs and feet of "a ballet bottom" and the dramatically expressive upper torso of "a modern top."

He had scribbled notes to himself back in Los Angeles about baptismal dance scenes. In New York, in Donald McKayle's *They Call Her Moses,* a piece about Harriet Tubman, Alvin danced a solo called *Run Brother Run* that McKayle believes may have been an inspiration for the *Sinner Man* trio in *Revelations.* Carrying a child on his shoulders, he also crossed a billowing river on his knees. On a visit to Los Angeles in 1958, Alvin saw a dance by James Truitte that was set to spirituals and ended with *Elijah Rock,* as *Revelations* did until Alvin saw that the audience responded more to *Rocka My Soul.*

"A theatrical form hits your eye and you say, 'I have an idea,' " McKayle said. "And you go from there."

Pressed for time and eager to see his performers' presence in the choreography, Alvin often pushed the dancers he trusted most to rework or even create parts of the choreography, which was then filtered through his own sensibility in rehearsal. Late one night in 1962, just before the company was to leave for Jacob's Pillow, Truitte recalled, Alvin prevailed on him to create a solo drawn from Truitte's Horton technique, to be incorporated in a performance of *Revelations* for the television show *Lamp Unto My Feet.*

That solo was *I Want to Be Ready,* one of the most haunting dances in *Revelations.* When Truitte taught the prayerful, yearning solo to Dudley Williams, the younger dancer reworked it with a substantial infusion of Graham style. Each man and each technique are powerfully present in the solo. And yet it retains its integrity, with very few differences between versions filmed before and after Williams took on the role.

An observant outsider in choreography as well as life, Alvin consciously appropriated and fused elements from the techniques of Lester Horton, Martha Graham and the jazz dance of Jack Cole to create a style that could express the visions of a humanist, a poet, or even an anthropologist. *Revelations* is, as Truitte saw it, a dance that contains the history of blacks in America.

A shared history is not necessary, however, to understand the piece. Alvin understood that the universal lay in the smallest, most everyday details of particular lives. The religious themes in *Revelations* meant little—or too much—to many of the Ailey dancers. Nat Horne, the southern-born son of an evangelical minister, at first felt a little sacrilegious dancing to the spirituals and worried, unnecessarily as it turned out, about his father's reaction to the piece. Some of the dancers, born up north, had had no experience of the southern black Baptist church. Claude Thompson, who rehearsed but did not perform in the premiere of the piece, recalled that he felt at first like "a Catholic nun at a Baptist convention." He was, after all, someone who passed by the black church in his neighborhood, heard tambourines and thought merely, "Nice rhythm!"

Nor is *Revelations* simply a " 'black' work," as the *New York Times* dance critic Anna Kisselgoff suggested in a 1981 essay, but a dance that also "addresses itself to a universal expression of faith—in religion perhaps, in faith in art itself." The dance has, Kisselgoff continued, "its own internal coherence."

Revelations has been largely impervious to changing fashions in dance. The piece has also been called dancer-proof. Veteran performers talk of how, surprisingly, it seldom seems a chore to dance the piece despite how often they are called upon to do so. Not only does *Revelations* seem unchanged by interpreters' greater or lesser technical or dramatic skills, but it has become a rich receptacle of living company history.

"There have been days where I've thought, 'Oh, God, not *Rev*,' " Williams said. "I had to wake up and look for new flavors." He asked Alvin if he could add or change a little something here or there. "Well, try it, let me see it, and I'll let you know if you can keep it," Alvin told him.

The success of *Revelations* dogged Alvin all his life. He knew the worth of the dance and cherished it in spite of himself, allowing only one other company to dance it, and that for a limited time. But he worried that impressionable young dancers, hearing the wild applause that invariably greets the piece, would assume that their performances were perfect. He worried that they could not understand its soul, coming as they did from worlds so different from those of the dancers for whom it was created. And, always, the singular and unrepeatable-seeming success of *Revelations* underscored Alvin's doubts about his gifts, driving him to compete uneasily with himself for his entire career.

"When was he going to do another one of those?" Linda Kent, an Ailey dancer of the late 1960s and 1970s, asked rhetorically at a seminar on the classic. "Well, there isn't 'another one of those.' "

In the early years, however, *Revelations* brought Alvin as close to a pure and joyful satisfaction in his work as he was ever to come. The future promised much. It was still possible then to envision successors to this outpouring of his heart and soul and craft. And there were later masterworks. But none was ever to have the same impact.

Revelations was a phenomenon, a work of raw emotion rendered with the innocent wholeheartedness and urgency of a first work into which all the experiences, thoughts and emotions of a young life are siphoned in an unquenchable, cathartic flow. At the same time, however, the dance captured the heart of Alvin's greatest gift and made it clear that he alone could have created it.

Both thrilling jazz dance and terrifying desperation can be seen simultaneously in the spins, darts, leaps and cross-stage skids of the *Sinner Man* trio. In the same way, the persistence of faith and survival instincts are the backbones of the outrageously giddy fan-flapping church ladies of *The Day Is Past and Gone*. "The most startling things can be said to an audience if they are said with humor," Alvin wrote in a note to himself not long after the premiere of *Revelations*.

From early on, movement was the one medium through which he could honestly express his innermost truths. "Some choreographers are chess manipulators," Charles Blackwell said. "And there's nothing wrong with that. Chess is a nice game. But Alvin excited body fluids. His things were about people. This in another choreographer might be a wave or an earth movement. But with Alvin it was a man and a woman reaching out. It was people. Everything was in the service of the emotions that he was dancing, or choreographing. It was not about showing off. It was always about what was being said. It was about tears, and perspiration, just reproduction. Mankind continuing."

That immediacy—that heart that opened itself unabashedly and without assumption to all in the privacy of Alvin's dances—is perhaps the key to *Revelations* and to the distinction of the best works to come.

twelve

A NEW YORK FAMILY

A door had opened for Alvin with *Revelations*, hurtling him through a decade of events and accomplishments that in their dizzying variety and number would have filled a normal life span. The big-headed baby who had bounced along on his mother's hip through Texas cotton fields was now an affable young man about town with a reputation for formidable intelligence and great choreographic promise. He performed lead roles on and off Broadway, appeared with his dance company at the two most prestigious dance festivals in America and saw that company serve as his country's cultural ambassador to the world. Somehow, Alvin managed to choreograph sixteen dances through it all, two of them classics, for a company that was steadily growing in size, professionalism and acclaim even as it mirrored the confusion about race that was becoming so integral a part of American culture.

Two of the company's most famous and best-loved dancers, Dudley Williams and Judith Jamison, joined the troupe during the 1960s, each very different from the other but equally expressive of the Ailey canon. And, hungry to see and experience everything the arts and life had to offer, Alvin boldly set about the realization of another dream: the modern dance company he intended to establish would not be the voice of a single choreographer but rather would perform and preserve some of the best and most interesting pieces by others.

127

American modern dance companies had historically been founded by choreographers—like Lester Horton, Ruth St. Denis and Ted Shawn, and Martha Graham—who were intent on expressing an individual vision. But not all choreographers had the means, resolute strength or personal charisma to forge such instruments of self-expression. What would happen to their dances?

Modern dance, Alvin believed, needed a living repository of its classics and curiosities. Choreographers with their own companies might be loath to share their dances, but many works were too easily forgotten after their annual Sunday afternoon performances by pickup groups at the Ninety-second Street Y. And so he set about, in typically unassuming fashion, to establish the first modern dance company that would perform the work of all choreographers, whether little known or famous.

Some wondered at Alvin's interest in choreographers who were often competitive with him. But he was a discerning fan as much as a shrewd dance professional. Pieces he had fallen in love with in his avid concert-going should find a home in the Ailey repertory, where he himself would get a chance to see and resee them at his will. His own taste and sense of potential would be Alvin's only guide.

A few of the choreographers whose work he chose had solid reputations in modern dance and ballet. Some were friends, and some were simply promising youngsters he wanted to encourage. None was a star. Just about anyone who had interesting or important things to say in dance—men and women, black or white—was worthy of consideration. He stubbornly ignored the pleas of reluctant producers. "Alvin, Alvin," Paul Szilard, who became the company's international booking agent in the 1970s, would groan. "Why not a Robbins, a Balanchine, a Graham? No one has ever heard of these Jimmy Smiths and Larry Browns."

One of the things that made it all possible was that Alvin and his dancers had a home at last. No more wearying searches for available spaces and snatched time in cheerless, filthy rented studios. No more gypsy caravan treks about town hauling stools, ladders, big straw hats and boxes of costumes and props from apartment to apartment and studio to studio to theater, negotiating for space on subways or, on days when Mickey Bord was free, cramming everything into the trunk of her huge, gas-guzzling 1957 Oldsmobile convertible, which could also hold all eight dancers.

The facilities at the Westside YWCA were not fancy. The women had no dressing room, and the men had to climb two flights of stairs to change before and after classes and rehearsals. But the studios were huge, clean and freshly painted white. The atmosphere was one of accommodation. For the first time, Alvin and the group could concentrate simply on creating dances and putting together performances. Now they could work in rehearsal sessions as extended as the dancers' daytime jobs permitted.

There was still no money. Edele Holtz resigned herself to the fact that the YWCA was not going to collect even the small fee she had asked for. She had been stunned by the performance at the Ninety-second Street Y and by the wild enthusiasm of the audience. She understood that this handsome, rather solitary young man had great potential. And she assumed that this arrangement, which she sold to the YWCA boardwomen on the grounds that it be of particular help to young black theater women, would be a short-term relationship.

That did not prove to be the case. The dance activities grew and grew, encompassing eventually a theater in which Alvin's dancers and others could perform. Clark Center for the Performing Arts at the YWCA would become the closest thing to the hectic, yeasty, welcoming Horton studio that Alvin would ever know, a place where he was enveloped in love and expectations so unwavering that he had almost no chance of failing. There he was accepted (and knew he was accepted) for what he was: black, homosexual, an impossibly imperfect mortal, and an artist.

Clark Center was born through the kind of lucky accident on which the theater thrives. Charles Blackwell had enlisted a friend, Bob Buccolo, to help him in his search for a solution to the Ailey rehearsal problem. Buccolo, whom Blackwell affectionately described as "a wonderful thug from the Yale Drama School," was the technical director of *Jamaica*.

"Charlie and Alvin were interested in one thing—rehearsals, and Bob was fascinated with us, with the setup, with the rehearsal space," Holtz remembered. "They said they wanted to have a serious meeting with us about starting a whole group of programs." Holtz asked the director of the YWCA cafeteria to find the four a quiet table where they could talk. They were seated, providentially, in what had been the loge of the hotel's big, old-fashioned auditorium on the first floor, where there had once been supper-club performances by Milton Berle. Bucculo looked at the space and saw a working theater.

Alvin sat through the meeting quietly, his mind apparently on other matters, as it frequently was. "Charlie and Bob were older and had more experience and they could see the possibilities," Holtz said. "They started to dig in to help me put this thing together. We didn't have any money at all for this kind of stuff." Buccolo assured her that it could all be done. "Alvin had very few ideas," Holtz recalled. "He was all worked up with the company. That was his mission."

The building's refurbished second floor clearly had possibilities as a center for classes and rehearsals. No one wanted to touch the little chapel. Simply furnished with a pretty blue rug, candlesticks and a couple of chairs, it proved to be the perfect place for meditation of all sorts. Alvin wrote in the room, as did a visiting poet, and actors memorized their scripts there. Holtz discovered an abandoned mattress room, which she emptied and turned into a women's dressing room, complete with showers and a full-length mirror donated by the Bonwit Teller department store.

Beautiful parquet floors had come with the hotel. Ves Harper helped design the finishing touches. Some of the white hallways acquired blue ceilings. Burlap-covered bulletin boards were installed for notices, which Alvin would suddenly begin to rearrange whenever he was choreographing.

Straight-backed hotel chairs scattered through the second floor were moved into the studios, where there were barres and mirrors and, in one studio, a baby grand piano. With no windows, there was no natural ventilation. The chief problem was not odiferousness, however, but a slight sense of imprisonment. "We'd be there for hours," Michele Murray, an Ailey dancer in the 1960s, recalled. "It would be like freedom when we got outdoors."

As the studios began to take shape, Buccolo turned his attention to the auditorium. Its tiny stage was so shallow that several dancers fell off in a test performance. But he was soon at work building a somewhat extended stage for dance, where Ailey could try out new works. Blackwell contributed a stage curtain, from a Broadway show that had closed. Everything was so small-scaled that Harper could run the lights and then dash down to prepare for the next piece.

The theater held 450 seats, folding chairs arranged on the floor below stage level. Sight lines were not good. The best view was from a little balcony at the back, although Holtz had a difficult time convincing some visiting dignitaries, including Agnes de Mille and a black reporter from the *Amsterdam News*, that they were not being shunted off to inferior seats at sold-out performances.

Clark Center, named after the family that had contributed funds for the theater renovation, had its formal opening in October 1960. The Ailey dancers performed on November 27 for the first time on its little stage, which looked full when occupied by six bodies. It was a perfect fit for James Truitte and Carmen de Lavallade, guest stars on that first program, who drew cheers as the preacher and his doomed young wife in Horton's *Beloved*. There were critical raves, too, for *Revelations* and for a dance by John Butler. Two new pieces by Alvin fared worse.

With his successes at the Ninety-second Street Y and his installment in Clark Center, Alvin and his work came under increasingly close critical scrutiny. *Three for Now*, performed to jazz by Jimmy Giuffre and John Lewis, was Alvin's attempt to move into more abstract choreography—and it was trounced. "Disturbingly trite for this greatly talented choreographer," Selma Jeanne Cohen wrote. The plotless jazz dance piece was "well-danced," she added, but aimed "for a style that never quite gelled." Walter Terry dismissed the piece as "a mild and rather aimless number." And Louis Horst, the outspoken terror of New York dance critics, responded to the piece's subtitle, *in the spirit of fun*, by observing that the dance "did not contain a ha-ha or a ho-ho in a carload."

Alvin also presented a preview performance of *Knoxville: Summer of 1915*, set to a score by Samuel Barber. Like the music, the dance was inspired by James Agee's tender, haunting prose poem *A Death in the Family*, and seems to have represented a way for Alvin to get at his childhood memories from a more abstracted point of view. The child Alvin was very much present in the dance and music, particularly in the evocative closing lullaby-like verse at the end of Barber's score.

Performed by Kevin Carlisle, a popular white Broadway and modern dance performer of the time, Agee's lost little boy was first seen silhouetted in front of the stage, separated by a scrim from his family and friends, who sat patiently waiting for him to join them. The scrim rose and the boy relived his life with them. By the end of the dance they were once more at their original places. Sitting motionless, they were again memories.

"Mr. Ailey is far too wise to treat the text literally," Cohen wrote in *Dance Magazine* in one of the most positive reviews of the new piece. "He has, instead, captured an atmosphere with the softly swaying, fluid bodies of the women-in-memory and the strong but gentle attentions of their men, pitted against the tenseness of the onlooker, who yearns to join them."

Terry felt that it took Alvin too long to hit his stride. "For a while it looked as though Ailey's grip on his material was not going to be firm enough to hold his images of the evening peace of a small town as it is remembered by someone looking back on himself as a child," he wrote. "But about half way through his imagination catches fire and he unfolds for us a passion of love and longing for days that are gone." Terry noted that there were some "lovely moments" in the dance, "such as the emergence of the Boy into his own dream . . . but music, words and dance action keep eluding formal integration." He commented on Alvin's casting of Carlisle as a possible problem, given the dancer's big, easy style of dancing and the way it shaped the choreography for the boy.

Alvin seemed to be searching for ways to expand the world of his dances as well as his reputation with works like the two premieres and the dances that followed, *Gillespiana* and his 1961 *Hermit Songs*, although he would return to his primal source in two other dances of the time. Performed to Barber's score of the same name, *Hermit Songs* was inspired, like the music, by small poems written by Irish monks and scholars between the eighth and thirteenth centuries. The religious fervor depicted in the solo has a heat comparable to that of the celebrants in *Revelations* but it is heat born of the exaltation of hedonistic religious pain.

Gillespiana, a suite of dances for three couples performed to music by Lalo Schifrin, was pretty, lyrical and a total departure for Alvin. Some of the dancers disliked the piece, but it charmed many of its early viewers. "In 'Gillespiana,' the dancers are concerned with projecting the movements of modern dance as they relate to the sounds of jazz," Terry wrote in the *Tribune*, stating what would prove to be a central but for a time little recognized tenet of Ailey's choreography. The result, Terry continued, was "an abstract creation concocted of stunning designs, varying rhythms (some almost poetic in their gentleness) and shifts of mood."

The piece, designed as a light opening dance, was a favorite of Holtz's. It looked elegant. Harper had dressed the women in black tops and white ruffled silk jersey skirts, which stretched and often had to be trimmed before performances. But Holtz also loved its froth and the way Alvin had made the women, whom he nicknamed "Edele's Clarkettes," look unaccustomedly cute. They responded by dancing with their tongues tucked happily into their cheeks. But audiences, for the most part, failed to respond.

Ella Thompson loved the experience of working on the dance, her first new work with Alvin. "He and I had a duet that was hilarious to do. He liked to lift me. He'd pay me no mind. He just snatched you up. I used to scream and holler. But then I knew he'd never let me fall." The genuinely frightening part was that, true to form, Alvin was never quite sure of the steps he had given himself in the dance. "He'd learn it at the end, when he was choreographing. He'd jump in and out. 'What's the next step? What's the next step?'"

By 1964, Clark Center had become known as an enormously imaginative and productive grassroots arts organization. The history of the Ailey company might have been very different without the center—and Holtz, who was to become the second muse of Alvin's career. And the feisty little home for the arts would have been a good deal less innovative and ambitious, Holtz suggests, without Alvin's ideas for programs.

Dance, drama, and opera and instrumental music were presented in the Y's little theater, with low-cost and even free admission, and were regularly reviewed. Since Sundays were a relatively inactive time of the week for performers, there were Sunday afternoon programs that featured concerts, workshop productions, films and lectures by arts figures such as José Quintero, the producer and director of Circle in the Square Theater; the actresses Mildred Dunnock and Geraldine Page; and Allen Hughes, dance critic for the *New York Times*.

Holtz's genial husband, Alwin, known to all as Al, frequently manned the box office and found himself serving on occasion as an ad hoc financial adviser to Ailey dancers. Free intermission espresso was served by volunteers such as Mickey Bord and Nese Harper, the wife of the Ailey designer, in three hundred dainty teacups someone had donated to the YWCA. Celebrities were sometimes in the audience and served as consultants to the center. One of them was Langston Hughes. Devoted to the children's programs, Hughes taught the youngsters about poetry and jazz.

Most of all, Clark Center was a lively, comfortable hangout. Holtz recalls running into an Ailey dancer, accompanied by two friends, who was then performing in a Broadway musical. "I'm just here to see who's here," the dancer told her after they had exchanged greetings.

"People came in and out because of the classes," Holtz said. Many of the students were black, drawn in part by the YWCA's reputation as a friendly place and a home for black theater, dance and music. And students—young and old, professional and amateur—found an astonishing variety of courses there. At $1 or $2 a class, the curriculum ranged from a preperformance dance warm-up for Broadway gypsies, taught by James Truitte, to training in acting styles through scene readings from Sophocles to Brecht. In 1965, Clark Center offered twenty-six courses. Some gave guidance on such subjects as audition techniques, musical sight-reading, stage makeup, stage accents, musical comedy techniques, and costume and lighting design. Students could learn how to play folk guitar or sing and perform in opera. The largest variety of courses was in dance. Anna Sokolow taught movement for actors. The modern dance choreographer Lucas Hoving helped performers learn how to make dances. There were classes in ballet and Hindu dance and in the modern dance techniques of Horton and Charles Weidman, the latter taught by Weidman himself, a major choreographer of the time.

Truitte was the chief draw of the adult beginner and children's classes, along with Thelma Hill, also an Ailey dancer and a widely known and beloved teacher. The two had a knack of making everyone feel comfortable, from children and "neighborhood ladies," as Holtz put it, to ambitious young professional dancers. Even the least likely candidate for a career in dance knew that Truitte was available after class for talk about the field.

Those, like Bord, who were a part of the sprawling Ailey inner circle enjoyed additional perks. She would sit in her car, dressed in her leotard for class and waiting until 6 P.M., when parking was allowed on Eighth Avenue. Then she raced out and into the studio for three hours of nonstop dancing. That was followed by fried clams across the avenue at Howard Johnson's with Alvin, Truitte, Hill and other members of the gang, who would order a sandwich for propriety's sake and then finish the free hors d'oeuvres left from the restaurant's happy hour.

Alvin grew more interested in participating in the everyday life of Clark Center as it became clear that his company was there to stay and grow. Never fussy about such things as food and dress, he ate many of his meals in the Y cafeteria. And he began to spread out comfortably through the center, adopting it as a secure second home.

The company was still a small family of friends, most of them his own age and all closer to Alvin than his dancers would ever be again. He was cosseted by the women who worked at Clark Center. A few wondered how they might wrench him away from men. Alvin was sublimely unaware of their plotting.

To Holtz's exasperation, Alvin made himself at home in the center's little second-floor office, sprawling behind whatever desk was handy as he wrote, chatted with the staff, kibitzed on passing conversations and threw out idea after brilliant, fully formed idea.

"When he became relaxed about his own company, he was terribly interested in Clark Center," Holtz said. "It was another thing for him to focus on. For a messy person, Alvin had a wonderful planning mind. He would come up with program ideas, outline designs, pull in people to cover them and leave us alone to execute it all." Somehow they got it all done, "in our magnificent ignorance!"

Alvin, who seemed to know everyone in the arts in New York, not only suggested theater and music projects but often suggested exactly the right people to direct them. He pressed Holtz to establish children's programs. He had charmed women at a fund-raising luncheon by telling them how he had been taken to an art exhibition in seventh grade and had never recovered. And he took formal education very seriously. Holtz recalls his fury as they talked one day of a plan then in the news to publish school texts written in "black English."

One of his most important and far-reaching ideas was the creation of a forum for new choreographers, who would be selected by audition and given practical training in producing dances and concerts in addition to a performance of their work on group programs at the Clark Center theater. Commonplace today, institutionalized, regular showcases like that were a new concept in the early 1960s.

Alvin kept insisting to Holtz that there were choreographers all over New York who had no way of showing their dances. Some of their work, he felt, was terrific, and they should be able to display and develop their talent. Dances needed to be seen.

He approached her about the showcase a few days before the Ailey company was to depart for a first tour, appearing in Holtz's office with every detail written down on one of his omnipresent yellow legal pads. When she tried to protest that she knew nothing about producing dance, he sat down and told her which critics to call and where they might be reached, whom to invite to join the panel that would choose the choreographers competing for places on the program, and places in Greenwich Village to put up mimeographed notices for the auditions. "I hate to tell you the mob we had," Holtz said, still wonderingly. All of them, as she recalled wryly, did a dance to the folk song "Where Have All the Flowers Gone." But the judges were patient and kind, and over the years several of the fledgling choreographers went on to become staples of the New York dance scene.

As early as the fall of 1960, Clark Center was becoming known primarily as the headquarters of the Alvin Ailey Dance Theater. Visitors flocked to the second floor to watch Alvin's rehearsals. Most were unwelcome, for he hated to work in front of an audience. Duke Ellington was an exception, and Alvin was pleased to learn that Ellington had particularly enjoyed *I Been Buked*, the opening of *Revelations*.

Holtz tried unsuccessfully to define the place as something more than just a dance center. But Alvin—sexy, sunny, brooding and a law unto himself—filled it with his relaxed presence. One administrator was forced to remove a photograph of him because it distracted young women applying for jobs. "Does *he* work here?" they would ask, gazing up at that sensuous and for once crisply attired member of the teaching staff.

The classes that Alvin taught were packed. Hilary Ostlere, an English-born dance writer and former dancer who taught ballet at Clark Center in the mid-1960s, took his class a few times. She had found it difficult to teach a roomful of students who ranged from rank beginners to professional level. And the neat but well-lived-in and utilitarian studios did not encourage flights of fancy. "Next door every so often I'd see this jolly jazz class, where everybody was having great fun," Ostlere remembered. "Alvin taught, when he felt like it. I'd go into his class to see how they did it, but I was hopeless at it and I realized almost immediately that it would ruin my knees. Some people who were smart wore kneepads.

"Alvin showed you what he wanted, a lot. As far as I remember, he didn't talk much, though there were digressions at times. I remember thinking how funny he looked because he wore a sort of little beanie hat. It was like a jazz class to some extent but with all the rather distinctive movements he had for his actual choreography. Shoulder and arm work. Things you see now."

Holtz had suggested offering dance classes as a way of establishing both the center and the Ailey company. But Alvin made little secret of his dislike for teaching, and failed with surprising frequency to show up as scheduled at Clark Center and other studios. That—and his habit of sneaking his company in for extra rehearsals when the building was closed—led to a series of irate letters from Holtz. "You know as well as I do that however limited your teaching may be, you just can't avoid it and still have your niche here," Holtz wrote Alvin on January 3, 1962, in a memo that suggests their loving, prickly relationship and Holtz's perceptive contributions to the establishment of the Ailey company:

In order to justify having your company here, storing your equipment, etc. etc., you really must make at least a token contribution to the life of the department. In fact the powers that be keep questioning me about when you will return so what it amounts to is that I am the one who must do the justifying.

Actually this is a more vital reason than the above and that is the importance of keeping your company together, challenged and inspired as only you can do it. At the present moment, company morale is not high and members are getting more disappointed and discouraged. Like you they want to *dance*— not just any old way but a la Alvin Ailey.

Without varnishing facts you must know yourself that you contribute a fantastic drive and motivation to a class (witness last week at the Henry Hudson) and you have your own special style. It is foolish to assume that your company—or students— can continue to develop and expand in that style without you around as a guide and inspiration. If you don't watch out you will come up with a tour or an engagement and no *real* AA company to carry it through! Let's face it—Thelma can only rehearse them the way you want it just so far.

I know that you are busy and distracted with other things right now. How about just considering this minimum schedule for awhile: one hour on Mondays and Wednesdays from 6:30 to 7:30 for advanced students and company only. Thelma says she'll warm up the class for you from 6 to 7 and leave the fun of the class for you.

So do think this over carefully over the weekend—especially for the sake of the company—noblesse oblige and all that!

It was not the first or the last of such memos. But Alvin's response, in a note printed on scrap paper, was persuasively contrite and accompanied, typically, by a small gift.

Edele, I apologize. You are of course right. I have been too much with myself and my own projects and thoughts. I will do everything I can for the dance here at the Center as I have of course always intended to—and will see that all the things are as well organized, taken care of, etc.—costumes, music, accompanists, letters, new ideas for all above, etc. etc.—

thirteen

BACK TO ACTING,

ON TO ASIA

The "projects and thoughts" that were preoccupying Alvin involved an exciting but unnerving new turn his life had taken. Late in 1960, he had been called out of a class he was teaching at Clark Center to take a telephone call from Michael Shurtleff. Would Alvin be interested, Shurtleff asked, in auditioning for a lead role in an Off-Broadway play that would also feature two young unknowns named Robert Duvall and Joan Hackett.

Shurtleff, then a casting director working with the Broadway producer David Merrick, had an eye for actors and loved dance. He had spotted Alvin in *Jamaica*, a Merrick show, and then met him when he sneaked over to watch Lena Horne rehearsing cabaret material between performances on matinee days. Shurtleff thought of Alvin when casting began for the role of a young black college student in his first play, *Call Me by My Rightful Name*, which was scheduled to open in January at One Sheridan Square in Greenwich Village.

"It was down to three finalists," Milton Katselas, the play's director, recalled. "We went to him. There was something magnetic, sexual, exciting about Alvin." Rehearsals began at Clark Center in November, about the time of the Ailey company's first performance there.

Call Me by My Rightful Name, inspired by the white playwright's passionate identification with his black friends and by an incident involving his own family, told a story that was explosive on more than one level. Alvin was Paul, a sensitive but wary young black college student rooming near Columbia University with Doug, played by Duvall, an equally sensitive white student who hates racial prejudice.

Bedeviled by troubling confrontations with the white world, Paul leaves New York for a time. While he is gone, Doug falls in love with Chris, his brother's fiancée, only to discover on his roommate's return that Paul and Chris had once been lovers. The two men, once so close, fight violently, Doug hurling racial epithets at Paul. Chris, played by Hackett, tries to bring the men together again but their friendship is over. Shurtleff's vision of a failure of liberalism was as unfashionable in 1961 as interracial dating, also a theme of the play.

The month's worth of rehearsals went smoothly enough, at least for the actors. Alvin became very fond of Hackett, whom he called his "golden girl," and she kept up with him and his career to the end of her life, writing him affectionate congratulatory notes now and then. Alvin also developed a lasting friendship with Duvall, with whom he shared a birthdate. Onlookers were amused when "Bobby," as everyone called the solemn and rather difficult young actor, developed a hopeless passion for Minnie Marshall, the pretty, long-limbed Ailey dancer, during the run of *Call Me by My Rightful Name.*

Alvin also got to know Duvall's real-life roommate, an acting student named Dustin Hoffman. In another seven years, *The Graduate* would make Hoffman famous, but he was an unprepossessing figure as he hung out in the theater, watching the three rehearse. For a long time, Katselas assumed that Hoffman, who always wore a leather jacket, had wandered in from the Sunoco gas station down the block.

The atmosphere was friendly, and Alvin was able to remember his lines more easily than the steps he gave himself in his dances. Nor did he have trouble opening up to his character despite his habitual secretiveness and desire for privacy. He was particularly convincing in the fight scene, during which Duvall ran up a seven-foot ladder only to have it knocked out from under him. Alvin prepared for the first rehearsal of that angry scene, in which the character is a little drunk, by downing several martinis, amusing the others by his misguided sense of verismo.

He clearly had a temper to match that of his character, although he usually lost it only in frustration during rehearsals. "The explosive power was in him, in his dance," Katselas, with whom Alvin later studied acting, said. "There was a bit of a fuse there and you never knew when it was going to go. And yet there was a sweetness in him beyond words. And a willingness to listen."

Alvin's chief problem, oddly enough, was moving in the natural fashion of an actor. "It came from a certain tension and self-consciousness," Katselas said. "He didn't really want to act, but it interested him. And the fact that he was a gorgeous man was also part of the self-consciousness, which he didn't have in dance." He suggested that Alvin trade the chukka boots he wore to rehearsal for shoes with thin leather soles through which he could feel the floor. That worked.

As in *House of Flowers*, last-minute adjustments to the script made for chaotic rehearsals. But opening night was electric. Katselas's reputation had drawn a number of celebrities, among them Shelley Winters, who astonished Alvin by advancing angrily on Shurtleff in the Green Room after the performance. First Winters slugged the playwright, then she burst into tears and embraced him. Why, the actress asked, had he given the play such an unhappy ending?

The *Times* review was mixed, describing the play and characters as unconvincing. Other reviews were raves of an unusually contemplative sort, and Alvin received his first real theater notices. Most of the comments about him were positive, although years later Alvin remembered them as having been "terrible." Writing in the *New York Post*, Richard Watts Jr. described the play as "an honest, thoughtful and probing study of the racial tensions potentially present even among men of good will, done in straightforward and unsentimental dramatic terms and admirably acted by a small and notably expert cast. . . . The young Negro is brilliantly played by Alvin Ailey, and Robert Duvall is excellent in the difficult and rather too complicated role of the other youth, while Joan Hackett gives a remarkably unhackneyed portrayal of the girl."

Whitney Bolton of the *Morning Telegraph* issued "an earnest and sincere plea that you go to see 'Call Me By My Rightful Name' as quickly as you can get there." Bolton rhapsodized over Shurtleff's "singing typewriter." "Robert Duvall, Alvin Ailey (a superb dancer making his first dramatic performance) and Joan Hackett are the principals," he continued. "I shan't try to tell you the exquisite detail of performance they have found. It is there and you have to see it."

The play ran for five months. Well before it closed, Alvin was involved in rehearsals for two new plays. One was a summer stock production of a play called *Ding Dong Bell*, in which he played a professor, that opened and closed without much ado at the Westport Country Playhouse. The other was an Off-Broadway production called *Two by Saroyan*, a pair of one-act plays by William Saroyan that was due to open in the fall. Alvin was a soft-hearted but dangerous prizefighter named Blackstone Boulevard in one of the plays, *Talking to You*, in preparation for which he had a few unsuccessful lessons in boxing from Al Holtz. Now studying with Stella Adler, Alvin was praised for his acting in both.

But he was not neglecting dance. He had had an important triumph earlier in 1961 at the Tenth Annual Boston Arts Festival, where he had been invited to present dance in the jazz idiom to live accompaniment in a retrospective of American dance since the turn of the century. Alvin put together *Roots of the Blues*, a four-part piece that was drawn in part from *Blues Suite* and incorporated that dance's *Backwater Blues* duet. He and de Lavallade "stalked each other and exploded into sultry frenzies so apparently spontaneous that they must have been calculated to a hair's breadth," one critic later observed.

Roots of the Blues was set to traditional music arranged and performed by Brother John Sellers, a singer from Mississippi whose earthy, roof-raising versions of the blues reminded Alvin powerfully of Texas days. Alvin had come to know Sellers after he wandered into a Village hangout called Gerde's Folk City on one of his rambling walks through the city earlier in the year, drawn by the singer's voice. He returned again and again to hear Sellers perform, and the two became friends in a relationship of careering highs and lows, Sellers wandering into Alvin's life at just the right moments, it seemed, to provide company on his wildest escapades. Something in Sellers's singing struck through Alvin's emotional defenses and into the core of his memories of his childhood. "A mans blues—a solo man—(maybe Ailey—maybe not)," he wrote around that time in a poem titled "John Sellers Sings."

The singer outdid himself at the festival, held outdoors on the Boston Common in mid-June to noisy applause. Sellers was used to improvising with jazz bands, and so, encouraged by the reception, he continued to sing well after the dance had ended, forcing Alvin and de Lavallade to keep moving until he and his musicians wound to a halt.

The new work was repeated in another outdoor performance in early July at Lewisohn Stadium in upper Manhattan, a vast old open-air arena where popular low-priced arts performances were once a staple of New York summers. But the dance writer Lillian Moore thought the piece looked better in the more intimate rustic setting of the Ted Shawn Theater at Jacob's Pillow, where the company returned in mid-July.

Once again, the response to *Roots of the Blues* was tumultuous. "Mr. Ailey and Miss de Lavallade just about stopped the show," Moore wrote. Describing the setting of *Roots of the Blues* as a "Harlem cellar," she praised Ves Harper's scenic design of high stepladders on which some of the action took place, and singled out de Lavallade for special praise: "Lithe as a reed, exotically beautiful, she can look like a slut or a Botticelli madonna at will. In 'Roots of the Blues' she was sullen, sultry, provocative; each sensuous or willful mood was danced with tempestuous intensity. Mr. Ailey, earthy and vigorous, met her on her own terms."

This year, too, the Pillow experience was like summer camp for the dancers. They shared the week's programs with ballet greats Maria Tallchief, Erik Bruhn, Lupe Serrano and Royes Fernandez, and Alvin taught Tallchief and Bruhn parts of *Revelations* at their request. He and Bruhn, the most elegant of classical danseurs nobles, gained a certain amount of notoriety for their impromptu dancing of a pas de deux from *Swan Lake*, with Alvin as the swan queen, in postperformance partying at a local roadhouse.

The Ailey dancers were intrigued by the larger-than-life backstage dramas that seemed to be an inherent part of preparing for ballet performances. And a teenager from Buffalo named Linda Kent, who would one day become a leading dancer with Alvin and with Paul Taylor, was as fascinated watching the Ailey dancers. Kent was a scholarship student at the Pillow and was working backstage when she first saw the company. The sight of Alvin in the *Sinner Man* section of *Revelations*, danced as a solo sometimes in the early years, astounded her with its desperate energy.

"Here was this incredible emotional impact," Kent recalled. "Pain, joy, rage. This was what I was looking for. I thought, 'Wow, this is about living.' I wanted to be a *person* onstage." Although she was white and the Ailey dancers black, Kent filed the thought away in her mind that when she one day made it to New York City, this might be a company with which she would like to dance.

Back home in New York, several possible projects awaited Alvin. Langston Hughes had asked him to choreograph a ballet based on his just-published poem "Ask Your Mama," and Alvin was due to choreograph Hughes's production of *Wasn't That a Mighty Day!*, a gospel retelling of the Christmas story directed by Vinnette Carroll, with whom

Alvin had worked the year before on *Dark of the Moon*. Renamed *Black Nativity*, the production opened at the Forty-first Street Theater in mid-December and was a runaway hit there and on tour in Europe. In addition to creating the dances, Alvin was to mime Joseph to de Lavallade's Mary, in a cast that also starred Cicely Tyson and two noted gospel singing groups.

In the end, however, the show went on without Alvin. " 'Black Nativity' was a product of Hughes's faith in the importance of a black racial sense, and as such—in the golden age of integration—it offended some blacks," Arnold Rampersad observed in *The Life of Langston Hughes*. De Lavallade was one of those offended, and Alvin followed her when she walked out of the show.

It had been a tumultuous year for Alvin. The pages of his 1961 appointment book are scrawled with reminders of acting classes with Katselas and Adler, a grande dame of American theater and an exponent of the Stanislavsky technique at whose studio he would teach "modern jazz" dance the following winter. "Adler—explain finances," one note reads poignantly, followed in later pages by lists of small debts to Mickey Bord and other friends, and reminders to show up for unemployment benefits.

Plays are listed from which Alvin might select scene studies for his classes. Dinner dates and tickets to *Call Me by My Rightful Name* had to be arranged for Arnold Saint Subber and other theater and dance friends. Alvin was both a new young actor and a celebrity. "Note to S.P. re show," a February memo reads, alluding to Sidney Poitier, by then a leading Hollywood actor who portrayed a new and more dignified kind of black male character on the screen. "Would be interested in his reaction to the perf in larger terms—i.e. racial." The conversation was not to be, but Ossie Davis and Ruby Dee, black royalty in the American theater, went backstage to congratulate him after one show.

Ideas for a film project on the blues and for numerous dances are jotted on the cramped pages, among them a dance-drama inspired by Beckett and pieces about Henri Christophe, the visionary Haitian painter, and the revivalist Aimee Semple McPherson. Then and later, Alvin was interested in putting the seamier side of life onstage. He contemplated a "massive dance work" that would be the "dolce vita of dance—massive destruction and negations—a sinking to perversions as an out," possibly featuring a "scene of a young man on a slab—offered up as part of a ritualistic ceremony." On the following page is a costume sketch, a typical feature of Alvin's notes on dances, of a robe for a

Carthusian monk, presumably for *Hermit Songs*. Throughout his career, the profane would compete with the sacred when Alvin contemplated themes for ballets. But his wilder and more ludicrously tasteless ideas served for the most part as simple fantasizing, a way, perhaps, of venting steam and even an outlet for his unruly sense of humor.

Pages of the date book are crammed with names, addresses and telephone numbers of possible new company members, musicians, composers and dance teachers and accompanists, along with reminders to himself to find a singing teacher and an agent, and a recipe for a sore throat remedy. Fighting for space are lists of "Jokes to Remember," mostly terrible. "War god Thor comes down to earth," one reads. " 'You're Thor!' 'I'm so thore I can hardly walk.' " Appointments with the psychiatrist Lawrence Hatterer are also noted.

Normand Maxon had been urging Alvin to see a psychoanalyst. Alvin spent less than a year with Hatterer, an admitting doctor at the Payne Whitney Clinic at New York Hospital as well as a painter, who was becoming known for his work with artists. Like many of the male artists Hatterer saw, Alvin had conflicts about his sexuality but none of the substance abuse problems that were also common among the patients. "A lot of his complaints had to do with his guilt and conflict about his sexuality, though he didn't need or want treatment," Hatterer recalled. "I don't think he talked much about his early life. He had a fair amount of intensity—he was an intense communicator—and certain charismatic elements even as a patient. He seemed rather advanced for someone so new in his career. My guess is that he was probably very aggressive about it."

Clark Center wasn't forgotten in all the hurly-burly of that steadily building career. "Get notebook to note progress of beg. class," Alvin reminded himself in his daily diary. Repertory and program order for performances are written out carefully. There are also frequent notations of dance rehearsals. And time was set aside for dealing with dance photographers, festival promoters, grant applications and auditions.

But there is no record of the major event of the year. In the early fall of 1961, Alvin was approached by American government officials who had seen his performances in Boston and at the Pillow. Would he and his company be interested and available to perform in Southeast Asia early the following year? The thirteen-week tour, produced by the President's Special International Program for Cultural Presentations, would open in Sydney and close three months later in Seoul, Korea, with stops along the way in Burma, South Vietnam, Malaya, Indonesia, the Philippines, Hong Kong, Taiwan and Japan.

Alvin accepted the invitation and planned for the tour with all his usual energy and sense of organization. The company must be enlarged, he saw, with the popular Carmen de Lavallade heading it as a guest star. Altogether, there would be ten dancers. He and de Lavallade would be joined by James Truitte and Don Martin from Horton days; Charles Moore and Ella Thompson, who would soon marry; Minnie Marshall, Thelma Hill, and Georgia Collins, a dancer with impressive technical skills honed at the New York City Ballet–affiliated School of American Ballet. Sensitive to his new and suddenly acquired role as cultural ambassador, he hired a white dancer, Connie Greco, to complete the group. Brother John would accompany them, with a musical trio composed of the guitarist Bruce Langhorne, the bass player Leslie Grinage and Horace Arnold on percussion.

The company must dance *Revelations*. That was clear. The repertory would also include *Roots of the Blues*, *Gillespiana* and the Horton classic *The Beloved*. Carmen would dance John Butler's *Letter to a Lady*. And another ballet choreographer, Glen Tetley, contributed a new work called *Mountainway Chant*, an American Indian fable danced to music by Carlos Chavez, which added a touch of another kind of Americana to the program.

What new Ailey works could he contribute? *Hermit Songs* could be given a dry run in December in the company's second concert at Clark Center. And he must finish *Been Here and Gone*, another blues piece with a juicily dramatic entrance for Brother John as a blind musician. Just three years into his formal career as a choreographer, Alvin was discovering the law that would govern his entire career. Art, he was now learning, is made not in splendid calm and isolation but in an unavoidable rush of commitments.

Alvin's company was not the first black dance group that the State Department sounded out about foreign touring in a time of racial conflict in the United States. But the dancers and their repertory succeeded beyond anyone's expectations as vibrant national propaganda. In a mere three years, Alvin had created a company and a body of work that would convince much of the world, on this and the countless tours that followed, of the beauty, importance and universality of black art and of its rightful place in American culture. His was not an overt preachment about racial harmony. Instead, Alvin addressed the riches of black life in America.

"The cultural heritage of the American Negro is one of America's richest treasures," he wrote in a program note for a later tour. "From his roots as a slave, the American Negro—sometimes sorrowing, sometimes jubilant but always hopeful—has touched, illuminated, and influenced the most remote preserves of world civilization. I and my dance theater celebrate this trembling beauty."

fourteen

"HOT AND PERFECT"

"Almost late to Eside Airline Terminal," Alvin wrote on January 30 in his diary for 1962, a journal for a memorable year and one of his last attempts at recording his increasingly hectic life in any detail. "Then onto bus to Idlewild. Drinks in Pan Am VIP room at Idlewild. Then off to L.A." Only a handful of well-wishers had shown up to see the Ailey dancers and musicians off on the 4 P.M. flight that would start their voyage around the world. Mickey Bord was there, and Susan Pimsleur and Gertrude Macy, general manager of the International Cultural Exchange Service of the American National Theatre and Academy (ANTA), the Manhattan-based acting school that served as the program agent for the State Department. But Alvin's family was waiting for him when the airplane touched down in Los Angeles, as were friends of James Truitte, Carmen de Lavallade's family and a few Horton stalwarts, as well as Alvin's solemn confidante of his Los Angeles years, Ella Hurd, who was now married and had brought her son to the airport.

"It was like old home week at the Los Angeles airport," Truitte recalled, "and a good time was had by all with lots of hugs and kisses."

Alvin's stepfather looked grayer. His mother was fatter but "wonderful-looking," he noted, and had come to the airport with chicken and cake for him to eat on the plane. His half-brother Calvin, now nine, had grown taller, wore glasses and was very excited about being at an airport, his glamorous older brother observed. At least one dancer was surprised to learn that Alvin had a brother, so secretive was he about his life. But this was for Alvin a rare chance to see the child whose birth had caused him such great pain.

There was not much time to visit, however, before the dancers had to reboard for the next leg of the journey, to Honolulu, where the warm weather reminded Alvin of Los Angeles. "We saw our scenery get onto plane," he wrote in his journal. "What an awful lot & and the joke is what a long way to go to a concert. We lost this day by passing over the International Date Line someplace between Sydney and the Fiji Islands—or was it between Honolulu & Fiji? Anyway, we lost an entire day. A long, long way between Honolulu and Fiji—seemed forever, everyone asleep and wondering what it will all be like—in the morning a very beautiful year-old-boy from Melbourne traveling with his parents from the U.S. to back home charms us all—his name is Bradley and he climbed over the seats of the plane and into the aisles—completely delighted with [Ailey musician] Horace Arnold especially and Thelma [Hill]—"

Another stopover on the twenty-eight-hour trip gave them a glimpse of Fiji, steaming hot, green and filled with "people (negroid they are) who look just like us!" Alvin wrote. An indefatigable shopper then and always, he made the first of many purchases on the trip, some of them carefully documented in the diary, even noting wonderingly that he had paid only $47 for a wood bowl, postcards, several wooden combs and three large bottles of Black and White Scotch. He and de Lavallade watched regretfully as the hazy mountains of Fiji receded into the distance as the plane took off once more, this time for the company's final destination. If only there had been time to explore. And, Alvin noted, "I'd like to see Tahiti and Samoa and all those fabled places."

The dancers shared his elation and a sense of unreality that must have grown exponentially when reporters from television and radio stations greeted the exhausted dancers and musicians as they climbed down the stairs of the airplane onto the tarmac at the Sydney airport. At a reception with local critics and the mayor of Sydney, Alvin was accosted by a "wild-haired man" who insisted on discussing the Aborigines. "I made a little speech to the effect that we are overjoyed to be in Sydney. Carmen looked exquisitely like a star." Then it was off to the hotel, which was in an area that reminded Alvin of Greenwich Village,

and the start of the dizzying round of receptions, rehearsals and performances that was to be the dancers' daily routine for the next three
months and many more years, with only the settings changing. The
atmosphere did not encourage reasonableness and undying camaraderie. It would not be long before exhaustion and a lack of privacy
erupted in painful friction. But for now the world was ripe for the
picking by the dancers of Alvin's important new company.

As solitary as ever, Alvin made a hasty getaway by himself from a
party at the American consul general's home, leaving de Lavallade and
the others to be escorted off to see a play. Back at the hotel, he was
drawn into conversation with a drug salesman from Queensland whom
he met in the lobby. "A young guy full of jokes—also met his friend
John—they talk about Chappel St and its whores which they are very
interested in. We go to my room and open the Fiji scotch and Gregg
drinks so much that he passes out and is dragged to his room by
John—Surely I can find better things to do with my time—"

His spirits improved, however, the following day when the company opened at the Palace Theater in Sydney for a seven-performance
engagement. There had been a colorful advance piece on the company
in the *Sydney Morning Herald,* a story that hit a precise balance between
wonder at the exoticism of Ailey dance and dancers and an appreciation of their humanity and expertise: "The elegant nineteenth century
gilt and plush atmosphere of Sydney's Palace Theater was shattered yes-
terday by the raw rhythms and pungent harmonies of Negro jazz and
'blues,' " the reporter wrote in a news story that ran the day of the Ailey
opening. "Rehearsing for their opening night, an American dance company—ten dancers, nine of them Negro—brought a new world to the
Palace stage, for months past occupied by comedy and musicals. In
worn practice clothes, and mainly barefooted, the company danced its
way through work and prison songs, hoe-downs and 'blues' . . . while
they rehearsed Ailey's dance version of 'Backwater Blues'—which commemorates a disastrous Mississippi flood—other members of the
company went through a series of muscle-knotting warm-up exercises
which were as far from the cold formality of classical ballet as New
Orleans is from Leningrad. As the rehearsal went on, the dancers created a lively picture of life in America's deep south—a share-farmer
mourning the loss of a crop ruined by boll-weevil, a blind folk-singer
being led through the streets by his guitarist. It was a world away from
the lunch-hour scramble outside in Pitt Street."

The city was blazingly hot. The theater was small, with no air-conditioning, and the stage was slightly raked. Halfway through the matinee Alvin wondered if he and de Lavallade weren't dancing too much on the programs. But there were congratulatory telegrams from the local producers and American well-wishers, and loving messages from home. "This telegram can't hold all the good things I wish for you," Bord cabled Alvin. And the gala performance in the evening ended with eighteen curtain calls for the dancers, an astounding ovation considering the small number of people in the audience. Looking back, Alvin estimated that 25 people sat in the 1,100-seat house. A long line waited at the box office the next day, however, and that night—and for the rest of the run—the theater aisles were filled with overflow audience. The box office staff stopped taking reservations the morning the reviews were published, for the engagement was quickly sold out.

Reviewers treated this new young dance company and its earthy, determinedly different repertory with respect, seldom succumbing to the temptation to see the dancers and their unfamiliar style simply as ethnic curiosities. "The American Dance Theatre show, which opened to a packed house at the Palace, is something not to be missed," Frank Harris, theater critic for the *Daily Mirror,* wrote. "Cheers and repeated curtain calls were a tribute from a crowd tormented by heat to highly skilled dancers who put over a fine show under tough conditions. It was a case of The Beat beating the heat." He singled out *The Beloved*, along with de Lavallade, Truitte, Alvin and the program closer, *Revelations*, "the most exciting of the lot, with its hepped-up spirituals and choral background."

Harris was not the only critic to fall in love with the company. Norman Kessell of the *Sun* raved about the "rare and exciting quality" of the program presented by the Ailey dancers at the Palace. "Half-savage jazz rhythms, the lament of the blues and the lilt of Negro spirituals are here brilliantly interpreted in dance form," Kessel continued. "It is an astonishing combination of live, willowy gyrations, and muscular posturing in which the whole body is constantly in fluid and vital movement. It retains the somewhat harsh idiom of the New World, yet absorbs some of the poetry and discipline of classical ballet." For Griffen Foley, writing in the *Daily Telegram*, the company was as exciting as the New York City Ballet had been in a visit to Sydney four years earlier.

There was a little time for play in the dancers' busy schedule of performances, photo sessions and interviews by reporters who were sometimes disappointingly uninformed. "Not properly organized," Alvin noted rather primly in his journal about one young interviewer.

Even social opportunities turned into business discussions. Alvin ran into Ernest Parham, who was in Sydney performing in *Little Mary Sunshine*. Parham seemed older but very happy, and the two discussed the difficulties of running a dance company. "Keep aloof, businesslike, impersonal and make one's own decisions and let co know they are one's own," Alvin recorded in his diary. Only four days into the company's international tour, he was critically examining the program, music and, in particular, his own dancing. But if he was already questioning his directorial abilities, the dancers were not aware of it.

The company saw the beauties of Sydney when Alvin and the dancers were taken to the city's best restaurants and prettiest beaches. At one beach, Alvin, who had forgotten to pack a bathing suit, wandered off by himself, thought of John Masefield and his sea poems, and saw, as he commemorated in his journal, "the most incredibly beautiful child scooping sand, with eyes as big and as clear as marbles."

He had ridden out to the beach with Roland Robinson, a critic for the *Herald Tribune*, and his wife, and had greatly enjoyed the talk of Australian aboriginal and Afro-American cultures, gladly agreeing to an exchange of indigenous songs. He suggested Robinson write to Langston Hughes in Harlem for more materials. Robinson, who became one of the company's most fervent admirers, later commented that Australians needed someone to show them how to make use of their own art forms.

"Judging by the reactions of the audience," he wrote in his first-night review, "this critic was not the only one who felt the urge to rush up on stage and join in the hand-clapping, singing and dancing." That was certainly the mood on the company's jubilant closing night.

As the performers stepped forward for their final curtain calls, they were showered for several minutes with streamers in every imaginable color, thrown from the balcony and orchestra in such quantities that it was impossible to dance an encore on the littered stage. There were huge bouquets for the women. Looking out over the cheering audience, Alvin found himself near tears. It was one of the most incredible theater experiences he had ever had, although the directorial part of him could not help but remark to himself that "BH&G" had been slightly off that night.

A quick side trip to Canberra for a performance proved to be memorable for a reason that had nothing to do with audiences but that forced the dancers to develop new social skills. The occasion was a cocktail party held in the company' honor at the American Embassy residence, a handsome place with an unfortunate proximity to sheep country. "There were enough flies to supply the world," Truitte recalled. "The Australians didn't seem to mind as flies landed on their faces, crawled across and took off for another landing. But if you have never tried to nibble an hors d'oeuvre, balance a glass of champagne and play 'shoo-fly' while conversing, you haven't lived."

The troupe opened in Melbourne on February 11 at the Princess Theatre, a movie house where the dancers performed between the matinee and evening shows of *The Sound of Music*. After Sydney and the Palace, the much larger Princess felt coldly formal and its stage was slippery. The company danced only reasonably well, for a small audience whose reserve made Truitte think of people attending a Boston tryout for a Broadway play.

Word went out quickly after the performance, however, and the next day the theater was filled. Scalpers moved in here as they had in Sydney. Local artists and critics followed the dancers around from rehearsal to dressing room and back, and by closing night the stage wings were so crowded that Alvin became annoyed.

Melbourne was a little like a second-night performance—worthy and interesting but a little less exciting than those first days in Australia. Alvin had plenty of time to reflect on the experience during the plane trip from Darwin, Australia, to Singapore, where, after a brief early-morning stop, the company was to fly on to Rangoon. Tired and a little self-conscious, perhaps, in his sudden new importance as an internationally acknowledged young American company director and cultural ambassador, he pondered his responsibilities to his work and to his dancers.

"Carmen is a great, intuitive actress—great poetry seems to come out of great feeling—great and deep feeling—

"Can the Stanislavski theories of sense-memory and all be made ready to work for dancers and communicate to the audiences—concentration certainly can.

"I will demand a great deal from dancers hereafter: they must be technically studied in a dance way & in an acting way. I would like dancers who have studied acting—who can use an image—their imaginations—animal exercises—preparations physical & mental.

"I must think about improving our programs—re refurbishing the company's ideas re what we are doing—each week a surprise—each week a new image with which to work—

"We are due at Singapore at 1 A.M. + Rangoon at 3:40 A.M."

The company almost lost two of its dancers at the stopover in Singapore, when Truitte and Hill wandered off to explore the airport. All of a sudden there were cries of "Back!" and they found themselves staring down gun barrels. "We drew a breath, executed a graceful turn and joined everybody else," Truitte remembered. "The funniest thing was that these guards were the heftiest Chinese women we had ever seen, and I do mean *big!*"

The travelers were met in Rangoon by American diplomats and several Burmese gentlemen whom Alvin found charming, noting details of their native dress even at that early hour. Once he had checked in at the Strand Hotel, he found it hard to sleep and went out for a meandering walk by himself. "Was too excited by being in really strange ctry [country] for 1st time to sleep—walked out into the morning city to dock and watched small ferries taking people across very muddy bay—then walked in city a few blocks then back to hotel to sleep."

Everything seemed remarkable. The huge open-air theater where the Ailey company was to perform did not have lights, but the company had brought along its own lighting equipment for such emergencies. Alvin's ten dancers would be competing against performances by a troupe of 250 Chinese ballet dancers presenting the classics, in a season that was quickly extended to provide the maximum competition for this American interloper. Alvin was intrigued to see large photographs of himself on posters beside a Chinese ballerina in *Swan Lake* tutu and feathered headpiece. At the hotel where he was staying with de Lavallade, Brother John Sellers and Dick Campbell, the company manager, he was served by "1000 Indian waiters in white bowing and scraping," as he put it in his journal.

For all the difficulties of the theater, the performances went well. They were met by an at first disconcerting lack of enthusiasm from all but the Americans in the audience. "Go back," Hill hissed at the other dancers as they swept forward in near silence for their first curtain calls. "Go back. Dim the lights." But many in the Burmese audience were monks, Alvin was told, and here a mere two claps of the hands was considered a tumultuous reception.

The reviews were politely positive, with one reporter going so far as to describe *The Beloved* and *Revelations* as "deeply moving." Backstage, the atmosphere was less civil. Only weeks into the three-month tour, Alvin was starting to have problems with his performers, who had begun to fight among themselves, split into cliques and indulge in sometimes messy love affairs. He took one of them aside to talk about the benefits of psychoanalysis, later worrying that he had revealed too much of himself.

But he took quickly to Rangoon, a shopper's paradise, he discovered, and a constant source of street scenes of startling beauty. He liked the people he noticed on his wanderings, too. They watched curiously wherever the dancers went, smiling always. The children were beautiful, and Alvin was delighted by the monks in their spectacular colored robes. He longed to snap photos of every child and monk he saw, but was uncertain how to work his new camera.

Burmese dance was a source of continuing pleasure to him, as was the sight of the bananas and coconuts placed backstage for good luck in the theaters where the company performed. On a side trip to Mandalay, Alvin and the dancers watched a special program at the State School of Fine Arts by impressive little performers—"mosquitos," as Alvin noted. He was entranced by one in particular, a very small dancer named Titi. Alvin promised to send their teacher American books on modern and Oriental dance. "And I must do it," he wrote. "Took 8 mm. movies of children dancing indoors and I cross my fingers and everything that they come out—also photo'd the little boy with the extraordinary face—but they really are *all* extraordinary—I must write something about them or they should come to America to represent Burmese culture."

The day before the company left the country, the minister of culture invited the dancers to tea and presented them with gifts of native clothing. Alvin and de Lavallade received a large silver bowl inscribed with the company's name, which Alvin thought of putting in a glass case back home at Clark Center as a symbol of the group's accomplishments. But there was chilling news to come. The day after the company left Burma, the government was deposed. "All the high officials we had been lunching with, etc. are now behind bars," he wrote Edele Holtz, stunned.

Bangkok, where the company stayed one day en route to Saigon, pleased him almost as much as Burma. "What a lovely, progressive city," Alvin wrote, with "clean streets & healthy looking dogs and small round faced brown people with almond eyes." There was a lot to buy, too, at a place called Johnny Siam's. De Lavallade bought rings set with brown and blue sapphires, Alvin noted. "John S. bought a $250 sapphire after much lamenting & I ended up with 3 loose grey sapphire stones & a pink sapphire ring with a hardly distinguishable star—$140! I must be crazy—by Manila I'll be starving I know—"

The dancers had narrowly avoided a plane accident arriving for a stopover at Phnom Penh, Cambodia, on the way to Saigon, and the airport authorities there were unpleasant. The stopover ended in an uproar when Alvin insisted that the company would not leave without its sets and costumes. It was an appropriate introduction to the next segment of the tour, for Saigon, where the troupe arrived on March 2 for a week's stay, was a low point.

Although the Vietnam War was not to escalate for another three years, America had begun to send troops to South Vietnam in 1961. There was everywhere an eerie atmosphere of impending battle. The United States Information Service representatives assigned to the performers in Saigon were for the most part officious but unhelpful. There had been no publicity for the program. The Ailey dancers were forced to perform at an out-of-the-way old movie house in the city's Chinese section after the theater where the company was scheduled to dance was bombed. After performing for depressingly tiny audiences, seated far apart in fear of terrorist attack, Alvin went on his own to the university and encouraged students to see the dances.

Reaching out to the young should have been a mandate of the tour, Alvin later told American reporters. He was dismayed by how few university students turned out to see the company perform abroad. The State Department ought to have recruited the young as audiences. Back in the United States, Alvin wasted no time in proposing ways of doing that on future modern dance tours.

Vietnamese students were generally mystified, however, by what they saw. Perhaps lectures, demonstrations and fuller program notes were needed, Alvin thought, or a narrator of the sort the company had had in Burma. But perhaps the time and place were more the problem. Saigon was a troubled city that, he wrote Holtz, looked dirty "and seems to have taken on the worst aspects of the many cultures that have been here—especially the French & the American."

American soldiers walked the streets, some dressed in flowered shirts and "regular pants—just like boys from Ohio," he observed. "They are on a 'training mission' here—but we are told that guns could be thrown into their hands at the slightest provocation," Alvin wrote in his journal. Gunfire could be heard at night. The old French hotel where the company was staying was barricaded against a demonstration one evening, and the dancers woke up one morning to find a loaded aircraft carrier docked close by.

It was troubling to walk through the streets. "This is a city of whores!" Alvin wrote. "The 'nice' Vietnamese girls are seldom in the streets—the ones sitting on barstools are overpainted and are available to the American soldiers here—and very cheaply." He was told that "almost anything can be bought for 100 piastres—about $1.50 American money."

For Alvin, the Vietnamese suffered by comparison with the Burmese. They were less friendly and looked tense and suspicious. Meeting students at a lunch at the house of an Information Service official, Alvin and the others sensed that this was probably the first time the Americans "had had many Viets not of a higher level in their house." His disillusionment with the country saddened Holtz, who had been to Vietnam and who wrote him regretfully on March 13 that the country wasn't "bad if you can get to the native sections." "The East after all IS dirty," she continued, "but the usual human and interesting things go on in spite of it." Someday they would all go back to visit the East together. "It has long been our ambition to engage all twelve places on a freighter and divide them among congenial friends and take a 4 month tour around the world," Holtz added. "It can be done you know."

As for news from home, the *Lamp Unto My Feet* television program that had included excerpts from *Revelations* had been nominated for an Emmy award, although it did not win. Stella Adler had called to invite Alvin to a cocktail party. And the dancer Myrna White, a Broadway gypsy who later joined the Ailey company, had stopped by to report that Alvin's teaching had given her an edge in a recent audition. And where, Holtz wondered in a postscript, were the newspaper clippings from Melbourne?

The company moved on to Malaya for performances in Kuala Lumpur, Seremban, Ipoh and Penang, where the tired dancers faced new difficulties. In Ipoh, their makeup soaked off in the afternoon heat. The costumes had to be hung out to dry on bushes around the theater after the performance. Minnie Marshall went sailing up into the flies of the ten-foot-high stage in a lift in the *Fix Me, Jesus* duet in *Revelations.* "She was up in the lights," Truitte recalled, "of which there were only two. Or three." In Penang, the Ailey dancers and musicians won hearts by appearing in a benefit for a local rural community service project, a gesture that a reporter for the Malaya and Straits *Times* found "as rare and noble as their programme is scintillating."

The critical response in Malaya was among the oddest on the tour. A reviewer in Kuala Lumpur, irritated by an overwhelming American presence in the audience, let fly with some of the severest and least coherent criticism of the tour, including a description of *The Beloved* as satire. The dancers' spirits rebounded, however, when they found a restaurant called the Oasis where American hamburgers, cheeseburgers, milkshakes and malteds were available. The young waiters were small and thin but eager to learn about the United States. Alvin struck up a conversation with one waiter, who stared up at him in awe at Alvin's size. Finish school, Alvin told the young man. They also discussed Elvis Presley. "How much we should meet more students!" Alvin commented in his diary.

The rifts building among the performers exploded into full-fledged battle in Kuala Lumpur. Alvin had tried to keep things calm, often pushing for extra time off for the dancers from their hectic daytime routine of formal functions in each new country so that they could shop or simply amble, as he did, through street fairs. But some of the dancers who had worked with Alvin before resented the better-known de Lavallade's place of honor. Alvin had been their friend. They had all grown up together as performers. De Lavallade, who had performed with the company only sporadically and as a guest artist before the tour, was an interloper.

Although billed in Australia as Alvin Ailey, Carmen de Lavallade and Their American Dance Company, the troupe was referred to as the De Lavallade–Ailey American Dance Company in many of the Asian tour stops, and de Lavallade was described in some news reports as the leader of the group. Her involvement in administrative and artistic decisions angered several dancers.

"Had decided that the dances were falling apart from lack of time to really rehearse & clean them so called early rehearsal at theater to work," Alvin wrote in his diary on March 10, a little over a month into the tour. "Chas Moore . . . became very defensive at Carmen because she criticized him and screamed that he would 'hurt' her if she didn't leave him alone . . . Carmen stormed out—furious & told D.C. she wanted to take the next plane out—went on with rehearsal to finish & arrived hotel to talk to a very hurt Carmen—decided to fire Charles and called him in to tell him so."

Alvin relented, however, and Moore continued to perform with the company through the tour. He and Ella Thompson did quit when the group returned to the United States, although they later resumed their friendship with Alvin and were among the few friends in whom Alvin confided in any depth.

"We would have killed for Alvin," Ella Thompson Moore remembered. "We'd do anything for him. We loved him. When Carmen came around, everything changed. We might as well have disappeared into the woodwork. He tried to be nice."

Some of the problem lay in Alvin's inexperienced management style. "He could be very kind and very gentle," Ves Harper said. "I have one or two things he gave me that we found in Korea. He came in one evening and said they were a gift from him and Carmen. It turns out that Carmen knew nothing about it. He thought he would give these small gifts in their name. But I must say he was extremely difficult."

Harper tried to convince Alvin to use Dick Campbell or himself as a buffer. "We were giving him the opportunity to be loved and then we would be the bad person. But it was difficult for him to do that. He wanted to be loved and to control."

Alvin redoubled his efforts to pull the company into shape as the long, difficult tour wound on. But the work, the endless heat and the rounds of parties and receptions eventually got the better of him.

He had chided Truitte for wearing his habitual dark green glasses at receptions, kicking him under banquet tables as the dancer's eyes closed peacefully behind those opaque glass curtains. Sometimes Truitte fell comfortably asleep, waking only to clap on cue at the end of speeches. But it was Alvin who in the end caused a disruption by collapsing from the heat at a formal function at the governor's palace in Kuala Lumpur. The dancers, their own clothes soaked with perspiration, were advised to carry him out quietly so as not to offend the speakers. Alvin was well enough to dance that night and attend a postperformance reception at the YMCA in Ipoh, whose theater and stagehands, he noted crossly, were unforgettably incompetent. "Show seems to be falling apart," he observed gloomily.

A stop at a snake temple lifted everyone's spirits, although Marshall was so terrified of reptiles that she fainted just looking at pictures of them. Alvin was intrigued by the way the snakes, drugged by incense, lolled about on tree branches. And there were reminders of home. Holtz called Alvin on the company's last night in Kuala Lumpur to discuss Clark Center business, and the mail was soon to include a lazily cheerful message from Langston Hughes. "Well, Alvin," the poet wrote on a postcard depicting the Rockefeller Center statue of Prometheus and fountain, "I sure love all the exotic cards from far-away places! So *cold* here!"

A gust of bracing March wind would have seemed like heaven to the beleaguered Ailey dancers. They had moved on from Kuala Lumpur to Djakarta, which, Alvin noted despairingly in his journal, more than lived up to its reputation as a hellhole.

The company would not soon forget opening night there. The dancers arrived just after the Dutch departure from Indonesia, when the country was in the throes of postrevolutionary turmoil. Chaos reigned. People were being killed in the streets. Passing through Customs, the company was delayed to almost an hour before performance, and the dancers arrived onstage about ninety minutes late. As they began to perform the opening number, *Gillespiana*, there were angry screams from the audience, many of whom were standing to yell things the dancers could not understand.

"Apologize!" the dancers were being told. When someone in the wings explained, they walked to the front of the stage, bowed and gestured their apology. The performance continued and ended with an ovation.

The hotel was filthy. The room Alvin shared with Brother John was hot and airless, not only without the promised air-conditioning but without even a fan. The restaurant, waiters and food were equally dirty. And when Alvin, Brother John and de Lavallade picked up the rest of the performers on the bus taking them to Bandung, they discovered that their hotel, too, was unlivable and that they had spent the night sleeping in the lobby.

A storm sprang up as the bus clambered along to the Bandung performances, stopping, starting, and finally grinding to a halt on a hill. The company waited in the terrible heat and humidity for another bus, enduring the stares of villagers who had gathered to see these strange creatures ensconced in their "sauna on wheels," as Truitte put it.

The costumes had had to be packed directly after the performance, still wet with perspiration, in already smelly wicker baskets, by a crew of three that was also responsible for setting up and taking down the lights and sound system. (At a humiliating eight pounds heavier than before the tour, Alvin split his pants at nearly every performance, so an extra pair was always put out for him in the wings.) Miraculously, however, the company presented some of the best performances of the tour in Indonesia. The audience response seemed to Alvin to be the most enthusiastic since Australia. And the dancers were tremendously touched when eggs were somehow secured to make bread for their last breakfast in Djakarta, as a gesture of appreciation.

Alvin was clearly the worse for wear at a stopover in Singapore en route to Manila. He had gotten up that morning at 3 A.M. to pack for the flight, after a closing night performance followed by dinner and letter-writing. In the airport, he scribbled out a poem in his journal that was inspired by the sight of an Indian man asleep near the hotel. "This is the way I sleep in Singapore," he wrote,

> (in singapore) in Singapore!
> With my feet stretched out +
> my face enshrouded
> You may think I'm dead in Singapore
> but I'm not!
>
> Oh but I can see in Singapore—
> (in Singapore) oh in Singapore
> my eyes are half opened +
> my ears are too,
> You may think I'm *dead* in
> Singapore but I'm not!
>
> The rains come at 5 here in
> Singapore and it darkens
> my short blue trousers
> and washes my big brown feet
> and makes the small bugs
> fly around my head but
> I'm alive—Singapore—

The planes carrying the performers from one small village to another in the Philippines took off from and landed at frighteningly tiny airports, one of which, Alvin noticed, had dangerous gravel runways. In Cebu, the people had an unnerving habit of staring unblinkingly at the dancers. The company had weathered intemperate climates, truculent soldiers, and cat-sized rats in one place they stayed along the tour. Now they were warned not to stray from the hotel, which was filled with huge flying cockroaches, because the Muslims of Cebu had a penchant for beheadings.

In a performance in a gymnasium in Cotabato, Alvin cut *Roots of the Blues* from the program because of the audience's raucous talking and laughter during *Mountainway Chant*, in which the dancers wore authentic American Indian designs but looked a little, Truitte observed, like "shuffling tepees." "They'd had almost nothing there ever," Alvin wrote Holtz. "When Truitte and I came out in our fur and feathers I thought the house would fall down."

His mind always at work, Alvin pondered ways to make such programs more appealing to unsophisticated audiences. Dance presentations, he felt, should be as theatrical as possible. The group leaders in each region must be prepared to speak to locals about how to look at dancing, preferably with demonstrations. Companies should arrive at each stop armed with press releases and cameras to record local functions.

But the Philippines, where the company had touched down for ten days on the last leg of the tour, was otherwise blessedly comfortable and civilized feeling. Nearly everywhere the Ailey performers went, artists expressed a great interest in introducing them to Philippine folk arts and, tired as they were, the dancers responded graciously, performing with a local folkloric group at one stop in the first such gesture to have ever been made by a visiting company. Alvin was given bamboo castenets and coconut shells and reminded himself in his diary that he must send dance books and programs to the country on his return to the States.

The audiences were generally enthusiastic. One of the most interesting reviews of the tour came from Rodrigo Perez III, who named Ailey's inspirations as Martha Graham, Katherine Dunham, Jerome Robbins and Gene Kelly. "He uses the human body with the outrageous freedom and ingenuity that recall Miss Graham; he uses folk material with the zest of Miss Dunham, and he has some of the smooth, appealing showmanship of Messrs. Robbins and Kelly. Modern dance is an affirmation of the immutable law of gravity. Modern dance breaks free, capitalizes on angularity, extreme vigor, rawness of feeling; and in Ailey's cast at least, employs convulsions of the head and torso; rather unlikely, but quite effective."

There was less than a month to go before the tired dancers returned home. The consummate actor, Alvin smiled thoughtfully for the photographer of the *South China Post-Herald* on the company's arrival in Hong Kong and observed, for a small interview that ran the following day, that he and his dancers greatly enjoyed "traveling to so many interesting countries, meeting so many different people, learning so much about the arts."

Modern dance, he added, had come from the East. "The best of everything in the dance comes from the Orient," he continued. "We learned the real basis of theatre, including songs, dance, lighting, costumes—everything that makes for the total theatre effect—from the East."

But with the last tour performances still ahead of them in Hong Kong, Japan and Korea, Alvin was becoming dangerously exasperated with the pressures of the tour, epitomized for him in "the same dull shell-shocked conversation" day after day with de Lavallade and Brother John.

Hong Kong was a gentle balm to the dancers' ragged spirits. The audiences were quiet and responsive at City Hall, where the company opened on April 9. The dressing rooms were "exquisite," Alvin noted, "the best so far." There were Spanish omelettes or eggs to order for breakfast at one hotel, and reviews ranged from polite to enthusiastic, with Brother John a special favorite—"A contortionist of a singer" was how an uncredited reviewer vividly described the singer in the *China Mail*, with a "hoarse, gravelly, gurgling, panting, rasping, rolling sound box" of a voice.

Alvin was running low on money and had to borrow $30 from Carmen to pay his hotel bill in Taipei, but that did not stop him from going on another shopping spree. He was getting more sleep now, writing in his diary less often, and meeting more friends of friends, including one young American sailor "with *problems!!*" he commented inscrutably.

The next-to-last stop on the tour was Tokyo. Tucked into Alvin's 1962 journal was a snapshot of Hughes, taken in the poet's Harlem apartment, smilingly holding up a poster emblazoned with a title in large Asian script. "Poster of my play, MULATTO, as performed in Tokyo, Kyoto, and other Japanese cities," Hughes had typed on the back of the photo.

If Alvin carried the card as a talisman, it worked. The company seemed to have a special bond with its Japanese audiences. The reviews were among the most touching of the tour, revealing something not only about how fresh eyes from another culture might view this American art form, but also about Japanese culture and Western dance of the day.

The Japanese reviews were also a validation of Alvin's belief in the universality of his dance. As he had told a reporter from the *Djakarta Daily Mail*, in what would prove to be a summary of his entire career, he envisioned the tour's objective as being "to reach the audience and make them a part of the dance." His work was "a communication of experience. We are always looking for that which will help us find a perfect harmony between the artist, the technique and the performance."

The tone of several reviews suggests that that kind of instinctive, seamless sharing had in fact occurred in Japan. One Western critic weighed in with a particularly probing response. Elise Grilli cited the company in the *Japan Times* for its humanity, imagination and training but also put the group into a historical context, suggesting that in many ways the repertory summed up historical influences from European court ballet to world ballet and modern dance as well as ethnic music and dance, but without a trace of obvious eclecticism. The Ailey dancers had taken black and American Indian folklore and transformed it into theater art. "There was nothing naive or 'folksy' about this performance, and no reportage of things-as-they-are," Grilli wrote. "A large accumulation of ideas and of history was translated into pure motion." Some of the other reviews were surprisingly abandoned, given the Japanese reputation for reserve, and they make for fascinating and colorful reading. "Hot and Perfect" was how the headline writer described the Ailey program in the April 23 evening edition of *Asahi Shimbun*.

A few reviewers seemed overwhelmed by the exoticism of it all. Masao Kageyasu singled out the "stupendous sensitivity" with which the dancers' bodies responded to the music. "The unusual length of the legs and arms of Carmen and Alvin were effectual and impressive in and of itself, but their movements were gushy outpouring of Negro vitality," Kageyasu continued.

De Lavallade repeatedly drew extra attention, as she had earlier on the tour. In one Japanese review, she was praised as a practitioner of an ancient Japanese theatrical technique. "The Queen de Lavallade shows her good sense of 'ma' " ("a Japanese term," the translator added, "that means timing in general and clever utilization of non-movement at certain significant moments in particular, an important concept in Noh, Kabuki and other traditional music") "in 'The Beloved.' "

Some of the most gripping description came from Nobuo Ikemiya, who followed the troupe to one of the tour stops outside Tokyo. Ikemiya's April 25 review in *Ongaku Buyo Shimbun* was written in the form of a letter to Alvin that began: "I am so grateful that we could meet you."

"Brother John Sellers was singing," Ikemiya continued. "He stood nonchalantly and started singing quietly. But when he sang the last number I saw a dark *Asura*" ("Sanskrit name," the translator explained, "a guardian of Gods with supernatural vehemence, an Oriental equivalent of Furies") "shouting 'Break down the walls, the barriers' . . . The de Lavallade–Ailey American Dance Company needs more careful scrutiny, for they show us the relationship between the impulse of love and the blues in a language beyond languages."

In a postscript to the sheaf—the bouquet, really—of reviews, the translator Sumio Kamabayashi wrote that the Ailey performances marked an epoch in Japanese dance history. Alvin's work had suggested to young ballet dancers ways of making their art "modern." Older Japanese modern dancers, trained largely in the German expressionist school, had new forms of communication to consider. One comment suggested that it was not only in New York that dance had become dry and in need of an infusion of theatricality.

"To young modern dancers who are influenced by *anti-theatre* and *anti-danse* and produce cerebral or sexual experiments, you pointed a way to a healthy *totaltheater* that includes general public," Kamabayashi observed.

The company moved on to Seoul and the tour's exuberantly received final performances. Alvin had been impressed by the subtlety and pinpoint focus of Japanese theater, he told *Dance Magazine*. But he was even more impressed, he said, by the "extreme originality" of Korean dance, a judgment seconded by American reviewers some two decades later when Korean dance and theater began to be seen with some regularity in New York City.

The tour ended explosively with a near riot at City Hall in Seoul on closing night, when would-be ticket buyers tried to push into the sold-out performance. The company left Seoul on May 12, returning to New York via Tokyo, where Alvin stayed on to teach at a local dance school for a week. On his way home, he stopped for another visit with his family in Los Angeles.

A spokeswoman for the State Department later described the tour as "a far greater success than we ever dared hope," and Alvin arrived in New York full of plans on how to improve future international dance tours.

Early American modern dance had looked to Asia for inspiration. But for many Asians, Alvin suggested, American culture was what they saw in American movies. They were surprised to hear about the variety of dance companies, dance forms and synthesis of forms, particularly in a country that offered almost no subsidies to its artists.

"Most of what they knew regarding the U.S. Negro previously was negative," he told Arthur Todd. "They all knew about Little Rock and the Freedom Riders. The Asians have a great identification with the American Negro, especially because they, too, have been involved with struggles for many years and have seen so many wars. There are, I believe, important political ramifications to this."

Some friends felt that Alvin had returned a harder, less innocent person. The pressure of the tour had taken its toll. Truitte, Bord and Hill watched and worried, concerned that for all Alvin's hard work success had come to him too soon, before he was prepared to take it—and failure—in his stride.

There were other casualties of the tour. De Lavallade drifted away from Alvin, although they never completely lost touch. She continued to be a source of comfort in difficult times, and performed with the company sporadically through the years as a glamorous guest artist. But their relationship had been strained by the pressures of living in such close and constant proximity and by Alvin's impatience at having to defend her against the antipathy some of the dancers felt toward her.

The company lost several other performers, a few of whom felt betrayed by what they saw as Alvin's greater loyalty to de Lavallade. But the tour had been a remarkable achievement for the young director, who felt an increased pride, he said, in belonging to the "exciting, brutal, horrible, glorious, exasperating, beautiful, terrible, and, most of all, frustrating" American dance scene.

The company had performed abroad for an estimated 146,791 people in sixty performances, most of which were exuberantly received. Armed with glowing reviews, Alvin and the dancers returned to find almost no work, a pattern that was to be repeated after every foreign triumph for another decade or so. Only abroad, it seemed, could the Ailey company and American modern dancers in general perform frequently, be considered important artists by audiences and earn a living with their art. Glory quickly faded for Alvin, replaced by the dull reality of struggling to keep the company going—and of facing what would prove to be one of the most painful experiences of his life as a performer.

fifteen

PROPHETS WITH
LITTLE HONOR

Alvin moved back immediately into the busy life of rehearsing and teaching at Clark Center. He returned a week before the first choreographers' showcase—after all the work had been done, but in time to witness a huge crowd pushing in on the afternoon of the free concert.

No one at the center had thought to print tickets. So the doors to the modest little theater were simply opened, the audience poured in and a tradition was born. That the reviews were positive did not surprise Alvin, but he had seen far past that horizon in the Far East.

Although the Ailey company was not in the kind of demand that might have been expected after the tour, success was clearly in the air. Everyone seemed to know about Alvin and his dancers and their headquarters on Eighth Avenue. Soon after his return, Alvin received a letter from Ruth St. Denis, still an icon of American modern dance, asking if she might rent office space at Clark Center. "I have written her that unfortunately I did not think it would be possible," Alvin told Edele Holtz in a note that asked, with the exquisite tact of which he was so capable, if she would be interested in also writing "Miss Ruth." "She'd appreciate it and to hear from you would help very much in my explanation of the reasons why not to her."

Sylvia Waters, later an Ailey dancer and the director of the Alvin Ailey Repertory Ensemble, the junior Ailey company, recalled a conversation she had around 1962 with Martha Hill, director of the Dance Division at the Juilliard School, where Waters was a student. They met in the street and Hill asked her about her plans. Waters told her about the choreographer she was then dancing with. Hill, a looming, ebullient dance midwife who coaxed many careers into being over a half-century career, had other ideas, expressed with a characteristically staccato emphasis that Waters never forgot. "Well, you *must* get with the Alvin Ailey company," she told the young dancer. "Now listen to me. You get with the Alvin Ailey company, because *that* company is going to be the *num*ber one company, especially for Negro dancers. And keep working on your ballet technique."

The company did have two prestigious bookings to look forward to in the summer and early fall of 1962. Alvin had been asked to teach a two-week class in "jazz forms" in mid-July and to perform with his company at the American Dance Festival on the rolling green campus of Connecticut College in New London, Connecticut. The Pillow, in Massachusetts, was known for its family feeling and sometimes scrappy eclecticism. The less intimate Connecticut festival, founded in 1948, was known for presenting high-caliber premieres by the greats of American modern dance.

The company was represented by some of its tour dances, including *Revelations*, on a program shared with the tap stylist Paul Draper. The idea was to focus on ethnic influences in dance. "The chances are, however, that hardly anyone in the audience bothered to reflect on the origins of anybody or anything," Allen Hughes wrote in the *New York Times*, "for the proceedings on stage were simply too engrossing most of the time to allow for meditation."

It was easier to cheer the dance and dancers than to put into words why everything worked well, Hughes continued in his affectionate and perceptive review. Their success might lie, he speculated, in "the galvanizing personality of Mr. Ailey himself. There, one might find sweetness and rage, hope and despair, the sacred and the profane, all battling with each other for ascendancy. Weakness, resignation and compromise would hardly have a chance." Hughes commended the dancers, singling out Alvin and James Truitte, for performing of "stunning directness and intensity."

The invitation to perform in New London meant that the company could not return that summer to the Pillow. Alvin had also been approached to play a lead role in a film to be shot that summer in the West Indies, which he apparently also turned down for the Connecticut engagement. But he did become involved in a project with Robert Joffrey while at the festival. Joffrey, a friend of several years who made a point of encouraging black dancers, had introduced Alvin to Rebekah Harkness, the poor little rich girl of American ballet. Alvin spent his time in Connecticut commuting to Holiday House, the heiress's lavishly appointed, fifty-two-room summer home in Watch Hill, to choreograph for the Robert Joffrey Ballet, which was in residence there.

Shy and petulant, a deluded dreamer who insisted on her way, Harkness was a would-be composer and a would-be dancer who longed for a ballet company of her own. Addicted at various times in her life to alcohol, drugs and sex, she nonetheless faithfully subjected herself to the discipline of daily piano practice and private ballet classes. She had taken on the Joffrey as a personal project, inviting the company to spend three months at her estate working on new ballets and helping to finance their tours of the Near East and the Soviet Union. In 1964, however, she took over Joffrey's dancers to form a troupe of her own, leaving him without a company and ensuring that dance audiences and critics saw her as nothing but a woman with large pockets, wild schemes and almost no taste.

But her 1962 invitation to Alvin gave him the chance to work with dancers whom critics considered to be among the best in the country. It was a bizarre and somewhat lonely experience. "Watch Hill Days," he wrote in notes for an autobiography. "Clam bakes & gold fixtures. Orgy upstairs. Once I was the only choreog in the hotel—the others were in the House on the Hill." The dancers did not always seem respectful to him, and at one point, stung by the begrudging minimal attention they paid to his requests in a rehearsal, he left abruptly and headed back to New York, to everyone's consternation.

That Alvin had tried hard to work with the troupe is evident in notes for a memo that he wrote to "Dancers" on the new ballet, a dance version of García Lorca's *House of Bernarda Alba* that Alvin called *Feast of Ashes*. "Seems I never have enough time to say all the things I want to say to you about this dance—and neither do you have time to listen what with all you are trying to accomplish in the time before you leave—I have written this about the dance hoping that it will help us all to communicate it better—" His memo analyzes the characters' behavior in a ballet "clothed in an air of religiosity—in a respect for things dictated, things much outside the manipulation of the characters themselves." The dancers should not worry about their technique, he told them. "You are all excellent dance technicians—but the dramatic values are as important as the dance values—who you are, what you are doing and why from one moment to the next dictate the texture of the work."

Alvin did finish the dance, a tale of a house inhabited by a family of repressed women. Not a major success, *Feast of Ashes* suffered from the turgid heat that sinks most dance interpretations of that apparently irresistible vehicle. But it held its own with ballets by some fairly accomplished choreographers, including Joffrey and Gerald Arpino, and was later praised in reviews of the Harkness Ballet's first European performances. The ballet had little to do with the Lorca play, Peter Williams observed, but it was nonetheless "a powerful and effective dance drama."

"So far I know Ailey's work only through the instrument of the Negro dancer and I have gained the impression that it derived its impetus through those particular qualities unique to the Negro—that strong rhythmic sense, that sculptural physical construction, that seeming bonelessness and that ability to perform technical feats in a manner almost denied to other dancers," Williams continued in a considered summarizing of Alvin's career, from a perspective thoroughly grounded in the classical ballet. "I was wrong. 'Feast of Ashes' has proved to me that Ailey had a very personal form of expression, using modern movement naturally based on a firm substructure of the academic classical vocabulary. The two forms do not fight together but are welded naturally together and his line is so sure that it is just as effective when performed by those lacking the special qualities of the Negro."

Harkness's largesse continued to flow. She invited Alvin and his company to perform at the Rebekah Harkness Foundation Dance Festival in early September in the open-air Delacorte Theater in Central Park. In exchange for the performances, Harkness provided the money for live accompaniment by Brother John Sellers and the Howard Roberts Chorale for *Roots of the Blues* and *Revelations*, new costumes by Ves Harper for *Revelations* and the restaging of *Creation of the World*, now a dance based on primitive ritual.

Alvin added improbable Soviet ballet–style high lifts to *Creation* on opening night in homage to some illustrious guests in the audience, dancers from the Bolshoi Ballet, and managed to put together a welcoming intermission speech in Russian for the occasion. Harkness provided special Russian programs.

The Russian dancers were a good audience, but the performance was not one of the company's best. Rain lifted the evening, however, to inspired heights. The first drops began to fall, gently but persistently, just as Alvin and Myrna White started *Roots of the Blues*. Alvin's pants split yet another time, during his *Jack of Diamonds* solo, and the gap widened as the rain increased. The stage grew slippery. White kicked off her shoes and the audience howled, for under her fishnet stockings were toes stuck with corn plasters. Alvin followed suit, but he had a few falls anyway as he went into one of his famous knee slides. The rain continued as Brother John sang about forty days and nights of rain in the *Backwater Blues* section. Then suddenly it abated, just as the two finished dancing.

Alvin shook his head in dismay at their performance, but the audience had loved their persevering spirit. The Russians applauded rhythmically, having sat stolidly through the rain as others left and umbrellas sprouted around them. At the end, they cheered the Ailey dancers, particularly Truitte, and were cheered in return from the stage.

Although Alvin's acting career was as encouraging at the moment, he would soon give it up. He had charmed political and cultural leaders across the world that year, but now he was to be undone by a handful of New York actors.

The theater director Josh Logan had seen Alvin perform a few years earlier and had gone backstage to ask him if he really wouldn't prefer to be an actor. That fall, Logan found a perfect vehicle, a play by Peter S. Feibleman called *Tiger Tiger Burning Bright* about a black matriarch in New Orleans in the 1940s who nearly destroys her children in her blind, ferocious attempt to raise them right.

Alvin auditioned successfully for the role of Clarence, the tiger of the title and the oldest son, a thief who tries hard to keep his mother's illusions alive. It was a meaty role that, under other circumstances, he might have enjoyed. But he was surrounded by trained, experienced actors—among them Claudia McNeil, who played the mother, and Diana Sands, Cicely Tyson, Ellen Holly, Al Freeman Jr. and Roscoe Lee Browne—who were for the most part intent on making sure Alvin did not forget his inexperience. That wasn't likely, for only Logan seemed to believe in him.

Could this untried youngster pull off a lead role in a Broadway play? people sitting in on rehearsals asked the director. He didn't move like a tiger. No, Logan told them, he didn't. He was Nijinsky. Nijinsky? they asked incredulously. What Logan needed was a black Brando.

The play went into rehearsal in mid-November for an opening on

Broadway on December 18 at the Booth Theater. It was soon discovered that Alvin could not be heard beyond the third row. And so he began every morning at 7 A.M. working for two hours with a speech coach and then went off to rehearsals, where the actors "bit me off, chewed me up, and spit me out," as he told an interviewer, although Logan was characteristically gentle. Alvin was awed by McNeil, whom he immediately saw as an Electra. Carried away, perhaps, by her success in *Raisin in the Sun* three years before, McNeil tortured everyone, including Logan, with her high-handed ways and sheer meanness.

She and Sands made a practice of upstaging Alvin, a mere dancer after all. Without a clue as to how to retaliate or even hold his own, he pulled into himself, dazed and zombielike, and guiltily began to fortify himself with wine before rehearsals. Logan called Milton Katselas, Alvin's director in *Call Me by My Rightful Name*. "Is Alvin on drugs?" Logan asked him. Not that he knew of, Katselas responded. Perhaps he was just scared.

The dam broke in a way that Logan was to long remember. Alvin had just finished rehearsing a scene with Sands, who played the role of a sexy, sympathetic prostitute. Suddenly he raced across the stage and buried his face behind the curtain. There was a moment's silence, followed by the terrible sound of howls of laughter and then uncontrollable weeping. No one moved. Eventually, McNeil went to him.

Someone joked about opening a tranquilizer concession. Logan, who had had two nervous breakdowns, said that he would take the pills himself. But at last, at last, he added, Alvin was doing what Logan wanted. He was lying down and crying. Soon he would gain control of himself and the role, Logan said. And he did.

But *Tiger Tiger Burning Bright* closed soon after it opened. Although the reviews were good, none of them appeared in anything but special broadsheet editions, for the play opened in the middle of a newspaper strike.

The dreadful experience of *Tiger Tiger Burning Bright* ended Alvin's fling with drama, although years later he would look back on his acting classes, and particularly the sense memory exercises, as extremely useful to him in choreographing and dancing. "After *Tiger* he just seemed to turn back to dance and dance seemed to consume him," Michael Shurtleff said. "I felt that idealization drove him. No doubt the terribly unhappy experience he had in *Tiger* was instrumental, but he was so driven with this concept of starting a black dance company."

Alvin had some rebuilding to do, for only three of the dancers from the Far East tour—Don Martin, Truitte and Thelma Hill—were left. They performed in April in a benefit concert at the Brooklyn Academy of Music that included the premiere of one of Alvin's most subtly beautiful works, *Reflections in D*, a lyrical solo danced to a piano piece of the same name by Duke Ellington. In program notes for *Modern Jazz Suite*, a group of three works that opened with *Gillespiana* and included *Reflections in D*, Alvin wrote of dances that explored the interrelationship of modern jazz scores and the contemporary dance idiom. The solo lived up to that premise in an understated physicalization of the score that caught all the music's subtle accents and rhythmic shifts, no matter the changes that different performers brought to it and handed on to other dancers.

He continued to be drawn as a choreographer to both "high" and "low" art in their many gradations. The trio of dances was completed by *Suspensions*, a formal quintet performed to music by Jimmy Giuffre, which was replaced the following year by the appropriately named *Light*, a celebration of social dancing performed to music by Ellington that was popular on tour but did not survive long in the repertory. Alvin had consulted Truitte and Hill, who were expert social dancers, in the creation of what one Philadelphia reviewer described as "a hilarious scamper of nose-tweaking and hip-wiggling." Another premiere was *Labyrinth*, an equally short-lived dance that seems to have been a dry run for a later Harkness ballet called *Ariadne*, drawn as both were from the Greek legend of Theseus and the Minotaur.

Alvin had not, however, abandoned his earliest pieces. *Revelations* burnished its growing reputation as a classic with two performances that spring and summer that some in the audience were never to forget. In early May, the city of New York invited the company to represent dance in Salute to Spring, produced by the city one breezy night in front of the imposing central public library building on Fifth Avenue and Forty-second Street. The oddball homage was a smorgasbord of puppeteering, dramatic readings, modern dance and popular and operatic singing. Colleen Dewhurst and Cab Calloway joined Casey Stengel, Mayor Robert Wagner and the city's Sanitation Department band in a program that included the processional, *Honor, Honor* and *Wading in the Water* from *Revelations*.

It was the best performance Holtz ever saw of *Wading in the Water*. Three decades later, in an era when the video documentation of the most fledgling of choreographic attempts is a matter of course, Holtz was saddened by the lack of any sort of record of that occasion. Why had it worked so well? she asked Alvin. The dancers had been rested and fresh, he told her, but most of all the music had been performed live rather than on tape.

A month later, the Ailey dancers performed in a packed Benefit for Birmingham concert at Clark Center. The idea of Geoffrey Holder, the concert raised money for the work of Martin Luther King Jr. in a time of gathering protests across the nation and a few weeks before King led the massive march on Washington. In that charged time, there was quiet sobbing in the dark auditorium during *Revelations*. At performances in mid-August at the Pillow, an exultant *Revelations* drew more applause than an elegant display of Spanish dance by a popular ethnic team and dancing by two leading members of the Royal Danish Ballet.

Dancers came and went throughout 1963. Three nonblack dancers who later established significant performing and choreographic careers of their own—Louis Falco, Sally Stackhouse and Mariko Sanjo—performed briefly with the company. Minnie Marshall was back, and two distinctive youngsters signed on: Michele Murray, who had some Horton training and had been spotted by Alvin when he taught in Boston the year before, and Loretta Abbott, who went on to one of the most varied and enduring careers in New York modern dance.

The company danced a few college performances that summer, arranged by Benjamin Jones, who appeared as one of those unassuming angels that tended to materialize as needed in Alvin's life. In this case, the relationship turned sour. A black sportsman and businessman who loved the theater and performers, Jones had seen that the company needed practical help. "He was a sweet man who turned over the profits from his dry cleaning business and set up an office for Alvin in New York," Harper recalled. "He gave us his station wagon and began to set up concert tours for us throughout America. That was how we subsisted.

"He was the impresario. He knew nothing about it, but he was so in love with the company and the idea of what it was doing that he was willing to risk everything he had to set them on their feet again. He provided the necessary money for new costumes. When the dancers had no money, who did they go to? They went to Ben. He supported the company in any way that was necessary at the moment." Jones even tried to convince the restless, rootless Alvin that he ought to invest in a home of his own and buy an inexpensive brownstone uptown.

On tour in the Midwest, Alvin and his dancers had a chance to work with Ellington in *My People*, created for the Black Centennial Exposition in Chicago. Marking "a century of Negro progress," the eighteen-day event marked the centennial of the Emancipation Proclamation. Ellington had agreed to contribute a piece that paid homage in music and dance to black heroes, among them Mary McLeod Bethune, Countee Cullen, Florence Mills, Jesse Owens, Medgar Evers and King. It was to be performed in the five-thousand-seat Arie Crown Theater in McCormick Place.

My People was a musical pageant rooted in sacred spirituals and the secular blues, incorporating parts of *Black, Brown and Beige*, a massive, ambitious jazz suite in which Ellington traced black music from African sources through American history. *My People* was intended to entertain, the composer cautioned wryly, and contained "only about one minute of social protest," although the text did include lines like Ellington's observation that "the foundation of the United States rests on the sweat of my people." There was also a finale called *King Fit the Battle of Alabam*, and to everyone's delight King himself attended a rehearsal.

Ellington had had several choreographers in mind to work with him on the piece but chose Talley Beatty, adding Alvin a little later. Beatty learned more about choreography from his work sessions with the composer at his New York office and in Chicago, he recalled, than from anyone else in his career. They disagreed about certain historical references, but Ellington had a strong feeling for what the accents and flavors of each moment should be.

Ellington set the mood precisely for Beatty in a scene in which a member of a chain gang figured. "You come in," Ellington told Beatty. "You're supposed to be here. It's early in the morning. But not dawn. So you can have a little attitude." Another time, he suggested just how a heavy hammer would be held so the weight could be seen in the arm and in the way the hammer dropped. The experience of working with Ellington was productive but "very hard," Beatty said, "a baptism by fire."

The composer was also a bit of a tease. When Beatty worried because he had run out of music for his dance, Ellington leaned close to tell him, "Well, that's all right. That's my job. I write music."

Both Ellington and Beatty had trouble producing the work fast enough. An anxious and vituperative perfectionist, Beatty worked with excruciating slowness. When Alvin arrived, he was pressed into rapid service of the sort he was learning of necessity to thrive on. But he was disappointed with the exposition and wrote to Holtz that it was poorly organized, boring and provincial. It was also not drawing the expected audience, and the huge theater was usually only about one-fifth full.

Alvin would later describe the experience as the time "Talley Beatty and myself both once did the same ballet," at Ellington's request. The bizarre setup brought out all Alvin's comic sense of the ludicrous. Describing the opening *Work Song* section of *My People*, one of two pieces his and Beatty's dancers performed in together, Alvin wrote to Al Holtz that "the combined dance companies make a rather spectacular entrance in African garb on an ascending orchestra with all the arms raised and heads back in I been 'buked style." In the second number— "integrated (if you'll excuse the expression)"—Ellington had the two choreograph to the same music in dances to be performed at the same time, Alvin's dancers on an upper level of the stage and Beatty's below. The effect promised to be stunning, Alvin told Holtz, but the two choreographers were horrified when they saw the finished result. Ellington told them it looked wonderful.

The Ailey dancers performed two other minor pieces that Alvin had also created on the spot, with *Light* completing his contribution to *My People*. Work went on late into the night, and Ellington talked with Alvin on the telephone early each morning. Alvin had brought "a trunkful of stuff" in the way of costumes and props, he wrote Holtz, and insisted that Harper be summoned to create costumes that were in the end worn not only by the Ailey dancers but by the singers and the Beatty company as well.

It was mayhem, with endless rehearsals and no one in either dance company expecting the piece to be finished in time. The first few shows were a shambles. "It's all pulled together now but Mr. E couldn't make up his mind if the show was for Broadway or the Apollo," Alvin wrote Holtz. "I had Broadway in mind of course and had asked for lots of effects—scrims, projections, fragmentary set-pieces, etc., you know me—and some of it got in—so the first part of the show has an air of production but the last half descends spectacularly to the level of vaudeville—tasteful—but vaudeville.

"Maybe after all that negative talk you'd like to hear something good—1) Duke Ellington <u>really</u> is a genius—what an incredible man! He never seems to sleep & new music pours out of him like water from a tap—not only was he constantly rewriting the show music but other things for the band to record while here—and the most gracious, tactful, charming human being I've ever met."

As it turned out, Chicago was a prelude to more disarray. Alvin and his dancers flew from Chicago to New York, where they picked up several musicians at the airport, and then went south to Brazil for the International Music Festival in Rio de Janeiro and some of the worst performances of their careers. They arrived just hours before the opening performance and found the theater locked. There were problems with the music. Alvin had hired the actor Louis Gossett to substitute for Brother John Sellers, who had a previous commitment in Australia. Gossett had sung before, but never for dance. Brought in at the last moment without rehearsal, the unfortunate actor was unprepared for the precise timing required for such a collaboration.

Confused, Gossett lost his way in the middle of the performance, and Alvin and Myrna White had to sing and dance their way through *The Blues Roll On*, a piece Alvin had made by combining segments of *Blues Suite* and *Roots of the Blues*. "It was truly a fiasco and those Brazilians were not ready for these black children in bare feet," Truitte recalled. The audience was dressed to the nines, expecting something pink or classically white, no doubt, for the troupe had been billed as Ballet Alvin Ailey.

Alvin later lost his temper violently, screaming at the dancers and slamming any open door he could find backstage, but he was as angry at himself as he was at anyone else. He was feeling sick and not up to performing at his best, he told Holtz. It had been a long time since he and White had rehearsed *Roots*, and ticket prices were high. There had been little advance publicity, and the Ailey dancers performed only one night after Igor Stravinsky and the London Philharmonic Orchestra. The theater was half full.

"The Alvin Ailey Dance Theater had several heavy bales to tote in its first appearance at Rio de Janeiro's music and dance festival and did not quite make it anyway," a correspondent observed in the *New York Times*, blithely attributing part of the company's lack of success to the fact that "Rio has many people singing and dancing sambas for fun and for free the year round."

Revelations did receive its usual good response, even on an opening night when the applause was otherwise seldom more than courteous. The company danced a third performance in São Paolo that was much more warmly received, but Rio was a nightmare that Alvin never forgot.

He took a week off to recuperate in Bahia, where he went to do research for *Macumba*, a new work for Harkness. He then embarked on the Ailey company's first national tour, six weeks of performances that would take them south for the first time. Traveling by station wagon, the dancers performed in one-night stands on stages whose condition often seemed to vary inversely with the warmth of the audience's response.

The most enthusiastic audiences were the southern blacks for whom the company performed, in a time of great change and not a little fear. In Jackson, Mississippi, the dancers met Gilbert Mosley, then director of the underground New Free Southern Theater, and visited a place that printed pamphlets designed to teach black farmers how to read.

The company was invited to several civil rights meetings, among them a frighteningly clandestine one held by the Student Nonviolent Coordinating Committee, a major mover in the push for equality for black southerners in the 1960s. "Like dummies, we went," Truitte remembered. "It was pitch black dark. We knocked on the door. This curtain moved and someone said, 'Come in.' When we got back to the hotel we were shaking like leaves."

Alvin kept up with Mosley and others over the years. Sending home some of the group's "contraband material" to Holtz, who he knew would be interested, he talked of offering the group help in the form of a benefit, old clothes, books "or something."

The dancers' experiences playing in the South—"Courage Country," as Alvin called it in a postcard to the Holtzes—were sometimes poignant. In one town, blacks on their way to work scattered when the company station wagon, its roof piled high with the ladder and stools for *Blues Suite* and *Revelations,* pulled over early one morning so the dancers could ask for directions to a hotel that would take them in. Eventually they realized that they looked as if they had come to participate in sit-ins. They left Mississippi with nervous anticipation, carefully driving a steady two miles below the speed limit until they got to the border, a highway patrol car tailing them all the way. There was a fervent sigh of "Hail, North" in the dancers' car, Truitte recalled, as they crossed the state line at last.

It was not a happy homecoming. After all the work, Alvin was left with almost no profit for the company and the suspicion that Jones and Susan Pimsleur, the company's agent, were unreliable. But an intriguing new project awaited him. He would be working again with Langston Hughes, who had asked him to help direct *Jericho–Jim Crow.*

Hughes, as always cheerfully intent on cashing in on the market and never averse to admitting it, was aware of a building enthusiasm for gospel music among the general public that had helped make his *Black Nativity* such a hit. But he, like Alvin, also felt an irrepressible delight in black people as he knew them best, not the political icons of the 1960s but men and women who squeezed all the juice and joy and sadness out of often impoverished, difficult lives.

Acting on that delight, Hughes alienated himself from those who believed that it was time for blacks to be portrayed as dignified and heroic, just as Alvin faced increasing charges of commercialism when his choreography seemed to stray too far outside the parameters of "serious" modern dance. Hughes had described another, earlier work, *Tambourines to Glory*, as "a singing, shouting, wailing drama of the old conflict between blatant Evil and quiet Good, with the Devil driving a Cadillac." For satirizing corrupt black storefront churches in the play, Hughes was branded as a politically irresponsible traitor to his race.

He took no chances with *Jericho–Jim Crow*, which opened on January 12, 1964, at the Greenwich Mews Theater on West Thirteenth Street, a church that served as a synagogue on Jewish holy days. Hughes called on ministers to vet the new gospel play for him. This time, he said, he was presenting "a serious but entertaining and optimistic play about the freedom movement" that dealt with "young people of all racial and religious backgrounds who are meeting, working, canvassing, petitioning, marching, picketing, sitting-in, singing and praying today to help make a better America for all, and especially for citizens of color." In addition, some proceeds from the box office were to go to several leading civil rights groups.

Jericho–Jim Crow was a hit that ran to the end of April and then went out to other theaters around the city. It was a good start to a promising year in which the Alvin Ailey American Dance Theater would take giant steps toward becoming an American institution.

sixteen

BACK ON THE
ROAD AGAIN

The company's move into the ranks of established modern dance in America went hand in hand with escalating pressures on Alvin, which, by early 1964, were becoming overwhelming. There was an increasingly popular company to run, and at least some of Alvin's obligations had to be fulfilled at Clark Center, where he and his dancers continued to teach and perform. And he knew he had to keep the momentum going by creating dances and performing.

In February, Michael Dorfman, an English impresario who had taken *Black Nativity* to Europe, contacted Alvin with an offer of a three-month fall tour to open in Paris in early September. Such a tour would give him the excuse to act on his idea of turning his company into a library for the dances by other choreographers that he loved and thought deserved attention.

He had already presented pieces by Horton, John Butler and Glen Tetley. He acquired James Truitte's *Variegations*, an evocation of the Horton technique that Truitte had created in 1958. Now Alvin set about creating in earnest his groundbreaking modern dance repertory company. He brought in Joyce Trisler, the former Horton dancer, who had come east to study at Juilliard and perform and choreograph. New

York had not rounded the sharp corners of Trisler's personality. She was as strong-willed and feisty as she had been back in Los Angeles. But another side of this tough-talking woman was suggested in her *Journey*, set to Charles Ives's haunting *Unanswered Question*. Alvin believed that *Journey*, lyrical and elegiac, had the potential to become a modern dance classic, and he acquired it for his repertory.

A dancer of extraordinary suppleness and resiliency, Trisler had created the solo for her "floppy" self, as Alvin loved to describe her, for a back that carved into a deep curve and legs that stretched out on a line that seemed to reach into infinity. Years later, in a time of terrible pain, he would find solace in that luminous arc and make use of it in *Memoria*, a tribute to Trisler that became one of the best-loved dances in the Ailey repertory.

As fond as ever of organizing everything but his own life, Alvin swung into full gear in preparation for the tour and for the company's new look. He might drag his feet going into the studio to teach or choreograph, but he loved the work of gauging audiences' interests and putting together programs and a repertory that would engage the widest range of people on as many levels as possible, each program building in an orderly, well-plotted way to an irresistible finale.

Sitting at whatever desk was handy at Clark Center and scribbling long notes on his pad of paper, oblivious most of the time to the hubbub around him, Alvin whittled his list of favorite dances down to four possibilities for the European tour, each the work of a distinctively individual creator. Louis Johnson's *Lament* was a delicate romantic piece in the ballet idiom. Horton's *To José Clemente Orozco*, inspired by the painter's homage to the Mexican Indian agrarian revolutionaries of the early twentieth century known as Zapatistas, was of the earth. Filled with a sense of mesmerizing stillness, it was a dance for two peasants pulled down by gravity as they work the land. In Paul Sanasardo's mysterious *Metallics*, a woman peers out from behind a curtain of metal tubes at a man and a woman dancing together and then draws close to them but remains outside their world. And Anna Sokolow's *Rooms* was a searing portrait of what one Australian critic would later describe as "outwardly conforming people in a large rooming-house living out their dark dreams and fantasies in the privacy of their own small rooms."

Rooms had a strong hold on Alvin, although it left the Ailey repertory soon after its first performances. The dance was loneliness and anguish laid bare. He loved it intellectually, admiring the piece for the way it reflected the paintings of Yves Tanguy that had been its inspiration, as Alvin told one interviewer, referring to his own work as "Rodin dance." *Rooms* "has a kind of linear sculpture to it. Everything is terribly simple, terribly honed, honed down to its finest elements, so that you see only what Anna Sokolow wants you to see."

He had not had the courage to ask Sokolow directly for such a major and difficult work. Instead, he wrote to her about acquiring another dance, adding that he felt it would be too much to ask for *Rooms.* She immediately proposed staging that signature piece for the Ailey company, although she was later a little disappointed, one company member recalled, that in rehearsals the Ailey dancers failed to respond with the meekness of her Juilliard students to Sokolow's fierce passion for detail and discipline. The dance nevertheless had a strong impact on its Ailey performers, and Truitte cited his role in *Rooms* as a highlight of his career.

There were only scattered performances in the months before the tour. Alvin went home to Los Angeles with his company to present a salute to Horton at the University of California at Los Angeles in mid-April. The dancers also participated in a benefit for the Young Women's Christian Association in late June at Clark Center, and Alvin was present in spirit at the 1964 Jacob's Pillow festival when Truitte and de Lavallade danced *Twelve Gates,* a pièce d'occasion he had created to celebrate the golden wedding anniversary of Ted Shawn and Ruth St. Denis.

Alvin had neglected himself as he plunged into his crowded schedule, balancing the demands of the company's work at home, its second international tour, and a return to Australia that would follow in December. Jacqueline Maskey commented in a review of the Clark Center benefit that Alvin was dancing a little sluggishly and getting by on "natural magnetism." Reviewing a second Harkness concert at the Delacorte in the *New York Times,* Allen Hughes observed that he looked heavier and slower, although Hughes added that Alvin's performing was still riveting.

Truitte was singled out at the Delacorte performance, as he had been all year, here for dancing that had had "the effect of smelling salts" on one critic. There was also a batch of recent recruits to enjoy, with reviewers giving special praise to Trisler and two incandescent new company members, William Louther, formerly with Martha Graham, and Hope Clarke, who would work with the Ailey company in a variety of capacities over the years. The audience was wildly exuberant, cheering and applauding not only at the end of dances but during them. It was a joyous send-off, for two days later the company would be leaving for Europe.

Revelations was presented at the Delacorte in its final form, with a poetic addition to the program notes. "The spirituals sing of woe triumphantly, knowing well that all rivers will be crossed and the Promised Land is just beyond the stream," Alvin's friend Langston Hughes wrote. "The spirituals ask no pity—for their words ride on the strongest of melodies, the melody of faith. That is why there is joy in their singing, peace in their music, and strength in their soul."

The Delacorte also served as a formal dress rehearsal for *The Road of the Phoebe Snow*, one of three pieces by Talley Beatty that Alvin had acquired for his "library." He had had his eye on the piece, which had been choreographed in a studio next to his at Michael's. And its theme was one Alvin could identify with. Danced to urgent, hurtling music by Duke Ellington and Billy Strayhorn, the jazz ballet depicted lives lived along a railroad track by men and women who are left behind by passing trains but who also turn away, Beatty later said, "from the empty, sterile places where they live."

Phoebe Snow was a cornerstone of the repertory Alvin was building, a piece by a master choreographer whose sleek, onrushing dance combined elements of jazz, ballet, modern dance and the kind of Afro-Caribbean dance made famous by Katherine Dunham, with whom Beatty had performed early on. But even the most abstract of Beatty's dances always carried an undercurrent of the kind of passion that Alvin wore on his sleeve.

Beatty continued to create dances for the company through 1988, wandering in and out of Alvin's life like a quizzical ghost. The two would remain somewhat wary friends for years. "I wasn't all that comfortable with Alvin," Beatty said. "I think he was guarded with me. Alvin would get screwy in certain areas; he'd act peculiar sometimes where peculiar was out of place. But he was about the nicest of the whole lot."

Beatty had not kept a company of his own going with any consistency. Alvin's interest in presenting Beatty's choreography may have been piqued by a chance meeting in 1960. Alvin was living with Ernest Parham in an apartment on Forty-sixth Street between Tenth and Eleventh Avenues, an area where black modern dancers and choreographers were settling at the time. Beatty had ambled over to tell Parham about an idea he had for a ballet, but his friend was out.

" 'Why don't you come in and tell me?' Alvin said, which was cute," an amused Beatty recalled. The two talked about what eventually became *Come and Get the Beauty of It Hot*. He was pleased when Alvin pronounced the idea "a poetic expression of life in the ghetto"—"something like that," Beatty said. "Very sweet."

Their paths would cross many times over the years, sometimes when Alvin invited Beatty to come in and tidy up the Ailey dancers' performances of his work. They went nightclubbing together in Germany and shared a hotel room in Portugal—for a few minutes. The friendship of these two quite different men lasted for professional reasons, of course, but also because each enjoyed the kinds of zany small adventures that Beatty found himself drawn into by Alvin.

"We were finishing the [1967] tour in Faro, in Portugal. We met at this hotel and had coffee or whatever at the swimming pool up at the top, then we went down to his suite. I unpacked my things and put them in the closet. Alvin said, 'See you at the theater.' " Beatty went out and on his return to the room bathed and went to the closet to get fresh clothes. The closet was full of dresses. Alvin had checked out, without telling Beatty.

But he found it hard not to be fond of Alvin, for all his exasperating heedlessness and self-involvement. "In Amsterdam, there was a big party after the performance. One of those down kind of parties like the company would give. A little man came up and asked if he could dance with one of the girls in the company." No, Alvin said teasingly, dance with me. And off they went across the dance floor, an interracial Mutt and Jeff. "It was so funny."

By the end of 1964, Alvin and his dancers were old pros at the exhausting business of touring. The phenomenon was still fresh when the company set out excitedly for Europe on September 4. Europe was new, although Europeans would soon grow to know the dancers better than most Americans. The English dance critic Clive Barnes, who joined the *New York Times* the following year, would comment that when he left England he had seen more performances by the Ailey dancers, and the companies of Paul Taylor and Merce Cunningham, than anyone could have seen in New York. In its 1964 season in London, the Ailey troupe performed at the Shaftesbury Theatre seven shows a week for six weeks. That year they had performed in New York four times.

The company opened in Paris on September 7 at the Théâtre des Champs Élysées, where it presented two programs in a three-week season. There were bravos and frenetic applause from the first-night audience. A headline writer for *l'Aurore* described the evening as a triumph. But it was too early in the season for an unfamiliar company to open, the critic Jacques Bourgeois commented, and the audiences were small. That was a pity, Bourgeois continued, for Beatty's choreography was much more original than most of the modern ballet seen at the Opera.

The reviews were generally favorable for all but *The Beloved*, which French critics found old-fashioned and, as a fastidious Bourgeois put it, a sample of the "frightful American esthetic" of realism that produced *Fall River Legend*, Agnes de Mille's narrative ballet about Lizzie Borden. "When Marcel Marceau takes time to come backstage to shake our hands and expresses his admiration for the choreography, all you can say is French critics be damned," Truitte retorted.

While the French saw overtones of *West Side Story* in the jazzier items in the Ailey repertory, English reviewers thought of classical ballet when the company, now billed as the Alvin Ailey American Dance Theater, arrived in London for a six-week engagement at the Shaftesbury Theatre. The frothing skirts of *Gillespiana* reminded one reviewer of the Russian ballerina Alexandra Danilova, the epitome of witty gaiety. Another, Peter Williams, thought of a famous pas de deux from *Swan Lake* when he saw the *Fix Me* duet in *Revelations*.

"Truitte behind Trisler like a guardian angel and there are some exquisite compositions with the two bodies moving as one, seldom in unison but with a lyrical fusion," Williams wrote in *Dance and Dancers*, an English monthly whose lengthy, double-issue coverage of the company's two programs provided some of the most informed, far-reaching and sympathetic analysis Alvin and the company were ever to receive.

Reviewing the company's second program, Williams invoked the names of George Balanchine and Antony Tudor. The conviction with which Truitte and Trisler danced *The Beloved* drew another odd but apt allusion from Williams, this time to the intensely committed dancing of two great Russian ballet stars, Tamara Karsavina and Vaslav Nijinsky, in another duet, *Le Spectre de la Rose*. The Ailey dancers' "stylish, throwaway expertise" reminded Barnes, also writing in *Dance and Dancers*, of the Kirov Ballet of Leningrad. It is clear from the reviews' general tone of respect and pleasure that this was not simple ethnocentricity but the impulse to analyze something loved by referring to another, more familiar love.

For London embraced Alvin, his dancers and his repertory with an intensity of focus and a passion they had seldom experienced. The Graham company had prepared the way the year before with a successful London season, after a trouncing by English dance audiences in 1954. The reappraisal of Graham opened the doors to other American dance companies, starting with Merce Cunningham and followed by the Ailey company and Paul Taylor. Even so, the Shaftesbury season started quietly, with the audience building slowly, by word of mouth.

The theater seated fifteen hundred, and the company was making an unexpectedly early start after a tour of the provinces fell through. The reviews were good but not "splashy," as the English critic Mary Clarke put it, although the always mischievous Richard Buckle compared the experience of watching the Ailey dancers to "basking in the sun." And A. V. Coton, who was not at all convinced by the company's opening program, ended his review of the second program with the comment that "the company danced like people possessed, but possessed of a great and glorious vision in which they wholly believed."

Williams even had evocative praise for Alvin's often neglected designers Nicholas Cernovitch and Ves Harper. "By his use of back projections and by a marvelous and exciting sense of colour he clothes the stage with magic yet scenically the only props in the whole show are a few chairs, stools, ladders and a hatstand," he wrote. "This combined with Ves Harper's simple yet stunningly effective costumes create some of the most beautiful stage pictures seen in London for a long time. I wish some of our lighting experts could inherit from Cernovitch the manner in which he can illuminate dancers so that none of this light ever spills on the backcloth."

English dancers and dance students, some of whom had taken special classes given by the Ailey performers, filled the theater each night. The audience was seldom less than enthusiastic, going so far in loosening the traditional English reserve as to clap along with the *Revelations* finale. Blessedly, several critics observed, there was real blues and jazz music to listen to rather than the symphonic pablum that tended to pass for jazz accompaniment in some British dance.

Too bad, some felt, that the music had to be performed by a pickup chorus of white English singers, although Brother John Sellers, who conducted them, was impressed. "We had to use these people," he said. "We couldn't find a black chorus to do it. But you never seen them, only me. And they could use 'dis' and 'dat.' They were excellent." But the prickly Sellers drew the line at participating in another piece on the program, *Been Here and Gone*, despite his star turn as the blind man. Alvin had added a solo for Louther, set to the song "Prettiest Train," but he was forced to sing the accompaniment for it himself after Sellers refused to sing "white music" he said he didn't understand or feel.

Michael Dorfman, whose tall, slender frame and reserved manner struck at least one of the dancers as quintessentially English, doubted that the Beatty and Horton dances were commercial enough for this new English audience. But Alvin pressed on with a showcase for critics in which he talked about the repertory before presenting it, offering a bit of *Congo Tango Palace* as well as *The Road of the Phoebe Snow* so that reviewers would have more than just one Beatty work by which to judge the choreographer. Williams and Barnes urged Alvin to go ahead.

What bothered the English more than any problem with Beatty's style was the insubstantiality of Alvin's *Been Here and Gone.* For most of the English audiences—as well as Americans—the Ailey programs were a first taste of "black modern dance," and there were some intense exchanges on race in print and in conversation. "There is no such thing as Negro dance," Alvin told Williams. "There are Negroes dancing and some things are suited to them and they perhaps do them better than anyone else," he insisted.

Williams responded in kind. "The path on which he is travelling, making the Negro dancer seriously accepted in the dance scene rather than merely being an exotic ornament is clearly revealed. He may today be self-effacing as a performer but his sense of good theatre and the way in which he can apply his modern schooling to the qualities of the fine artists he assembles is infinitely valuable not only to the Negro cause but the world of dance as a whole."

Barnes weighed in on the nature of black art, a question that continued to provoke heated public discussion well into the 1990s, when it was tackled head-on by choreographers, dancers and critics participating in the American Dance Festival's Black Tradition in American Modern Dance project. "One of the most odd aspects of Ailey's work is that he is neither a Negro dancer, nor a modern dancer, but a Negro modern dancer," Barnes wrote in *Dance and Dancers.* "Basically his technical background seems to be pure modern dance, but one of his purposes is to explore the cultural values of the American Negro. Thus in a sense he is no more a Negro artist than James Baldwin is a Negro novelist (no one ever called Henry James a 'white novelist,' did they?) but, often like Baldwin, he seems naturally concerned with the Negro heritage."

The English critics made much of the company's outstanding male contingent. Once again, William Louther made a strong impression. He had been praised by one giddy Paris reviewer as a dancer to make the great Rudolf Nureyev jealous. In London, Marie Rambert, a keen-witted and formidable presence in English ballet and the founder of one of the country's two great ballet troupes, talked admiringly of "Lucifer," as she nicknamed the sensuous Louther.

Rambert, a voluble fan of the Ailey company, had given Tudor the encouragement that led to his establishment as the major practitioner of dramatic ballet in England and America. She discussed with Alvin the exchange of *The Beloved* for Tudor's *Dark Elegies*. He coveted the ballet, a bleak but haunting portrait of villagers reconciling themselves to the loss of loved ones after an unspecified disaster. Alvin asked that Tudor allow his dancers to perform the piece, which did not require virtuoso ballet technique, in flat shoes rather than on point. But the exchange never occurred, in one of the great missed opportunities in American dance.

Performing less and less, Alvin seldom danced in London, to the disappointment of the English audiences. Whether consciously or not, he had begun to withdraw from the stage, always a place that tested his meager technical skills and confidence and a place, too, where a side of himself was revealed that had disturbed his mother enough to have slapped him all those years ago at Horton. Alvin could get by on the animal sensuousness and the power, so strangely unself-conscious, of the way he moved and inhabited the stage. True, he sometimes felt an unexpected sense of exultant extra life onstage. But mistakes and inadequacies could not be fixed there, in the rush of the moment. In the studio, there was time to reflect, to tinker. It was hard, too, to pour himself into performing with all the necessary controlled abandon when so much else needed to be done to keep the company going.

Alvin's reluctance benefited Dudley Williams, who found himself suddenly assigned the exquisite *Reflections in D*, ordinarily danced by Alvin, right before one Paris performance. Williams had come to the Ailey company from Graham. Like Louther and Ailey guest artist Takako Asakawa, also former Graham dancers, he had developed a physical control that made the most difficult, demanding moves seem a mere rippling of energy. But at the heart of Williams's artistry was a subtlety and refinement that even then, in a relatively inexperienced performer in his early twenties, made for dancing of an "elusive, unobtrusive brilliance."

Alvin had first spotted Williams, then a student at the High School of Performing Arts in Manhattan, in a performance of dances by Eleo Pomare. He cast the teenager in his balletic *Sonera*, which he had submitted to the choreographers' competition at City Center sponsored by Lincoln Kirstein and George Balanchine.

"How do you get into your company?" Williams asked him. Under the impression that Williams was a ballet dancer, Alvin told him that the Ailey company performed modern dance. "What do you think I've been doing all these years?" Williams exclaimed.

He had come of age in a time when to be a professional dancer was no longer so unrealistic a dream for black youngsters. Now there was an Ailey company for modern dancers. There were idols, like Alvin. "I went to Karel Shook and I saw all these black dancers, taking class, there," Williams recalled. "I went, Oh, my God. I was praying to them. Not even seeing them onstage, just in class, and there I was, eyes like saucers. And then I saw Alvin. Your heart stood still. And he was nose down, looking down on you. He had that aura, like, who are you? Because he was beautiful. He was here."

But there were no nibbles from Alvin, so Williams joined the Graham company in 1963. He had a moment of glory as a soloist in *Secular Games*, drawing praise from London critics, but he soon began to look into the future and see himself as a perennial spear carrier. About to take off on a Greek freighter for Europe, where he thought he might have more opportunities to dance, he received a call from Alvin. A replacement dancer was needed for a tour of Europe to begin in a few weeks, Alvin said, and Williams had performed Beatty's work. Williams's mother talked him out of his plan to travel by sea to Europe. "At least I'll know where you'll be," she told her son.

"So I went to rehearsal the next day and I fit like a glove," Williams said, still recalling his awe at being in the presence of star dancers like Truitte. The Ailey environment was different. Graham had been kind to him, but the atmosphere could be forbidding in her studio. "You dared not move in a Graham freeze," Williams recalls. "You dared not blink an eye. If you did, the dancers who were dancing in front of you would scream, 'He's moving.' " In contrast, the Ailey company seemed like a family. Most of the twelve dancers in this group had worked together for a relatively sustained period of time. "With the other companies Alvin had before that, it was 'Are you busy? Would you like to come to Singapore?' "

There was almost no time to learn the ropes. Dancers were gener-

ally hired during the rush to prepare for a new season, with little time
to rehearse with Alvin and the senior performers. Williams was soon
dancing with the company at the Delacorte, where not so long ago he
had seen and fallen in love with Alvin's work. But he was in for a shock
in Paris when, out of the blue, Alvin told the young dancer that he was
to replace him in *Reflections in D*. Alvin would not be able to dance the
solo much longer, he told the nervous Williams as he escorted him into
a nearby studio and taught him the difficult solo.

"He said, 'Okay, let's take it from the top' and I took it again,
deedly deedly doo. Then he told me I was going to do it that afternoon.
Of course I panicked." Williams had heard that the theater would be
filled with many of the best American modern dancers then working in
Paris. "I think Alvin knew they were coming. Maybe he didn't want to
do it. Maybe he wanted me. I don't know. But he made me do it.

"I told Alvin I didn't even really know it. He said, 'Just make it up,
darling. You know, put in the Williams touch. Yes, you can.' And it's
true. It sounds so corny. But you can. If you believe in yourself." Many
times over the years Williams doubted he could pull off something that
Alvin wanted him to dance. "I'd tell him it felt so strange. And he'd say,
'Do it.'"

And so Williams went on in *Reflections in D* that afternoon in
Paris, managing almost numbly to get through the piece as a small and
not very vocal audience watched. Over the years he continued to make
something distinctively his own of the solo that he thought of as a
poem. And he taught it to others, like a gravely elegant young member
of the Ailey junior company named Derrick Minter, who would in turn
make it his own three decades later. Talking of that lineage, Truitte offered Williams a dancer's ultimate compliment. "To this day I don't feel
that any dancer of great talent, even after being taught by Dudley, will
ever bring to *Reflections in D* the supreme serenity, sophistication, elegance and musicality that he brought to that choreography," Truitte
said. "Dudley is one of those rare dancers born with those qualities."

Alvin and the dancers returned to New York in mid-November for
a few weeks before leaving for Australia. Johnson's *Lament* and Sokolow's *Rooms* were added to the repertory, and Alvin restaged *Hermit
Songs*, his sensuous dance for a monk of the Middle Ages. There was
even a little time for Alvin to begin work on *Ariadne* for the Harkness,
to be performed in Paris. Then it was back onto a plane in early January of 1965 for another six weeks on tour.

The company opened at the Tivoli Theatre in Sydney and was

received only a little less exuberantly than before. There were some giggles at *Been Here and Gone*, whose superficiality Williams loathed and mocked occasionally in difficult moments with Alvin. But the rest of the repertory, including *Rooms*, was praised.

Foreseeing trouble, Alvin had taken pains to prepare Sydney audiences for the bleakness of the Sokolow piece, describing it in an interview in the *Australian* as "penetrating, soulful, shocking, almost terrifying." But Sydney audiences took the piece in stride, and reviews ranged from respectful to intensely admiring.

Alvin was amused by the differences in the audiences for each of the two programs the company presented. The first consisted of "black blues and jazz and all the pretty costumes," Alvin told an American interviewer. "In the second program, the curtain went up, and there I was in my monk's robes crawling all over the floor—then comes 'Lament,' a ballet! then fifty minutes of psychosis in Sokolow's 'Rooms.' The art critics called 'Rooms' one of the most important things that had ever happened to the Australians—I think the management lost money. The first few weeks the audience came eating popcorn and so on—after we changed the programs, the audience became very intellectual and the whole affair became an art event."

Although some of the bloom of Australia had worn off on this return trip, Alvin enjoyed his encounters with the Australians. "They treat us like celebrities—I mean many interviews and the lot—and I do believe some of the kids are already being touched by the Australian accent—God help us!" he wrote to Edele Holtz. "The kids gave me a surprise birthday party on Jan 5 (my 34th!) complete with presents, champagne and American hamburgers (the biggest treat of all since the food here is beyond all description) and was lorded over by the owners of their hotel—a lady of 40 or thereabouts with wine-colored hair and her mother a lady of seemingly-seventy with bright pink hair."

Melbourne was a disaster, however, with the company drawing smaller crowds than before, in part, Alvin felt, because of poor publicity by the local management. *Rooms* was performed only once in Melbourne, and then as a last-minute replacement for *The Road of the Phoebe Snow* after an injury to Louther. Alvin could have substituted the pretty *Gillespiana* but stubbornly seized the chance to test the producers. The management of the Tivoli theater chain, which owned the house where the Ailey company was performing in Melbourne, had forbidden an angry Alvin to present the Sokolow piece for fear its bleakness would turn away audiences.

He had been tempted "out of defiance," he later said, to present the kind of difficult choreography created by rolls of dice or other chance procedures that was then fashionable among young avant-gardists in America. But at least one Melbournian had been equal to the challenge of *Rooms*, describing the dance as "one of the best things Ailey has done."

Truitte was dismayed when *Rooms* was removed from the repertory. He would have been willing to suffer for the piece and did, eventually, in Rome. "I finished my beautiful solo, which I loved doing. And that audience went 'Boooooo.' So I walked very quietly off and said, 'I've arrived.' "

Business picked up in Melbourne, and the season was extended by two weeks. But before its close, Harkness summoned Alvin to France to finish *Ariadne*. To get him there, she was forced to pay the Tivoli management $5,000 to release her procrastinating choreographer from his contract. It was the sort of tangled dispute that only Alvin, it seemed to his friends, could get himself into and then, a charmed creature, extricate himself from without much problem.

Alvin had started *Ariadne* at Watch Hill in a workshop in July and August when he was there restaging *Feast of Ashes*. Everyone was impressed with the new piece, and Harkness gave him a $1,000 fee in addition to the negligible pay of $500 for the two months, with the agreement that Alvin would go to Paris in November to continue work on the ballet. The music was not ready, however, and Alvin was forced to leave for Australia.

He promised to return later, sure that Dorfman and the Tivoli management in Melbourne would relent and give him the leave they had said they would not grant. Harkness sent Alvin another $1,000 to come work in Cannes, where the company was to open. But Dorfman and the Tivoli stood firm. "Telephone calls are coming from Harkness pleading Ailey's release," the Ailey company manager wrote nervously to Al Holtz, who was acting as treasurer for the group, "page-long telegram from Rebecca [*sic*] Harkness calling Alvin everything from black muslim to culture hater (actually all very friendly)."

When the theater demanded that Harkness pay from $30,000 to $50,000 to let Alvin go off to France for ten days, plans were begun to send Truitte, who could be released for a mere $62.50 per missed performance, to work out the style of the dance with the Harkness company. In the end, the $5,000 agreement was struck and Alvin was flown last minute to Cannes. "Alvin says, and I agree with him to a certain extent, that this kind of juggling is the only way that he has been able to do what he has done for the past five years," the manager wrote.

It was money well spent, for *Ariadne* was the hit of the Harkness Ballet's Paris season at the Opera Comique in March. It was also Alvin's first big commission for a major dance company and a collaboration with the chic French composer André Jolivet and a then unknown scenic designer named Ming Cho Lee.

Ariadne was based on the Greek myth in which Theseus, the hero king of Athens, slays the powerful Minotaur for love of Ariadne, whose father has installed the monster in his lair. The psychological possibilities of the story had been explored by Graham in 1947 in *Errand into the Maze*. Like her, Alvin told the story from Ariadne's point of view, in a ballet of unaccustomed scenic extravagance.

Alvin completed work on the ballet during the Harkness company's debut season in Cannes, where he stayed at the beautiful old Majestic Hotel and enjoyed watching "ancient English ladies in enormous mink coats," as he wrote Edele Holtz. He met Princess Grace of Monaco one afternoon as she sat sipping champagne with Harkness "surrounded by more photographers than there were people at the performance that evening."

The curtain rose on an enormous bare-breasted statue of Pasiphae, the mother of the Minotaur. Theseus fought a chorus of bulls under red ribbons representing the thread Ariadne has given him to find his way back through the Minotaur's labyrinth. Alvin marveled at the decor in a letter to Holtz, describing it as "all brass poles and enormous pieces of shattered rock."

"The ballet is a strange creature," he continued. " 'Ariadne,' I mean. I have decided to admit to myself that I am a miserably slow choreographer. Took me a month in New York City to do the first fifteen minutes of the work and that is not bad—but the last half is rather like television choreography. Too fast."

He had started working with the music bar by bar to get the texture of the ballet right, Alvin told an English interviewer in a rather more elegant version of his account to Holtz, but then ran out of time. He was pleased with some things in the ballet, he said. But he thought the piece needed more work, and he wanted to get a better feeling for the classical ballet. It had also been difficult working with the Harkness "kids," Alvin added grandly. "I'm so used to working with our own kids and literally wrenching something out of them. But these classical kids just stood around in rehearsal waiting to be shown what to do. It's a hard life."

The ballet stood out, however, in a season considered more notable for the dancers than for the overall quality of the repertory. "For a brand-new ballet company to be blessed with so many fine dancers and at least one strong original choreographer is a most excellent portent," Cynthia Grenier wrote in the *New York Herald Tribune*, referring to Alvin, whose *Feast of Ashes* was also being performed by the Harkness dancers.

And so Alvin returned to Melbourne, two days before the close of the Australian tour, with another success behind him. The company was scheduled to return to London for two weeks, to be followed by the European tour. There were still few engagements at home.

Relentless international touring was to keep the company afloat financially for three years. To be a member of a successful, relatively busy major American dance company was to live out of a suitcase, with little privacy or sense of self-determination. And the Ailey company of 1965 was a small group of strong individualists who seldom hesitated to speak their minds to one another and to the titular patriarch of the group, with sometimes angry and hurtful results. Wandering for months through foreign lands, the dancers must have wondered if performing with the Alvin Ailey American Dance Theater was the equivalent to taking a vow of rootlessness. Home was on the road. Family was the company, in happy times and in squabbling disarray.

seventeen

"THREW ALL DANCE CLOTHES INTO WASTEBASKET"

The outbursts among the Ailey dancers—and Alvin's own bursts of restlessness and temper when the pressures of his increasing responsibilities became too much—reflected an unrest then building in American dance. Change was in the air in the mid-1960s, although it would not make itself felt in any clearly discernible way for another few years. The first tremor of the coming dance boom in America had occurred in 1963, when the Ford Foundation began a $7 million program to strengthen ballet in the United States, an unprecedented amount of money for dance. A year later, the federal government began its greatest involvement with the arts since the depression, culminating in the formation in 1965 of the National Endowment for the Arts.

Eventually the National Endowment would develop programs to encourage artists to create new work, to shore up financially weak institutions and to introduce the arts to new audiences through touring performances and exhibitions. In 1965, all that was up to the institutions themselves. The growing pains felt by Alvin and his company were not unusual, although in his complex mix of vision, astuteness and quick-shifting moods, Alvin may have been less equipped to deal with those pains than choreographers working simply to create dances and a company of their own. Alvin's duties also included participation in the programs of Clark Center, shaping a repertory that was to suggest the range of all modern dance and not just his own, working as a freelance choreographer, and acting as a bright young ambassador of culture, bearing the message of racial harmony to the world at large.

Nonetheless, the years were good for Alvin, both personally and professionally. The Ailey company was in growing demand abroad, as were Alvin's services as a choreographer and director. And he was involved in what would prove to be one of the most stable romantic relationships of his life, living with a handsome, idealistic younger white schoolteacher who had almost as hot a temper as he but who was also possessed of an apparently unshakable loyalty toward this unpredictable, immensely gifted bear of a man with whom he had fallen deeply in love.

Alvin did not attempt to hide the relationship, but, typically, he was loath to discuss it in any detail with friends and colleagues. This was his private life, and people could take it or leave it. For all the intensity of their involvement, on every level, Christopher was a fait accompli and nobody's business but his own.

The two met in a bar. Christopher came from a very different background, that of a comfortable family of upper-middle-class achievers. He was well read and knowledgeable about the arts, sharing Alvin's love for poetry, and dreamed of becoming an actor. Christopher's family grew fond of Alvin and Alvin's friends loved Christopher, appreciating in him the virility that Alvin preferred in men and laughing, years later, over the tremendous battles that would suddenly erupt in public over seemingly inconsequential matters.

This was not a time when an ambitious young modern dance pioneer could devote much energy to a personal life and home of any sort. Dance was becoming an increasingly professionalized field in the mid-1960s in America, but the business side of running dance companies tended to be taken care of by loyal volunteers or by professionals who were often almost as untested. At the same time, dealing with dancers as members of an affectionate if unruly small family was becoming more difficult, for they had begun to insist on their rights as professionals.

By the late 1980s, dancers no longer were just "boys" and "girls" who pointed their feet and followed directions. They had families of their own with mortgages, automobile loans and college tuition to pay. In 1965, Alvin found himself faced with newly intractable young artists' egos.

He was also having problems with Ben Jones and Susan Pimsleur. "Would you—or you and Al be interested in taking on the enormous task of booking the AADT in colleges, universities, community centers, or wherever we might play?" Alvin wrote in mid-January from Australia in a memo to Edele Holtz appropriately titled "A hundred thousand questions all in a row." "I do agree with Al that Pimsleur's hold on the booking of modern dance should be broken," he continued, "and that she is really only a glorified and brilliantly disorganized public relations person with a certain amount of contacts she's built up over the years, but I see no reason why someone else—providing you really want to dissolve yourself into the enormity of this project, shouldn't be able to book us—or other groups. This, among the thousands of other things, means doing things like having a new brochure designed for us (badly needed) and sending out a mailing list to whomever might be interested in having us.

". . . Also would mean probably putting an ad in Dance Magazine and other publications to reaffirm the fact of our severance with Sue P. and to advertise our new address to be reached at. Also this means doing enormous pub relations work on our behalf with State Dept., State Council on the Arts, and some of the foundations. Did I just frighten you beyond belief? Completely understandable! Also, not to eschew money—we should, if you decide to do this, work out an agreeable financial arrangement for your work and time investment."

Though no longer at Clark Center, Holtz looked into touring setups with typical efficiency and energy and was soon busy designing a brochure, analyzing the company's far-flung travel routes on earlier tours and investigating college booking conventions and contract deadlines. She put together a list of two hundred colleges in New England and New York State alone, an area chosen for its proximity to New York City "in view of your varied interests," leaving Alvin free to go back and forth as professional obligations dictated. Catalogs were on their way.

"I am convinced what with careful planning you could make an excellent income annually in four concentrated months which would leave you free for more creative things the rest of the time," Holtz wrote. "Charlie Blackwell used to say that given one year for planning he could cut the costs of any off-Broadway show in half and I am thoroughly convinced of it; it is the last minute frantic expedient moves that make the mistakes and cost money."

Holtz was also working on two brochures, one to advertise the company and the other "on and about you: director, dancer (?), choreographer teacher etc. etc. It would be false modesty to fail to recognize that it is you that is selling . . . I also want to stress that we CANNOT sell a college tour without you, even if you only dance a little. . . . I think you certainly aim for that some time, maybe in the near future, but not *quite* yet. You must ease out of the dancing slowly, not all at once." Holtz had left Clark Center in 1964 for graduate study in social work at Columbia University, but she and her husband planned to work on Ailey projects over weekends and refused to accept money for their work.

The rest of Alvin's six-page January memo is filled with suggestions about publicity, people to contact—and a somewhat unconvincing apology for having roared off on tour leaving his apartment in a terrible mess of clothes-strewn floors and boxes of office files, records, books, photographs and personal possessions that infuriated the older couple. The Holtzes were the perfect people to enlist in Alvin's projects, however. Not only did they care immensely for him as a young friend, no matter how inexplicable or demanding his behavior might sometimes be, but they believed in what he had set out to do. Energetic Quakers who had had experience in the United States and the Middle East in social service and political resettlement, the Holtzes tended to have a longer vision than most. They played an immensely important role in the creation of the Alvin Ailey American Dance Theater.

Al Holtz had become involved with the Ailey company almost accidentally. A businessman, he was interested in the performing arts, and his wife discussed with him the day-to-day problems of running Clark Center. Stopping by to pick her up in the evening, he would put himself to any task that needed doing at the moment. Soon he was working with Alvin as unofficial company treasurer and saw the troupe through its early investigations of legal incorporation. Now he found himself trying to work his way through four years' worth of unfiled income tax returns for Alvin, complicated by Ben Jones's poor or nonexistent record keeping, and even helped one of Alvin's dancers with her tax problems. "Since it has gone on this long and they can only put you in jail once," Holtz wrote her, "I think you should enjoy yourself, dance well and we'll worry about it when you get back. O.K.???"

A small, rotund man with the unfailingly cheerful demeanor of a vaudeville song-and-dance man, Holtz had a great deal of patience and empathy, as well as a shrewd practicality about the ways of the world. By 1964 he had put himself at Alvin's disposal, even though he had a full-time job.

"I was always working," Holtz recalled wryly. "Instead of going out with the boys after work, I went and did something with Ailey." Sometimes his extracurricular activities spilled over. "It got to be ridiculous when I was working on Wall Street. I'm supposed to be calling customers on the phone and everyone's turning around to look at me because I'm calling some agent trying to book Ailey. It got pretty bad."

Holtz could see that Alvin was very talented, and he was impressed by the scope of his plans. Ask Alvin for a solution to a specific problem and you would also hear his ideas about a repertory theater, a dance school, a larger company, more spectacular pieces and ideas for whatever dance he was working on at the moment. His mind was always racing over, under and ahead of whatever anyone else was thinking, it seemed to Holtz. "He knew exactly what he wanted and he had no intention of having anybody turn him away from his big ideals. Nothing was going to do that. I appreciated that. I have the same nature.

"I always encouraged Alvin to think big. I'd tell him, 'It doesn't make any difference. We can do it or we can't do it. If we can, we'll do it. But don't hold it in yourself. Tell us about it. What is the biggest thing you can do?'"

At times Holtz was a little too forthright, as he was when Alvin's problems with Susan Pimsleur came to a head. "I went up to Clark Center one night. Alvin was in a big tizzy. Edele shoveled me in to talk with him. It turned out that Sue Pimsleur was holding back some money on him. She said she had expenses, etc. etc. He complained to me about how terrible it was. He couldn't pay the dancers because she was holding out the money. 'Want me to go see her?' I asked him. So I went over to see if she couldn't make out some amiable arrangement about Alvin." But Pimsleur was not in the mood to be amiable, Holtz discovered. "She tried to get tough with me. I got tougher and dismissed her."

He returned to Clark Center. "What did she say?" Alvin asked. Holtz told him he had fired Pimsleur. "What am I going to do now?" Alvin asked, horrified.

"I didn't know Alvin well enough to know he wasn't on the business end of it at all," Holtz recalled. "I told him I'd do it for him in the meantime. Of course, that was the end of it as far as he was concerned. He never even attempted to get anyone else."

Letters flew back and forth across the world, sometimes daily, between the Holtzes and Alvin's lover, who was doggedly learning on the job how to manage the company during its second international tour. The day-to-day details to be mastered were almost overwhelming. A single letter written to Al Holtz in mid-January 1965 raises questions about Australian tax provisions, air transfers to the United States of pay from the Australian theater management to the company, and deductions from the dancers' pay to cover their debts. There were also questions about back salary for himself and Alvin, costume expenses and his half of that month's rent for their apartment on West Eighty-third Street.

Pimsleur was claiming thousands of dollars in unpaid fees. What to do about the English impresario Michael Dorfman's insistence on deducting hefty weekly sums from the company's tour fees to pay Pimsleur off? Were the dancers liable for Australian taxes, and how could they get receipts for that? And could Holtz send him information to prepare last year's income tax returns? "These petty, angry details are so endless I feel that I am in some purgatory of tawdry slips of paper," Christopher raged.

"Perhaps you also can claim a costume expense in the U.S.," he wrote, adding worriedly, "Al: do you think me very dishonest?"

Holtz answered the next day. His paragraph on the company bank account alone suggests the daily life of the troupe as well as the way it managed to roll along, Rube Goldberg machinery made up of overworked and underpaid mortals all trying to function as a smooth-running whole.

"As for the bank account," Holtz wrote, "I've had a few small minor problems mostly because it is difficult for me to get up there so the business has been on the phone. I finally got the statement for the new account, but not the old. I understand that you ordered new checks but I have not yet received them, instead I got two huge batches of Deposit slips. This will all work itself out. At the moment you have about $950 in the account. 910.00 original, 220.42 from the old account, 90.00 from Bud, less the rent and 125.00 to Thelma for tights. As soon as I get the new check book you will have bills from Dance Magazine for 211.06, Carl Winkel 50.00, Talley Beatty 315.00." The Selva costume supply company had called to say a designer's check for $33.70 had bounced. Was it for a company expense? If so, Holtz would pay it immediately. And a seamstress who had worked for a few days on costumes had inquired if the company was covered by Workers' Compensation. She also wanted the $10 she was owed when a second check bounced. "Now what?" Holtz exclaimed before plowing on to the even thornier question of taxes, sweetened with news of an impressive-seeming communication from the White House.

"Believe me this is nothing to be messed with. If nothing has been done about 1964 taxes we better think about doing something. . . . We sent you a cable about the invitation to the Inaugural, realizing there was little to be done about it, but we did want you to know of the honor in a historic sense. In some ways it is a shame you can't make it, everybody doesn't get one every day."

The Holtzes were also pressed into mailing checks to dancers' landlords, insurance companies and mothers, finding music, getting composers' releases for music, mailing fabric swatches for costumes to the touring company and finding tapes of scores. What did they think of a proposal by a not-too-trustworthy-sounding agent that Alvin involve himself in the founding of an American Negro Arts Theater in Australia? Could they send material on the Ailey company to Rudolf Nureyev, whom Alvin had met in London?

"Practically speaking Nureyev is rather vague and although he has often excited AA's imagination by off the cuff plans about ballets etc. I don't think that he would ever get organized to work with AA unless there were some third agent involved," Christopher wrote. "However, Eric [sic] Bruhn is organized enough and serious enough to sometime offer AA an interesting collaboration."

There were even impromptu lessons in high and low finance. "Try to visualize the corporation as a thing separate from the individuals," Holtz wrote patiently to the young company-manager-in-spite-of-himself. "The corp. is an entity unto itself. It receives income, pays bills, pays taxes, etc. all separate from 'Alvin Ailey-Person, James Truitte, Brother John.'

"I didn't mention this to you before because I didn't realize there would be so much money passed back and forth. Get Yourself a Receipt Book (in any stationery store). Get it in duplicate. For ALL monies received (actually or in theory) make a receipt. Even if the individual doesn't want it or throws it away YOU KEEP THE DUPLICATE." Occasionally, Holtz's composure cracked. "Both Edele and I have gone through the envelopes with back bills and receipts and all I can say is FEE-you," he wrote, unable even in his desperation to bring himself to type the raw expletive that he was thinking of. "I couldn't begin to start asking all the questions I have."

But no one lost sight, at least for long, of why all this mattered. "Yes, I agree that Alvin must get his nerves together at some point,"

Christopher wrote the Holtzes. "It's all a blur after a while, but there seems little you can do to stop good or bad tides. He is always behind the 8 ball and never in a good bargaining position with anybody and consequently never able to turn anything down when it comes along."

On the other hand, in the matter of Alvin's personal finances, "I can only think of budget control as a feasible idea if Alvin never sees, hears or knows that he has more than 45.00 in the bank and he knows that he will have to go through six months of bureaucratic tape to get it out."

Characteristically, Alvin rarely wrote about finances, concentrating instead on touring conditions, reviews and his many plans for the company. The European tour had gotten off to an unnerving start. The company had taken off for London on a Sunday at noon, arriving Monday at noon for a Tuesday night opening. The costumes, traveling on another plane, arrived ninety minutes before the curtain, "pressed and repaired by an army of costume ladies recruited from everywhere and somehow we got on," Alvin wrote Edele Holtz on April 7, in a letter headed "THE PERILS OF ALVIN AILEY OR HOW NOT TO RUN A DANCE COMPANY CHAPTER 2."

But London, where the company opened on March 23 at the Saville Theatre for a two-week season, proved once more to be a triumph. "As an occasion of the finest kind of wholly theatrical and totally professional dancing the evening invited comparison with the first impact here of the Bolshoi Ballet," A. V. Coton wrote in the *Daily Telegraph* and *Morning Post*. It was high praise, considering Coton's reputation as a critic not prone to hyperbole and given the Bolshoi's exotic glamour and the reverence accorded that major Soviet troupe by the ballet-mad English.

Alvin had put together two programs, each featuring *Revelations* and Louis Johnson's *Lament*. The first program also included *Gillespiana*, *Reflections in D* danced by Dudley Williams, and *Rooms*, all replaced on the second program by Talley Beatty's *Congo Tango Palace* and *The Road of the Phoebe Snow*, and Alvin's solo *Hermit Songs*, which he taught to Kelvin Rotardier and William Louther.

Williams and Louther got a strong dose of Alvin's distinctive approach to directing dancers, which was much less relaxed than in the simpler-seeming, more intimate relationships of Horton and early Ailey days. The two younger dancers, good friends of about the same age, had discussed and knew each other's solos. Williams asked Louther to watch his performance of *Reflections in D*. He would watch Louther dancing *Hermit Songs*, and each would offer feedback to the other.

Louther agreed and watched from the shadowy wings just off the stage. As he stood there, Alvin suddenly materialized behind him and whispered, "You should be doing that, not him." Flustered, Louther did not repeat the comment to Williams. Then came his own performance of *Hermit Songs*. Williams stood watching from the wings and was startled to hear Alvin whispering, "You should be doing that, not him." Eventually, Williams confided in Louther and discovered he had had the same experience. "I said, Ah, ha, he's trying to pit us against each other," Williams recalled. "And then Jimmie [Truitte] confirmed it by saying that Alvin liked to bring up that stuff and make you fight. He felt the company danced better when there was tension."

Alvin would regularly provoke Hope Clarke backstage before the two danced the *Backwater Blues* duet in *Blues Suite*. Angry, she would slap him hard with her shawl as the characters battled onstage. "That's what I want," Alvin would say happily. "Fire."

"He didn't want you to come out there and just do the steps," Williams remembered. "He wanted a reason behind it. And I tell you, I learned something from this. I learned something from his shooting us down onstage. One by one, he'd line us up after a performance and complain. 'You didn't do this and you didn't do that.' Or before a performance. He'd say, 'Why did you fall out of your pirouette last night?' Just line us up and read us to filth." Alvin mellowed a great deal as he grew older, but one habit persisted. "All the dancers and Dudley," he would call out slyly, naming the performer who had made a mistake as he directed everyone to go through the steps again in rehearsal.

Alvin also believed in the element of surprise to strengthen performances and keep them fresh. In that small a company, each dancer had to know more than one role in every piece. With no casting sheets or even bulletin boards backstage, the dancers often did not know what roles they would be performing that night until Alvin stuck his head into the dressing room at the half-hour mark before the performance.

Sometimes he would keep them in rehearsal until the backstage call that alerted performers that there were only fifteen minutes to curtain. Even then, the dancers might get a last-minute dressing-room visit. "You're trying to put on your makeup, all this cookie dust, we used to call it, and eyelashes," Williams said. "Or you're trying to warm up. And he would go, 'What are you dancing about? What is Phoebe Snow? What is your part? How do you feel towards this person?' I learned something, because I had to stop and think in case he asked me what a piece was about."

In this "mean old man phase," as Williams put it, Alvin did not believe in mincing words. When he spotted a mistake in rehearsal, he would turn off the tape deck and shout, "What the hell was that?" Even the loyal Truitte, who had known Alvin as a much sweeter and more companionable budding choreographer back in Los Angeles, found him impossible at times.

Back in New York, Truitte had discussed Alvin's difficult personality with Thelma Hill and Minnie Marshall but then had vowed to continue working with him no matter what. That vow was sorely tested during the tour. When Alvin let loose a tirade against the dancers in a rehearsal during a 1965 engagement in Yugoslavia, Truitte calmly faced him down. Raising his hand, he stepped forward. "I have never in my life given a hideous performance and I never will," he told Alvin. "Take ten," Alvin told the dancers and then went over to Truitte. Did he talk too much? he asked him. "You sure do," Truitte replied.

Two years later, hurried by Alvin from one ballet to another in a soaking costume in ninety-four-degree heat in Tel Aviv, Truitte slipped and hurt himself while crossing the stage as the blind man in *Roots of the Blues*. He wasn't able to dance for a time and was extremely angry at Alvin. But at the next stop, in Haifa, he asked Alvin if there was anything he could do to help. "If you can't dance, you're no value to me," Alvin told him coldly.

Yet somehow it was impossible to stay angry at Alvin for long. "He was so much fun," Truitte remembered many years later. And even when Alvin was at his worst, the dancers looked forward to his rehearsals. Strangely, they saw there was no ego involved in his rages and no pretense in his direction of his dancers.

"Sometimes there was a level of tenseness with other choreographers, who had different ways of responding when they were stuck," Linda Kent, who joined the Ailey company in 1968, remembered. "Sometimes they nitpick, go over and over the same two steps. Alvin liked things loose. You could tell when he was stuck because he'd start getting silly, as a tension breaker. Or he'd throw silly stuff at you, like making up a bad nightclub routine as a joke, or twirling around like he was Carmen Miranda."

The 1964–1965 tour occurred at a vulnerable point in Alvin's life. At thirty-four, he was well known and respected in his field, but the sensuous faun was beginning to age and put on weight. Alvin had danced out onto the edge of too many limbs of the tree, called on with increasing frequency and little preparation to test his footing in one insecure environment after another. He could breeze through almost any public situation. He was quotable. He was authoritative. He had visions. And it was clear to his dancers that no matter how pressured he felt or how much he growled at them, he still loved the life and work of the studio. But there was very little he could take immediate comfort and pleasure in, and whatever buffers he had managed to develop were painfully thin. His armor of affable authority was easily pierced.

Sylvia Waters learned that when she bumped into Alvin at the bar of the Paris theater where the Harkness was performing in March 1965. "You two want a beer?" he asked Waters and the friend accompanying her. The two nodded and Alvin ordered for them. A silence followed and Waters mentioned *Ariadne*, which she assumed he realized was not very good.

"I don't remember what I said about it, but I guess it was taken as very patronizing. He looked at me, took a swallow of beer, put the glass down, excused himself and left. He never said he'd see me later, or good-bye. He must have been in terrible pain."

The tightrope path that stretched before him was both frightening and exhilarating. Soon after the encounter with Waters, the company embarked on another tour of Europe, performing at major festivals and in an endless succession of one-night stands in nine countries, from Belgium to Italy via Denmark, Sweden, Finland, Switzerland, Yugoslavia, Germany and France. In mid-April Alvin dashed off a note to Edele Holtz about "incredible Copenhagen."

"Thought I was in love with London & Paris but this city and its charming people have stolen my heart. . . . Press parties, press & photo calls, publicity functions right & left & an opening last nite in the Falkoner Centret here—an incredible theatre—a marvelous stamping & shouting audience and critics this morning not yet completely translated. . . ." The Danes would one day prove to be among the company's most loyal supporters. But the untranslated reviews Alvin mentioned were the most negative the dancers had received in Europe.

There was praise for the lighting designs of Nicholas Cernovitch here and on the rest of the Scandinavian tour stops. The critics were less impressed by the dances. Svend Kragh-Jacobsen, the dean of Copenhagen dance critics and normally a kindly, avuncular sort, had particularly harsh words, leveling the unusual charge of coldness and too much virtuosity against the Ailey dancers. "Especially during the first part of the rather longish programme you were disappointed not to see anything but an excellent technique displayed by a few of the dancers and artful tricks by Mr. Ailey, who did not even prove to be one of the best dancers of his group," Kragh-Jacobsen wrote.

"Revelations," he observed, had "a certain warmth and submission to the dance," but he was disturbed by the "outward virtuosity and arranged effects which seemed to cover an inner emptiness" in other dances on the program. "You were missing an inner spontaneity in all this superficial vital body glamor and jazz ballet technique," Kragh-Jacobsen continued. "The best dancers also had a fine classical ballet training, which gave them great advantages over the dancers who displayed their temperament only."

Stockholm audiences were, Alvin reported, "beautifully receptive." "I must say that we have had some of the most thunderous acclaim of the tour in Stockholm & Helsinki," he wrote to Edele Holtz on April 29. "We played state theatres in both places—found an enormously active dance scene in Stockholm. . . . We even performed 'Rooms' two of the four performances to great acclaim by critics and audiences. In Helsinki, the audiences stamped and cheered and speeches were made closing nite about having us back—"

Germany was a dream that the dancers on the 1965 tour would never forget. The company rode by bus to Hamburg and arrived at the theater there at 5 A.M. for a 10 A.M. performance, on a floor on which a rug had been laid out. The exhausted dancers were amazed to see a full—and noisily excited—house when the curtain rose. Energized by applause that started with the rising curtain, they performed to the hilt and were rewarded with gifts of flowers and candy that the audience placed on the edge of the stage. In large theaters in two German cities audiences paid a top ticket price of $54.50, unheard of in New York, to see "this formerly unknown American Negro group," as the theater trade paper *Variety* put it.

In Muenster, the audience applauded *Revelations* for forty minutes and would not go home no matter how many times the dancers repeated the *Rocka My Soul* finale. Alvin was pleased but slightly cynical about the reception. "Not a step of [Revelations] was together at all— they applauded for 40 minutes at the final curtain—80 curtain calls!" he wrote to the Holtzes. "Scandalous! I mean one begins to doubt either their eyesight or to suspect a slight favoritism for the color brown—& so on & so on & so on & etc."

Edele Holtz had a measured response. "The success in Germany is marvelous of course but like London really predictable," she wrote Alvin on May 16. "Europe has been brainwashed into thinking that all American modern dance is like Merce Cunningham and Negro artists produce only jazz and gospel singing."

The troupe returned to France and performed in late May at the Sarah Bernhardt Theatre, where the Ailey company represented the United States at the Paris Festival of Nations. The immensely popular company was the only one on the bill, Alvin noted, that was not subsidized by its country.

Italy was last on the tour, luckily, for the dancers were tired and the reviews mixed. Alvin was particularly bothered by poor reviews in Rome. "As for the Rome notices, you can't expect a perfect batting average after all," Edele Holtz observed in a consoling letter written in mid-June. "Someone is bound not to like you sometimes. I hope for all your sakes that Florence turns out well—if not there will be other times."

But worse was in store. In Como, Louther was having "star problems," as Alvin put it. In Pisa, Alvin and Christopher had one of their worst blowups. In Florence, Louther quit and Alvin had to take over his roles in *Rooms* and *Revelations* at the last moment, after which he "threw all dance clothes into wastebasket," Alvin wrote long after the experience, "and that was that."

Louther had been singled out by reviewers in many countries. But when *The Road of the Phoebe Snow* was badly received by Italian critics and audiences, Alvin pulled the dance from the repertory when the company reached Rome. Louther, who had had a lead in the piece, refused to perform at all, saying that he had a back problem. He left suddenly just before the Maggio Musicale festival in Florence, a star-studded event that Alvin felt was one of the most important stops on the tour. An out-of-shape Alvin was forced to step into Louther's roles in four ballets, and the company got into legal trouble with Italian authorities for having one dancer too few to fulfill their contractual obligations.

Louther was not the only problem. "These dancers have suddenly turned extraordinary!!" Alvin wrote Edele Holtz from Torino in unusually large handwriting that looks as if it is about to shoot off the margins of the page. "Inflated egos such as one cannot imagine!—Now this was expected but to such a degree!"

Fed up, Alvin decided not only to give up what little dancing he was now doing but to dissolve the company and concentrate on choreographing when he returned to New York in September after a brief Mediterranean vacation. At the same time, Edele Holtz wrote him with gentle but firm encouragement that she was "so glad you are not (or are you?) making definite plans for the summer. There is so much to be done in the way of just THINKING about what you have just done and how to plan the future intelligently."

eighteen

BACK IN BUSINESS,
SEVERAL TIMES

The well-organized college tour Edele Holtz had begun to plan the year before never did materialize, a victim of her inexperience, the difficulties of transatlantic communication and the pressures of her own work. But faced with an already booked smaller college tour when he returned to the United States in June 1965, Alvin was forced to abandon his plan to dissolve the company. He hired five new dancers for the performances, three of whom became Ailey stars.

One was Clive Thompson, a tall, elegant Jamaican who had previously danced with Martha Graham. Another was Miguel Godreau, a wiry little Broadway show dancer from Puerto Rico who came and went in the Ailey company over the next four years, cheered vociferously by audiences around the world for his explosive performing. And the third was Judith Jamison.

Like Dudley Williams, Jamison threw in her lot with Alvin early on, at the start of her career. Both grew from self-involved young adults to artists of rare individuality. Molded by Alvin in his laissez-faire sort of way, Williams and Jamison eventually helped to mold his dance. Each came to represent an opposite pole of the wide Ailey choreographic spectrum: Williams, the quiet intensity of Ailey dancing, and Jamison its go-for-broke ebulliency.

Three years younger than Williams, Jamison had begun her training at an unusually early age and, as unusually for a black dancer of the time, her training was almost exclusively in ballet. Most black dance students of the time tended to be steered by well-meaning teachers into the more welcoming field of modern dance.

The product of a close-knit blue-collar family, Jamison attended Fisk University in Nashville for three semesters as a psychology major but returned to study dance in Philadelphia. From there, Agnes de Mille whisked her off to New York to appear in *The Four Marys*, a dramatic tale of seduction and miscegenation in the antebellum South presented by the American Ballet Theatre in its 1965 spring season. Like most of de Mille's work, the piece dealt with serious social themes—here, inequities of race and class in America. Jamison played one of four "Marys," pretty young housemaids who enter into a conspiracy of silence with their mistress when one of them, played by Carmen de Lavallade, is hung for the murder of a baby conceived with the mistress's suitor.

Jamison's job did not lead to a contract with the company, which had once before employed black dancers at de Mille's behest but subsequently had a poor record that reflected American ballet hiring in general into the 1990s. Regardless of her skin color, it would have been surprising if Jamison had ended up with Ballet Theatre or any other ballet company. Rising up past six feet in toe shoes, she would have dwarfed her partners.

Jamison would stand out in modern dance companies, too, but Alvin saw something—he was never sure exactly what—in the untried young ballet giantess who arrived to audition in late summer for a television show to be choreographed by Donald McKayle. Dressed in ballet leotards, tights and knit leg warmers, and without makeup, she was even more an anomaly in that group of flashy, easy-going Broadway gypsies.

Alvin had heard about Jamison from de Lavallade, but he had not seen her until the audition. McKayle kept Jamison dancing until the last cut as an act of kindness, she later wrongly surmised. Hurrying out with a profound sense of failure, she brushed by a man watching from the stairs of the rehearsal studio. It took Alvin some time to track her down, but three days later she heard from him. Would she join his company? Jamison answered yes, and on November 30, 1965, she was onstage performing with the Alvin Ailey American Dance Theater at the Harper Theater in Chicago in an all-star ballet and modern dance festival whose roster also included the companies of Paul Taylor, Robert Joffrey and Merce Cunningham, as well as the New York City Ballet stars Edward Villella and Patricia McBride.

The company traveled on to engagements at Howard University in Washington, D.C., where Alvin was able to do some catching up with Ruby Phillips, the sister of Moses Alexander, the beloved surrogate father of his Texas childhood. He took time to write his mother that he had seen Ruby, carefully sending her a new address and telephone number for Phillips. Then the troupe journeyed to New York City, where the Ailey dancers were engaged for two performances in mid-December at the Hunter College Playhouse, a theater with nearly as prestigious a dance history as the Ninety-second Street Y. It was a heartening invitation, for Norman Singer, the theater's administrator, was attempting to create a home for new and important American modern dance troupes at Hunter by producing engagements rather than simply renting the theater to the companies.

Alvin and his dances were becoming known in the United States, but the demand for them was still much greater in Europe. In February 1966, he and his dancers embarked on yet another European tour. This one opened in Muenster, where, Truitte wrote to Al Holtz, the audience "adored" *Rooms*, and Alvin noted happily that the curtain calls extended from the forty minutes of the company's triumph the year before to a full hour. Performances in Rome were received well, too, with a great deal more enthusiasm from audiences this time.

Alvin took off soon after for Cannes, where he was to finish *Macumba*—"Becky's little extravaganza," as Truitte put it—for Rebekah Harkness, who had composed the samba score and commissioned the ballet for herself and her dancers with the idea of presenting it in May in Barcelona. Truitte had taken over as associate director of the Ailey company. "I'll be in charge of the monsters," he told Holtz. "Yipe!! So far the morale is good but this is only the beginning." Soon he was worrying about "a couple of star complexes" that were developing in the company and needed nipping in the bud.

"Till later, J.T., C.P.A., Ballet-master, Dancer, etc. but it's fun," he signed one of his many letters to Holtz, most of which began with a cheerful "Hi there!"

The company toured by bus, earning extra money performing its repertory in television programs filmed in Berlin, Koln and Amsterdam. It was not a great deal of money, however, and the meticulous Truitte felt that anything extra should be saved for emergencies, exhibiting a caution that would soon prove to be well founded.

Alvin's dispute with Susan Pimsleur had gone to arbitration in March and she had won, claiming nearly $8,000 in unpaid fees. And when a troupe of black performers that Dorfman was touring just ahead of the Ailey dancers failed to please audiences, several Ailey engagements were canceled, and the dancers were stranded in Milan.

There were enough engagements elsewhere to keep the troupe performing, at least on paper. Every week two or three requests arrived for Ailey performances back home. A Canadian tour was possible, Holtz wrote, although one in Israel had fallen through. And it looked as if there might be a booking for the company in April at the First World Festival of Negro Arts in Dakar, Senegal, a three-week celebration of black culture designed to increase awareness in the artists themselves and in the world at large of black contributions to world culture.

Arthur Mitchell, who chaired the dance division of the festival's American advisory committee and served on it with Alvin and Katherine Dunham, had put together a festival dance company and programs. But in the end there was not enough money to fly performers over from the United States to Africa. The Ailey dancers, already in Europe, would be cheaper to transport. Alvin was at that point struggling to find ways to keep the company intact. He reasoned that if Dakar came through, the dancers could travel on with him afterward to Barcelona, where the Harkness company would be performing, and fling themselves on Harkness's mercy.

"This compulsion to keep the company together no matter what the risk or headaches is nutty to me," the practical-minded Al Holtz wrote Truitte in March 1966, "but I guess Alvin is always going to have it, so that's life. If it was me I'd explore all the possibilities and if it wasn't working out, I'd ship the whole crew back, and forget it." But he tried to reassure Truitte the following month about the Harkness scheme. "You should know by now that Alvin moves in his mysterious way 'his wonders to perform,' and he usually is thinking far ahead and not communicating it to anyone. The gag to move in on Harkness is clever and chancey but he'll pull it off."

In addition to his worries about bills, balancing the books, problems with the dancers and forwarding to Holtz a never-ending stream of carefully numbered petty cash vouchers, Truitte was concerned about Alvin and his tendency to spend any extra money on "some outlandish thing." "I'm really trying to keep these finances straight and I count the damned money every day to be sure that I'm in balance," Truitte wrote. "The most difficult thing afoot is to keep our problem child from blowing it in one fell swoop. Somehow I manage, but only heaven knows how."

The days of carefree foreign shopping sprees were mostly a thing of the past, however, as the company grew more famous and Alvin worked even harder to maintain it. His temper had grown more perilously short. "Just spoke to Alvin this morning and he is in one of his petulant, sarcastic, facetious, I've had it moods," Truitte wrote Holtz. "He said he'll not rehearse the dancers until we get to Dakar and he doesn't care if we look awful. So I've just ignored him which is the only thing to do."

Most of Truitte's book balancing and letter writing took place in the early hours of the morning after performances. During one of those sessions Alvin had called him, hurt and angry over something a dancer had said in one of the periodic meetings that were a distinctive part of Ailey company life.

"At 2:00 A.M. this morning he called me ranting and raving on the phone but all I could do was hold the receiver and be a sounding board for his outburst," Truitte told Holtz. "As the French say, Il est quelque chose!! I told him you said you had funds which you weren't using as yet but he probably didn't hear me. These kids have made the sacrifice he has asked of them such as the half salary and on maintenance for a week because they believe in what he is trying to do and then he turns around and says they are money-hungry in so many words. Quel enfant! I'll survive through all of this. When we get to Dakar his tune will change believe me because his reputation is at stake and in spite of his tirade at the moment he is concerned about that."

Truitte did recognize that Alvin deserved occasional pampering. "There's a pair of cuff links that Alvin has his eye on and he really wants them but he says he can't afford them," Truitte wrote Holtz. "I think they're about $60. They are really beautiful and I really think he should have them. Do you think it would be OK if I bought them out of Petty Cash and we could write it off as personal expenses. I think he owes them to himself. Write me an O.K. and I'll get them and surprise him. I'm sure he would be shocked."

Holtz told him to go ahead, and put a voucher in for the amount for "costumes." He would think of something. And enclose a little note with the gift, he added, saying that it was from "The Corp" for service beyond the call of duty.

Alvin, Holtz later recalled, "could never hold on to a dollar." "He'd give it away. He was the softest touch in the world. Some ne'er-do-well dancer would ask for $20 and he'd never get it back. He never remembered who he gave it to."

The company made it to Dakar, where the Ailey dancers were a hit. The festival was the idea of Leopold Sedar Senghor, the poet-president of Senegal. Endorsed by the United Nations, it was a poorly organized but unparalleled gathering of black artists from around the world, drawing delegates from fifty countries. Langston Hughes was there, his usual imperturbable, charming self as he led a group of more than one hundred representatives of the United States. The Ailey dancers were impressed to discover that he was staying at their hotel and that Josephine Baker was among the visiting American celebrities. They themselves had been welcomed at the airport by "a group of dancers and musicians carrying on," as Truitte reported in a letter home to Holtz.

Alvin had arrived in a bad mood. He hadn't told Truitte that the dancers needed visas and yellow fever shots until they took off for Dakar. Truitte was covered by his shots for the Far East tour in 1962, but Alvin had no proof of his innoculations because his passport had been stolen. Other calamities were soon to follow.

Thompson had been called home to New York by his wife, who had just had a baby. Another dancer became sick during the opening night performance, threw up onstage just as the curtain fell on *The Road of the Phoebe Snow*, and had to be pulled out of *Revelations*. In a company without understudies, this presented a problem, but the Ailey dancers were used to last-minute adjustments.

The dancer collapsed again early in the second performance. Williams took on his roles, and Godreau filled in for Williams until his shoulder popped out of its socket not once but three times, the last time in *Revelations*. There was only one "sinner man" left for that trio, so it was cut, and there were at times three dancers on the stage in place of the usual eight. The delighted audience seemed not to notice.

The end of the festival meant that the company needed to embark on its uncertain pilgrimage to Barcelona, where Alvin hoped his dancers could work with the Harkness Ballet and go on to Paris with the company. But they were stranded in Madrid when it developed that there were no seats on flights to Barcelona for another few days. Alvin was able to fly on alone to book rooms for the dancers, who would travel by train.

His attempt to bring a sick dancer ahead with him failed, and he was again in a foul mood, blaming Truitte for the mess. "Then he started the facetious routine which is really beginning to grate on my nerves," Truitte wrote Al Holtz on April 27. "There's so much you can stand. It's really a good thing I like and admire him or I would have thrown the money belt in long ago. I have told him that he is being very unfunny. I've almost been at the point of blowing my top but then I say, Why? The things that he says he is going to do he doesn't do, which I should know by now. Then of course since he didn't do them it seems as though it's my fault, but like I say, that's 'show biz.' "

Blessedly, the wandering performers found a place to rest in Barcelona. Williams and two other dancers left the company, impatient at the week it took Harkness to make up her mind and angry that they had not been paid for the week after Dakar. Alvin worked anxiously on *Macumba*, and filled the cast with as many of his own dancers as possible. But there was little else for them to do except take daily ballet classes with the fifty-one-year-old Harkness, who would be performing in *Macumba* with Alvin as her partner. They were getting a little less than their Ailey salaries from her, but at least it was work.

Macumba, a bit of ersatz latinalia, was the lackluster embarrassment that almost everyone expected from Harkness, and no one blamed Alvin. The piece died a quick and quiet death. Never a model of good taste, Harkness was becoming increasingly uncontrollable in her dealings with her ballet company, which continued to be praised for its first-rate dancers but not for its repertory.

While in Barcelona, Alvin began work on a new piece for Marjorie Tallchief, the American Indian ballerina who had played the title role in *Ariadne* the year before. Neither *Ariadne* nor *El Amor Brujo*, the second premiere Alvin created for the Harkness dancers that year, would be received with much initial enthusiasm at the Festival de la Marais in Paris, where the now-augmented Harkness Ballet was to perform in early June. But Alvin had a good deal else on his mind.

He was thinking again of disbanding the company he had struggled so hard to keep together. He was tired of the battle, of the endless tours and the dancers' equally endless squabbles. Tantrum prone himself these days, Alvin was regularly starting the day with an aperitif in an outdoor café in Las Ramblas in Barcelona, and he drank right through the evening. He was not alone in this. Drinking was common in the company at the time. Alvin needed alcohol to soothe his exhaustion, it seemed, and to ease his humiliation at the weight he was putting on.

He had started work on yet another new project. The $45 million Metropolitan Opera House at Lincoln Center was to open on September 16 with *Antony and Cleopatra*, an opera commissioned from Samuel Barber, as the highlight of the sumptuous, celebrity-laden opening night festivities. Franco Zeffirelli, hired to direct the production, had so far participated only minimally, and Alvin was asked to fly to Rome to discuss the progress of the opera. After that, he was to work for a short time at Watch Hill with the Harkness company, fly back to Europe to teach in Cologne, and then return to New York for the opera rehearsals, which were scheduled to begin in late August.

The Holtzes were vacationing in Europe and had a rendezvous with Alvin in Paris before this latest odyssey began. The two men straggled behind Edele Holtz talking shop, following her blindly into one boutique after another without breaking the conversation. "We dined in small cafés and in all had a lovely relaxed time—not too usual in Alvin's life," she said. Alvin invited them to a rehearsal at the outdoor amphitheater in the handsomely weathered old Paris neighborhood where the Marais festival took place, and one day they found themselves settling in to watch from their favorite spot, high up at the back of the theater.

"They were beginning rehearsals of *The House of Bernarda Alba* [*Feast of Ashes*], and thanks to Mrs. Harkness there was a Spanish orchestra to back it up," Edele Holtz recalled. "To the horror of the very elegant musicians, as the rehearsal started out came this enormous man in a gray sweat suit, lumbering toward them to give directions. But by the time Alvin had spoken to them clearly in Spanish, to the stagehands in French and the dancers in English, it was clear who was in charge!"

His meeting with the Holtzes seemed to have refreshed Alvin and cleared his mind. Three days after the festival ended, Alvin wrote lovingly and with unusual reflection to his two New York friends. "First let me say that seeing the two of you here even in so brief a time served immeasurably to reassure me that the enormous fantasy of having a dance company *is* possible and somehow from you and your belief in me and my possibilities as a human being and an artist has been born a new faith—a disorganized one—but a faith.

"Secondly let me say that to finally have the company and Harkness finished for the moment after so long a period—Macumba, co. problems, new ballet, Marais Festival, etc., etc.—is something more than a big bird let out of a cage—I feel free, light, (only <u>slightly</u> troubled) and am now beginning to see, hear & feel Paris—the city I despised before seems now a different thing—do you think it was me all along and <u>not</u> Paris?

"<u>Marais</u> finished really gloriously for us and I only wish you & Louis [Johnson] could have been there to see his ballet on that great open stage with the gleaming wood the 8 celli, 2 violas—the musicians all in tails & gleaming white shirts—the conductor—elegant & salt & pepper haired—the young & quite beautiful soprano from the Paris Opera—(what a glorious voice!) all on the stage on the elevated platform stage right and the dancers below them dancing wonderfully. . . . Even Ariadne—which I still do not like—looked good there—"

The mood of radiant tranquility and hope was short-lived, however, for although Alvin was reassured by his visit in Rome with Zeffirelli, the rehearsals for *Antony and Cleopatra* were a nightmare.

The first plan for the gala that would open the Metropolitan had been to commission a purely American opera. Tennessee Williams and James Baldwin had been considered briefly as librettists. "Moby-Dick" had been suggested as a subject to Barber. "Too much water for an opera," the acerbic composer responded, "and too much wind." Eventually, Zeffirelli created a libretto in fifteen days, breezily providing Barber with an extra "bunch" of words to draw on if needed.

The detached, fastidious Barber—as great a procrastinator as Alvin, Edele Holtz noted wryly—was still at work on the score at home in Mt. Kisco, New York, as rehearsals progressed. At times Alvin had to work without any music, improvising rhythms in an attempt to do some sort of honor to this glittering assignment. But *Tony and Cleo*, as one music writer renamed the production, was savaged by critics, with most of the blame piled on Zeffirelli. Alvin's contribution was one of the few elements of the lavish, moribund opera that received any praise.

Alvin was once more back at what felt distinctly like a starting point. He could choreograph for the company that was coming to feel like a millstone, and he could tour. But money remained a problem. Plans had fallen through for merging the Ailey company with the well-endowed Harkness Ballet. He was a world-famous choreographer with little but debts to show for all his work. And he was tired.

nineteen

AFRICAN ODYSSEY

The Alvin Ailey American Dance Theater seemed to have an unquenchable life of its own as it moved into the late 1960s. The company might stagger from crisis to crisis. Its still-young founder might yearn at times to shake free of the endless responsibilities of running a dance troupe in America. But Alvin's "family" was growing up and becoming an institution in spite of it all.

Al Holtz had recognized that the troupe could not sustain itself on Alvin's commissions and on box office receipts alone. Each tour added a new dimension of some kind to the picture, as Al Holtz wrote to Alvin in the summer of 1967, adding prophetically that "it would be unthinkable if some gains were not made in the organization, and I suppose after you do it ten more years it will run by itself." But as he and Alvin investigated foundations and other sources of money, it became increasingly clear that if the company was to continue, it must become a good deal more of a business.

Over the years, Alvin had talked to Edele Holtz and others about the importance of a school. He might hate teaching and be unconvincing in that role, but he could see the necessity for a training center for children and young dancers. In late April 1967, plans were begun to incorporate the company as the not-for-profit Dance Theater Foundation. According to the Certificate of Incorporation, the organization was eventually to include a school with classes for "the Young American Negro dancer . . . to provide a continuing source and outlet for the talented professional Negro dancers to the world of Dance."

There was talk about finding a permanent home for the company and a school, but not a great deal of activity. Alvin contemplated a half-formed invitation from Rebekah Harkness to open a small school in a hall in the Yorkville section of Manhattan, many blocks to the east of the Harkness center proper. As Edele Holtz pointed out, however, the physical separation of the Ailey school from the Harkness academy had unpalatable overtones of racial segregation. In any case, ties with Harkness were irreparably broken later that year when Alvin, summoned to Watch Hill to restage *Ariadne* for the Harkness Ballet's Broadway season, walked out on the second day of rehearsal, tired of the piece and feeling as if he was forever to be at Harkness's beck and call.

Alvin and the long-suffering Christopher had at last broken up, although they would keep in sporadic contact over the years, surprised, a little, at how little catching up they seemed to need to do. On the rebound, perhaps, Alvin decided to give himself a hedonistic vacation in Morocco. He had long been intrigued by Arab cultures in which homosexuality was considered a perfectly normal premarital sexual activity. Morocco, he knew, had also been a mecca for artists in exile. In 1967, Alvin took the plunge and sought out the easy, nonjudgmental world of the male prostitutes of Algiers, so different from his demanding and relatively straitlaced life back in New York City.

It was a world he returned to twice and then abandoned, a world where this big, boisterous, crazy American was remembered long after he left. Smoking kif, partying and making love with their clients in numbered rooms, his boys sang out the rock songs that Alvin, seldom able to be completely serious, had taught them. "I'm caming, hold on," they caroled at appropriate moments, as one of the men wrote Alvin in New York in somewhat precarious English.

Some were married and had children. Some had other jobs, although their lives tended to be bleak out of tourist season. Some wrote to Alvin, and he kept their letters. There is a hint of sweetness to some of the letters, and Alvin—also known to the men as "Alevin" and "Azi"—responded in turn with a sort of teasing, quasi-avuncular fondness.

Looking back, Christopher suggested that Alvin was capable of feeling enormous love and enormous self-hatred simultaneously in these fleeting sexual encounters. "I think inside that self-hatred was a real connectedness with whom he loved and what it was for him to love somebody—a man, a boy, whoever he was loving. He could open that up and pour it out and get it."

There was at times a certain wistfulness to Alvin's adventuring, captured in a poem he jotted down in the mid-1960s:

> several hard-hipped hustlers
> and more I am I will always
> be queers gazing
> at the crotches of
> small thick-thighed
> magazines—
> sighing
> "oh"—

At home in gray, prosaic New York, Alvin and Al Holtz found a ground-floor apartment in a brownstone at 28 West Sixty-fifth Street, where they set up an office for the company with living space in the back for Alvin. Each had a desk in one of the front rooms. Alvin's living quarters were spartan. The bed was a mattress placed on the floor so Alvin, who thrashed in his sleep, would not fall. His television was borrowed, and seldom used, and he did not bother much about any other amenities. His idea of dinner was to open a can of spaghetti or chili, inevitably trailed over the kitchen and behind him as he walked about the apartment eating. Despite the simplicity of his lifestyle, Alvin was messy to a degree that drove Holtz to add housekeeping to his duties.

Alvin bore the cleaning but little else. It was not a setup for someone who treasured his privacy. His frustration boiled over one night when he returned to the apartment two hours later than scheduled and found five or six people waiting to talk to him about auditions and other company business. Holtz had made them comfortable, and Alvin walked in on a roomful of chatting strangers. A looming presence in the hall, he turned on his heel without saying a word and disappeared back out into the street. Holtz got rid of the visitors. Gradually he was coming to understand that Alvin would do what he had to do when he felt he had to do it, as Holtz put it, whatever anyone else thought. His moods were often hard to read. But Holtz never again made appointments for him.

In any case, the company was soon off on yet another long tour to Israel and through eight European countries. The dancers left New

York in late May and returned in early September, just in time to embark on a tour of Africa. Why did a New York critic have to travel abroad to see a New York company? Clive Barnes complained. "When is Mr. Ailey going to have a Broadway season?"

Judith Jamison had stayed on with the Harkness for a few uncomfortable months after the Paris performances but returned to the fold, rejoining a very strong company that also boasted Consuelo Atlas, Kelvin Rotardier and James Truitte, three of the most eloquent dancers ever to perform with the Ailey. Williams returned to work his quiet magic in *Reflections in D*, one of only three Ailey dances in the tour repertory. Miguel Godreau stirred audiences to new paroxysms of excitement in Geoffrey Holder's *Prodigal Prince*, a dance based on real and imagined events in the life of the Haitian painter Hector Hipployte, a subject Alvin had long ago contemplated for a piece. As he often did, Holder created not only the choreography but also vivid music and costume and set designs. The ballet was a popular success, establishing Godreau as one of Alvin's most bankable stars.

For all the vibrancy of the performing and the wide-ranging and choice repertory, which also included dances by Talley Beatty, Lester Horton, Louis Johnson and Paul Sanasardo, the European tour was a nightmarish, poorly organized and exhausting experience for the dancers. Through it all, however, Alvin was strangely peaceful. The angry, anxious creature of the preceding tour seemed largely to have disappeared, replaced by a serene and often contented seeming man.

It was not to be the happiest of years, however. Minnie Marshall and Langston Hughes both died in the summer of 1967, Marshall of cancer and Hughes of infections in the urinary tract and upper respiratory system that he had not bothered to have treated. Both deaths were unexpected, and both had to be reported long distance by a sorrowing Edele Holtz. "Dear Beleaguered Boss and Blonde Dragon Lady," Alvin wrote in an unusually tender postcard from the Netherlands. "What can I say of Minnie except that I'm happy the end came soon & that she did not suffer." Also uncharacteristically, it was signed with a gentle "All my love to you both."

Alvin's new serenity might have been an outgrowth of intensive treatment he was undergoing with the psychotherapist Carl Goldman, whom he had come to worship as a wise authority on life. It was one of the few times in Alvin's life when he was able to unburden himself in a more meaningful way than his usual exuberant wails and groans about work or angry exclamations about his mother, which were less self-revelation than a smokescreen designed to maintain his sense of privacy. He was able to pour out his soul to Goldman, not only about his problems with wanting and not wanting success and fame but also about quieting the ghosts of his childhood and his problems with his sexual identity.

A gay analyst and concentration camp survivor, Goldman had established a practice on Waverly Place in Greenwich Village, becoming something of a guru among gay men and artists. His apartment "became a drop-in salon; of an evening you could ring his bell and usually find a congenial group gathered in the living room," Martin Duberman wrote in *Stonewall*. "He sometimes cooked for the more 'interesting' gay men he collected . . . discoursing at length after dinner on existentialism or the meaning of paranoid psychosis. A genuine intellectual, Goldman was also tight and aloof, literally hunched over with tension and incapable of looking anyone directly in the eye. He could be archly patronizing, effectively using his wide-ranging knowledge to cow those who were younger or more impressionable (but really to establish his own right to exist)."

Alvin's unaccustomed peacefulness shines out, along with a touch of weariness, in a long letter to the Holtzes in early July. "Sometime after the war, after the <u>real</u> history of the world is written and after I've been a much longer time with the well-known shrink," Alvin wrote, "I'll probably learn why it is I cannot write from tours anymore, buy clothes, lose weight or keep from tiring of dance companies after six weeks in the field. So no more excuses from me about not having taken pen to hand except for muddled airport postcards.

"Actually this time all has gone very well. Much much better in an organizational level (actually <u>all</u> levels) than ever before—too we are all older and calmer—at least I am—and I don't really care as much. I am remembering, boss, your plea to keep the sense of humor—and short of the theater's caving in because Elbert Morris's arms just <u>won't be right</u> or Dudley's glowering at the world because Prodigal Prince has made Miguel the star of our show—the laugh prevails. Even a threat or two from our beloved and much-saved Skeets [the company's nickname for Matthew Cameron, its wardrobe master] that he will go home on the next plane has simply brought an 'it's your life baby—do with it what you like'—and the same I'm afraid will go for everyone. On with the laugh—"

Alvin's dancers would probably have been surprised to hear the tour described as organized. It had started well. "Hello my darlings,"

Alvin wrote the Holtzes from Pula. "The Yugoslavians had adopted us and don't want us to leave—beautiful people. receptions & cities." But the dancers almost mutinied later after two consecutive weeks of one-night stands through Portugal and Germany.

"A slave camp on the march" was how Truitte referred to their arduous travels in a letter home in June, blaming the poor tour arrangements on Alvin's new company manager, Gil Shiva. A suave and elegantly dressed Israeli, Shiva had given Alvin a revitalized sense of possibilities for the troupe. But he exasperated Truitte. Shiva was to join the dancers in Italy, and he wouldn't want to be in Shiva's shoes, Truitte added cheerily, when the dancers saw him.

There were also terrible new alarms about the company's earnings, some of which had simply not been accounted for in the bicontinental chaos of the tour. Truitte had had to pool the dancers' tax deductions, Alvin's salary and what little was left in petty cash at times for such pressing necessities as bus rentals and cargo shipment from country to country. "We should become solvent in Sweden, thank goodness," he wrote Al Holtz.

At one point Truitte realized that he had been underpaying Alvin by a large amount. He had waved away Alvin's plaintive questions about the size of his salary with a sunny "that's how it goes with Uncle Sam." "This will be my story to A.A.," Truitte wrote conspiratorially to Holtz on July 12. "I decided to do it that way so he would have some extra money knowing how it slips through his fingers." At any rate, he observed in another letter, he was determined to see that Alvin came out of the tour with some money in hand.

Audiences and reviews were for the most part enthusiastic as the company traveled across Europe. The reception in Muenster was as delirious as ever, but Alvin had a minor set-to with the director of the theater. "Go out on stage, just jump around some more, do something," the man told Alvin when the applause showed no signs of abating after a performance of *Revelations* and an encore of *Rocka My Soul.* Why not book the company for longer? Alvin responded coolly. Then he'd see more.

In Stockholm, the company had a tiring but enjoyable time filming dances for Swedish television. Alvin created a piece for television that he later named *Riedaiglia,* a word made from the names of the three collaborators—Georg Riedel, the Swedish composer, Alvin, and Lars Egler, the producer. "In some ways it is a very beautiful show," Alvin wrote the Holtzes, in a rare mood of self-approval. "Very sad too.

It has an inner kind of philosophical line but I'm not sure what I mean. It is in the shape of the 7 deadly sins—Anger, Sloth, etc.—a suite really of differently conceived dances but also costumed chronologically to pass thru time from beginning history to Middle Ages to present day. It is clothed in a kind of 'hippie' beginning and ending with everyone dressed East Village and Jimmie kind of an Ingmar Bergman devil or (Saint?) in black suit, dark glasses, cross on a chain, and cape."

Riedaiglia was praised by Swedish critics, went on to win the Grand Prix Italia, the most prestigious European award for television productions, and then sank into an oblivion that Truitte and others thought was well deserved. The piece was not one of Alvin's most considered or profound works. It was during this tour, in the Netherlands and Israel, that sustained criticism of the company's theatricality began to appear. Reviewers suggested that Alvin was promoting black stereotypes, particularly in *Blues Suite* and *Revelations* and in Holder's *Prodigal Prince*. The Dutch reviews, Alvin speculated, might have been a response to two questionable touring black theater programs that had preceded the company. In any case, they opened up heated arguments between the press and the public.

Several critics accused the company of being too commercial. "It must be quite a new experience for one of our leading dance companies to be regarded as commercial, and one hopes it will not go to their heads," Barnes commented sardonically. Looking back, Edele Holtz wondered if the Dutch had any notion of there being a distinctive black culture in America that claimed what seemed like stereotypes as its own.

But there was a similar response in Israel. Audiences thundered their approval, yet critics questioned the company's appeal. One of the most outspoken reviews was that by Meir Ronnen, writing in the *Jerusalem Post*. "There is no doubt a great deal of sympathy here for largely Negro companies; and the four men of the group are all superb hoofers of demanding Broadway standards and equally superbly built," Ronnen wrote. "The two works choreographed by Ailey have regrettably little to offer where dance idioms are concerned. The Blues Suite, danced to vocalized Duke Ellington [*sic*], is of the level of Parisian cabaret and subscribes to all the cliches of Negro movement and costume that should have died with the Broadway of the twenties; I find it difficult to appreciate how a Negro can lend himself to perpetuating this form of unflattering cliche. 'Revelations' is only a little better."

There were no such academic subtleties about the experience Alvin had on a short trip home, a brutal reminder of what it was to be even a famous black man in America. It occurred, ironically enough, just before a state-sponsored tour of Africa that was of cultural importance to the United States and of considerable emotional significance to Alvin and his dancers. Back in New York in late summer after his abortive session with the Harkness Ballet in Watch Hill, Alvin had had dinner with friends at the Ginger Man, a fashionable restaurant near Lincoln Center, and was walking home shortly after midnight when he became aware that a police car was following him. The car pulled up and one of the policemen called to Alvin to come over. Suddenly a flashlight was beamed into his eyes and he heard a voice saying, "This is the guy. I recognize him."

Alvin later discovered that "the guy" was a black man with a mustache and beard, like him, who had murdered four policemen in Cincinnati. In what seemed like only moments, he found himself on the floor of a police station, handcuffed and being kicked in places, he later observed, that didn't show bruises. No one knew where he was. Frightened and helpless, Alvin wondered if he might be killed. But he was carrying his passport in his briefcase, and when it was discovered, the police decided they had the wrong man. Alvin was charged with pushing a policeman and spent the night in jail before an outraged lawyer hired by Al Holtz freed him.

A man of the world and a representative of his country, Alvin had not traveled so far after all, it seemed, from rural Texas and Los Angeles, where the specter of imprisonment was a part of the racial unconscious of black men. He did not press charges against the police as the lawyer urged him to. Two days later, he rejoined the company, catching up with it in Athens for the African tour. But Edele Holtz noticed that for a long time after, when Alvin was upset he would rub his wrists as if they were handcuffed.

The dancers toured through nine countries in two months, performing everywhere from rural community centers and movie houses to state-of-the-art theaters in Senegal and Ghana. In some towns the company had to tap into municipal street lighting systems, and the stage lights would then dim and flicker when too many people turned on their lights at home.

In Africa, Alvin was able to fulfill his earlier dream and reach out to students with low-priced performances and lecture-demonstrations in which the dancers presented examples of jazz, ballet, ethnic and modern dance styles. He noted that the audiences were not terribly surprised by the Beatty works or *Revelations*, with their fairly clear

American black themes. What did surprise them was the range of the other dances on the program and what they saw as the experimentalist look of Paul Sanasardo's *Metallics*. "I only wish I could have shown them the sort of things our really far-out young choreographers are doing!" Alvin observed in an article he wrote for *Dance Magazine* on his return to New York. But not all the audiences were such blank slates. "You have discovered how to stylize your passions for a technological era," the Senegalese president Leopold Senghor astutely told the company.

Some interpretations of the plotless dances in the repertory were intriguing. *Metallics*, with its woman peeping out at a couple dancing before her, seemed to one Ghanian "to be about a shy person who longed to fly, but who was held back by the spirits of her ancestors."

The atmosphere in Africa would not have encouraged romantics in the company to think of the tour as a return to their roots. Although the troupe was the first American dance company to tour the continent for any length of time, the accommodations and arrangements had not been well taken care of by the State Department. And the reception was cool, at first, at each new stop. The audiences were large, but, as was true in a later tour of Russia, they seemed to need time to adjust to the Ailey dancers. The dancers were black Americans, and most of what African audiences knew about American blacks had come from the desperate lives depicted in films such as *Porgy and Bess* and *Carmen Jones*. But these were black American men and women who lived different and comparatively easy lives. Still, many of the dancers felt strangely at home walking through the streets of the Ghanian capital, Accra, an area from which many black American slaves had come.

The temperature warmed when the American visitors asked about African lives and culture and attended performances by local groups. The dancers bought enough sculptures, animal skins, drums, jewelry, fabrics and shoes to stock a museum, Alvin noted, worrying a little that the Ghanians might be offended by the sight of the Ailey women wearing the traditional Ghanian shirt as a miniskirt. He was relieved to see that they were amused.

Jamison's presence added to the company's appeal, for she was as tall, regal and dark skinned as any African goddess, with the dark gums that were considered a sign of beauty in much of Africa. In Kenya, Alvin was approached by President Jomo Kenyatta, in whose gardens the dancers gave a private performance, about leaving Jamison behind with him when the company departed.

Everything he saw and heard fascinated Alvin. He was intrigued to learn that the bumps he felt on one rural road were probably pythons, bounced over by the car transporting him to a reception. He was struck by the "unusual beauty" of the Congolese. "They manage to preserve a pride and a delicate gentility even in conditions of civil strife," he wrote in *Dance Magazine*. "There is a feeling of tension about the Congo which is ominous and, yet, somehow invigorating." And he had a warning for Americans: "The issue of colonialism is of extreme importance; I cannot stress this too much. It colors the Africans' outlook on almost all topics. For example, many people, hearing of racial strife in the United States, assumed that our country must be like South Africa, a nation of brutal apartheid. A few people thought that in the United States Negroes were chained to posts in the street. People kept asking us: What does it really mean? What's really happening in Newark and Detroit? What did the riots in Watts accomplish? . . . Cultural exchange can do much to clear up misunderstandings. And never suppose that the other great world powers are unaware of the effects exchange programs can have. Our engagement in Dar es Salaam overlapped that of a ballet troupe from Communist China. That was surely no coincidence."

There were long ovations at the end of many of the programs. The reviews were favorable, one of the most heartwarming by a critic in Accra. "Something breathtaking did come to town!" Togbi Yao wrote in the *Sunday Mirror* in a review titled "It Was a Sight to Live for a Life Time." "It was the Alvin Ailey dance troupe. For a suspenseful two and a half-hour 'age,' a ladder as it were, was thrown over the Atlantic (echoes of Jacob's dream ladder of the Old Testament), linking the people of Ghana to the people of the United States.

"It was a sight to live for a lifetime in memory! These Afro-Americans, our brothers and sisters of many generations removed, are our relations still. The dynamism and vitality which they have contributed to American culture comes as no surprise to us in Africa.

"This element of American culture strikes a common chord in the hearts of Africans. As ambassadors of goodwill, they are most welcome to Ghana. May the cultural exchange grow and flourish."

twenty

BUDGETS, BOARDS AND
TWO GOOD-BYES

A year of promising public gains, 1968 was a turning point for Alvin and for the company. The Alvin Ailey American Dance Theater was back in New York for its first performances there in four years, followed by a long American tour of the sort Edele Holtz had envisioned. Large grants from major foundations signaled a new acceptance of the company as a successful, businesslike arts institution to a degree beyond what Alvin had ever imagined. The White House beckoned. And the third of Alvin's unlikely muses entered his life.

There were gathering clouds in his private life, however, for Alvin was to lose the steady, loving support of the Holtzes, who left New York that year. Absorbed in the work of running his company, he had very little life of his own. And the lack of time to himself added to the pressures building within him. The assassination of Martin Luther King Jr. in April shook him more deeply, friends felt, than he let on. And it became increasingly clear to his closest friends that he could not live comfortably with success. Over the next decade, as he became one of the most important and beloved figures in American dance, a part of Alvin was engaged in a slow crawl into a dark and solitary place where he could exist on his own terms.

Looking back, he was to characterize 1968 as the year "we spent more than we had." But it started promisingly in mid-January with a three-month tour that took the dancers on a crisscross trek through forty-seven towns and cities along the East Coast, into the Midwest and on to the West Coast, where the company performed at seven university campuses in California in what was a triumphant homecoming for Alvin.

Performances in New York City on January 19 and 20 at Hunter College were also a jubilant return home. Only one of Alvin's dances—*Revelations*, of course—was presented. He had designed the program to show the company's full range of styles and to reestablish its reputation among city dance audiences. Talley Beatty was represented by *Congo Tango Palace* and Louis Johnson by *Lament*, with a taste of Lester Horton, still rare for New Yorkers, in *The Beloved*. *Metallics* and *Prodigal Prince* were also performed, and both were warmly received. Walter Terry wrote excitedly about the Holder ballet and its performers. Clive Barnes ranked the Beatty piece as an indisputable jazz-dance classic, but he once more sounded a cautionary note: "Without question this company, which has made its way triumphantly through Europe, deserves a properly extended, indeed a properly extensive New York season. Why are we so regardless of our own treasures? It is only a rather sad question."

The Ailey dancers wound their way through one-night stands in Massachusetts, Connecticut and New York State, moving on to Pennsylvania, Ohio, Indiana and Kansas before reaching California late in February. Alvin stayed behind for part of the tour, spending three lonely but productive weeks at the Wellington Hotel working out project proposals for the company and letting Truitte oversee the dancers.

Alvin was learning how to navigate the tricky waters of dance funding. He was hopeful, he wrote to Edele Holtz, that meetings he had attended at the Guggenheim Foundation might be productive. "We made a rather neat & concise proposal to them and the guy in charge (a Mr. Mathias) even had me to his office several times helping me to phrase the proposal and its figures properly," Alvin wrote.

"He also has on the walls of the room (where the deciding committee meets) an enormous exhibit of Jack Mitchell and Dominic photos of the company very very elegantly displayed. I have the very distinct feeling that I am going to get a fellowship from them in late March for about $10,000. This will of course be used for a company rehearsal period & for me to produce—repeat ME—to produce two—

count 'em <u>TWO</u>—new ballets in May and early June." One, he added, was to be about Malcolm X. "Don't shudder," he reassured Holtz. "It'll be non-violent."

He had also met with the Rockefeller Foundation about establishing a school. Alvin dreamed of buying a house in San Francisco and setting up a school there and a second home for the company, a novel concept then in dance, with a network of smaller residences in other cities in America. But for the moment, he wrote, his "rat race" continued.

Alvin had accepted an invitation to stage *Revelations* for Ballet Folklorico de Mexico in Mexico City for the 1968 Olympics, the only time he permitted the dance to be performed by a company other than his own. He returned for performances in late March and early April around Washington, D.C., and at the Brooklyn Academy of Music in New York. A European tour, Australian commissions and the Edinburgh Festival were in the offing for the summer.

On April 4, however, as the company was preparing for a performance in New Jersey, the terrible news came over the radio that King had been shot on the balcony of a motel in Memphis, Tennessee. "There is not a word that could describe the pall and devastating hush that fell over us," Truitte recalled. Alvin called Al Holtz, whom he knew to be a great admirer of the civil rights leader, to offer his condolences. Then he made his way back to New York as planned.

Watching the funeral services on television, Edele Holtz thought of calling Alvin to talk. "I rushed to the phone to call him," she remembers. "And then I put the phone down and I said to myself, 'Alvin's in Atlanta.' And he was. He had gotten back to New York, and in the airport discovered some people rushing onto a plane for Atlanta. He got on some way, in his lucky fashion. Everyone wanted to go." Once in Atlanta, unable to reach any friends who had flown down for the funeral, a travel-rumpled Alvin simply merged with the thousands of anonymous mourners, young and old, black and white, militant and pacifist. The tightly packed crowd wound through the sweltering streets of Atlanta behind the battered farm wagon on which King's mahogany coffin rested, along the four-mile route to the overflowing Ebenezer Baptist Church and on to the open-air memorial at Morehouse College. Then Alvin endured a long, dispirited wait for a flight back to New York late that night.

At home, at least, solid work was going on with the company. The minutes for a board meeting on April 30 suggest a somewhat greater degree of sophistication in the direction of what was now a senior American modern dance troupe. Alvin opened the meeting—which was attended also by Gil Shiva and four members of the haphazardly organized board, one of them the writer Anita Loos, a loyal fan of the company—with comments about the kind of school he wanted to create and how to raise money for it. There was discussion about moving into studios on Broadway at Eighty-first Street that had been occupied by the New York City Ballet and its School of American Ballet, a place where George Balanchine had choreographed some of his most famous works.

The perennial problem of recruiting new board members was addressed, and lists of affluent and influential possibilities, both black and white, were put together. How about contacting the editor of the *Amsterdam News* for additional names of prominent blacks? What about approaching corporations with an involvement in what the minutes described as "the Negro community, who have a high percentage of Negroes in their employ," for board members? Chock-Full-o'-Nuts, whose vice president was Jackie Robinson, might be a good start. There was talk, too, about bringing black audiences into the performances.

The most pressing concern was the need to raise $100,000 for the commissioning of much-needed new repertory and new music and for company expenses through its European summer tour. The money would pay for seven weeks of rehearsal before the tour and the preparation of six new pieces, two major and four smaller, as well as fees for choreographers, music and production personnel, and transportation on tour. It would also cover a deficit of about $45,000.

With a Broadway engagement on the horizon, late in the year at the Billy Rose Theater, a "preview" performance might be a good fund-raising event. The budget for the past year had been $250,000, almost all of it earned. As the fiscal year ended, the company was just breaking even.

Alvin had heard that he would receive a $12,000 fellowship from the Guggenheim Foundation. In May and June, he learned that the company would receive $10,000 from the National Endowment for the Arts and $5,000 from the Rockefeller Foundation. Never before had he had so much money to spend on his work.

Now, at last, free of some of the financial problems facing the company, he could return to the studio to create new pieces for his own dancers, the first in seven years. He also commissioned a dance from

Beatty and asked Lucas Hoving for his *Icarus*, a shimmering retelling of the myth with an almost oriental economy of means and stunning costumes. Some of the company's costumes and sets badly needed refurbishing.

Alvin flew into a flurry of activity, managing to overspend the grants without finishing his own projects. Suddenly it became obvious that the company was in serious financial trouble. Gil Shiva was managing the troupe's finances, but Alvin needed more administrative help. Truitte was an obvious candidate. The only problem was that he was still dancing.

Alvin had been thinking of asking Truitte, now in his mid-forties, to retire from the stage. He had written teasingly of his friend's aches and pains to Edele Holtz the year before. Truitte had, after all, been performing for a good two decades with one group or another, although his craggy, authoritative presence onstage still had a theatrical power that excited audiences in a way that no other Ailey dancer could quite match.

Friends had noticed that Alvin was not as close to Truitte as he had once been. The two had fewer long, friendly talks than in the past. Alvin approached Al Holtz and asked him to talk to Truitte about retiring, but Holtz refused, insisting that Alvin should do it himself, as a friend of so many years.

Truitte had had a presentiment that something was up when a close friend of his in California received a disturbing telephone message earlier in the year, from an unrecognizable voice, that "Jimmie should leave the company." And when he walked into the small office at Clark Center where contract negotiations were being held that May, Truitte looked at Alvin's face and sensed that something was wrong.

Had Alvin talked to him? Shiva asked, sitting behind a table next to a silent Alvin. Truitte said no. Then Shiva told him bluntly that his contract would not be renewed. "Oh, well, this is a hell of a way to tell me," Truitte said angrily, grabbing his things and pushing out the door through a group of waiting dancers.

Truitte remembered the conversation as lasting about seven minutes, a quick, relatively cool severance of an eight-year relationship. One dancer standing outside the door recalls screams and curses. Many, especially the older company members, were shaken. "If I had known Alvin was going to get Gil to do it, I would have done it myself," Al Holtz says. "Jimmie hated Gil. And Jimmie had committed himself to

Alvin. He was always sort of brotherly and fatherly with him. He knew Alvin was talented and could do the thing, so when push came to shove he would just shake his head and go along with it."

Truitte found teaching work elsewhere, going on to a busy and distinguished career as a teacher of the Horton technique. Looking back, he was philosophical about the way his enforced retirement was handled. Alvin simply could not handle unpleasant situations. "An eighth of an inch of confrontation and he'd be in the next state," he said ruefully many years later. "I thought about it for about two days and then I said to myself, 'Okay, it's over.' And little beknownst to anybody, and no one will believe me to this day, I was only going to dance another year anyway. There was life after Alvin Ailey. I wasn't going to slit my wrists." Truitte felt, mistakenly, that it was Shiva who had engineered the firing. He was polite but chill when Shiva called a few weeks later to ask Truitte if he would become company manager. Truitte declined.

He didn't see Alvin again for a long time. "I knew he had done what he thought he had to do. He was still my friend. When he decided to talk to me, he would. And it would be as if nothing had happened in the interim." Two years after their break, Truitte was approached by Jacqueline Moore Lathem, a graduate student doing her doctoral thesis on Alvin and on Arthur Mitchell. Alvin had given her several names, Lathem told Truitte, but had suggested that he would be the most objective. Soon after, the two met on East Fifty-ninth Street. For a moment Truitte didn't recognize Alvin, for he had lost a lot of weight. But Alvin cried out "Jimmie!" and hugged him as if nothing had ever come between them. They stood and talked, and Alvin asked when Truitte was coming to teach at the school he had opened nearby. Whenever you want me to, Truitte answered. And so he rejoined the Ailey family.

"That's how Alvin is. He was my dear friend. And he had his faults. He certainly had his good points. If it's friendship, if you can accept the good then you can accept the bad. And to this day, I still don't hold it against him. I can't. Life's too short."

The company went off on its fifth European tour without Truitte. There was a new crop of dancers and a new repertory that included a piece by Beatty called *Black Belt* and two Ailey novelties—a revival of *Knoxville: Summer of 1915* and a new work to be called *Quintet*—as soon as Alvin finished them. The tour went well. "Certainly this is one of the world's most beautiful cities," Alvin wrote the Holtzes from Dubrovnik in early August. "Sunny, ancient & charming & I believe we are the smash of the festival so far."

The reception was as good in the Netherlands this time around. "Well, so far the luck has been holding out," Alvin wrote the Holtzes with his usual mix of exuberance and foreboding. "As far as I can see this has been the most dangerous tempting of fate yet—so far we've made it—standing ovations for Black Belt—(new Talley) & Revelations—Love &—"

Critics were less enthusiastic. The English dance writer Nicholas Dromgoole wrote fastidiously about *Black Belt*, danced to an Ellington score, which presented an unsparing look at race relations in the United States. Its finale was a race riot. "At the end of the ballet the dancers wave lights at us and scream in a crescendo of sounds that they are going to murder every one of us," Dromgoole observed in the *Sunday Telegraph* of London, in a review of the premiere at the Edinburgh Festival. "The piece has ceased to be a dance work, even to be a dramatic one and becomes almost a public meeting, and a very didactic one at that."

It was an uncomfortable period for the Ailey troupe, necessarily a microcosm in many ways of the society it had sprung from and liable, therefore, to the same confusions over racial issues. For some in the company, as for many in the outside world, racial separatism had replaced the goal of integration by 1968. Alvin had always made it plain that his company existed in large part to provide work for black dancers. Although he had feelings of uneasiness and even anger toward the white world in which he lived, he believed in integrating his company. Linda Kent, who had joined the company just before the European tour, was an example of that policy. Alvin would probably have received more grants and more attention at the time, Kent suggests, if he had been opposed politically to hiring white dancers like her. But he was not about to make that distinction. Alvin could be cruel to friends. He could be sloppy about the details of running a dance company. But at heart he remained an idealist about social issues.

Some company members were unfriendly to the new recruit. Dancers are often unpopular when they join a company, and Kent had a firm sense from the start of who she was and what she wanted. She wondered if she sometimes felt unliked because of her race or the fact that she might be kicking higher than another dancer. "But I think we should all be put in the spot of being a minority. We take so frigging much for granted."

Kent's determination to make things work was tested sorely during rehearsals for *Black Belt*. As was his custom, Beatty had taught everyone the choreography and then chosen the dancers for each section. He used Kent in several places, including a riot scene where, dressed in a neat orange suit in a group of black women wearing fishnet tights, Kent tossed her long hair and joined in shouts of "We're going to burn you whitey." There were times in rehearsal, however, when Beatty announced, "All the women—not you," gesturing toward her. It was hard for Kent, a new and very young company member as well as white, not to feel excluded.

Alvin had taken her aside earlier to talk about the subject matter and setting of the piece and try to ease her into the difficulties of the situation. "The man was very giving," Kent said. She understood, however, that Alvin was committed to providing work for black dancers. She could find a place for herself somewhere and eventually did. Looking back, though, she felt she would have welcomed more directness from the two. "Alvin couldn't come out and tell you the bad stuff. He couldn't have told me he didn't want a white girl in a particular role."

It was not in general an easy time for the company, which had bad news when it reached London in September. The season there had suddenly fallen through because of the unavailability of an appropriate theater. The dancers could stay on to perform in a television special, Alvin wrote in a letter to the Holtzes, and he might still find a way to keep the company in London.

But the television project did not materialize. Without work, it was impossible to stay for five weeks until the time arrived to move on to the Israel Festival. When it became evident that no salaries or per diem payments were left "in the shoebox," as one dancer put it, and that they would have to live on their own in England until it was time to leave for Israel, many asked for their tickets home.

There was nothing to be done but cancel the company's appearance at the Israel Festival, for which Alvin was sued for breach of contract. The dancers dispersed. After a two-week idyll in Morocco, Alvin also headed home—to face another kind of wreckage.

Edele Holtz had accepted a job in New Orleans and would be leaving New York. Hard to believe or accept, her departure increased Alvin's sense of isolation. He had not kept in close touch with the performers who had danced in his first little group. He was becoming very much a company director to his current dancers, a relationship that would not have allowed for much soul-easing conversation even if Alvin had been a more open, forthcoming person. Without the Holtzes, he would be much more alone.

A rupture had already occurred earlier when, during a dinner together at a restaurant near Lincoln Center, Edele Holtz lectured Alvin about his thoughtless treatment of his dancers. "The Quakers say 'I have concern about thee' and then they proceed to tell you dreadful things," Holtz said, laughing wryly as she recalled the conversation and its effect on Alvin.

Two or three people, including Sidney Poitier, had stopped to say hello during their meal, which pleased Holtz. "Alvin was always surprised when that happened," she said. "And it often happened, because by that time he was pretty well known." But the evening ended less happily when Holtz hesitantly began to talk about Alvin's behavior with the dancers. "He wasn't a happy person, and he was kind of rough with them," Holtz recalled. "His first dancers could have said anything to him, but these couldn't. He'd yell at them in auditions and rehearsals because he couldn't say no or reprimand anyone. And it was building up, so I thought he should start thinking about it, and no one else was in a position to say that to him. But his feelings were really badly hurt and he made that clear, and so I felt bad and wished I'd kept my mouth shut. I went home and he went off to Africa. I didn't write, because he didn't write to me."

The silence ended suddenly and unexpectedly when Alvin called her Brooklyn office and asked if he might stop by. The two went out for a long walk, talking easily again although it had been six months since Holtz had heard from him. They walked all over the neighborhood, stopping for lunch and talk of the African tour. It was as if nothing had happened since their last conversation. Alvin had, Holtz could see, a great need for friends.

And now that the Holtzes were leaving, he refused to believe that they really intended to move out of New York. "Surely you can't be serious about New Orleans," Alvin wrote from Dubrovnik when he heard the news—then, a little plaintively from London, "Will I have to come to N.O. to see you?" In response, he received what must have been one of the most saddening letters of his life, in effect a farewell that was filled with love and concern not only for Alvin but for the world they shared, in a time of perilous change.

Yes, it was now certain that she and her husband were going to New Orleans, Holtz wrote to Alvin on August 11, 1968, two weeks before her move:

There were so many things we would have liked to have talked to you about these past two years but there was never time. I, especially, felt that much was happening that you were not completely aware of though surely on the college tour you must have seen the changes in American life that have taken place even in the last year.

The brute fact is that NYC is becoming—and has become—one of the most racially polarized cities in the country—certainly as far as social agencies are concerned. Because there is no united fund raising as in other cities, boards of directors of private agencies are all from the wealthy white structure in order to raise money. We have reverted to an awful colonialism where the wealthy white is now raising money for all black staffs and all black clientele. I must confess that that is why I was so disturbed at the board composition of AAADT—I thought here we go again—white wealth raising money for black causes. If I am part of a board I want to be part of the action.

Don't misunderstand. I am much in sympathy with the black nationalist movement—much more so than many of my black middle class friends. . . . It is time that the black community handles its own affairs. The isolation of black children terrifies me as well as the hate being engendered but the historical fact of all this "insularity" as you call it, is undeniable. . . .

Many of our friends will never be able to understand our moving south—and maybe we can be of no help here either but I don't think that I, at least, will feel as impotent as I do now.

She was not burning her bridges, Holtz assured Alvin, adding that she and her husband had been talking with Truitte and Hill about buying a house together in New York City. The four-page letter ended with typically practical housecleaning details. Holtz had put together a book of Alvin's dance photographs. "With your permission I will make a book of the duplicates and send to your mother—or maybe you would like to do it at xmas or some other time."

The two would continue their friendship long distance, mostly via unexpected telephone calls from Alvin, through the mid-1970s. But, although Al Holtz was on call to help out as needed during that time, the warm Clark Center family was disbanding. And Edele Holtz's involvement in Alvin's life—as indulgent in her much sparer way as his mother's attention all those years ago on walks through Texas woods—was something that Alvin would never again experience to quite that degree.

twenty-one

AN ANGER IN THE AIR

Edele Holtz had come into Alvin's life just as he needed unwavering emotional support and a home for his new little company. Before Holtz, Mickey Bord had appeared when Alvin needed a loving and admiring friend to help him with the scattered, endless chores of founding the company. Now, in the late fall of 1968, the third of Alvin's muses materialized in Ivy Clarke, who would serve as a feisty midwife in the company's final birth throes.

Alvin knew Clarke through her sister, Leu Camacho, who danced in *House of Flowers.* Clarke had a large and welcoming apartment far west on Forty-sixth Street that functioned as an informal hostel for black dancers, Alvin among them in the 1960s. When they could pay rent, they did. Otherwise, they kept the apartment clean, although Alvin was never very committed to such chores.

A tiny, stylish black woman with a habitually watchful air, Clarke was nineteen years older than Alvin, although she looked much younger and kept her age a secret. She served willingly as his confidante in the years he lived with her, listening to his talk about his mother, his lovers and his plans for his company. Clarke saw the depth of the churning emotions that lay under his shell of mostly easy amiability. She found it hard to accept some of those emotions and the ways Alvin acted on them. He was drinking too much, she felt, and was associating with street people, drug dealers and hustlers among them. And she watched, more than a little sadly, as he seemed to grow harder and less innocent with success.

Bord, still very much a part of the Ailey inner group, had known not to learn to work a sewing machine when she offered her help at Clark Center. But Clarke was an expert seamstress as well as a committed Ailey volunteer when Alvin pressed her into service as the company's unofficial wardrobe mistress in 1967. Bord loved Alvin, his dancers and the kind of heightened life they led, and considered it all an extension of her own life. Clarke loved Alvin, too, but in more intense and much more complicated ways that she never acknowledged in herself.

Like an elegant small herding dog nipping at the heels of a shambling crowd of sheep, Clarke browbeat costume designers and seamstresses into working at a professional level despite the minuscule and usually late pay they received. Although she had trained and worked as an X-ray technologist, she was also an avid traveler and signed on as an Ailey staff member without hesitation in exchange for free passage to Europe that year, soon proving her worth when she helped track down costumes and sets seized by customs for nonpayment of reentry taxes when the company returned to New York.

When Gil Shiva left in 1968, Clarke took over his work, learning as she went along to draw up contracts, deal with dancers and booking agents, and put together tours. She helped Alvin shape the company well into the crucial 1970s when the excitement of its astonishing accomplishments had worn off and the job was to keep the institutional momentum going. Clarke could be a martinet, and as such was frequently a buffer for Alvin. And she loved him and believed fiercely in his vision. "Alvin was the conduit through which I could work at building something for minorities. I wanted him to have control, black control. No blacks had control at that time. I wanted something to show people that it could be done. Because all these people said black people would never amount to anything. I wanted to show them that if you work hard at it, you can do anything. I don't care what the uniform is."

Clarke had a vision of company-run studios where youngsters could learn the recording business, film or choreography. She wanted to draw black children into the world of dance to see and touch and hear it firsthand. "Once when we were in Chicago, the black people wanted us to come down to the inner-city schools. I said positively not. Those kids never got out of the environment. They came to us, and Alvin was wonderful to them. And they said, 'Could we get on the stage?' 'Could we touch the curtain?' 'Could we touch Judith Jamison?' 'Could we be like her?' Of course they could. When they saw this massive stage, they wanted to do it."

Alvin shared Clarke's enthusiasm, and she loved the pleasure he took in the simplest pleasures of everyday living. "Alvin loved life. Anything that was in life he really loved. Animals. Colors. People. He was curious about things, about other people, what they did and how they did it. And he lived, even when he didn't have money."

There were times when she came close to despair about his habits, when the company's financial problems drove her to uncharacteristic tears over its needs and how to meet them. On occasion, she doled out money to Alvin from their joint business account only to see him squander it on food and milk for the stray cats that lived in the desolate surrounds of the train tracks near her apartment, or on a lavish gift to appease someone with whom he had quarreled.

Their work together got off to a shaky start. Alvin was living in a hotel at the time and asked Clarke if he could use her apartment as an office. She was willing, and even took calls for him in an offhanded sort of way.

One day the telephone rang and a rather plummy voice announced that it was calling from the White House. "Isn't that interesting," Clarke said tartly. "You've just reached the Black House." There was a brief pause, then the caller tried again. Clarke assumed it was a prank but promised to give Alvin the message. When she told him about the call, he roared with laughter. "But she was serious, Ivy," he told her. "President Johnson wants us to perform at the White House."

The occasion was a salute on November 21 to the National Council on the Arts, the federal umbrella agency for the National Endowments for the Arts and the Humanities. Alvin was able to round up only six members of the company to perform *Revelations*. George Faison ended up dancing the *Sinner Man* trio alone, and *I Want to Be Ready* had to be cut altogether. The dancers were flown to Washington, with Talley Beatty going along for the ride. Although the invitation was obviously an honor, Beatty never forgot his disappointment when the president passed by without a word as he sat alone in a White House corridor. A commemorative photograph of the occasion shows Alvin, who had had almost no time to rehearse the company, looking as if he wanted nothing more than to race for the nearest exit.

Surprisingly, the command performance did not help with fundraising, although people were happy to lend their prestige to company activities. "Please use my name as a sponsor of the Alvin Ailey Dance Group," Helen Hayes wrote to her friend Anita Loos. "I shall be most proud." The cream of society had turned out earlier that year for an open rehearsal of "the predominantly Negro Afro-modern ballet company," as the society columnist Suzy, hedging all bets, reported on June 19. And other black arts organizations had willingly shared their patron lists. Letter after letter from potential corporate contributors expressed unwillingness, however, to help underwrite a gala to be held for the company during its engagement in late January on Broadway at the Billy Rose Theater. The company's cause was not helped, perhaps, by the absence of a strong Ailey board and by Alvin's reputation for independence.

The Broadway season was only a week, which was bemoaned by reviewers who saw it as much too short a time, but it introduced mostly new audiences to first-rate professionals in newly refurbished ballets. Dance fans could find their way to theaters like the Hunter College Playhouse or even the Brooklyn Academy of Music, where, it had just been announced, the Ailey company would become one of three resident dance troupes, along with the Merce Cunningham Dance Company and young Eliot Feld's new American Ballet Company. But everybody knew their way to the glitteringly inescapable New York theater district. The houses were packed, and Alvin saved and treasured a sign that read "This Performance Sold Out" that someone had filched for him.

The Alvin Ailey American Dance Theater belonged on Broadway, several critics noted. "The material is so theatrical that some of it could be a part of a Broadway musical—a superior one, that is," Frances Herridge wrote in the *New York Post.*

Alvin's *Quintet* and Beatty's *Black Belt* were two of the most theatrical pieces. *Quintet*, a dance set to songs by Laura Nyro and danced by five Supremes look-alikes, had not appealed to English critics the fall before any more than had *Black Belt*. A. V. Coton, writing in the *Daily Telegraph* and *Morning Post* of London, approached the piece with particular—and comic—squeamishness, describing the women as "five very worldly wise ladies obviously of the Harlem entertainment milieu." Dressed exotically, he continued, "they celebrated in weird, luminous and occasionally tedious dancing, the banal sentiments of the accompanying music." The two dances also received mixed notices at the Billy Rose. But *Quintet*, although rarely performed in ensuing years, is in its way a small masterwork and one that differed significantly from other Ailey signature works before it.

Like *Blues Suite* and *Revelations*, *Quintet* was a suite of dances, and, like *Revelations*, it dealt at least superficially with a "black" subject. Like *Reflections in D*, the piece was an imaginative and sensitive reading of its score, and it offered yet more proof of Alvin's distinctive gift for blending serious choreography and themes with affectionate teasing of his characters. In the new piece, however, Alvin explored for the first time the private being behind a highly public face, a subject he would return to repeatedly.

Audiences of the time might have been forgiven for thinking the dance was a spoof. The five women in the piece did have a certain tawdry ridiculousness, dressed as they were in high heels, extravagant blond wigs and tight dresses. But their shedding of that public personna, their naked exposure, is stunningly abrupt and almost cruel in its completeness. Some saw a deeper level to the dance. "Alvin was a black man who grew up in this country and chose the most racist business," George Faison said. "The business of self-promotion, of making a statement, or suppressing who you really are. *Quintet* was all about that masking, taking off that veneer that allowed us to go to Europe, to be in cocktail parties, drinking champagne."

The look of the dance is simple. The five "singers" enter and stand, rocking to the music and gesturing in the manner of girl-group singers of the 1960s. With each new song, a woman is left alone onstage to grope her way through some private emptiness or sorrow as she dances to Nyro's haunted voice and lyrics. The staging is subtly effective, weaving the women through meetings and separations, as a group and individually, in ways that accustom the eye to slight dissymmetry so that the unobtrusive entrances and exits are simply a part of a seamless, shifting whole. Alvin works against the music at times, as when a dancer is motionless or moving very gradually to pushing, lapping rhythms. At times there is almost no dancing, per se, just a body stretched and stretching against the floor in yearning and despair.

Alvin had talked to the dancers about Nyro and about doing a piece about girl groups. He arrived at rehearsal fairly sure of what he wanted, gave his dancers some movement and then, as always, left them a certain amount of interpretive leeway. "He told me I was Marilyn Monroe," Michele Murray recalls. "That was my subtext. But not all of the women were suffering." Alvin's notes for *Quintet* suggest that he saw a degree of pathos in each of them, for he wrote of the "sad charm" of Murray and her character and compared another performer to "Billie Holiday—hard, hurt and bitter."

The balletic solo danced by Linda Kent, the least persuasive of the sections, was choreographed last on the day of the premiere. "That happened quite often," Kent said. "I have a theory: Alvin was so generous with time for other choreographers. He wanted young choreographers to have a venue, and old dances to be preserved. Generally the man had just two weeks to make a twenty- to thirty-minute dance."

The popularity of dances like *Quintet* on Broadway and the mere fact of their presentation there made it even more obvious that the company had outgrown Clark Center. Alvin jumped at the invitation to become a resident at the Brooklyn Academy, a handsome old opera house that had been turned into a theater, studio and office complex. It offered storage and rehearsal space, and regular seasons to begin that spring with the then-innovative concept of a shared subscription series, including performances by twelve modern dance companies in eighty works over three-and-a-half months at the Billy Rose Theater and the academy.

The contents of the Ailey offices at Clark Center were moved to the academy just before the dancers went off on a six-week national tour early in 1969. By the time the company returned, in April, it was clear that the move had been a mistake. There was too little room and only the performances were materializing. A promised school for needy neighborhood children was established only when Clarke went out to look for a place herself. The academy did provide money for one summer at a welcoming church down the block, found by Clarke and Wade Williams, yet another Ailey volunteer who had been swept inexorably onto the staff. Williams's cousin was the pastor of the nearby Hansen Place Central Methodist Church. Not long after the company's move to Brooklyn, four hundred children from working class and low-income homes around the academy were taking classes in ethnic, jazz and modern dance in the church basement.

The audiences proved to be small and relatively unenthusiastic, as they had been for most of the inaugural academy dance series, which ended in late April with the Ailey performances. Alvin had appeared before a small group of middle-class black Brooklynites in late February in an attempt to raise $30,000 for the company. A little defensively, he talked of a dance he planned to create—a work about Malcolm X was still on his mind, now to be three acts and created in collaboration with the painter Larry Rivers and the jazz composer and instrumentalist Charles Mingus—but only slightly under $4,000 was donated.

It was frustrating. "Everybody thinks I've got it made," Alvin told Ellen Cohn in an interview before that first season. "The foundations think so, my friends think so, even I thought so. But it's a fallacy, a big fallacy."

The setup at the theater troubled him. Why, for instance, should the academy send buses to Manhattan to lure audiences across the river? Why not go out into Brooklyn and bring back audiences from the largely minority areas of Bedford-Stuyvesant and Fort Greene? Why not establish an official school in a nearby church or settlement house?

Asked about the integrated "family" of the company, Alvin spoke of his vision with new eloquence, in words that would be quoted throughout his life. "I feel an obligation to use black dancers because there must be more opportunities for them but not because I'm a black choreographer talking to black people," Alvin told Cohn. " 'Revelations' comes from Negro spirituals and gospels. Its roots are in American Negro culture, which is part of the whole country's heritage. The dance speaks to everyone—to Yugoslavs, to Poles, to the Chinese. Otherwise it wouldn't work. . . .

"We talk too much of black art when we should be talking about art, just art. Black composers must be free to write rondos and fugues, not only protest songs. I use Ellington and I want to use more of his music, but it's music. I also want to use Amram. Again, *mu-sic.* James Baldwin probably wants to write 12th-century epistolary novels, but he can't because everyone wants him to be a spokesman. It's terrifying in this day and time to keep after the black community to support my company. What about my white dancers? Should the academy ask white businessmen to pay their salaries? . . .

"The modern dance has traditionally been down in the dirt. We've always said if it costs $50,000 for the ballet to get it on, the modern dance can do it for five. But we have to think differently. After every tour, I lose a few dancers. They're faithful, but they have to eat. I need the same dancers and I need them trained daily. I need Rouben Ter-Arutunian and the best young designers. I need Vivaldi and Mozart, and to have new scores commissioned. I need an orchestra and a conductor and a clean hall to rehearse in. I need. I want good things. I want to grow. Don't treat us like modern dancers, treat us like a dance company, like an artistic entity, treat us like something that's worthwhile, like something that's contributing to the culture of the country."

The Ailey dancers went back out on the road in May to continue their national tour of mostly one-night stands. By August, Alvin's mood had darkened again and he had become bitter over the disappointments of a year that had promised so much. Temperament and discord were in the air, too, and they erupted during a brief residency in Up-state New York.

The company still gathered regularly to air difficulties and differences of opinion or simply, as Sylvia Waters put it, "to tell Alvin how we felt, how we needed him to tell us what he was seeing, what we were doing." The dancers, she said, "all had very deep feelings about Alvin and the company." And he encouraged them to be outspoken. The meetings were generally impromptu, called by Alvin on the spur of the moment, and until union rules became a fact of life and the company grew too large, they tended to run on for hours like open-ended group therapy sessions.

One such meeting was called during a stop at Skidmore College in Saratoga Springs, New York, to talk about how the dancers could communicate with one another despite racial barriers, in a changing climate for black performers. "We were the last of a generation that could have seemed exotic to Europeans," Faison said. "The last of an elite group." But Alvin's increasingly bad temper did not make for constructive discussion.

The optimism of those struggling in the early 1960s to achieve racial equality in the United States had dulled by 1969 as the nation became increasingly polarized, affecting both Alvin and the dancers. A mood of pessimism had lodged in him. There seemed to be so few substantial gains in his own country. And if his own dancers couldn't get along together, who could?

Alvin's views on race were an eloquent model of the integrationist philosophy of the 1960s in America, and he continued to hold them through changing eras, but from time to time there would be flashes of emotions that were at once more complicated and simpler. In "Instructions: How to Play the Drums," jotted in a notebook that appears to be from the mid-1960s, Alvin wrote:

Be born in Africa
(even centuries ago)
Run free on the white sand of
the beach—
Laugh! Throw your black body
against the white sand—
Pick up a tiny stone—
Throw it out toward an island—
(a world you know is there
but cannot see—)

Wait and see if the waves
bring it back—(they do not)
Splash in the water like a
Black Fish—walk slowly
home thru the green leaves
Becoming emerald with nite—
Then—
　　Try to run away when they
come for you with whips &
guns & nets
　　Feel anguish & terror as they
lash you together with others of
your kind in a dark ships hold—
Sweat, get sick, vomit—
Become thin & weak &
your eyes yellow & empty—
No more sand
no trees—
only perpetual night in a
forest of malignant Black
Bodies—caged like sweaty
panthers in a cave without light—
Then—
Arrive & be sold
Stand on a block

Work

Do not speak your own language
Sing his songs—not yours
Do not dance—its bad they say—

wonder

think
going home to "<u>his</u>" Jesus—not Obatala

Go to Memphis, New Orleans, Atlanta

sing

blues

spirituals

Be jazz

and that is how to play drums

In this time that tested the most resolute racial equanimity, Alvin's private anguish was to spill over later that year when he heard the news of the shooting of Fred Hampton. Hampton, the Illinois chairman of the Black Panther Party, was shot and killed in his Chicago home with another Panther official in a predawn police raid in December 1969. "How can people just go into someone's house and kill them? What is this country about?" Alvin railed at his dancers. "How can you not be angry? How can you not be bitter? How can you expect to just—act like it never happened?" He was beside himself. "The same rage, although he didn't say it, was in *Blues Suite*," Waters observed. "But at least there was more hope there, perhaps."

Earlier that year, Alvin had begun work on a new piece that would prove to be among his most important dances. *Masekela Langage* was a brooding depiction of broken, weary lives lived in a dusty little roadside café. As with much of Alvin's work, it was also an evocation of its score, by Hugh Masekela, the South African trumpeter and composer. Many have seen the dance as an indictment of apartheid and its effects on black South Africans. But the piece could just as easily have been taking place in a shabby Dew Drop Inn in the American South, a vision of de facto apartheid that would soon be confirmed by the killing of Hampton. "Alvin masked the fact that he was talking about America," Faison said.

Work began on the piece at the American Dance Festival at Connecticut College in New London, where *Masekela Langage* received its premiere in August 1969. The air was hot and humid, generating a comparable heat among the dancers. Finally, the tension that had been building since Skidmore erupted into an explosion between Alvin and the even more volatile Faison, with the two nearly coming to blows at one rehearsal. As the argument escalated, Faison lost his temper completely and told Alvin that he wanted to leave the company. Alvin never listened to anybody, Faison said. He felt everything the company did was about him. He didn't believe that the dancers could think. The dancers had begun to feel like Alvin's doormats.

In the old days, Alvin might have arranged the fight to sharpen the dancers' performances in an angry new piece. But this fight was real, and it was vicious. Many of the dancers, male and female, cried. Dudley Williams, veteran that he was, looked on in amazement from the sidelines. They were getting paid, weren't they? he thought. What more did they want? In the end, Faison stayed on, although only for another year. And the premiere of *Masekela Langage* seethed with passion so strong you could almost smell acrid smoke in the comfortable, antiseptic college auditorium.

Alvin had been listening to Masekela's searing, soaring African-flavored jazz without any clear idea of the kind of dance he wanted to make. The composer thought of the music as songs of protest. The score made Alvin think of decay, and used-up people. He started work on the piece by calling the dancers into a dowdy dormitory lounge at the women's college and asking them to move to the music. They pushed the chairs back and danced as Alvin watched thoughtfully. Over the next few days, he took individuals and groups into the festival studios and started the formal choreographing of the dance.

In *Masekela Langage*, men and women sit vacantly, staring out into empty space. They stride and stumble, punching a jukebox that company manager William Hammond had hunted down at Alvin's request, finding it in a secondhand store in seedy downtown New London. An angry, tough woman rebuffs the men she has beckoned close. (So convincing was one later interpreter—or so present in the choreography was that original anger—that someone in the audience yelled out "Hit her back!" in a 1978 performance.) A man who might be a salesman, preacher or politician harangues the seated dancers. A dreamer reveals the despair underlying her fantasies. Another woman, comically strung-out, is interrupted in her jitters by a wounded man who tumbles hard through the café doors. He leaps and plunges like a wounded stag through agonizing death throes. But the men and women return to their chairs at the end, angrily gazing once more into a nonfuture.

Alvin captured the innate qualities of at least two of his dancers in the roles he gave them. Lithe, distant and almost casually sensual, Kelvin Rotardier was unparalleled as the snakelike speaker, with the tempestuous, fast-spinning Faison as the dying man. And once again, each dancer had a character to work with. One of the women had been inspired, he said, by a despondent neighbor in California. Another was modeled after a schoolteacher he had known. A third was drawn from Katherine Dunham although, as Alvin told the dancers, there was something of Dunham in all the women. "He said she was very angry, very very adamant and very passionate, and that she could motivate people," Waters said of the character.

Alvin was less helpful to Rotardier at first. Standing a little outside the storm in rehearsal, Rotardier pondered his character and decided he needed advice. "Who am I?" he asked in a quiet moment. "You're a son of a bitch," Alvin told him.

"I said to myself, 'Oh, okay,' " Rotardier recalled. "And I used that. I took it." He worked patiently on this mysterious character, trying to figure out and capture that quality in his performance, only to discover later that Alvin had not been talking about the role.

"You're so angry you could spit on these people," Alvin told Rotardier, talking seriously then about the character. "You're afraid of them. They're afraid of you. You are a worldly man in your mind. A man who has traveled. You are able to manipulate these people." Alvin compared the man to a politician, and Rotardier began to build the role on Adam Clayton Powell.

Like *Quintet*, the new dance had moments of startling stillness, its choreography an unself-conscious blending of everyday gesture with the jazz and modern dance technique that were the work's medium of physical expression. "He would have us pick up a chair and throw it back," Waters remembered. "He had us do this little walking—walking up and down—and I remember him saying that we had to work out the interaction between each other." Much to Faison's regret, Alvin threw out the dance's dramatic original ending, in which his voice on tape murmured eerily and repeatedly, "Thank you ladies and gentlemen, thank you very much." It was too reminiscent of the way John Butler had ended *Portrait of Billie*.

Even without that last moment, *Masekela Langage* was an emotionally draining dance. "It was one of the most intense things Alvin did, for everybody," Waters said. "I remember when you had just finished dancing it, you couldn't really talk to anyone and people couldn't talk to you."

The Ailey company finished 1969 with television dates in Hollywood, another national tour and performances, providentially, in December in Latin America, where the dancers could spend cold winter days in a warm climate. While they toured the United States, Alvin went to work choreographing a Broadway musical, *La Strada*, that was due to open in mid-December at the Lunt-Fontanne Theater.

Based on the Fellini movie classic, the musical told the story of the waiflike Gelsomina, assistant to the circus strongman Zampano, and their descent into violence and death. *La Strada* was the first Broadway musical directed by Alan Schneider, renowned for his directing of straight dramatic plays, and critics generally praised the acting and Schneider's fluid staging, as well as Alvin's choreography.

His elaborate notes, which chart every move, gesture and manipulation of a prop in the most minute detail, testify to the amount of painstaking work Alvin did on the musical, which starred a promising newcomer named Bernadette Peters as Gelsomina and Larry Kert, the original Tony in *West Side Story*, as Mario, the guileless trapeze performer who loves Gelsomina.

The musical's script was banal, however, as were its score and lyrics, the latter by Lionel Bart, whose only previous Broadway credit was *Oliver!* Still, Alvin's friends were excited. "If this is not to be the year of the Pucci at least let it be the year of the Kleins," Bord and Clarke teased in a giddy opening night telegram. But *La Strada* closed after only one performance.

twenty-two

CLIMBING

"This year of 1970 has been extraordinarily interesting for me from many points of view," Alvin wrote rather dutifully in a thick bound diary he began to keep in September. Few entries followed, however, for he and his company were in steadily increasing demand.

Money continued to be tight, but the company had its home at the Brooklyn Academy. Back there after a national tour early in 1970, Alvin had three weeks to create the three premieres he had promised for the academy's spring season. The American Ballet Theatre had invited him to choreograph a ballet, to be danced to a commissioned symphonic jazz score by Duke Ellington, for the company's summer engagement at the New York State Theater at Lincoln Center. And the State Department was planning a tour of the Soviet Union for the Ailey company, a dream of Alvin's ever since the Bolshoi Ballet dancers had been so moved by the company in Central Park in 1962. Such a tour would be a tremendous coup.

Alvin and his dancers were welcomed back to the academy as homecoming heroes. One of his premieres, *Streams*, was a success. Performed to a percussion score by the Czech composer Miloslav Kabelac, the group piece was cool with a slightly turbulent subtext, and suggested Alvin's renewed interest in abstraction and formalism, although the work's abstraction gave way toward the end in true Ailey fashion to a hint of male-female interaction and a muted plea for love.

Streams drew a revealing analysis of the best and worst tendencies in Alvin's choreography as a whole from Deborah Jowitt, critic for the *Village Voice*. "Ailey has always been an extremely stylish choreographer," she wrote in 1970, adding that his use of unison movement could be annoying. "For me, therefore, the finale of 'Streams' leaves an unpleasant taste—a sock-it-to-'em Broadway chorus that shamelessly wraps up the dance and bats it across the pit to make the crowd howl.

"The other thing Ailey does that can be good or bad depending on context has to do with rhythm. He seizes on the pulse of the music and drives it along in rich, spacious movement. This keeps you on the edge of your seat. But every now and then, you wish he'd use a little stillness for contrast, or be a little more strange with rhythm."

Jowitt praised a meditative solo for Consuelo Atlas and a slow section for entwining couples that filled the stage with "a soft, unhasty sensuality." Some sections were less exciting choreographically, she observed. "But even when Ailey isn't doing his best choreography, he always creates dancing—that is, he makes something that the dancers can tear away with, delighting you by their spirit and beauty."

With Truitte gone, Alvin had asked Dudley Williams and Judith Jamison to oversee the rehearsals as company ballet masters. Each had developed the habit of absorbing all that went on around them, and neither was cowed by Alvin's formidable charm or temper. Both continued to perform, and Williams had a large role in *Streams* that he remembered with special pleasure.

Alvin had wanted to do a piece that drew on the solid, theatrical technique of Martha Graham, which most of the Ailey dancers had studied. Money for costumes was short, so the new work was performed in simple gray tights and leotards. But the piece felt good to dance. "Good good good good movement," Williams said. "Sink-your-teeth-into movement, and on top of that, trying to say something." It had an all-star cast that included John Parks, a tall, lean dancer with a shaved head and an air of understated, passionate intensity, and the firebrand Miguel Godreau, who had returned to the fold.

Alvin was up to his old tricks, Williams recalled laughingly. "Miguel and I danced the scherzo together. We didn't like each other in those days. Alvin was plotting and planning against us constantly, like what Bill Louther and I went through." This time, however, his machinations were short-lived, for Williams suffered an injury just before he

was to dance in Alvin's new *Gymnopedies*, the second and last premiere
he was able to complete for the academy season.

Created for Williams, the solo was instead performed by Keith
Lee, a capable black dancer with the American Ballet Theatre. Continuing his exploration of Williams's gifts, Alvin had put together a suite of
three dances that were as dreamily idling as their Satie piano accompaniment, yet provocatively odd. Starting with meditative everyday movement, the piece then became balletic and finally floorbound.

Alvin placed the pianist onstage. Another "piano" ballet, Jerome
Robbins's *Dances at a Gathering*, had been an enormous hit for the
New York City Ballet the year before. Alvin may have had that in mind,
although *Gymnopedies*, with its intimate, almost casual atmosphere and
onstage pianist, was created well before the genre became a cliché.

His always theatrical sense of programming had sharpened over
the years. Programs must be exciting, of course, and must build as a
whole to become something more than the sum of the parts. Opening
dances must be light or even pretty and the closing piece dynamic, with
a "difficult" dance stuffed into the middle like a nourishing sandwich
filling. The academy repertory as a whole was well-balanced, too, showing off a variety of moods and styles that was greater than anything
offered by other companies performing in New York that season.

The dances and guest choreographers Alvin had chosen ranged
from the lyricism of *Poeme* by Pauline Koner to the spare and mysterious orientalisms of Lucas Hoving's *Icarus*, to the Afro-Caribbean flash
and theatricality of Geoffrey Holder's *Prodigal Prince*. The company included senior performers who would long be remembered for the dramatic nuance and distinctive personal qualities they brought to all that
they danced in what was seen in later years as a golden Ailey age.

Alvin himself recognized that. "All begins well & Blues is sensa-
tional & new & free with Kelvin in all those foreign places it has a
vitality that it has seldom had for a few years," Alvin wrote in his 1970
diary when Kelvin Rotardier replaced injured younger dancers on tour
in new roles in *Blues Suite*. "It almost all looks improvised. During it I
begin to feel sure of the old feeling."

From his long perspective, Clive Barnes saw a larger message in
that spring engagement. "Ailey is black and proud of it," Barnes wrote.
"But he understands that the African culture is as much part of American life as European culture. He is no black apostle of apartheid, and I
love him for it. Today his nonblack dancers can keep up in his company's idiom, which, for the most part, is Afro-American. As a result—

and I wouldn't stress this but rather take it as it comes—every performance he gives is the greatest lesson in race relations you are going to get in a month of Sundays."

It was—and continues to be—easier for many to accept black performers in "white" roles than whites playing black characters. The sight of Linda Kent as a "Bible-thumping, fanwagging black matron" in *Revelations* was initially unnerving, Barnes commented. But why the hell not, he asked himself rhetorically, if Cleavon Little could play Hamlet?

"Ailey is an equal opportunity employer in a field and at a time when equal opportunity is not that fashionable," Barnes wrote. "He shows guts as an administrator (for these whites are not at all comparable to your token black with a Harvard accent in the front office) and that same gutsy quality emerges in his choreography. It would be easier—more acceptable—for Ailey to form an all-Black company, for then, as the obvious black leader in American dance, guilty foundations would have to beat a path to his door. But Ailey goes the hard way of his conscience. It is a very old-fashioned kind of militancy and, I suspect, it brings in less cash, yet there is the individuality of genius here. Also, when Ailey, I think our black leader in American dance, demands such ethnic variety, and so successfully achieves this racial mix, can our 'white' companies afford to stand aside?" And Alvin, he continued, not only presented a racially integrated company but "also employs indiscriminately black and white choreographers."

The following Sunday, however, Barnes suddenly found himself contemplating the demise of the Ailey troupe. Alvin had announced that he was considering dissolving the company because of financial problems, effective at the close of the academy season. He and his dancers had been forced to tour interminably, he said, under terrible conditions and "a constantly worsening situation." He had explored every alternative before deciding to "quit while we are ahead and to leave the financially troubled dance scene to those who are stronger."

A bombshell, the announcement drew cries of anguish from critics and fans. Letters poured in. "It's a great loss of dance to the whole world and to the Black world of dance especially," a friend from California days wrote Alvin. "We have no company to brag on any more. No yardstick for the mediocre companies to strive to. All of us here are really saddened." The most succinct critical comment came from Joseph Gale, critic of the *Newark News*. "The death of the Alvin Ailey American Dance Theater would be a stain on the country's artistic conscience," Gale wrote.

The dancers were horrified. What was so different about the present situation? they asked Alvin. They'd rehearsed before for no pay. What was so different now? The difference, Alvin told them, was that he had come to the point where he couldn't ask them to do that anymore. If he did, nothing would ever change. So perhaps it was time for him to do something else. But what about us? the dancers asked.

Looking back, Sylvia Waters felt that a good part of Alvin's motivation was sheer exhaustion. "He said to us, 'You don't realize. Since 1958, I've been trying to put this thing together. Here it is, 1970, and here I still am.' "

Alvin was increasingly angry about the situation at the academy. A comparatively late arriver, his company had to carve out the promised office, storage and rehearsal room from space already taken up by the companies of Merce Cunningham and Eliot Feld. The promised school had still not materialized.

The ornate old academy was a huge step up in prestige from the small, often poorly equipped theaters in which the company frequently performed on tour and in New York City. But Alvin had had a taste of Broadway and success at the Billy Rose the year before. He was disappointed, too, that the academy audience continued to be small and unrepresentative of the theater's Brooklyn constituency, although the company had been invited to become a resident in part to reach out to black theatergoers and generally broaden the academy's audience in the borough.

"We were just trying to get it going," Harvey Lichtenstein, director of the academy, recalled. "They were hard years. The thing we wanted to give Alvin was performance space, and we tried to help them raise money from the community. We did more with the other companies, for no particular reason." Lichtenstein, a former dancer sympathetic to the struggles of dance companies, remembers having many talks with Alvin, pacing up and down the long dim corridors upstairs at the academy. "He really felt the need to be in Manhattan. So he pulled away. But I had heart-to-heart talks with Alvin."

There was more on Alvin's mind than a move to Manhattan, for he was involved in a complicated larger game. Although he resisted the restrictions placed on him by his increasing fame and the demands of running a company, he was politically astute and growing more canny with each success. At the request of the State Department, he had kept the company's schedule clear for the proposed Soviet tour, which had been under discussion on and off since 1965. Suddenly, however, he was told that the tour was off. Buoyed by critical acclaim for the 1970 Brooklyn season, Alvin and his dancers faced a year without any significant employment. It was the last straw. Alvin threw down the threat of closing like a gauntlet.

William Hammond recalls Alvin speculating that if he could embarrass the State Department into reinstating the tour, the company could keep going until a possible Broadway season. The tour abruptly materialized again, although it was postponed until the fall. To fill the gap, the State Department offered a July tour of North Africa to keep the Ailey dancers working and even provided money for two weeks of rehearsal. The company was back in business.

There had never been a question of Alvin being without work. He traveled back and forth now between Brooklyn and Manhattan, dividing his time between his company and the cast of *The River*. Scheduled for the American Ballet Theatre's opening night at the State Theater, the premiere was eventually postponed to June 25, less than a week before his own company's departure for North Africa.

The creation of the ballet was a nerve-wracking business. Unfinished, the piece was presented as a work-in-progress, but since *The River* was a plotless suite of dances, Alvin easily added two of the promised sections to the original six for Ballet Theatre's 1971 New York season.

Although flattered when Lucia Chase, the ballet troupe's indomitable director, had approached him about choreographing an Ellington ballet for the company's thirtieth anniversary, Alvin had approached the project with misgivings that deepened as the premiere date drew closer. He wanted to explore the classical idiom in *The River*, putting the ballerinas on toe and giving them ballet steps, although in the end the overall group configurations reminded some of *Revelations*. (He was convincing enough in the idiom, however, that Herbert Ross asked for a solo from *The River* for his movie *The Turning Point* to suggest a plum assignment for Emilia, the young ballerina on the rise in the film. Amusingly, the character who choreographs the ballet is played as an arrogant, very un-Alvinish sort of avant-gardist.)

Alvin was not slowed by having to work in the unfamiliar classical ballet vocabulary and style, for Jamison was on hand much of the time to translate. "I want something like this," he would tell the dancers. "Then Judy would get into point shoes and demonstrate," Cynthia Gregory, who danced the *Lake* duet, recalled. "So you got it from both. From him, the feeling. She would solidify it. I think he was maybe a little afraid because it was on point."

Alvin teasingly nicknamed the *Lake* section "Hungarian Jazz" in honor of Ivan Nagy, Gregory's Hungarian partner. An elegant classicist, Nagy was not, as Gregory puts it, "the jazziest person in the world." But both dancers laughed as they worked. "All I remember is having a good time," Gregory said. "You never felt the pressure you felt from other choreographers. And Alvin never kept you waiting while he pondered. Basically, he was pretty fast. I think he had a general idea of what he wanted."

Alvin's notes and drawings for the ballet suggest that he was full of visionary ideas for the new piece, although many remained unused. Working through *Spring*, the opening group section of *The River*, Alvin wrote first of the image of "a magnet offstage <u>RIGHT</u>. Being drawn into life . . . into the future reaching always up & out carried on shoulders—girls frightened—sheltered by men." "Young people of U.S.A. moving toward a new freedom," he added.

None of this is evident in the finished *Spring* dance. In later notes Alvin writes of *Spring* more recognizably as "<u>linear</u> & light. . . . MALES Image of leading—seeking out—fluttery beats of legs in lift carry crossing statement. 1st arabesque & pull away toward line of direction. Sporadic lifts from cluster."

His first musings on what became the quick-darting *Meander* section are surprising, given the unemotional, almost abstract nature of that dance. "A woman torn between two equally possessive loves," he writes, "a gallant gentleman—a rough young poet—Her movements show her consternation. Arms frustrated around her smooth bourrees. Cavalier looks as if wooing her, helping her. Young man walks demandingly—beside with rough arms."

For the most part, Alvin could not help but imbue the most abstract of movements with drama and emotion. It takes very little to create a sense of dramatic incident on a dance stage. The placing of a single dancer on an empty stage makes a world of the space around that body. A relationship is suggested the moment a second dancer enters. And just the presence of a few bodies, motionless, even, in empty space, suggests incident. "<u>Important</u>," he observes. "The choreographer as storyteller, story inventor as ideas invented . . . as people created situations created."

Much as he had for his first little company, Alvin even planned for the distribution of "nosegays for girls from me, small roses for boys, individual cards" for the Ballet Theatre dancers who performed his piece. (His own dancers now often found gifts of small plants in their dressing rooms on nights they had danced premieres as well, sometimes, as the carefully chosen trinkets that he loved to give to them.)

Clearly, he was approaching this all-important commission for a world-class ballet troupe with as much equanimity as he was ever able to summon. The problem was not with Alvin but, once again, with a composer. Alvin had been moved by Ellington's ideas for a ballet about water and the life cycle in their early discussions of the piece. The composer had played him some beautiful music he was thinking of for *The River*. But the rest of the forty-four-minute score was late and arrived in pieces, sometimes brought to the sixth floor studios at City Center by Ellington himself to the delight of the dancers and a nervously watchful Chase, who was growing worried that *The River* would never be completed. "Ah, we have a few more bars here," Alvin would slyly announce to the dancers after such a visit. "Let's go on."

He had worked out several sections with Jamison and Godreau before arriving at Ballet Theatre, but there was a point beyond which he could not go without the music. He and the confused ballet stage manager were thrown into a panic as Ellington nonchalantly sent along pages of music nearly up to performance time. When Alvin was finally ready to walk out on the project, he threw open the studio door in a rage and was confronted with a smiling Ellington, who handed him a tape of the completed score. What was Alvin carrying on about? That was how he always composed.

The tension got to the dancers, too, and many expected the ballet to be a fiasco. It was one thing to tell his own dancers just to get out onstage and give a piece their own personal touch, but quite another to expect that level of invention from performers who were unfamiliar with his style and ways of choreographing.

Dennis Nahat remembers with amusement the creation of the famous solo in the *Riba* section of *The River*. His role had not been completed by the premiere night, and Alvin told Nahat, who had started to choreograph the year before, just to get out on the vast stage and do something. To his horror, Nahat watched the others bounce out into the wings when their choreography was done. He waved bravely as they left, and then discovered that, alone onstage, he was being followed by the spotlight. He sashayed slowly to the back, trying to fill up the endless-seeming music with dance that might look as if Alvin had made it. At last Nahat was up against the backdrop with the spotlight breathing down his neck. He turned to wave it away just as his music was ending, with an irritability that came across as comic insouciance. And the solo was over.

The River was an enormous and immediate popular and critical success. Balletomanes got to see their favorite dancers let down their hair. Critics had the opportunity to write poetically of the ceaseless, easy flow of rivers and this one in particular. And Alvin could be proud that he had successfully bridged the gap between ballet and modern dance, although as usual he disappeared quickly after the curtain fell on the first performance.

Several choreographic passages were Ailey at his most accomplished. The wistful closing section, *Two Cities*, is one of his most hauntingly beautiful and simple duets, a dance for a man and a woman who remain apart in their separate spotlighted worlds, the woman's back arching like the deep curve of bow without its communicating arrow.

On June 29, Alvin and the dancers took off for a five-week tour through eight cities in Algeria, Tunisia and Morocco. Their audiences this time were large and enthusiastic and included Alvin's stepfather, Fred Cooper, whom he had invited along on the tour. Happy, although silent, and never without his camera, Cooper tumbled into an entirely new world. He and Alvin didn't talk much. The tour was difficult, taking the company into all kinds of backwoods towns and makeshift theaters. Pleased and touched by the invitation, Cooper seemed content to travel as a tourist with his stepson's exotic colleagues.

Alvin's escalating fame had enabled him to step back a little from his complicated relationship with his mother, dealing with her for the most part with the faintest hint of noblesse oblige and getting away with it because of her pride in his accomplishments. That fame also enabled him to be more generous with the gentle, inoffensive Cooper. Some of his friends saw Alvin's invitation as a loving gesture. A few, more cynical, felt it was his way of saying to his stepfather, I'm something. Here I am. I'm important.

Ivy Clarke had stayed behind in New York to work on company business and soon faced a terrible decision. A young dance impresario named Charles Reinhart, later the director of the American Dance Festival, had been involved in the Billy Rose season the year before. Excited by the Ailey dancers and repertory and by their tremendous success at the Billy Rose, Reinhart invited the company to perform in another Broadway season, this time presented by City Center at the ANTA Theatre. If the company accepted his offer, however, it would be forced to give up the academy, which had exclusive New York rights to its resident troupes.

Clarke was as disappointed as Alvin in the way the Brooklyn residency had turned out, and she had begun to dread her trips to and from Brooklyn two and three times a day. She was eager to accept Reinhart's invitation, but first she would have to talk it over with Alvin in North Africa.

It was difficult to get through by telephone to Morocco, where the company was performing at the time, and Alvin sounded strange to Clarke when she finally reached him. "He didn't make any sense at all," she remembered. "Whatever it was, he seemed to be strung out." Unable to obtain a clear decision from Alvin, Clarke consulted a theater friend, who urged her to accept Reinhart's invitation. So she did, knowing that it would mean the company would lose its base at the academy. "But when Alvin came back I thought he was going to beat me to a pulp. We had no place to put anything. I told him I was sorry I had accepted it if he didn't want it."

The break between the Ailey company and the academy was formally announced the following month, in July. Clarke had made the only decision that might eventually lead to an invitation to City Center, an important theater for dance, a longtime dream she had shared with Alvin. But they would be homeless for a time. The days of transporting scenery and costumes in Mickey Bord's convertible, now with the accumulations of twelve years of performing, had returned. Louise Roberts, director of Clark Center, agreed to give the company space until a new headquarters could be found. Alvin was crushed.

"He hated going back," Clarke said. "He told me that it emasculated him." For a long time Alvin refused to go upstairs to the little room where the company had settled in. He had loving and grateful memories of the YWCA and did not hesitate to speak out in support of it when asked. The company still gathered there to board the buses that would take them out on tour. But much had changed. There had been so much growth, and so much effort, since those early days.

Clarke ignored Alvin, and she and her secretary, Mary Colquhoun, went to work sprucing up the space, painting it in theatrical colors. It became a cozy, happy center of operations, but Alvin insisted on meeting people downstairs or somewhere else entirely. Finally the two women refused to fill out any more grant applications with him in coffee shops and on the street. He straggled upstairs, an angry, stubborn child of thirty-nine. "His eyes got big as a saucer," Clarke said. "He couldn't believe how professional it looked. And after a while he wasn't ashamed to come back. He never really felt okay about being back there, but he felt we were doing something meaningful. It was only temporary. I told him we were not going to stay there. And we didn't."

A few months later, Clarke heard that the Graham dancer and choreographer Pearl Lang had found space on East Fifty-ninth Street between Second and Third Avenues in a building owned by the All Saints Church and once used as a settlement house. Lang and her dancers moved into the ground floor, but the two floors above were empty and could be used for rehearsals and classes. The only renovation required was the installation of a new floor in the third-floor gymnasium and the clearing of second-floor debris that included old iron cribs from the time the church ran a nursery for babies born out of wedlock. The Rockefeller Fund provided $37,000 for the work, and the two floors were soon filled with the hubbub of rehearsing and auditions.

To add to the tumult, the company was busily preparing for the Soviet tour, the first visit of a major American modern dance company to the land that had given birth to *Swan Lake* and other ballet classics, a country that cherished its ballet traditions and turned away, at least officially, from the new.

"Today at 5 PM the company gathered at the YWCA—at Clark Center at 51st Street and Eighth Avenue—our former home," Alvin wrote on September 21, 1970, in a detailed journal he would keep through most of the Russian tour. An attempt, clearly, to record this latest adventure for possible publication, the diary is written in a somewhat more self-conscious and less vivid style than Alvin's notes on the first tour, in 1962. But the pages are crammed with heartfelt comments on failed stage equipment in the Soviet theaters, frequently dreary and inadequate food, and dancers' injuries and rebellions. Everyone was in a fairly constant state of edgy anticipation and nervousness throughout the tour.

For one dancer, the terrible pressures and hardships gave new meaning to an Ailey classic. "It was the *blues*," Jamison would later write. "It was what the blues were about. You think we didn't know how to dance 'Blues Suite' after all the things we went through? It was as if we were being treated like a bunch of cattle. Alvin was very upset about that. Within the company, there were little explosions of personality at being treated like third-class citizens. Alvin took the brunt of it all."

No longer performing, Alvin was less directly involved with the unhappiness than he had been in the company's equally difficult first tours. So much had changed. "In 1963 we had met Ben Jones here at the YWCA, gotten in his station wagon (along with the costumes & scenery (our stools, ladders, fans for Revelations and Blues)—then we were 6," Alvin wrote in his Russian journal. "Now in 1970 we were 16 dancers and 8 technicians with 4000 pounds of cargo. The years have really gone—we have travelled so much, seen so much, heard much applause, danced before thousands of people on many many tours at home and abroad and here we were again—but this time enroute to the Soviet Union—fearful, anxious."

Huddling in the YWCA lobby that September afternoon, Alvin worked feverishly with Reinhart and Meg Gordean, the company publicist, remaking the schedule for the upcoming ANTA season just moments before the bus to the airport pulled away from the curb. Onboard, he scrutinized the faces he was to come to know almost too well during the arduous adventure ahead. "Brother John, Judy, Miguel," he wrote, carefully delineating his cast of characters, "Dudley. Kelvin (beautiful faithful Kelvin—the longest standing member of the company. A real friend. A devoted dancer. Kelvin who had met at the YWCA so many times before. My age but still dancing beautifully. Thin, elegant, calm. A rock in a sometimes troubled sea. (Or should I say always troubled sea?) Dudley who complains so much. Such a prima in certain ways—but he too in his way a rock—a pillar of the company—he too had almost always been there. . . . Ghosts survive around departing from the YWCA. Minnie Marshall—beautiful black tall—now gone. In the same year as Langston. Thelma Hill (grown too fat to be lifted). James Truitte (a long story but gone since 1967). How many more!—a who's who of black dance ghosts.

"Ivy Clarke—our administrator since 1968 when she took over out of exigency. In a new Afro wig & looking very chic. Good friend in addition to being administrator. Indispensable in the life of the company."

There was a layover in Copenhagen—"Erik Bruhn territory!" Alvin noted—and then on to Russia. "I feel we are on the threshold of a great adventure," he wrote, "not only artistically but personally." He scrutinized passengers who looked Russian, searching for glimpses of what might await the company. "Are they serious people? Or is there laughter under the rather rigid look? It is a look of experience. Or is it age? And what of the young Russians? Are they hippies? What kind of music do they dig? do they boogaloo? are they a groove—or self-serious? What do they really know of what is going on in the USA—or for that matter what do we know of their life-style? Thoughts. Behavior. We shall see."

The first land he sighted beneath the plane looked disappointingly like New Jersey, and the terminal in Moscow reminded him of ones he had seen in Milwaukee and Omaha—"simple, clean, not elaborate." Volodya, the young Soviet tour guide who met the company at the airport, reminded Alvin of Frank Eng all those years ago in Los Angeles. There was also a "Mr. Bougaslavsky(?)," a representative from the Soviet Gosconcert producing agency, whom Alvin was soon referring to in his diary as "Mr. Boogaloo." Volodya quickly became "the snake," and the two Intourist guides, both named Natasha, were the "Bolshoi sisters."

Alvin was intrigued by the omnipresence of blond, often buxom women as maids, concierges and guides. He had been reading John Steinbeck's Russian journals in preparation for the trip and was disappointed that the country looked so different from what Steinbeck had reported. Despite his exhaustion after the long trip, however, he found the streets, the hotels, the interiors of the planes, cars and buses, endlessly absorbing.

The company opened in the Soviet Union on September 24, in a small city called Zaporoche, where the lights and sound failed and the dancers took two or three bows to merely polite applause. "This has been a bad performance," Alvin wrote. "The worst! The worst in spirit I have ever experienced." The technical problems were unavoidable, he soon realized. He promised himself he would begin to train his own technicians from now on, in the Horton way. "I have a feeling that I am going to be Lester Horton's most famous offspring," he continued. "I would be very proud of that."

The technical problems continued. Tempers grew frayed, and audience and critical response was measured. The company turned to Miguel Godreau's tapes of American rock groups for a soothing dose of home, and Alvin found solace in a Mae West tape belonging to Dudley Williams, listened to in Williams's hotel room over a quick glass of Scotch as he attempted to relax after one particularly difficult performance. He was relieved to discover that the very good folk dance companies he had seen performing in Zaporoche at the same time were the cream of the nation and not routine competition. One less thing to dread. "I have the feeling," he wrote, "that in this tour I will get to know myself much better as a person & as a choreographer."

In each city, Soviet dancers showed up at the rehearsal studios to watch the Ailey dancers take their daily class. Once again, as in the earlier tours, Alvin was saddened by how much more he felt could have been exchanged with foreign dancers. There were passionate discussions about the respective virtues of ballet and modern dance. "We do those things in bed," one amused ballerina said of a steamy duet in the Ailey repertory. Increasingly, however, there were encounters with ordinary Russians that warmed Alvin's heart.

He had arrived prepared with gifts of American music tapes and dance books for Russian artists and enthusiastically handed them out early in the tour, depleting his stock well before the company reached its major stops in Moscow and Leningrad. In return, Alvin and the dancers were given Russian dance books and small personal gifts like a cufflink or a medal. In one hotel, a restaurant pianist performed a piece of music he had composed on the spot called "Alvin's Song."

Other experiences were not as pleasant. Audiences were kept away from the dancers outside the theater after performances, sometimes brutally. A young man who talked in halting English to Alvin about American jazz during one intermission had disappeared by the program's end. A woman who followed the company to its next tour stop was gone by morning.

"The women—just as black women were—are able to communicate more with us than the men. The men are reserved (because if they make a mistake their families can be hurt?) but the women open up to us & really communicate as they can. The men are all cautious, stern, reserved." In vain, Alvin and the dancers protested to the tour guides.

Some fans did manage to talk to the dancers without harm, watching and waiting for their chance. Two students approached Alvin one night in Donetsk, the second stop on the tour and an industrial city that had long been closed to outsiders, and offered him an old card, postmarked 1915. "They want to meet & drink with us & talk about friendship," Alvin wrote in his journal. "After the evening performance groups of young men wait in the dark for us across the street— to look at us—and only approach after a long interval. One comes to have his program signed and then another and finally all. It is difficult to tell whether they have been told to stay away from us or whether they are shy because they do not speak English or what."

Alvin began to have chaotic nightmares, brought on, he conjectured, by Russian vodka. In one, Martha Graham died and a friend of Alvin's became president of the United States and might thus be able, Alvin dreamed, to be of considerable help to the Ailey company. His waking hours tended to be nearly as disturbing. He worried that the white dancers had started to band together in a clique. "We Americans are all colors & are working together," Alvin wrote. "We must, or we will destroy ourselves."

Sightseeing was not much of a respite in the smaller cities. Proudly conducted tours frequently consisted of stops at factories and housing complexes. In one town, the company was shown a six-hundred-year-old tree and heard a rote recitation by local children of the tree's history. It was getting hard, Alvin noted, to continue smiling.

The Russian audiences began to have clear preferences in the repertory. The grim subject matter of *Masekela Langage* might have been expected to fit very neatly into Soviet propaganda about black lives in the United States. But the piece was not a favorite, Alvin was sorry to see. Unsurprisingly, the Russians were no different from audiences around the world in their delight in spirit-lifting dramatic modern dance. But *Masekela Langage* needed to be seen, Alvin believed, and he refused to drop it, fighting hardest to keep the piece in the repertory in the relatively cosmopolitan Moscow.

By the time they reached Donetsk, the dancers had discovered the spirit-reviving properties of vodka. An equally warming sensation began to well up more dependably from the Soviet audiences. Alvin's sense of humor returned. "The deputy director makes one of those peace & friendship speeches & I respond with one of mine," he wrote of a visit to one local dance school. "Something about our countries being more alike than different. . . . Profuse goodbyes & back-slapping."

The theater sold out in Kiev. The Ailey dancers were the toast of the town in Voroshilovgrad, where the audience gathered shyly beside the company bus after one performance, mutely staring up at the dancers until Williams leaned out. Bits of paper and even a package of cigarettes were suddenly proffered for autographing. The walls fell. The dancers left the city with rhythmic closing-night changes of "Al-vin Ai-ley" ringing in their ears. And then came Moscow, or the Big Cabbage, as the nervous dancers began to call the city as that all-important opening night approached.

Everyone in the company had a cold, it seemed. Several dancers had painful injuries. The opening night performance did not go all that well, Alvin thought, but the response was everything that he and his dancers could have dreamed of.

"Thursday—The day we conquered Moscow!" Alvin exulted in a scrawled entry that races along for thirteen pages. "I am writing this on

Saturday morning in my hotel room in Moscow & let me say first that I would never have believed what happened at the end of the 1st Moscow performance—our reception was like Germany with at least 20 minutes of applause & the audience coming down to shake hands with us! Fantastic! A success the likes of which people say they have never seen in this city! and it seemed all very genuine. We took at least 20 curtain calls then went in front of the curtain innumerable times, applauded the audience & then with our repertoire of bows exhausted shook the hands of the audience from the edge of the stage. The dancers nor anyone backstage could quite believe it had happened. We are a great great success in Moscow!" American dignitaries, Alvin noted happily, had also been present. "It was indeed one of the finest receptions we ever received anywhere & on opening night in Moscow. We shall see what the history books write of this evening."

Tickets for the Ailey engagement suddenly became scarce, but the company performed on Moscow television to even larger audiences. People calling out "vodka" as a universally understandable cry of "thank you" began to follow the dancers down the streets. "I am having a hell of a time keeping this journal up—tiredness, anxiousness, too much to drink—too much to put down—etc etc," Alvin wrote.

His jottings grew even sparser as the company moved on to Leningrad for the final performances of the tour. The food was terrible, he noted. The architecture and the city were of overwhelming beauty. And the performances? The response to them was recorded in American newspapers, which spread the news back home that on closing night a determined overflow of young people without tickets were allowed to pack the theater's aisles. Shouts of "thank you" and "come back" rang through the air at the final bows. No one would leave the theater. Alvin climbed down into the orchestra pit and signed programs, calendars and even arms held out to him.

He had hoped to ride the wave of enthusiasm on to Europe after the Russian tour. That seemed unlikely, but seasons in Paris and London did materialize piecemeal, arranged from the Soviet Union by a nervous but determined Clarke, who had never before engaged in such international wheeling and dealing. In Paris, where the company performed at an international dance summit at the Théâtre des Champs Élysées, Alvin was awarded the festival's prestigious Étoile d'Or for best modern dance group and choreography.

The company traveled on to London. The fee there was to be a percent of the box office receipts, and the two-week engagement was an ambitious one. Clarke was frightened. But the season, the troupe's first there in five years, was a success, and the company earned a munificent $8,000. Clarke hurried to Alvin with the check tucked safely under her arm.

There would be more—and greater—successes through the coming year. *The River* was one of Ballet Theatre's biggest hits in Europe, and the company decided to present it during its winter season at City Center. Alvin would choreograph *Cry*, the dance of his that came closest to rivaling *Revelations* in popularity. But in this triumphant moment, standing close to Alvin in a London street with a huge check for a season she had booked, Clarke felt as happily companionable and as close as she would ever feel to this burly, exasperating genius.

twenty-three

FAMILY MATTERS

The wisdom of leaving the safety of the Brooklyn Academy of Music for another season on Broadway was proved the night the company opened at the ANTA Theater, on January 18, 1971, the first of nine modern dance and ballet companies to perform in the two-month City Center American Dance Marathon. Alvin had come up with the requisite premiere, *Flowers*, in which he took another look at the soul-killing demands of fame. The company classics were popular. But in the end it was the dancers' season. Fresh from their tour of the Soviet Union and cosseted by affectionate European audiences, they seemed to glow with new assurance and pride. On opening night, the audience responded in kind, cheering the dancers through bow after bow.

The company performed on television on NBC's *Today* show during the first week of the ANTA season. "The next night the lobby was so full of people I couldn't get in," Ivy Clarke recalled. "Leonard Bernstein was there, the Beautiful People were there, *people* were there. At the end of the performance they were all screaming. By Monday of the second week there wasn't a ticket left. Nothing. I couldn't believe it. I couldn't believe it."

The Ailey company was finally off and running at home. Four days after the close of the ANTA engagement, it embarked on a two-month national tour, followed by a spring season at City Center and then another national tour that ended with a return to New York in August after performances in Bermuda. In September, the company became the first modern dance troupe to perform at the new Kennedy Center for the Performing Arts in Washington, D.C., when it appeared in October in Leonard Bernstein's *Mass.*

Then the dancers returned to City Center for two weeks, establishing a pattern of twice-yearly seasons at the theater that was to last twelve years and create a considerable burden for Alvin, who was expected to contribute at least one premiere per season. Now there was work in New York City, and, increasingly, touring filled most of the months between. Six months out of every year on the road did not do much, Alvin commented in later years, for one's personal relationships.

The longer and more continuous performance schedule and more efficiently organized tours were accompanied by a sense of greater stability within the company. Alvin's fascination with the classical ballet idiom was increasing, as was his interest in exploring it as a choreographic style. To the disgust of some in the company who saw ballet as a rarefied white art form, he required his dancers to undergo regular, strengthening ballet training with two former Harkness Ballet dancers, Ali Pourfarrokh and Ramon Segarra, who was then dancing with the Ailey troupe and whom Alvin had his eye on for a possible administrative post.

Alvin turned to ballet once more in *Flowers*, created for the English ballerina Lynn Seymour, although it did not draw on her classical technique as *The River* had on the Ballet Theatre dancers. A portrait of a tragic rock star, *Flowers* was inspired by the story of Janis Joplin, who had died recently of a drug overdose and whose songs were part of the dance's rock-music score. Its tale of a star's descent into drugs and death was told straightforwardly and with a maximum of theatricality, glaringly illuminated by the flash of cameras. In the stunning final scene, photographers close in on the woman as she writhes on the floor, alone and dying.

Seymour herself, a charismatic star of the Royal Ballet in London, was Alvin's other inspiration. He had seen her perform and had fallen in love with her presence, so different from the reserved, well-schooled image of English classical ballet. Her huge dark eyes, her softly rounded prettiness and the lyricism of her dancing belied a down-to-earth manner on and off the stage. A gifted and outspoken actress who did not at all mind looking tough and ugly in the dramatic ballets that choreographers fell over themselves to create for her, Seymour also had an underlying vulnerability tinged with humor. She seemed always to be a victim of rape, insane or madly in love with the wrong prince in the ballets choreographed for her. What better to throw herself into than *Flowers*, and in toe shoes yet?

Seymour saw it as a "formidable acting role" in which she drank, snorted cocaine, and had a lover who was a pimp, and danced in high heels as well as on point, smoking a cigarette and moving to raucous rock music. She and Alvin developed the character together—a combination, he told Seymour, of Judy Garland, Marilyn Monroe, Bessie Smith and Joplin—and analyzed the emotional implications of every move and gesture. "Just remember to keep that child real heavy," Alvin told her. "She's got a lot of *baaad* habits."

She worked hard and successfully to overcome any resentment of her as an imported star. She survived the usual flurry of last-minute choreographing only minutes before the curtain rose on the premiere on January 25, as well as an opening night mishap that nearly sank the whole enterprise when the wrong part of the score was played. "The curtain went up and I sauntered out smoking an outrageous 'pretend' joint," Seymour recalled. "With an extravagant gesture, I cued the canned music. Instead of Janis Joplin, however, the stage manager put on Bessie Smith. I held my position—a foolish mummified object. The tape screeched to a halt after fifteen horrendous seconds. Then Joplin began singing and I had to hop into character, knowing the show was finished before it had started." Alvin was reassuring, as always. "Baby, stop worrying," he told Seymour. "I can't see anyone else in the role."

Looking back over a long and varied career, Seymour described her time with Alvin as "my happiest time ever." "It was just so sort of free yet full of intent," she said. "And it was hard work. And we were getting somewhere. And it was fun. Alvin was incredibly kind, and so sensitive to what you might be going through. He was fascinated with pointwork and pirouettes. Ballet was something interesting for him, something new. Like a really interesting *other way* to explore.

"He was a fabulous partner. We were doing some of these quite amazing lifts in rehearsal and I remember him lifting me. At that time he was quite big, but I never felt so safe. It was just right. He had this wonderful big, broad back and he sensed where your weight was. He tossed me around like a wee leaf—a wonderful feeling!" There were other amusing memories of that time, one of them the sight of Segarra, who played the sleekly savage pimp in *Flowers*, teaching class while standing on an electric blanket in a studio at Fifty-ninth Street that Seymour remembers as being "fucking freezing."

She was disturbed, however, by some of what she saw during her time in New York. "We had gone to quite a smart party of the ballet world. A whole bunch of people like Natasha [Makarova]. All very nice and all that." As the party ended, Alvin offered to take Seymour home. "He was in black tie and looked like a million dollars. So handsome. We walked over to Central Park. Everyone leapt into cabs but no one would stop for Alvin." Finally one slowed. "It's gonna be a black cat," Alvin told Seymour. And the driver was black.

The same thing happened later with Arthur Mitchell, Seymour recalled, as they tried to hail a cab in Greenwich Village. But Williams, one of her favorite Ailey dancers, provided a memorable antidote to the sadness she felt at seeing her friends treated so badly in the city where they lived. "And Dudley! The cabs in New York were about to raise their rates and people were refusing to use them. Dudley told me in his inimitable way, 'I was walking on Fifth Avenue and I spat and a cab stopped.' "

Although Alvin had wanted to enlist Seymour as a permanent guest artist with his company, he never told her, and she returned to England after the ANTA season. But when the Ailey dancers performed in London, she once again portrayed the doomed singer. "By that time he'd had some other people doing it. I asked him how it went. He said that originally he hadn't thought anyone else could do it. 'But it worked,' he said. 'I guess it must be a good ballet.' "

Like all well-wrought star turns, the role of the singer in *Flowers* brought out new qualities or heightened familiar ones in new interpreters. Linda Kent made the role her own by becoming an uncharacteristically wild, exhausted wraith, even setting her long hair on fire by accident as she flung her cigarette to the ground.

Then and later, Alvin tended to see specific performers in roles, even in dances with large casts. A good company director, he often chose dancers who were not being used by guest choreographers that season and so had time to work with him. Sometimes simple seniority determined the lead dancers for new works.

By the time of *Flowers*, he was famous enough to be considered a creator of vehicles rather than a choreographer favored by stars. And in *Cry*, a new piece for the City Center spring 1971 season, Alvin went a step further and established Judith Jamison once and for all as an unquestionable diva of the dance. The two-week season had come about at the last moment, an invitation extended by Norman Singer, executive director of City Center, as a result of the company's runaway popularity at ANTA. Announced publicly in mid-March to begin a mere six weeks later, the season featured specially priced low-cost tickets that ranged from $2 in the second balcony to $6.50 in the orchestra.

Cry was the perfect start to the company's long relationship with City Center. Danced to impassioned popular and gospel music by Alice Coltrane, Laura Nyro and the Voices of East Harlem, the solo was a gift for Jamison, so idiosyncratic and so difficult to choreograph for—and for Alvin's mother. Dedicated to "all black women everywhere—especially our mothers," the three-part solo took Jamison from oppressive drudgery to emotional anguish and finally to wrenching joy in sixteen exhausting minutes.

Alvin told Jamison nothing of the dance's dedication or its theme during their rehearsals. If she had known she was to represent all black women in the world, she later said, she would have walked off the stage immediately.

Almost everything that could go wrong did in the eight days they created the dance together in a studio at Fifty-ninth Street. There were battles of will between the two, who were both dieting hard and working under the gun to get the dance done quickly. They had had a love-hate relationship for much of Jamison's time in the company, a relationship that was not improved by Alvin's frequent teasing of her as bourgeois. In some ways she and Alvin were very much alike. And she was at first unwilling to give an inch.

Jamison went onstage on opening night dressed in a white leotard and her worn and slightly baggy *Wading in the Water* skirt, a makeshift and ill-fitting substitution for a late costume that Alvin felt was unsuitable. She had never danced the entire solo through and was totally unprepared for the physical demands of the dance, recalling that "my lungs were on one side of the stage and my heart on the other" by its end.

Years after the premiere, Lula Cooper brimmed with fierce pride as she talked of the dance. Alvin had brought her east from Los Angeles for the occasion, in her first trip to New York City. "I *did* cry," Cooper said, thinking of her life as reflected in the solo, "but it made no difference how hard you worked, you could get up and dance. Made no difference how I could scrub floors. I could always get up and shimmy in the shoulders." Encouraged by the success of the new work, she put in a request to her famous son for a piece celebrating one of her favorite social dances. "What was that cotton-picking thing? I wanted him to do something on the Black Bottom. But he didn't get around to it."

Consuelo Atlas had learned *Cry* as an understudy but she seldom got a chance to perform it, so popular was Jamison in the dance. Eventually different dancers did take on the solo, although Alvin never allowed a white dancer to perform it, and he began to share his thoughts about the piece as he watched them learn it. He was haunted by the image of a person carrying a heavy body that lay crosswise on her outstretched arms, an image that was buried in dances that included the *Wading in the Water* section of *Revelations* and surfaced again in *Cry*. He saw the woman in *Cry* as a slave on the auction block in another moment in the solo, but a slave who knew herself to be beyond price. When she washed the floor, she was actually wiping up blood. And a desire to become clean was the motivation for one walking sequence in the piece. In the notebook in which he wrote his rhythmic counts for the dance, Alvin alluded simply to "more food. caress & smooth body. scrub floors. wash windows. beg. have sex. beauty of African heritage. cradling. dignified. get rid of scarf."

Jamison recognized some of the movement from dancing she and Alvin had seen on tour in a club in Zaire in 1967. The long white turban had been suggested by her habitual headwear, which one admirer saw as her "black woman's stately tiara." On its most immediate and simplest level, *Cry* was Jamison in all her large spirit, cheerful flamboyance and sometimes lonely determination.

It was clear from the moment the curtain fell that the company had an enormous hit on its hands. Cheers escalated to screams as a perspiring, breathless Jamison took bow after bow during an ovation that lasted almost ten minutes. Watching and listening in the audience, both Clarke and Al Holtz realized immediately what Alvin had accomplished. *Cry* was not another *Revelations*, but it would come close for many.

Alvin made his way backstage and congratulated Jamison on her performance. Then he looked at her, in what she recalled as exasperation, and asked what he could possibly choreograph for her next. Worrying already, he nonetheless wept at what they had achieved.

Her phone rang at 4 A.M. the morning after the premiere. Alvin was on the other end, jubilant over Clive Barnes's late-edition review in the *New York Times*. The headline alone was thrilling: "Judith Jamison's Triumph." Describing her body, her face, her way of moving and her reserve in vivid superlatives, Barnes called the new work "a sensation."

One of the most telling analyses was written by Marcia B. Siegel, a New York correspondent for the *Boston Herald Traveler*. "This kind of mood dance works best when the dancer is strong enough to live in the choreography, to wear it like his own skin, which is the way Ailey himself performed solos, and probably still conceives of them for others," Siegel wrote.

"I saw 'Cry' performed by Judith Jamison, and she tore the place apart. Jamison is a statuesque woman with close-cropped hair and incredibly long arms and legs, who can do dumb-broad comedy or an indecently beautiful arabesque. She's an original, she's gutsy; she causes a sensation just by walking out on the stage. . . . You could say 'Cry' is just Judith Jamison doing her things, which is all right too. Ailey knew the right way to pull them out of her without allowing the piece to slide across the delicate boundary into nightclub or TV entertainment."

Cry was not Alvin's only triumph in 1971, a year that was one of his most productive as a choreographer. The dances he created for the company were startlingly varied in mood, theme and music, almost as if he were allowing himself to stretch rather than reach. "One thing was clear last night," Anna Kisselgoff wrote that April. "One cannot type the company and one certainly cannot type Alvin Ailey as a choreographer."

He continued to explore plotless, relatively abstract movement in *Archipelago*, the third of his pure-dance "water" pieces. André Boucourechiev, the composer of the piano and percussion score, had provided sections in which the orchestra had alternatives to choose from. It was a fashionable compositional device then, and Alvin rose to the occasion by creating a dance set to two recorded versions of the score, performed by two mostly different casts. Four more new pieces followed, created for spring and winter seasons at City Center that, combined with the ANTA season, gave the Ailey company an unprecedented three dance seasons at two major New York theaters over a single year.

Only one of the year's six new works, *Archipelago*, was considered a failure. Opinion was evenly divided on *Flowers*, with Laura Shapiro, a Boston critic, writing of "a few stock attitudes that occur every few bars" in a piece realized more through mime than dance. But the mysterious and poetic new *Choral Dances* was, like *Cry*, eventually considered a major work, although the group piece had nothing like the popular success of the Jamison tour de force.

Performed to six choral dances from a Benjamin Britten opera,

Choral Dances was choreographed in an abstracted folk dance style with faint echoes of *Revelations* and overtones of *Dark Elegies*, the dance by Antony Tudor that Alvin had so loved. Like the Tudor piece, *Choral Dances* was a celebration of community in all its moods, led by Rotardier as a patriarchal figure. "These Choral dances will be another Revelations—but universal," Alvin wrote hopefully in his work notes for the piece.

His way of working with the performers had not changed much since that elusive early success. They were portraying people who had been walking for a very long time, he told the dancers, before they reached a little village. What happened in the piece were things that happened in little villages. The men played games. They fought. They teased one another. The performers were setting up tents and living for a while in the little village and then moving on. "He wanted that more than just the technique," Williams recalls. "We had been traveling for a long time to get to this space."

Lula Cooper stayed on in New York after the premiere of *Cry* and then left for Los Angeles at the end of the City Center season, happier than she had ever been with her astonishing son and convinced that it was time for her two offspring to get to know each other better. She had been worrying over Calvin's teenaged rebelliousness and had had long telephone conversations seeking guidance from her older son. What could be better than to expose Calvin to Alvin and his work?

The boy arrived in New York in July for a month's stay. Alvin was as frantically busy as ever. His eighteen-year-old "little bro'," as Alvin had called Calvin for many years, did a good deal of tagging along and chauffeuring. He met Alvin's dancers and some even more exotic and rather disreputable friends, shopowners and hustlers who operated for the most part at the fringes of the tawdry life of Times Square. Alvin had come to know them partly through his always active sense of curiosity and in part from the street people who were now a fairly constant element in Alvin's other life outside the company, and they amiably escorted the teenager around town. At times, Calvin was left happily to his own devices, but he and Alvin spent enough hours together to get to know each other, face to face. Up to this point there had been only brief visits at airports and during California tour dates, although they talked frequently by telephone.

Alvin told Calvin a little about his own childhood and about how he, too, had once run around with the wrong crowd and gotten into trouble as an adolescent. What had he done? Calvin asked, fascinated.

"You don't want to know, little bro', you don't want to know," Alvin said solemnly, seizing on a prerogative of older siblings. He also talked of his mixed feelings about Calvin's father. There was no question that Fred Cooper had been very good to him. His own father had beaten him and his mother, too, he confided. It was just that it had hurt Alvin to see his mother turning away from him to another man. He made no mention, however, of his pain at seeing his mother give her love to another son.

They talked of Calvin's future. Why not come to New York, Alvin suggested, and work with the Ailey company backstage? But Calvin did not feel entirely comfortable with his brother's life in show business and as a gay man, although he did not tell Alvin. He had already enlisted in the marines. He would go through with it. "Alvin got very upset," Calvin remembered. So angry was he at his younger brother that he refused to let the boy come backstage when the company performed later in California. "We didn't really know each other before I came to New York. I felt I knew him better after that. But he didn't talk to me for a long time."

Alvin's professional life continued at a frenetic but mostly satisfying pace. By the spring of 1971, the company had officially settled into the American Dance Center, its new headquarters on East Fifty-ninth Street. Cigarette smoke, exhaust fumes from the nearby traffic approaches to the Queensboro Bridge and the smell of hardworking, sweaty bodies filled the air. But there was a comfortable feeling to the place, shared with the company and school of Pearl Lang, who had left the Martha Graham Company to focus her energies on her own career as a choreographer. Barres, mirrors and special dance floors had been put in, but there was otherwise little major renovation. The walls were repainted regularly, however, and decorated with drawings of dancers and other figures made by student artists.

This would be home until 1979, when the building was torn down, not only for the company but for two junior performing groups and for a school that within the next two decades would become one of the nation's best-known and most popular modern dance training facilities. Everyone seemed to pass through, from actors, musicians and dance stars to reviewers for whom a short-lived series of classes was arranged. The hundreds of young New Yorkers and would-be dancers from around the country who converged on the school included a solemn, rather mousy young woman later known as Madonna, who was briefly an apprentice in an Ailey student company directed by Kelvin

Rotardier. Years later, fund-raisers encouraged Alvin to approach the singer. He didn't remember her as an Ailey dancer, he told them annoyedly, as averse as always to "begging." He had a black company. If there had been a "white prima donna ballerina" in that company, he would have known it.

Classes in ballet, jazz and modern dance were taught by a staff that included dancers from the Ailey and Lang companies and starry guests. The school became a hangout for black performers, choreographers and teachers. Soon the Lang and Ailey companies were competing with the school for rehearsal space, forced to work at night after a daily ten hours of classes in the studios they needed. The planning meetings were endless, Lang recalled, and Alvin could be uncooperative. "Alvin, you're going to have to teach," she told him once, knowing that he would be a big draw. "I can't," he told her. "Try," she responded firmly. And he did, occasionally.

Alvin started out with an office on the second floor—"for about a minute," Sylvia Waters recalled, "before he was bumped upstairs to a kind of attic office. Or bumped himself." But he seldom remained in the relatively quiet upper quarters for long. A frequent visitor to Clarke's downstairs office when the company was in town and rehearsing, he would arrive just in time to work out details of touring, repertory and hiring with her, or simply to hang out as happily as he had at Clark Center. The small room was the hub of activity, and it was often crowded with people, with several meetings and conversations going on at the same time. Laughter tended to punctuate meetings in which Alvin took part.

Deciding to take charge in a moment of manic hyperenergy, Alvin at one point announced that he alone would run the organization. He opened his door and invited everyone to come in and talk to him about their needs. That lasted about a week. Much as he liked to apply himself to the solutions of other people's problems, Alvin was not at all a father confessor. But he was unvaryingly kind to the students and interested in what they were doing and what they thought and felt, despite his distaste for teaching. The students, in turn, felt very much at home at the center, crowding into studio doorways for clandestine looks at what the grown-ups were rehearsing. Sarita Allen, a prim young ballet dancer from Oregon who later became a leading Ailey performer, loved the sheer tumultuous variety of the place. "There were so many different types of people there," Allen said. "There was different music in each studio. Different parts of the body were used in class. We were there from early morning until late at night."

Some were intimidated by Alvin's roving figure. Raquelle Chavis, a member of the first children's classes on Fifty-ninth Street, looked up at him looming over her and wondered if he was crazy. "He used to scare me. He was so intense. He came into our class one day and sat there. I think he must have been arguing with the first company. He sat. And then he told us to point our feet and almost broke our ankles showing us." But Alvin was also an impressive role model. Chavis watched with awe as this "black individual who spoke so well" strode about his kingdom.

Chavis grew up in the studio watching dances being made. Her mother would drop her off at the school and then go shopping at the nearby Bloomingdale's department store. When class finished early, the tiny child, small even as an adult, sat with company member Marilyn Banks and watched rehearsals. "Dancers, whose little girl is this?" Alvin would sometimes boom out. She was waiting for her mother, Banks reassured him.

"Alvin intermingled then," Chavis said. "He knew all the parents. We were his babies." He also watched as the babies grew up. It wasn't long before Chavis wanted to join the older dancers onstage. Her tenacity amused and pleased Alvin, and when she sneaked into a company audition she was accepted. "Oh, Alvin, she's still in school," someone told him. Back she was bounced to the ranks of student dancers. But she watched for him in the hallways, and when he passed, she posed for him and they laughed together. Somehow, Alvin heard about Chavis's vivid imitation of Judith Jamison dancing *Cry*. "Miss Chavis," he told her when she later graduated from the school into the junior company, "I'm sorry *Cry* is not in the repertory. I hear you do a fabulous *Cry*."

Alvin's reputation as a choreographer was continuing to grow. He had begun to receive royalties for work performed by other companies, although they were often for relatively small amounts, like the $60 the London Contemporary Dance Theatre paid him that year for four performances of *Hermit Songs*. His own company, now up to twenty-one dancers, was larger than ever, and dancers from other countries were turning up more regularly at auditions.

Masazumi Chaya, who was eventually appointed associate artistic director of the Ailey troupe, was one of them. The Japanese dancer was surprised by the relative informality of his audition at Fifty-ninth

Street and by the warmth of the place itself. No panel of auditioners stared out impassively, scribbling notes about anonymous dancers, as they were wont to do at other tryouts. "There was Judy wearing a leotard and jeans and a tight, tight, tight turban, doing a crossword puzzle. And there was Dudley, with shirt and jeans, running around, walking around, holding a cigarette. He demonstrated the movement and Judy looked at it. Often Alvin talked with Judy about who he liked. Dudley was 100 percent giving. He'd take time with us with little things."

Watching Williams, Chaya ached to become a part of this family. "That audition took only an hour and a half, two hours. But I saw someone teach not only movement but what the movement was supposed to be. What looked good on you. I thought, Oh, my God, I want to join this company and work with him. Because he cared about the nonprofessional dancers in the room. He tried to make them look good. That kind of effort in an audition! He could have just said, 'Oh, you couldn't get that step. You go.'"

The Ailey company had reached the age where it had a generation of older dancers to pass along traditions. "When I joined," Chaya said, "I just hung out around Dudley. Where Dudley go, I follow. And when he talked about dancing, we just listened, listened, listened."

Alvin had a similarly strong effect on Chaya, who noted his brown corduroy pants, the fact that he wasn't wearing shoes and the way his abundant hair was pulled back. He was intrigued by the way Alvin blinked at people as he talked to them. "Because of his size, he spoke very gently. That fascinated me. Because when I came to the United States I didn't have any friends among so-called black people. I grew up with only Japanese people.

"When I started taking class and seeing dancers, they were never Alvin's size. And always they were quite loud. Always talking. And then to see this guy, with such a gentle, gentle voice. And something about his hand gestures. A magician, kind of. His fingers never straight out, always some kind of bent finger. I remember he liked to hold himself, combing his beard with his fingers."

Chaya's father had died when he was very young. "I imagined a lot what looked like a father. I thought this guy could be like that. That was kind of what I felt. Because he was something very special."

It was hard to feel lonely at Fifty-ninth Street, even for someone with Chaya's teetering command of the English language. "The building was always *packed* with people," Sylvia Waters said. "You had all kinds of people coming there. The energy was incredible. There was just something about the place. It made you want to dance. And it was accessible. The neighborhood was great. In the summer, you could walk through Bloomingdale's and enjoy the air-conditioning, and feast your eyes at the same time on all the little corner restaurants and coffee shops." For Alvin, the department store was a handy resource.

In a panic, he had dispatched Clarke to buy bed linen there when his mother insisted she stay at his apartment during her first visit to New York. Once installed, Cooper quickly reverted to her early habit of snooping when her son was safely away from home and opened a closet door. Down came a cascade of dirty linen. It was not that Alvin needed new sheets. What he needed were clean sheets.

He had grown even worse about clothes since the days when he had infuriated Edele Holtz with his lack of attention to the way he looked. Now he wore what Mickey Bord despairingly called a "clutch duffel," a coat he had to hold closed or pin together because the buttons had all fallen off. Once or twice she caught him wearing socks that didn't match to elegant social functions, or saw him wander off to appointments with important fund-raisers in pants whose cuffs gleamed with safety pins. His weight zoomed up and down as his frequent dieting worked and then failed him. When he was in one of his thin phases, Alvin splurged on magnificent suits, usually for special occasions, first showing them off at the office. But the buying sprees sometimes got out of hand, and finally the company, which by agreement with Alvin oversaw his personal expenses, took away his credit card.

He was a creature of extreme ups and downs. Given his larger-than-life personality, it is not surprising that no one wondered if Alvin might be suffering from clinical depression. His rages and his buoyant, loving moods were all part of the eccentric who spun through the hectic, last-minute creative sessions that produced the necessary premieres each year and who somehow knew how to keep a popular school and company—too funky to be thought of as the institutions that they were—alive and growing.

His behavior had begun to worry some, however. From time to time he would suddenly appear with a young, unsavory-looking male stranger in tow and talk of hiring the man to work in the office. "Alvin was awesome," one observer said. "He was brilliant. He had an incredible, incredible talent. He could be an incredibly kind, caring, sensitive person. But whatever demons there were, he never exorcised them. There were times when he was there, but not there. There was a lot you didn't know about him and his personal life and a lot you didn't want to know."

Much of Alvin's eccentricity could have been the result of the escalating pressures on him at the time. Never one to complain over the worst problems in his life, he announced cheerfully at one meeting that he was planning a new ballet about life in the theater, to be called *Straaassss*, or *stress* as he drawled the word out.

New and previously unimaginable situations were arising as the company became more professional, competitive and unionized. Williams and other older dancers had once infuriated Alvin with their grumbling, but it was of a personal sort. Now dancers began to appear in Clarke's office with increasing frequency to argue or plead for more money and better roles. "Try Las Vegas," she told Chaya and his friend Michihiko Oka when they nervously approached her about the possibility of earning just a little more—but a good raise appeared in their paychecks the following year. Two other visitors were Linda Kent and Sylvia Waters, who were unhappy because they received the same pay for rehearsal as for performing. "Could you manage to pay me a dollar more for performing, so it looks different on paper?" Waters asked a surprised Clarke. "It's not about money," she explained. "But somehow that will do something for my ego."

Clarke was usually designated to fire dancers, a job Alvin was not good at unless he was "in a manic mood," as one observer put it. Williams still shudders over one rout, after six young performers staged a protest over their pay. "Fire them," Alvin told Clarke, and she did. Williams begged him to take the dancers back. "Alvin, you can't do that," he said. "We just cleaned everything up. Everyone is ready to go." But Alvin was adamant.

His relationship to his choreography was also problematical. Deep down, a small but persistent voice was always telling him that he could not make the steps that would together make a dance. After all, he had had little formal training and even if he had, he would probably not have been a good dancer anyway. It didn't matter that Chaya and others pointed out to him how gifted he was at visualizing what might happen on a stage, as well as where and how. He was almost deaf to reassurances that he had a genius for theater, for creating powerful mood and atmosphere. He had only to look into the next studio, where Talley Beatty or Donald McKayle or some new young choreographer was working, to feel his own skill was meager and his successes accidental.

Yet despite his doubts, Alvin was often happiest and most absorbed in the studio. Choreographing remained as satisfyingly draining as performing had been when he was able to forget himself onstage. He still found great pleasure in his intense feeling of connection to music and in the access it provided him to the emotions of a dance. "For me relax more in choreography," he wrote in a battered three-ring note-book sometime in the early 1970s. "Let it come out a bit more sponta-neously—don't cerebralize—good music is of the essence and music which for me has real feelings."

Such theories of choreography were put to the test once again when Alvin began work on the dances for the Bernstein *Mass*. The composer had approached him about a month before the premiere. Jerome Robbins had left the production. Would Alvin be interested?

It was an unnerving assignment. Subtitled "A Theater Piece for Singers, Players and Dancers," the full-evening *Mass* had a cast of more than two hundred performers, which included the Ailey company as "street people" and acolytes.

The opera followed the form of a Catholic mass and incorporated rock, blues and folk music to tell its iconoclastic story of a young gui-tarist who becomes a priest but turns his back on his ungrateful, world-sized congregation, casting off divine authority and leaving everyone to their own devices. The work was full of choice Bernstein touches, in-cluding a mad scene in which the priest dances on the altar like a curate on a bad LSD trip, as one critic put it.

The sentimental liberal who inspired the term *radical chic*, Bern-stein saw the piece as an attack on President Nixon, the Catholic Church and the war in Vietnam. At the end, young men in the cast moved out in the audience and squeezed the hands of people sitting on the aisles, whispering "Pass it on." The reviews were mixed, with judg-ments ranging from trivial and superficial to a work that captured its era. Once again, however, Alvin escaped unscathed and even received some quiet praise. He seemed genuinely pleased about the production when friends came backstage to congratulate him. Later that year, how-ever, he told Anna Kisselgoff the dancers had been bored to death be-cause they were "second class performers in a production where the dancers sang and the singers danced."

Once more, Alvin had found himself working with a procrastinat-ing composer. Unceasingly ebullient, Bernstein bounced gleefully in and out of rehearsals as Alvin attempted to work on movement in mo-ments snatched from the general chaos, sometimes simply to announce that he had just written some glorious new music for the piece. Alvin occasionally reciprocated. "We were in the rehearsal studio working on some segment," Kent remembered. "It always got reduced to three hours on who took the bench over here and who sat on it." Bernstein suddenly appeared. "Oh Alvin," he cried, "I have some more music for you." What should he do with it? Alvin wondered aloud. "Oh, just do some of those stock Ailey moves," Bernstein advised him.

"Okay, let's take it from here," Alvin told the performers, singing out a bit of the girls' cheeping chorus in *In America* from *West Side Story* as accompaniment. Bernstein retreated.

In the midst of all this, Alvin somehow also managed to finish *Mingus Dances* for the Joffrey Ballet, a relatively overt political piece made up of five dances and four vaudeville episodes suggested by the music of Charles Mingus. Splitting the stage into two separate worlds, Alvin had front-of-scrim vaudeville characters parading in front of ballet dancers enacting scenes of love and death. Even the sympathetic Barnes was confounded, commenting gently on the dance's obscurity. Alvin continued to tinker with the ballet after its premiere, shortening it with some success. He felt he had failed Mingus, although in a prepremiere interview, the composer described the ballet as having "raised me from the dead."

"It wasn't very good really, and Alvin knew it," Al Holtz said. At the final rehearsal, as he finished choreographing the last moments of the ballet, the Joffrey dancers began to clap for him. Alvin walked over to a corner and quietly cried. "I don't think he ever blamed the dancers," Holtz said. "It wasn't their fault. And they were just appalled, standing around the floor and looking sad. It wasn't that bad."

Mingus was angry, blaming the dancers for Alvin's despair. "He went over and put his arm around Alvin," Holtz recalled. "We went downstairs and sat in a bar and Mingus was going on about these tight-assed white dancers. Alvin didn't have much to say, but little by little he got a couple of drinks inside him and was consoled and we went off.

"It's just another example of how no matter how critical Alvin was of things, and he was, he knew himself when it was not right. He saw some things that nobody else saw that he thought he could do better."

Alvin's mood of despair carried over to his work on *Mary Lou's Mass*, a celebration of the jazz composer and pianist Mary Lou Williams, whose score for the dance Alvin described as "a sum total of black music." Joyous and wry, this *Mass* delighted audiences and critics, but Alvin was never to be satisfied with it and eventually the dance left the repertory when Williams was no longer available to conduct and play the piano as stipulated, at considerable expense, in her contract.

Myth, the slight but evocative Stravinsky quartet that completed the year's premieres, was essentially a gift to Consuelo Atlas, whose almost indefinable gifts Barnes summed up with teasing admiration. "Miss Atlas, superbly womanly, looking at an only faintly hostile world with a finely sexual arrogance and flaring nostrils, is superb," Barnes wrote in his first-night review. "She has a manner with her that is not only indisputable but also beyond criticism. You do not vote for a queen, you accept her—and mere criticism is a lowly form of suffrage."

In the press of developing new pieces, Alvin had not forgotten his mission to keep alive some of the underappreciated beauties of American modern dance. He acquired *Suspensions*, a rarely seen modern dance classic choreographed by the former Martha Graham dancer May O'Donnell. And the following year would bring revivals of dances by Katherine Dunham, Alvin's spiritual mother, and Ted Shawn, who had so cruelly hurt him as a fledgling choreographer heading the Horton company in 1954 at the Jacob's Pillow Dance Festival. Their relationship was now quite different.

"I have been so happy with your great and continued successes everywhere," Shawn had written Alvin early in 1971, signing himself "your loving Papa," in a note about the planned revival of his *Kinetic Molpai*. "I only wish we could <u>afford</u> you at the Pillow."

twenty-four

"THE BOARD" ARRIVES

The Alvin Ailey American Dance Theater might have become higher priced, but as always it had its money problems. Ivy Clarke performed a good deal of last-minute patching and taping of budgets and debts. The company had a $30,000 deficit, however, for the fiscal year ending March 1972. "Compare that with any ballet company and that's nothing," Alvin told the interviewer Ellen Cohn. "One foundation gave us money for a new Ailey work. I used it to pay old bills. Did they get their new Ailey work? Of course, but they wouldn't have if we hadn't paid the phone bill first. Somewhere it may not be legal. But neither is not paying dancers. I think people should be told the facts." In his direct and defiant way, Alvin was enunciating an unspoken truth about arts funding. An articulate member of two minorities, one racial and the other artistic, he had a forum and he used it.

The company would falter time after time in the years to come, but by 1972 it had become a juggernaut that slowly picked up speed as it went on its unstoppable-seeming way. The ANTA festival, which had identified the Ailey troupe as a major New York company, was discontinued a year later for lack of money. But Alvin and the company had found a home theater of sorts at City Center, in a relationship that was cemented when the company became a dance constituent there in early August, joining the City Center Joffrey Ballet as a resident.

The arrangement lasted only a year, when budget cuts made it necessary for the Ailey and then the Joffrey to revert to tenancy. But for the time being, the Ailey company had a theater of its own with considerable cachet and some institutional sponsorship. In addition to a fee and a share in any box office receipts over its production costs, the theater provided advertising, musicians and the services of front-of-the-house and backstage personnel. "The two most urgent problems confronting us have been the need for a home base and relief from insurmountable financial pressures," Alvin said bluntly, using the announcement of the company's new status to bring once again to public attention the difficulties faced by his troupe and dance in general in the United States. "I am most grateful that the first has been completely resolved by joining the City Center family, and the second somewhat alleviated."

The residency probably came about at least in part because of the company's success in its winter 1971 engagement at City Center. Not only was it a record third season for the company at that theater, but the box office reported its largest ever advance sale. Encouraged by that success, Alvin dreamed of reviving dances by Ruth St. Denis, Lester Horton, Doris Humphrey and Sophie Maslow. He was thinking again of a three-act dance about Malcolm X, as well as an improbable-sounding strip-tease ballet to music by Charles Ives and a dance, to be set to music by Samuel Barber, about his former lover Christopher, whom he continued to see occasionally.

He fantasized about two other intriguing projects: a production of *Le Sacre du Printemps* to star Judith Jamison, and a version of *Afternoon of a Faun* for the ballet star Igor Youskevitch. He might also create another dance for Jamison, to music arranged by Max Roach. Called *Motherless Child*, it would be "the true description of the suffering of the black people," as Alvin observed in a note to himself.

In the end, there were three Ailey premieres that year, none a major work. One was a simple, yearning dance for Dudley Williams to Donny Hathaway's singing of "A Song for You," to which Alvin later added two solos to create a suite called *Love Songs*. Performed to music sung by Hathaway and Nina Simone, the piece became a staple of the Ailey repertory, giving Williams a chance to move eloquently through a variety of quietly expressed moods. The dance was as much an homage as *Cry*, exploiting Williams's great delicacy and control, but was without the Jamison solo's wider connotations.

Williams grew into *Love Songs* over the years, exploring, adding to it and refining it as he danced. One refinement came from Alvin, although it was very much delayed. "I would hold this arabesque, this one penché arabesque, and hold it to the last minute," Williams recalled. "I could hear the beat of the music just ready to go and then chhhhh, I'd catch it on the next one. And Alvin came to me and said 'You know, I've been meaning to tell you. Don't hold that arabesque.' I said, 'Alvin, this is almost ten years I've been doing this!' He said 'Yes, but I always wanted to tell you: Don't hold that arabesque.'"

The second premiere was the more ambitious *Lark Ascending*. The lyrical group dance received mixed reviews, including one from Anna Kisselgoff that remarked on its Grahamesque look. But then, articulating the largely unacknowledged truth in the arts that almost nothing is truly new, Alvin had never made any secret of his admiration for Martha Graham or of his borrowings from her work.

Jamison was featured in the first performance, but she soon stopped dancing the role. In his attempt to create something different for his new star, Alvin had choreographed a piece much better suited to the talents of Sara Yarborough, who had learned the work with Jamison and took over the part. Although both women were ballet trained, they were as different as two performers could possibly be. Each represented an aspect of Alvin and his dances. Onstage, Jamison was his ebullient, extroverted self and a performer firmly rooted in the reality of the moment. Yarborough was soft and sweet looking onstage, a dream of a dancer, with a melting lyricism and fluidity that had an almost hypnotic effect on Alvin. One of the few choreographers of the time who blended classical and modern dance with any success, Alvin continued to be fascinated by ballet, and Yarborough symbolized it for him in much the same way that Carmen de Lavallade had been his symbol of idealized womanhood.

Yarborough herself was torn between the two worlds. She had studied ballet all her life, first in Haiti with her mother, a former Katherine Dunham dancer, and then at the New York City Ballet–affiliated School of American Ballet and the school of the Harkness Ballet. She came and went at the Ailey company during her eleven years there, joining in 1971 and then leaving to dance with the Joffrey. In *Lark*, Alvin captured her presence and effectively suspended it in amber.

Not only did Alvin now have two compelling stars in his company; he was no longer considered only as good as his last dance. He was well on his way to becoming a major force in the American arts, despite cries of commercialism from some critics and dancegoers. The summer of 1972 he received an honorary degree from Princeton University. His company was invited to participate in the twenty-fifth anniversary season of the American Dance Festival at Connecticut College. And he was one of a number of celebrities, among them Arthur Miller, Harold Prince and Dustin Hoffman, who were asked to sign a letter published in the *New York Times* protesting the dismissal of the Jewish dancer Valery Panov from the Kirov Ballet after his attempt to leave the Soviet Union for Israel, a cause célèbre in the dance world.

Alvin was in something of a creative slump, though, after his outpouring of dances the year before. *Shaken Angels*, a minor and rather tawdry duet for Dennis Wayne and Bonnie Mathis, had the two ballet dancers playing characters who smoked pot and mainlined heroin to rock music in a performance at the Delacorte Theater in Central Park. Works he created for other institutional projects were similarly inconsequential. And Alvin was not able to surmount the difficulties of a "tough assignment," as one newspaper headline succinctly put it, a commission from the Juilliard American Opera Center to choreograph a dance sequence for Virgil Thomson's new *Lord Byron*. *Sea Change*, announced for the Ballet Theatre's summer season at the New York State Theater in 1972, was delayed until October, when the piece about death and the sea received lukewarm reviews. The response was somewhat better to dances that Alvin had choreographed for a new production of *Carmen* at the Metropolitan Opera that fall.

In a dizzying but enjoyable burst of activity, the Ailey dancers performed in the last ANTA marathon, a mere two weeks before the start of the company's December season at City Center. And Alvin oversaw the revivals of two long-lost jewels of American modern dance, Dunham's *Choros* and Ted Shawn's *Kinetic Molpai*. The Dunham dance was a success—a pretty, high-spirited yet demanding staging of old Brazilian ballroom and folk dances, the first traditionally performed by aristocrats and the second by slaves. But *Kinetic Molpai* was a failure.

Shawn, who had died in January, created the piece in 1935 for his Men Dancers group, a bold venture designed to display the power and virtuosity of male dancing. Makeshift filmed records of dances he created for his company suggest a vigorous simplicity and sheer energy that would not look out of place in a modern dance repertory of the 1990s. But *Kinetic Molpai* did not transfer well. Danced by the Ailey company on the City Center stage, it had a look of kitschy heroics that set audiences to giggling and outright laughter.

It was a brave failed experiment in a year whose demands were alluded to in a worried note from Alvin's mother. "Hello there," her July 14 letter began, written after a long and alarming silence from her famous son during which she felt, with her nearly infallible second sense about him, that Alvin had been under the weather. "Know you are feeling better since you got some rest. We are all well. You will feel better after you loose weigh. That a funny thing. I knew you were either in hosp. are not feeling good are something. Can't fool the old coon. Smile. I told Fred. He said Stop thinking like that. Alvin working."

Alvin's stepfather was right. But more was going on in Alvin's life than the rehearsals and performances Fred Cooper might have envisioned. In the fall of 1972, he moved into what would be his first real home since East Thirty-fourth Street, and his last. On the top floor of 467 Central Park West, the apartment was ringed on two sides by a terrace that looked out over Central Park and south. Alvin had found a nest, a floating cloud, an inviolable cell, a daring Arabian Nights cave of an apartment. The few people who were ever allowed a glimpse of it remember the penthouse—though that seems too formal a word for so intimate and idiosyncratic a place—as a home that measured his accomplishments in the world.

The place was dark and the five rooms small, even by New York apartment standards, and Alvin looked at times like a giant in a dollhouse as he followed the twisting route from room to room. But the tiny bathroom and sliver of functional white kitchen had windows, through which light poured. The bedroom was bigger, with ample closet space, and the living room, although angular and narrow, opened out onto an L-shaped section of terrace from which a handsome wooden water tower zoomed upward like a sheltering, peculiarly urban tree. There was even a room, too tiny for a dining table or bed, where he could store the honorary plaques and awards he had earned over the years.

After all the years of moving around the city, living with friends and in office quarters, Alvin was happier than he had ever been. His lease specified that there should be "no dancing, rehearsals, singing, acting, instrument-playing or group activity" in the apartment. But he could run his dog in the park that beckoned, solid green hillocks and rocky outcroppings, from across the street. The surrounding neighborhood was excitingly dangerous. And he threw himself into decorating the place with unusual domesticity.

He had taken Apartment 17-C unpainted and without repairs, bringing the monthly rental down to $329. It was cheaper to hire someone to clean and paint the place, the decorating overseen by Normand Maxon and Alvin's mother while Alvin was out on tour with the company. But most of the decor was his work. Bookshelves sprouted everywhere and were soon filled. Lists of the most minute repairs, written in a flowing, optimistic hand, cover several pages of a green notebook of the sort he still used for everything from memos about Christmas presents and counts for dances to jottings on psychotherapy sessions and a few bizarre asides about possible staff plots against him at Ailey headquarters. There were bedsheets to buy, and a digital clock, a color television and silverware. The bathroom shower rod needed to be painted. Trees must be bought for the terrace and plants—swamp lily, pepper and English ivy—for inside and out.

Brother John Sellers, the old friend who had toured with the Ailey company as a singer, lived in the building. Sellers accompanied Alvin on some of his barhopping adventures around the city and was a frequent visitor to Alvin's new home. "It was a lovely little apartment," Sellers recalled. "We used to set out there and talk. This and that." There were parties, almost always for friends who had nothing to do with dance. Alvin loved the idea of serving meals to his intrepid visitors, although he seldom did, Sellers said. There were almost never any clean dishes, and guests had to step over piles of clothes and other belongings on their way from one room to another.

Alvin didn't want to be bothered with cleaning, Sellers could see, and he hated the idea of anyone cleaning the place for him. "I guess he just felt as if 'This is my way and this is the way I want it and this is the way I'm going to have it and we'll leave it at that.' " But every so often Sellers went on a rampage, sweeping through the refrigerator with surprisingly little resistance from Alvin. "All the time I had to be throwing food out. I just can't stand certain things. I'd say, 'Alvin, you don't need this, you don't need that. How long you had this? Throw it out.' "

Miguel Algarin, a theater director and another barhopping pal, was also allowed to visit regularly. "I think Alvin liked living in chaos," Algarin said. "The tidiness of the ballets was as much tidiness as he could afford in his life."

Alvin was casual and stubborn to a sometimes comical degree. He had loaned pictures to another friend in the building to help decorate his apartment and then left them for so long that Sellers assumed they belonged to the friend. One day, Alvin summoned the singer to help him remove the pictures, without warning, surging through the apartment with Sellers in tow as the friend stared openmouthed.

"Good-bye, I'll see you soon," Alvin sang out as he left, his arms full, followed by a similarly encumbered Brother John.

His joy in the apartment did not carry over to the office, where Alvin was increasingly troubled by internal problems with the company and its administration. He was angry at Clarke, in particular, who he felt had become bossy and intransigent. A letter from Carl Goldman, Alvin's psychotherapist, suggests that those problems were an important topic of discussion.

"Last week we had a long discussion about your self-destructiveness," Goldman wrote in mid-February 1973, after Alvin had stormed out of a session. "This issue is complex and subtle and manifests itself most of the time in devious ways and in a manner which superficially looks like moves which are positive and beneficial to growth. Your organization might or might not be as you would like it to be. It might even survive a drastic step such as letting those go you dislike. . . . You feel ready for expansion. This is good and as it should be. You want a better cosmetics job. Beautiful if the price is right. Your price as you delineated it last night is exorbitant in terms of self-respect and emotional feed-back. I told you once that the Billie Holiday bit [John Butler's *Portrait of Billie*] is just not good enough, not for you and not for your dancers. Alvin, you know yourself only too well, how easily you can be intimidated by anyone you consider superior to you. You know how readily you respond to taking on artistic endeavors, not because of what they mean to you but because of what they represent with regard to status and success as you see it. Are you that sure that the people you will be working with in the future will not bring out the worst in you. You say you have to take this risk. Fine. But with it consider some of the poor judgments you made before. And don't forget the vindictiveness and cruelty you hand out to 'superior' people."

Alvin had walked out ten minutes into the session, Goldman noted. "At no point did you consider looking into yourself, your own suffering and turmoil. And you could not get yourself to bring that out in you which is the true Alvin, the person who feels compassion for others, who can be generous to a fault and who wants to give beauty and nobility to the world. We all are petty, ego-centric, greedy and pushy. There is nothing wrong with it. The real question is what is it we permit to take the upper hand."

He must face his problems with Clarke, the therapist added. "Alvin, we discussed your emotional instability and your more than frequent erratic behavior over and over again. You are stuck with Ivy.

Without her, you'll have nothing. Yes, she is irksome, domineering and possessive. But, Alvin, she also protects you from your own worst enemy and that is you. Right now, and I am not telling you anything new, you are falling, you are falling deeper and deeper. And your rage becomes more and more destructive." Alvin returned for another session.

His feelings about Clarke might have been brought into sharper focus by the establishment of a new and more businesslike board for the company. Two lawyers, Howard Squadron and Stanley Plesent, convinced Alvin that such a board would help bring new corporate and foundation money to the company. There had been a first stab at creating a board in 1964, and then a slightly more serious attempt in 1971. "Alvin got a little lawyer from the Village who was a performing arts devotee to run the papers through for $50," Al Holtz said of the last attempt. "There were nice people on the board, but hangers-on."

A friend of Alvin's at the New York State Council on the Arts had recommended Squadron, who had served as special counsel on several of the arts agency's projects and had also worked with the Joffrey Ballet and represented a few other dance companies with Plesent, a partner in the corporate law firm of Squadron, Gartenberg, Ellenoff and Plesent.

"There is this company called Alvin Ailey that is about to go bankrupt," Squadron told Plesent. "Do you know them?" Plesent could not believe his ears. "I saw them just the other night at ANTA," Plesent told him. "They're fabulous. The audience loved them. Why would they need help?" Looking back some two decades after, Plesent laughed ruefully. "That's the tune I got years later. 'Stanley, why do they need money? Everybody loves them.' "

He and Squadron met first with Clarke and then with her and Alvin. "Howard and I agreed to see if we could put together a board and help them become more stable," Plesent said. "Howard made particular use of the Interracial Council for Business Opportunity, which was put together by the American Jewish Congress. We agreed the board should be interracial." After a year Plesent succeeded Squadron as acting board chairman, "and they could never get rid of me after that." Plesent stayed with the company for seventeen years, pressed into service as a personal legal adviser to Alvin in everything from negotiating his apartment lease to bailing a relative out of prison and for a time even serving as Alvin's legal guardian.

The company did not draw big names or the very wealthy to the board, but the new members were professionals who were willing to contribute their skills. None could write out large checks to reduce a deficit or produce a new dance, but each pledged personal guaranties for bank loans.

Outsiders like Singer, who looked at the situation from the perspective of the director of City Center and a major dance producer, saw the company's need for structure. But some, including Clarke, were uneasy about the new arrangement, feeling that it would have been better to recruit famous friends of the company like Bobby Short, Lena Horne or Harry Belafonte as board members.

Clarke realized that the company needed a skilled fund-raiser. Money, she knew, attracted more money. But she believed that Alvin was reluctant to create a strong board that might conceivably take the company over. And she was filled with foreboding when, at the first meeting she attended with Alvin and the lawyers, Plesent recommended they hire a Joffrey Ballet administrator with whom Clarke had had a falling-out over Alvin's relaxed work habits. "A lot of those people somehow didn't have respect for us," Clarke said of the blowup. "I don't know why. Maybe because I was black, but I don't want to think that. I'd rather think it was because I was a woman."

She gave as good as she got from the man. "He was yelling at me about Alvin. I said, 'Listen, I'm going to tell you something. Alvin Ailey and Bob Joffrey are two of a kind. They're exactly alike. But you know what? One is cut from white cloth. And the other is cut from brown cloth. But there's no difference between these men.'"

She walked out of that first meeting with Squadron and Plesent with a sinking feeling. "Alvin and I were waiting to cross the street and I said, 'Alvin, these people are going to get rid of me the first chance they get. And the sad part is you're going to allow it.' And he turned to me and asked me why I was so paranoid. I said that I wasn't paranoid, but the handwriting was on the wall. And he would be in a straitjacket. He might not understand now but that was what was going to be."

The company was taking its first tentative steps into the new world of professional dance boards and administrators that had been ushered in by the growing popularity of dance in the 1970s and 1980s. But Alvin's creative life continued in a lull. His contribution to the Metropolitan Opera's miniproduction of Virgil Thomson's *Four Saints in Three Acts*, which opened in February 1973 at the Beaumont Theater in Lincoln Center, was as minimal as his choreographic opportunities had proved to be in the fall production of *Carmen*. And Alvin's only new dance of the year, *Hidden Rites*, did not add much to the Ailey canon. Performed to a score by Patrice Sciortino that reminded one English reviewer of a blend of movie music and *Turandot*, *Hidden Rites* essentially abstracted ritual from a series of loving and warlike encounters that seemed to one critic to be taking place in an African village.

For Alvin, the dance had to do with "private primordial moments of the soul," as he wrote in one of his notebooks. "These are our hidden rites." He continued with his revivals of modern dance classics, presenting José Limón's heroic *Missa Brevis* in a winter season at City Center that also included a gala benefit featuring Dustin Hoffman and Rebekah Harkness. And he seized the opportunity for a chance at arranging another ambitious foreign tour during a backstage visit to City Center by twenty-one Chinese journalists who had just attended an Ailey matinee.

"We are very lucky to have you here," Alvin told them in an uncharacteristically formal welcoming speech, adding quickly that "we would like to perform in your country." The journalists thought that might be possible. Then they asked to pose with the dancers. "Okay, let's clump together," Alvin said amiably, and proceeded to give a one-minute history of American modern dance, which, he explained, started out at the turn of the century as a revolt against the classical tradition of ballet, with its princes and gods. "We want to do away with kings and emperors," one journalist replied, "and ministers."

Increasingly, Alvin's charming facade hid a restless and troubled soul. As the year wound down, his notebooks were crammed with more and more memos about appointments with doctors, new dances, old friends in trouble and purchases for his apartment, new diets and new drugs, the latter alluded to in cryptic jottings. Some juxtapositions are comical, as when notes for his therapist regarding his difficult relationship with Normand Maxon, still an intermittent and adoring presence in Alvin's life, are followed directly by a reminder to himself to arrange for the Broadway dancer Hinton Battle to teach a Saturday children's class at the Ailey school before his matinee.

On a sheet of yellow legal paper tucked into one of the books, Alvin scrawled a defiant announcement he thought of making to his dancers: "Next Spring we'll pull a coup. Black Roots. All Black Choreographers. Co Question: Why are you here. Are you growing artistically, spiritually, personally. Don't know." Would the experience of performing with the Ailey company affect the dancers in any way when they were no longer able to perform? he asked himself. "I consider you all a bunch of problems. You don't appreciate where we've come from. Let me tell you where we're going—to the State Theater and then to the Met."

twenty-five

"DADDY WORE KHAKI PANTS"

On May 11, 1974, Alvin Ailey Sr. died in a nursing home in Wichita Falls, Texas. He was sixty-three years old.

Alvin Jr., as he had always hated to be called, had talked to his father the year before, after a silence of nearly four decades. His father had telephoned and left a message at the office. Wondering bleakly if he wanted money, Alvin returned the call. Their conversation was brief. The family had been keeping up with Alvin's accomplishments in *Jet* magazine. He'd like to see him, his father told Alvin, and could he send a poster of the company?

Lula Cooper worried her son would feel obliged to give him money, but Alvin never sent the poster or spoke to his father again. He did carefully jot down his father's address on a page filled with notes on dances. Within the year, Alvin Ailey Sr. was dead.

Alvin sent money to bury his father in Burkburnett Cemetery in Wichita Falls. He did not attend the funeral and did not open many of the condolence cards that made their way north from Texas. But he began to search out his family history, calling relatives and making rough charts for a family tree, which were found, after Alvin's death, saved with his father's funeral program and two photographs of the man.

One set of notes is a sketchy listing of several generations of relatives, including, on his father's side, a preacher, the singer Joe Tex, the

manager of a K Mart store and a graduate of the Peabody Conservatory
of Music. Alvin carefully noted the addresses and phone numbers of a
few relatives, as well as that of Amos Alexander, who was still living in
Navasota. Another set of much neater notes shape a poignant portrait
of a man he knew almost nothing about, shreds of information gathered in conversations with one of Alvin's uncles.

Alvin Sr. was five feet nine inches tall and weighed about two
hundred pounds. His birthdate was August 15, 1911. "Virgo!" Alvin
wrote. "Mathematical, musical—played by ear. Moved from Ft. Worth
to Burke Burnett then to Wichita Falls. Daddy wore khaki pts, black
shoes, white shirt, black hat. Pressed! Loved to gamble. Needed female
attention—loved baseball—-worked at Strand Theater from 50–73 as a
janitor—6 brothers. 7th son."

His father was divorced from his wife Rosalee, Alvin recorded.
"Got shot in 59 by a woman he was living with. Shot him 3 times with
38. 1959—48 yrs old. 3 mos in Hosp. 3 mos in bed. Didn't [take] care
of himself—hated doctors—pulled his own teeth—Rosalee stayed.
Routine: wk—6 AM–12:30 aft. Party—streets—gambling—kept piano
at house beside his bed.

"Bubba brought him white shoes—& then after always wore white
shoes—wore them year around. Loved white shoes. Aft gunshot was in
constant pain bet 48 & 55 yrs but wouldn't go to doctor—In hosp 5 Feb
to 1st May. Died May 11 1974. Still owe 400. Headstone 500."

Alvin must have talked to his therapist about this important, now
twice-lost figure in his life. He mentioned his father's call to Al Holtz.
But he seems to have shared the news of his father's death with no one
else in New York—happier, perhaps, to hug to himself such fragile,
vivid bits of life as a piano, white shoes, pressed khakis and the image of
a gambler who loved women and sounded every bit as devastatingly
attractive as Eddie Warfield, the man he had thought was his real father
all those years ago in Texas.

It was easy, too, to submerge himself in the flow of work. Less
than a week before his father's death, Alvin and the company had been
featured in its first American television special, "Alvin Ailey: Memories
and Visions," on the Soul! series, put together by Alvin's longtime
friend, the producer Ellis Haizlip. And he had his hands full dealing
with Janet Collins and Pearl Primus, idols whom he teasingly called his
"crazy black ladies," who were each to present two pieces at the City
Center spring season.

Inspirations to a generation of black dancemakers, the elegant and introspective Collins and the more extroverted Primus were both strong individualists. Primus, who like Katherine Dunham was both an anthropologist and a dancer, revived her pulsating *Fanga,* a famous 1949 solo based on a West African women's dance of greeting and performed by Judith Jamison to drum music, and *The Wedding,* a ritual from Zaire that the choreographer re-created for the concert stage in 1961. Performed exuberantly and with a canny sense of colorful detail, the group piece told of a wedding nearly disrupted by a demon and his henchman. Both dances were based on Primus's research into African and Caribbean dance and ritual, the details of which she shared with the dancers in intense discussion that Linda Kent, who played the comical little sister of the bride, remembers as being at least as thrilling as what unfolded on the stage.

Collins, the older cousin whom Carmen de Lavallade had revered as a child, revived her 1949 solo *Spirituals* and created a new work, *Canticle of the Elements.* Known as "a beauty, a diva," in the words of her friend and early dance partner Talley Beatty, Collins had almost single-handedly pushed down the doors barring her from the classical ballet in the 1950s to become the first black artist to perform at the Metropolitan Opera House.

"I was always an enigma," she told Anna Kisselgoff in an interview in May of 1974. "People never heard of someone doing point work and then Negro spirituals." But Collins seemed unsure of herself when it came to choreography. When the Ailey dancers arrived for the first rehearsals of *Canticle of the Elements,* a celebration by four archangels of earth, air, fire and water, they found the legendary former ballerina to be, confusingly, both indecisive and insistent.

There were daily changes in casting, and Collins would go over and over the same few details in rehearsals. A worried Alvin called Beatty for help. "They were rehearsing the dance at the Ballet Theatre studios at Columbus Circle," Beatty recalled. "Alvin asked me to come up there but he was nowhere in sight. Then he kind of pushed me in and locked the door. Janet asked me if I had come to help. I said I just came to offer her moral support. The dancers were kind of chilly."

Several company members went to Alvin to ask that the premiere be postponed. He could or would not do that. *Canticle of the Elements* was billed as a work-in-progress, to which Clive Barnes quipped in his opening night review that "possibly not quite enough progress has been made." Collins's solo, *Spirituals,* fared better. Performed by Jamison, the dance had for at least one critic the moving simplicity and directness of the three religious songs to which it was set.

In artistic terms, the formation of the Alvin Ailey Repertory Ensemble meant more for the future of the company than any other activities of the busy summer of 1974. Alvin had been thinking of starting a junior troupe to give gifted students a chance to learn how to perform and to prepare them for the senior company. He often watched the children's classes at Fifty-ninth Street and to the teachers' consternation occasionally popped up among the students in the studio, wryly begging one teacher not to embarrass him with too many corrections. He also took an active interest in the progress of the students who seemed to be professional material, whether as dancers or as choreographers. "I don't know if you're a dancer, but you're interesting," he told Donald Byrd, who had entered the school as a young adult and with Alvin's encouragement became a noted modern dance choreographer.

This new group was also to function as a workshop in which Alvin and promising young choreographers could work with trained dancers without the pressure of union time restrictions and without overtaxing senior dancers already busy learning pieces for City Center seasons and for tours. But the workshop concept did not last long. The Repertory Ensemble was soon performing across the United States in theaters that could not afford or were not well enough equipped to present the larger first company. A year later a third group, the Alvin Ailey Student Workshop, would be formed under the direction of Kelvin Rotardier to provide other handpicked students with performing experiences and extra training opportunities.

The formation of the Repertory Ensemble dovetailed with a spectacular new project that Alvin had been contemplating for some time. The New York City Ballet had celebrated Igor Stravinsky and his music in its 1972 Stravinsky Festival. Why not a festival to celebrate Duke Ellington, while he was still alive? Ellington was not sure he wanted to hear that much of his music, he told Alvin. The idea began to take shape, though, when Herman Krawitz approached Alvin about doing a special for CBS television.

Krawitz had worked with Alvin on a Central Park production of *Carmen Jones* in the late 1950s and, as assistant general manager of the Metropolitan, on *Antony and Cleopatra*. He was now looking for independent programs to produce for television. He and Alvin talked of *Revelations*, but it had been substantially filmed already. Alvin mentioned his interest in Ellington, who had died that May of lung cancer. He had paid his last respects to that grand yet whimsical American artist in a packed funeral at the Cathedral of Saint John the Divine in upper Manhattan. Here was an opportunity to celebrate Ellington's contributions with an homage now and an even more splendid festival timed, appropriately, for the American Bicentennial.

He and Krawitz came up with "Ailey Celebrates Ellington," a television special created for the CBS Festival of Lively Arts for Young People. Shown in late November 1974, it featured five new Ailey pieces, narration by Alvin and the rock singer Gladys Knight, performing by the Repertory Ensemble and even a rare glimpse of Alvin dancing. As Krawitz and Ivy Clarke worked out the details, Alvin settled into the job of choreographing for a small and eager group of malleable new dancers.

Unconvinced at first of the promise of the group, Alvin questioned the talents of some of its dancers in a flurry of mostly irritable memos he wrote in mid-September. Within a week of proposing to drop the television show so as not to hurt the feelings of these inept youngsters, however, Alvin was already planning detailed tours for the new company by February and talking of acquiring historic modern dance pieces like Paul Taylor's *3 Epitaphs* for the group. A few days after that, Alvin proposed again to drop the television project, in part because rehearsals were less than a week away and decisions had not been made about what music to use. The show went on, however, and from it emerged two popular Ailey dances, a haunting record of Alvin as a performer, and an interesting glimpse of several dancers who were later to become staples of the New York dance scene.

The first company was on tour, Sarita Allen remembered, when she and the other junior dancers began to work with Alvin. It was an experience that would change her life. "I was seventeen at the time. This little ballerina. I had gone to private school, ballet classes. I had no boyfriends. I'd never dated. Nothing. Alvin was like my father. I kind of grew up with him. At the time, we weren't doing so many technical dances. They were all about personalities." Alvin cast her as Marie Bryant, one of the black women singers and dancers alluded to in *The Mooche*.

"My character was kind of a sexy dancer, and I didn't understand why he would choose me for this role," Allen, who later became one of the senior company's earthiest and most glamorous dancers, said. "It was kind of typical of Alvin. He'd pick dancers a lot of times who people couldn't see in certain parts. And it worked out more times than not."

Woe to the Ailey woman who dressed in what Alvin considered an unfeminine way, or to the man who didn't look virile onstage. And "whining," as he put it, exasperated him. But he tended to have a soft spot for dancers who were rebellious and seemed hungry for something more than the life they knew. "Alvin always said you have to experience things," Allen said. "You have to go out and *do* it. And for a time I was kind of wild. I never messed up with my work with the company. But I thought I had to see what it feels like to have a heartache, to be sad and really miserable.

"One of the things I really loved about Alvin was that he never reprimanded me. He wouldn't say, Don't hang out with these people. He would tell me, 'You know, you should try to cultivate friends like artists. Maybe some painters and musicians.' He would treat a street person the same as he did the president when we went to the White House. He wanted everybody. Say somebody really funky-looking wandered into the studio. He'd say, 'Okay, come on in.' I think that's why people really loved him."

Alvin's eventual faith in Allen and his other young dancers was repaid, for the Ellington television special was a success. It did not win the Emmy it was nominated for, but Alvin received a cherished note from the Broadway director Harold Prince that praised the production as "easily the best of its kind I have ever seen—or hoped to see. . . . The company, the costumes, the camera work—all extraordinary."

Only two of the television dances survived—*The Mooche* and the shimmering *Night Creature,* one of Alvin's wittiest and most ravishingly pretty dances. "This piece will be our lyrical beautiful piece," he wrote in notes for the television production. And it was, with a sassy yet wistful undertone that perfectly caught Ellington's gift for slyly fugitive melody. A smooth-flowing suite of three sections performed by a blithe free spirit, the men who compete for her attention and a corps of dancers in dappled silver-white dresses, shirts and sleek pants, *Night Creature* shifts moods as mercurially as the music. At one moment it is comical, a split second later it becomes yearningly lyrical and the next moment the stage is filled with impudent, undulating bodies.

There are groupings, arm gestures and bits of action that look as if they have been lifted intact from *Revelations* and *The River.* But *Night Creature,* named after a score Ellington created in 1955, has a kind of conscious authority that the other two pieces lack. Alvin seems at ease here, with choreography that is as much ballet as modern dance flowing from him with a sure sense of the inherent expressive style. His use of fleet ballet footwork and bobbing bodies in one brief female trio perfectly captures, for instance, the music's bubbling, soaring excitement. And at the heart of the dance is an essential truth of the art of Langston Hughes, Ellington and Ailey.

In their earthier moments, Alvin's "night creatures" suggest a kinship with Jesse B. Semple, known to the world as Simple in Hughes's short stories, essays and drama. In Simple the poet celebrated the enduring life force that American blacks cultivated within themselves in order to survive the peculiarities of their history and position in their native country. Simple is in spite of himself a moral hero, a man who is innocent yet knowing, ridiculous yet dignified, and possessed of unassuming wisdom.

In *Night Creature*, Alvin's dancers move to music that celebrates that double nature so cherished by Hughes, Ellington and Ailey.

The sections of the dance performed on television differ slightly in detail from the finished piece, but the mood is the same. The young performers move like colts bolting through a starting gate, pushed by all their recently recognized love for dancing and display and released from the discipline of hard-earned technique to spring up out of the floor into soft, free air. They and the older and more experienced dancers who later took over the roles are truly the "night creatures" Ellington wrote of, who, "unlike stars, do not come out at night—they come on, each thinking that before the night is out he or she will be the star."

Alvin performed with the group, although it had been nine years since he had last danced. He wanted to do it in part because he would be partnering a protegée, Agnes Johnson, for whom he had great hopes, although Johnson did not subsequently join the senior company. Alvin's presence, particularly in a duet with Johnson that weaves and floats in and out of one section of the piece, is both hypnotic and poignant. The husky, sensuous peasant in Lester Horton's *To José Clemente Orozco* and the doe-eyed charmer of early theater photographs have grown into a lean, chisel-faced, somewhat tired looking giant with uneven teeth and an oddly distant half-smile.

There is no distance to his dancing, however, and certainly none of the practiced wit and grace of Alvin's eloquent speechmaking. Here is a man who has merged completely with what he dances, flowing with it like a stream that has poured into a pushing river. As before, he does not sell the movement. It is the entire body that registers the emotion of the dance, rather than just the face.

His lifting and guiding of Johnson is never obviously attentive, although there are hints of the gallant solicitude of an older man and the pragmatism of a teacher demonstrating a step. The two dancers are almost extensions of a shared body. Alvin himself performs with a simplicity and selflessness that are impossible to look away from.

Absorbed in this work and away from the crowd, Alvin put the youngsters through their paces in rehearsals that had a little of the adventurous feel of his company's earliest days. For once he was happy with a new dance, and his instincts were right, for *Night Creature* became a staple of the Ailey repertory and one of his most popular pieces.

But there was also a sadness to him these days, and a terrible quickness to his temper. Little things set him off. His anger often had an edge of paranoia. No longer the worthy newcomer, he had begun to receive his share of negative reviews in recent years, one of the most devastating of them from Arlene Croce, critic of the *New Yorker*.

"At one time 'Revelations' was plausibly the signature work of the Ailey company," Croce wrote that year in an essay titled "Standing Still." "Now it might almost be taken for a fluke. . . . Ailey either doesn't realize or doesn't care anymore what makes 'Revelations' so popular, and the work he now does is marked by an incredible inconsistency and slackness of design. However, Ailey is remarkably consistent in trying to capitalize on 'Revelations' as if it were a *formula* success." She went on to describe his choreographed gestures as "decorative chatter" created for the audience rather than the performers.

Scattered charges of commercialism continued to appear, epitomized by Marcia B. Siegel's description of two Ailey performances as managing "to stay just this side of schlock." Early on, Alvin had framed a searingly negative review and hung it up in his apartment. Now he was only wounded by such criticism.

Siegel had questioned the effects of the company's frequent international touring in an earlier review. "The business of performing night after night to houses full of strangers in foreign cities has taught the dancers how to make instant contact," she wrote. "Under their electric spell, even American audiences forget to ask whether they are contemporary, relevant, profound, or even honest." But, she continued, for the Ailey company those questions matter greatly, and "this kind of commercialism cannot be justified."

Even more disheartening, the sound of yawning could be detected. "New Dances, Same Old Steps," a headline read in the *Christian Science Monitor*. "The works are pale from over-exposure," a critic wrote in the *Washington Star-News*.

At the same time, in the usual topsy-turvy way of Alvin's world, prizes and honors were coming his way with increasing frequency. In 1975, he received the *Dance Magazine* Award, one of three top honors in the field. The following year, he was named the winner of the Spingarn Medal of the National Association for the Advancement of Colored People, awarded annually to honor achievement by a black American.

Dressed in an eye-popping backless gown, Jamison accompanied him to the black-tie reception at the Hilton Hotel. Another friend was no longer at his side to enjoy the event, however, for in September 1975, in the midst of preparations for the Ellington festival, Alvin's simmering feelings about Ivy Clarke had come to a head.

Clarke had sensed her position was threatened when a suave young black administrator, Ed Landers, was hired in May that year. "Alvin called me up and said, 'Sweetheart, don't give him a hard time,' " Clarke said. Landers eventually made the rounds of the office, armed with a large pad and asking staff members for job descriptions. She brushed him off, telling him she was too busy and that everyone did everything in that office—an honest estimation of the sort that professional arts administrators tend not to understand. "He'd ask me things and I'd say, 'Well, how would you handle that?' He was making so much more money, I'd throw it back at him." Then came the suggestion that Clarke leave her job as general manager of the company and work as a personal assistant to Alvin or as the director of the school. She refused, despite Alvin's attempts to prepare her for the changes and present them in the best possible light.

"I knew the board was trying to get rid of me," Clarke said many years later. "They would talk to Alvin and tell him things. They didn't realize that Alvin would come back and tell me exactly what they said." But she was stunned, despite her premonitions, by a visit from Landers one Friday afternoon, just before the senior company was to leave for California. "You . . . are . . . fired," Clarke remembered him telling her, pausing between each softly deliberate word. "I'll give you a week to clear things out."

"There were so many things I was doing to try to pull things together for California," she recalled. "I knew Alvin was talking to some of the dancers, so I went to the restaurant where he was. I said, 'Alvin, I need to talk to you.' He said, 'Yeah, sweetheart, yeah, but I don't have time.' He was so cold, so different. I went back and packed my things. I never went back. I just couldn't." It was four months before Alvin called her, Clarke said. She refused to talk with him. It wasn't Landers she blamed, or even Alvin, but the board.

Plesent, chairman of the board, told a different story. "Ivy did not have the training," Plesent said. "She was not up to the job. But the record needs to be clear. It was not the board. Ivy's leaving was because of Alvin."

At an emergency board meeting at East Fifty-ninth Street before the firing, Alvin had made cruel accusations against Clarke. "I think not a single one was true, but they were a reflection of how Alvin was taking out his frustrations at Ivy," Plesent recalled. "He insisted we fire her. He couldn't do it himself. It was fairly clear at the time of Ivy's firing that something was going on with Alvin. There was a piercing quality to his eyes. He was very harsh."

Some saw it as a matter of Alvin listening to the wrong people, as one observer put it. His therapist, who might have saved him from himself, had died that year, murdered by a patient. And on a larger scale it was true, as one dance producer saw it, that artistic and social institutions tend eventually to cut off the leaders they could not survive without and cannot grow with. "No one should ever take any credit away from Ivy," Al Holtz says. "She was in some ways difficult. But she can take the credit for holding that outfit together in that period when we were just going into the dance center. The school. Getting more bookings. She did it very very well. But she could never get used to Alvin."

The seat-of-the-pants governance of dance institutions that had seen them through their founding and growth was becoming a thing of the past by the mid-1970s. The Ivy Clarkes of that world had once been able to keep everything going by sheer tenacity. "I always believe that regardless of how much money you owe, there comes a time when you can get it and things can get better," Clarke said years later. "I don't think anything's impossible. It might be hard, and it might be inconvenient, but it's not impossible." But by the mid-1970s, dance had become a matter of multimillion dollar budgets, and the money necessary for survival went to organizations with balanced books and five-year plans.

The dancers, many of whom had had their run-ins with Clarke, took her firing in stride, although some were troubled. Chaya recalled that he and his friend the dancer Michihiko Oka felt frightened. If Alvin was a kind of father to them, Clarke had been a starchy but dependable mother figure in a world that didn't always make much sense. But there was work to do and an extra excitement in the air as the formal opening of the Ellington festival drew nearer.

twenty-six

ELLINGTONIA

Alvin had scheduled the second phase of the Ailey Celebrates Ellington festival enough ahead—for 1976 and the Bicentennial—to raise the money he estimated he would need. His planning was even more methodical than usual. The television special was the first of several prefestival events. By the time of the festival, to be held in August at the New York State Theater at Lincoln Center, the senior company would be fully rehearsed, having already performed many of the Ellington pieces during its City Center seasons. The tactic robbed the event of some glamour but ensured a polished and less costly presentation.

Alvin had trouble sleeping as the festival drew closer. His always active imagination went into overdrive, contemplating other kinds of projects for the year. "Bi Centennial Ideas. Re-naming theaters airports rivers," he wrote in an agitated flow of ideas on one page in a small notebook. "Rename streets, malls, parks, new sites after great American esp. black creative & performing artists: in black communities but not solely. Billie Holiday Ave. Ellington Ave. Blvd. The Ives River. Roger Sessions Park. Stravinsky Blvd. The Martha Graham Dance Theater. Katherine Dunham Hill. Louis Armstrong Ave. St. Denis St. Shawn Blvd. In every major Amn city of . . . certain population rename a major thorofare after an American creative artist. Eugene O'Neill Blvd. Duke Ellington Airport. Railroad stations. . . . Central Ave renamed—

Bessie Smith Blvd. Lester Horton Lane Blvd." Around the same time, in another notebook, a rare burst of racial anger is recorded, heightened or released, perhaps, by his living within music that was for its composer inherently political.

He was not playing jazz, Ellington told a reporter in 1930; he was "trying to play the natural feelings" of black people. "Our music is always intended to be definitely and purely racial," Ellington observed in an article in *Down Beat* magazine nine years later. It was a vision Ellington shared with Langston Hughes, but for Alvin the matter may have been more complicated.

"Next fall in August change to all black co—with publicity—rehearse for two mos," Alvin wrote. "Re-emerge with new statements of Blackness!! In the co only <u>modern classes</u> or classic classes adapted to modern dance. Let go all white dcrs. Replace with black & P.R. Very RACIST? <u>No</u>."

Alvin never acted on those scrawled plans. A part of him was pulled to the look and formal values of the European art of classical ballet and the interesting puzzles it presented. Another part—the well from which he had drawn up *Revelations*—rejoiced in the rich and abundant emotional life and culture of his people. Alvin had had no sustained contact with whites during his formative young years. He had known discrimination as a child and as an adult black male. And yet he had moved with apparent ease into a white world and learned how to navigate and beat it amiably at some of its own games.

Alvin spoke out against categorizing art in racial terms while continuing to concentrate on "black" themes, insisting on their universality. He might refuse to come up with a new piece requested by an English ballet company for a terrific black ballerina, asking slyly why she wasn't dancing *Swan Lake* if she was so good. He might chafe eloquently at statements suggesting the limits of black dancers' skills, as when he told the interviewer Ellen Cohn in 1973 that he was tired of hearing that his repertory was wonderful but that only black dancers could do jazz. But a nearly career-long dream was, after all, to choreograph a major work about Malcolm X. And the heroes he did celebrate most notably were Martin Luther King, Nelson and Winnie Mandela, Charlie Parker, and the friends and neighbors of his childhood.

"I know it sounds so corny," he told Cohn, "but I hope I can look back in a few years and think what we're doing here with our school and our company is celebrating the beauty of the human spirit, of people coming together and accomplishing something. I think people are sanest when they're working together creatively. That's the act we live every day in the studio."

He was troubled when some of his black dancers seemed to exclude white dancers from the daily life of the company. He talked to the white dancers at what he felt might be difficult times, and worried when they, too, seemed to pull away. "Politically, in philosophical terms, he had a liberal soul," Plesent said. "And interracial? Alvin lived interracial. We had some pressure early on from one board member about giving priority to blacks. Alvin lived out his beliefs about lovingness, humanity." But that genuinely humane man could feel divided, a black man making his way in a world of white-determined rules and customs.

Some problems, however, were universal among choreographers, whether black or white. Where was the money to come from for the festival? He made a note to himself at one point to tell Barbara Jordan, the Texas congresswoman and a friend and idol, that "Alvin needs some Texas oil money." "Those big oil companies in Texas to help keep his company alive," he wrote. "He needs $250,000 by end of June—and one million to put on Ellington Festival." And, just as pressing, where was he to get the time and peace and inspiration to create his contributions to the festival?

"There may have been many points when he felt dry," Sylvia Waters said. "One of those points was when he was putting together the Ellington festival, and Talley and Donny were not interested in collaborating on *Black, Brown and Beige* with him. None of them liked the Ellington music. He really had a hard time with it. He didn't trust himself. I remember going to one of the rehearsals and the music just seemed to meander on and on.

"Alvin hadn't expected to do the whole thing by himself. But because it was budgeted to do, he had to follow through. There he was, snapping his fingers, trying to find the music. He would always, somehow, come out—good, bad or indifferent. The dancers would help him turn it around.

"God, I need some movement," Waters heard him tell himself in one rehearsal. No more "lateral, lateral, attitude, step, step arabesque," as Alvin put it. "My God, I can't do that stuff again."

Dudley Williams looked up one day in a rehearsal for his solo in *Three Black Kings* and was astonished to see tears in Alvin's eyes. "He was just sitting there quietly. And I looked over to him to see if I was doing the right stuff, to get his approval, and he was crying. It blew me away." Williams asked what was going on. "Oh, you're so beautiful," Alvin answered. "Everything just moves so beautifully."

Typically, Alvin had planned the one-week festival to be a mix of the proud and the humble, the new and the old. Ballet Theatre would dance *The River*, which, to Alvin's disappointment, Ellington had never seen. Five new works by lesser-known black choreographers, including Alvin's old friend Cristyne Lawson, would be performed by the Repertory Ensemble. Lester Horton's *Liberian Suite* would be revived by James Truitte. Talley Beatty would be represented by *The Road of the Phoebe Snow*. And there would be new Ellington pieces by Milton Myers, a fluent young black choreographic protégé of Alvin's, and Louis Falco, who had performed early on as a guest with the Ailey dancers and was now a major younger choreographer known for his hip irreverence and the lushness of his dances.

Alvin would contribute most of the other fourteen ballets and three new pieces, including a fifteen-minute duet for Mikhail Baryshnikov and Judith Jamison that he contemplated calling *Ellingtonia* or *Kinda Dukish* but finally named *Pas de Duke*. A charged encounter for two stars, one representing classical ballet and the other modern dance, the duet was a pièce d'occasion that lost a little of its bubbly fun but demonstrated solid choreographic underpinnings when it resurfaced in the Ailey repertory with other dancers.

Baryshnikov, who had defected from the Soviet Union two years earlier, had frequently talked of a desire to explore Western dance. He had seen and loved the Ailey dancers when they performed in Leningrad. But his musings on *Pas de Duke* suggest he got more than he bargained for. He looked, he knew, "like a cow on ice" as he tried to grab hold of the slippery truths of jazz dancing. He spent hours, it seemed, standing behind Alvin and trying to copy his moves over the nearly monthlong rehearsal period.

"I remember thinking 'Could I do this?'" Baryshnikov said, laughing as he looked back on the experience two decades later. "But it was after I had worked with Twyla [Tharp] the first time, so the risk was not that big. I was afraid it would be barefoot. I never danced in bare feet."

Alvin immediately created a relaxed mood by walking into the studio for the first rehearsal, kicking off his shoes and proceeding to demonstrate steps in his street clothes. "He was full of humor," Baryshnikov recalled. "He put the music on and said 'Just follow me.' So I just followed, with him correcting me. There were certain Grahamish contrac-

The company in "Blue Suite" in Paris, 1964. Alvin lying in front; Lucinda Ransom (reclining); Loretta Abbott, Brother John Sellers (row 2); Morton Winston, Hope Clarke (row 3); Dudley Williams, Joan Peters, James Truitte (row 4); Kelvin Rotardier (center back); William Louther (back, left) and unidentified blues singer (back, right). *Source: Archives of the Alvin Ailey American Dance Theater; photo by Zoë Dominic*

Carmen de Lavallade and James Truitte in Lester Horton's "The Beloved," 1961.
Source: Photo © Jack Mitchell

The famed opening pose in "Revelations," 1961. From left: Alvin, Myrna White, James Truitte, Ella Thompson, Minnie Marshall and Don Martin. *Source: Photo © Jack Mitchell*

Gary DeLoatch, Donna Wood and Alistair Butler rehearsing "Memoria," 1979. *Source: Photo © Jack Mitchell*

Alvin Ailey, 1979. *Source: Photo © Jack Mitchell*

tions. I did them over and over and over until it was sort of semiright. He wanted me to use elements of my jump, but he used that a lot himself in his work."

Baryshnikov saw right away that a good part of the dance's humor came from the disparity in height between him and Jamison. "Everything was based on the odd couple of Judy and me. From the entrance, I could see that this was not for real, it was for fun. With gorgeous music." After rehearsals, he and Alvin often took off for a night's adventuring accompanied by some of Alvin's dancers or friends, sometimes with Jamison coming along for dinner. "We used to go out on drinking sprees, from one restaurant and one bar to another, until we finished about four or five o'clock in the morning in some really very strange places."

Alvin scheduled the premiere of the duet for a single performance on May 11 during the company's spring season at City Center, as the highlight of a benefit gala, to be followed by performances during the Ellington festival at Lincoln Center three months later. Fearful of the City Center premiere, Baryshnikov relived the performer's traditional nightmare of finding himself onstage without his clothes. In the heat of the performance, he reverted to what he knew best, smoothing the corners of the choreography and making it a little more familiar feeling. In the end, an injury prevented him from performing *Pas de Duke* on opening night at Lincoln Center.

Alvin was absent from the State Theater, too, hospitalized for appendicitis. That was not the only disappointment. Well before, he had had to abandon at least one dream for the festival, which he talked about in an interview with Joseph H. Mazo. "Maybe you shouldn't say this—no, go ahead, let them know how big the dream really is—I want the first night to start with a Cotton Club act with Lena Horne and the Ellington orchestra in white tuxedos, and eight chorus boys in the costumes of the era," Alvin told Mazo. "The chorus boys should be men like George Balanchine and Jerome Robbins and Talley Beatty. Duke Ellington deserves that kind of tribute. I just wish I could have done the festival while he was still alive."

As it happened, Horne paid affectionate tribute to Alvin in a speech at the gala opening of the company's spring season at City Center, calling him the definitive American institution and being called in turn a legend by her former dancing partner.

Alvin did assemble a fairly starry roster of hosts for the Ellington festival at the State Theater, although they did not quite measure up to his earlier fantasies. Betty Ford, once a student of Martha Graham, and Ruth Ellington, the composer's sister, were on hand for the opening, followed on other nights by black political figures and performers. *Three Black Kings* was introduced by Coretta Scott King, whose slain husband was commemorated in the dance. Each night, the Ellington orchestra performed a medley of his music.

"What I really want to do is to bring to audiences the profundity of this man's contribution—to illustrate not only his music, but his philosophy of life," Alvin said that spring, referring to Ellington as "the first authentic genius I ever met." "The public knows him only by his pop pieces. Black composers have a way of disappearing and we want very much for this man to take his rightful place in American and international music history."

By August 10, the festival's opening day, a special Ailey Celebrates Ellington flag was flying high over the front steps up to Lincoln Center. Alvin had pulled it all off. If the excitement of the festival was mostly generated by the mere fact of its occurrence, given that only one premiere was presented, he had succeeded in honoring and embracing a hero. "For the next few years, when people mention Alvin Ailey," Mazo wrote, "they're going to have to mention Duke Ellington, too."

twenty-seven

"NONE BUT MY CALLING"

The Ailey Celebrates Ellington festival was one of the few unquestionable accomplishments of Alvin's life in the late 1970s. It loomed large and bright over a steadily darkening landscape, together with an exuberant family reunion of the company onstage at City Center in 1978, in celebration of the company's twentieth anniversary.

Alvin had by now done everything he had set out to do. There were twenty-nine dancers in the Alvin Ailey American Dance Theater, a large number for a modern dance company. The budget had more than tripled to $3 million from 1973 to 1977, and, according to *Variety*, the Ailey company was now earning more at the box office than any other dance company in the United States, despite its relatively low ticket prices.

Performances, tours and premieres were now scheduled at least a year ahead. Alvin was making more money than ever before. His tax returns for 1976 and 1977 show gross income totals of $54,045 and $62,641, including annual salaries of $39,940 and $45,817 and film, television and guest choreography fees and royalties. The school on East 59th Street, where enrollment would build to five thousand students by 1980, had begun a determined fund-raising program as a first step toward establishing itself as a professional training academy.

There were cracks in that smooth facade, however. He had created forty-two dances for his company since 1958, averaging at least one new piece a year for his own and other dancers. But there were no premieres in 1975, a time of consolidation for the Ellington festival the following year. In 1977, the company presented work by new and newly popular choreographers of dance ranging from the lushly physical to funk and cool postmodernist experimentation—but, again, no Ailey. Around that time Alvin told Lelia Goldoni, his friend from Horton days, that he was so busy being an administrator he had no time to be a choreographer.

There was a distance now between Alvin and the family of friends who had loved and supported him through all the crazy ups and downs of the early years, throwing their lot in with him not because he might one day be famous but because of his teasing, sympathetic warmth, his extravagant humor and his stubborn vision. "The whole relationship changed, though not necessarily friends-wise," Mickey Bord said sadly. "I would go to all the performances. I would see Alvin and I would speak to him. But it was not the same. What could you say? And I was not allowed to do anything. He had unions. I could not wash the costumes and dye the costumes and go shopping for him and do things like that. I wasn't allowed to."

The company had a worrisome deficit in 1977, and in late June, Alvin was forced to cancel a two-week August engagement at the New York State Theater. True, the company performed its scheduled two seasons at City Center. It had its usual triumphs abroad on a spring tour of the Far East, Africa and Europe, and the dancers were booked for an eight-week tour of the United States in the fall. Such a packed performance and rehearsal schedule would have been pure fantasy even ten years earlier—as would the fact, ironic under the circumstances, that in a ceremony at Alice Tully Hall in Lincoln Center just four months before the canceled season, Alvin had been one of fifteen leading city arts figures chosen to receive a newly established Mayor's Award of Honor in Arts and Culture, in the company of Lincoln Kirstein and Robert Joffrey.

Once again, Alvin seized the chance to talk of the problems facing dance. "It is sad and frustrating that our company must now join the Joffrey Ballet, Dance Theatre of Harlem and American Ballet Theatre in having to reduce public appearances for economic reasons," he said in late June in a public announcement of the cancellation.

He was seeing a psychotherapist regularly again. But it was hard to keep up with the routine demands of daily life. There are several uncashed checks tucked into an address book for the year, one a Christmas present from his mother, as well as a notice from Con Edison warning that his electricity was about to be turned off. Judith Jamison noticed that Alvin looked tired and withdrawn all spring, although he cheered up considerably during the summer. Some of the younger dancers, among them Sarita Allen and Donna Wood, sensed that he was suffering and longed to know what to do or say. Observant Ailey office personnel also worried that something was badly troubling Alvin.

He was on and off a variety of diets, with the help of a variety of diet pills, in an attempt to get himself into "reunion" shape for the twentieth-anniversary gala. He could be an endearingly enthusiastic dieter who thought nothing of beginning a newspaper interview by earnestly sharing tips on weight loss. But this time he worked doggedly and with little cheer, admonishing himself in almost fanatically stern notes to exercise and give up cigarettes, drugs and fatty foods.

Life was closing in on him, as Alvin's increasingly bizarre notes to himself testify. "Make list of co who drk smoke etc.," he wrote, his thoughts of changing the behavior of others sounding like a desperate attempt to control his own. "People who smoke pot suffer loss of memory also. People who drink alcohol . . . can be controlled & are fat." Lists follow of dancers and company personnel, many of the names with home telephone numbers scrawled beside them. "THE SCHOOL RULES," another note reads in large bold print too impatient to slow for punctuation.

> Students of the school must
> not smoke, cigarettes, marijuana,
> pot, hashish, angel dust
> marlboro kent etc
>
> Schship students
> No Colt 45   No Boone's Farm
> Beer Angel Dust
> Hashish
> No marijuana
> heroin
> No cigarettes on school premises
>
> will call For immediate dismissal
>   Alvin
>
> NO LEG WARMERS
> NO COVERING OF BODY PARTS
> NO SWEATERS

Over the next few pages of the notebook are reminders to be given to one staff member to "Get some detailed literature on alcohol & its effects," "Leave school and come to work for us part time including new children's Ailey-Lewis depth percep #1," and, on a third page, "measure pieces in childs park at 100th build one on terrace." "I have some deep hangup about him," Alvin writes to himself, about a staff member, on a page lined with columns of random-seeming numbers. "Why?"

Yet he seemed normal to most of the people he worked with, and he continued to do an enormous amount of work, building the company and its repertory and developing dancers. In retrospect, William Hammond said, there must have been two totally different Alvins.

When the company was in New York, Alvin would arrive at the office mornings around ten, go off to rehearsal and then return for lunch ordered by staff members from nearby delis. Then he would go back to rehearsals, his workday ending in the early evening. He sat through lengthy production meetings in which details of lighting, costumes and other technical and design elements of new and repertory pieces were discussed. He met with Hammond, then company manager, to talk over complicated matters of budgeting and programming for City Center seasons and tour dates. He handled his own schedule, having lost his personal assistant after the company discovered the assistant couldn't curb Alvin's bursts of sometimes grandiose spending.

Alvin was also involved in a formal attempt to develop audiences by finding out who came to see the Ailey company dance. A survey commissioned by the board and completed in March 1978 by Young & Rubicam New York revealed that much of the Ailey audience went to the theater in "unmarried pairs," and that two-thirds of the audience was already familiar with his work. Those who liked the company were habitual theatergoers who also liked drama but not opera or pop or other music concerts. They were not impulse ticket buyers and usually went to only one performance a season. They tended to be over thirty-five with "higher educational backgrounds" and annual incomes hovering around $25,000. The leading competition seemed to be the Joffrey and New York City Ballet.

Alvin knew his audience. But who was Alvin Ailey? At forty-seven, he hardly knew.

If he could have put all that he had accomplished aside and started again, Edele Holtz suggested, Alvin might have saved himself from the fast-approaching cataclysm. With the upcoming twentieth anniversary, Alvin was forced to confront a central fact of his life as it was now. Nothing new was left to be done. There were no challenges of the sort that had fueled his passion and ambition in the 1960s.

That passion was now fixed on smaller battles—skirmishes, really—that seldom had anything to do with goals. In late June 1978, Alvin took on the city government, backstage technicians and the cream of society in Rio de Janeiro during a stop on a Latin American tour sponsored in part by the State Department. The company had already performed in Mexico, Peru, Chile and Uruguay when it arrived in Rio to dance at the newly refurbished turn-of-the-century municipal opera theater, where all major arts groups performed before the most elegantly dressed of society audiences.

Alvin issued his usual invitation to local dance students, teachers and performers to come watch rehearsals and take class with the Ailey dancers, and even to teach class on the stage. The first upheaval occurred when the visiting students, invited by the American Embassy, turned out to be white and from the city's ballet schools. Where were the dancers from the samba schools? Alvin asked.

He sent for them. They arrived, with their teachers, and proceeded with Alvin's encouragement to use the theater's ornate new dressing rooms. When they showed up the next day, the samba dancers were barred from the theater until Alvin insisted they be allowed in, threatening to cancel performances unless the doors were opened. "Well, the opera administration had a fit!" Sylvia Waters remembered. "A fit! They were just beside themselves and wanted to keep these people—These People—out of the theater.

"Plus we were there the day of the soccer matches. The World Cup. Every stagehand had a radio, and they could hardly get anything done. Every time somebody won a goal, they would all go 'Yeahhhhhh!' in the middle of rehearsal."

There were arguments with the backstage crew about a fire curtain that suddenly, mysteriously, would not rise the afternoon of the opening performance. "What do you mean it can't go up?" Alvin roared, convinced that this was a case of sabotage. "It went up last night. Why can't it go up for our opening night?" He finally had a meeting with the dancers. He had been through this kind of thing before, he told them. It was all very well to preach about all nations being one. If the curtain didn't go up by 5 P.M., they would leave the theater.

The curtain did rise at last. But friends whom Alvin had invited backstage were barred until Paul Szilard, Alvin's agent, pushed them through the stage door. Alvin finally exploded, losing his last shred of diplomatic decorum as he raged against the deficiencies of the theater and its staff and the ways he himself had been slighted. Theater personnel had treated him like a minor personage in the company and not its founder and director. He was ignored again, he felt, at the opening night party.

"I felt a lot of rage, a lot of hurt, a lot of anger," Alvin told a *New York Times* reporter two weeks later in São Paulo, after wildly popular performances and wide reporting of the disturbance in Rio, in part because Alvin brought the subject up at every interview. "I mean the sort of thing you get from being in the South, I mean really put down as a person." A local reporter suggested that the problems might have occurred because of "the uncommon fact that so many people at one time displayed interest in the dance in Brazil." Perhaps, Alvin speculated, the opera house might now be more comfortable about presenting popular theater and mass audiences might be more comfortable going there. But he doubted it, he said.

He was almost as angry—although more measured in tone—in one of the many interviews he sat through before the twentieth anniversary gala at City Center in late November. The months and weeks leading up to the gala had been crammed not only with rehearsals and informal get-togethers with returning Ailey alumni but with conversation after conversation about the past.

Was race still an issue in American dance? Ken Sandler asked Alvin for a feature for the *SoHo Weekly News*. Talking of the presence of only token blacks in New York's two biggest ballet companies, the American Ballet Theatre and the New York City Ballet, Alvin told Sandler that he believed black dancers now knew there was almost no hope of dancing classical ballet and so didn't bother to train in the field. And he wondered aloud, with a calm that was almost more chilling than his anger, whether it was racism that made him feel that the value of his company had to be proven anew each time onstage. That endless need to prove himself was a recurrent theme in the anniversary interviews.

Alvin was always shrewdly aware of the political ramifications of speaking out on one issue or another. He was seldom averse to addressing loaded subjects when asked for an opinion, however, and he did in these interview sessions, without self-pity or sentimentality. His almost offhanded eloquence, the popularity of his company, Alvin's race and his gift for universalizing specific complaints ensured an audience of readers as he addressed the larger problems that most of the major New

York dance companies faced. Almost in spite of himself, Alvin had become a singularly apt spokesman for dance as the profession nervously embraced new standards of greatness too often measured less by artistry than by fiscal responsibility and corporate efficiency.

The Ailey company was to become famous for its anniversary reunions, gala benefits that celebrated the company's twentieth, twenty-fifth and thirtieth anniversaries with what were in effect onstage parties at which the great mingled familiarly with the small, and the most honored guests were often founding members of the company who had come back for the occasion. On their return, many settled in to work with current company members on Alvin's early pieces, helping the younger dancers to deepen dramatic nuances and fine-tune telling details that had gotten lost or submerged in the general quest for show-stopping technical expertise.

It had become harder for more recent company members to understand some of the underlying emotions of the earliest Ailey dances. They had certainly experienced painful and frightening racist incidents, but such incidents were largely aberrations in an at least superficially egalitarian culture.

How to explain to them the kind of deeply ingrained pain that made the first Ailey dancers know in their bones exactly how and why Alvin wanted hands to fist and strain in one section of *Blues Suite* so tightly that arms trembled? It wasn't the misery of losing one's wallet, as Masazumi Chaya put it. It was the pain of being told that there were suddenly no rooms when you walked into a hotel lobby in all your black glory after a thirteen-hour overnight bus trip on tour. It was the shame of going into a restaurant in Atlanta with a black fellow dancer and friend, having the waitress hand only white-skinned you a menu, and then not knowing what to say to that friend when you left together without ordering. Most of all, it was being shocked but not surprised by such behavior.

Working with the older dancers and listening to them trade anecdotes was an eye-opening process, particularly in rehearsals for *Revelations*. "Oh, *that's* why!" Gary DeLoatch remembered thinking as he watched the "old-timers" talk about bits of business in the dance's finale.

Few of the older dancers turned Alvin down, although Ivy Clarke refused to participate despite his public recognition of her importance to the company in at least one interview. For a few, the gala represented a resumption or strengthening of long-ago friendships with

Alvin. "It will be interesting to see what this antiquated mechanism will be able to perform," James Truitte wrote Alvin from Cincinnati. "However, I'm looking forward to seeing familiar faces and doing dances I love."

Carmen de Lavallade came back, as did Hope Clarke, Charles and Ella Moore and Dorene Richardson from the earliest companies. Miguel Godreau and William Louther returned to the fold for the evening. And Alvin lovingly dedicated the performance to three pioneering "ladies"—Katherine Dunham, Pearl Primus and Beryl McBurnie, a major figure in the revival and preservation of Caribbean folkloric dance in Trinidad in the 1930s and 1940s.

Once the shouting and embraces and teasing were over, Alvin went back to his preoccupations, now underscored by a deepening sense of the passage of time and of his isolation from friends like Truitte and de Lavallade. Dizzyingly, a large matching grant of $175,000 from the National Endowment for the Arts—a fortune in the years when the three toiled at Michael's Studio, preparing for the Ninety-second Street Y—was now a mere drop in the bucket of the company's needs. And Alvin talked increasingly about feeling like a stranger in his own house to friends who, accustomed to his theatricality, downplayed his genuine pain.

Well before the announcement came of the impending demolition of the East Fifty-ninth Street building, Clarke and others had begun a search for new headquarters for the school and company. Clarke had had her eye on the building that had once housed the Columbia University School of Pharmacy on the southern edge of Harlem, and Alvin badly wanted to acquire the palatial nineteenth-century building that had once been the New York Cancer Hospital but was now long abandoned. A ravaged beauty overgrown with weeds and rubbish, it drew Alvin's attention as he took his dog Lucky walking around the block on which it stood, just south of his apartment at 107th Street and Central Park West.

That site also had the advantage of being close to Harlem, living repository that it was of a vital history of black culture. But both buildings would have been far too expensive to renovate. Costs would have been even more prohibitive for another of Alvin's dreams, the construction of a dance center built to the company's specifications. The board had begun negotiations to lease Town Hall on West Forty-third Street when affordable space was suddenly found on three floors of the gleaming new Minskoff building on Broadway between Forty-fourth and Forty-fifth Streets, whose owner, Jerome Minskoff, was a member of the Ailey board.

The anniversary year ended on an even more upbeat note when the entire company was enlisted to help King Hassan II of Morocco bring in the new year. The invitation had come at a command performance by the company at the White House on November 12, in a reception given by President Jimmy Carter for the Moroccan leader. The dancers were to be flown to Rabat where they would entertain the king's guests on New Year's Eve, perform outdoors the following day as a gift from Hassan to his people and then vacation for a week in Morocco, all expenses paid. Describing the offer as "the most fantastic Christmas present we could ever get," Alvin quipped to a reporter: "What an answer I have now to the old question everyone gets at this time of the year. 'What are you doing New Year's Eve?' Dancing for the King of Morocco, that's all."

It was certainly a memorable night. The concert was scheduled for 9:30 in the evening. The dancers had been feted all day long, stuffed with so much food and drink that one of them fell off the stage as they gathered to perform. When at last it was curtain time, the performance was moved to 11 P.M. The dancers were plied with "buckets of caviar and champagne," Hammond recalled. The hour rolled by once more, with the concert rescheduled for 1, then 2 A.M. At 3 A.M., the company found itself finally dancing *Revelations*—in a tent outdoors in the cool desert air—and then was obliged to improvise the dance all over again with the king's musicians and the king himself, who had decided to join in the encore.

Did Alvin find himself making New Year's resolutions that gaudy night? There would have been no point in wishing for anything for his company. It seemed set to roll along through 1979 as if on automatic pilot, with its usual two seasons at City Center and an ambitious two-month, eleven-country tour of Europe in the summer. Alvin received the second of the three major American dance honors that year, too, when he was named to receive the 1979 Capezio Dance Award. Established in 1952 to honor significant contributions in dance, the prize was given to Alvin for his work "as an actor-dancer, director of a company unprecedented in its impact throughout the world, and as a humanist who has interpreted the black heritage as a powerful and unusual expression common to all."

George Faison and Roberta Flack, a member of the Ailey board, were on hand to present the award in a private ceremony on April 23 at the New York Public Library for the Performing Arts at Lincoln Center. Alvin had put a little weight back on since the anniversary celebration five months earlier, and it made him look rugged and powerful, his face exuding the weary wisdom of the humanistic leader described in the award citation. He had taken pains with his clothes and looked stylish as he paused to chat with all comers.

He was at his bashful, disgruntled best, admitting that the award made him "well, nervous." "I hate this kind of thing. It makes you assess, and all that kind of stuff." But he used the opportunity to address several favorite themes. "Not very dignified, is it, to see all the dance companies *scrambling* for foundation funds," he said to the greatest applause in a speech frequently interrupted by affectionate laughter and clapping. He had become more "commercial," he conceded, but "people in this country equate commercial with things that are bad. All it means is that it's popular. I want to reach a broad public. I *still* want to play Madison Square Garden."

The company had begun to move into its new headquarters, a rather fancy home for someone with such populist ideals. Raw space had been carved into a ground-floor school that was a honeycomb of offices, dressing rooms and four enormous studios, its entrance just off the fabled Shubert Alley in the heart of the theater district. Company staff members worked in airy, light-filled, square-box modern offices upstairs. The overall effect was chill, but it was hard not to feel successful and important in such a place.

Minskoff had arranged for the Ailey company to rent office space on the eighth floor and pay back studio construction costs over the ten-year lease. Eventually the four vaulting studios—expanses of gray dance floor, large bright-painted pipes high above and windows that looked out over blazing neon theater marquees—were in demand for the lucrative rehearsing and filming of television dance specials. Here, a little incongruously, children from the city's public schools would learn about modern dance and ballet just hours before Mikhail Baryshnikov might arrive for a television rehearsal. Blind and deaf children and adults would be encouraged to relax and move freely in a room that would be filled that night with blasé Broadway chorus dancers. Here, too, a new generation of Ailey dancers would come of age, in surroundings that outdid Clarke's stubborn dreams for the future.

Upstairs, in a corner office that he claimed was bigger than the space where he had choreographed *Revelations*, Alvin sat at a large, handsome hammered-metal desk once owned by Helena Rubenstein.

His back to the soaring, light-strewn panorama of Times Square beyond his floor-to-ceiling corner windows, he was ensconced in a glittering small island afloat in a sea of dark streets, bars and greasy-spoon
restaurants in which he felt much more at home. Books and artifacts
from his travels were stacked haphazardly around him. There was even
a battered trunk or two on the floor.

Alvin felt more isolated than ever, however—the scrappy vitality
and informality of East Fifty-ninth Street were now a part of the past—
and, perhaps predictably, Alvin was soon miserable. He wandered
through the halls, settling into Waters's office to talk whenever she was
there. His own office had become sacrosanct. "He became an icon," Ella
Thompson Moore said. "People were told 'Oh, don't go in there,' but he
would have loved them to bother him."

De Lavallade was profoundly disturbed by a late-night telephone
call she received from Alvin during this time. He thrived on such calls,
coming to life in the early morning hours as he talked about business
with a select few company members and about life in general with a
few friends, chief among them Joyce Trisler of Horton days, who now
taught at the school and who shared his irrepressible sense of humor.
But de Lavallade was not used to this habit of Alvin's, and his call came
at a difficult time. She was working as an actress with the American
Repertory Theater in Cambridge. "He called to say he wanted me to
come back and teach classes. He kept saying, 'The way *I* want to do it.' I
hadn't seen Alvin in a long, long time. I was at Yale. My career had
taken off. I didn't know what to do to calm him down. He sounded so
out of it. And what I kept hearing was 'the way *I* want to do it.'"

Alvin talked frequently, in interviews as well as in private conversation, of feeling overwhelmed by the bigness of what he had wrought.
Friends and colleagues continued to shrug off or smile at his protesta-
tions. His groans were as long, loud and exuberant, after all, as the big
rich laughter that generally signaled Alvin's approach. He still enjoyed
the work of rehearsals and observing classes. With its bustling life and
relatively comfortable demands, the studio was an oasis. But there began to be murmurs of drug use, distantly heard by some of the dancers
and a few of the older students.

The atmosphere lightened somewhat when Alvin took off with
the dancers on the long European tour. But in early October, a few days
before the company was to return to New York, there was shocking
news. Joyce Trisler—drinker, worrier, smart and peppery observer of
life and friend, Alvin's "crazy floppy girl from down the street, loose as

a goose"—was found dead in her New York apartment. The official cause of death was a heart attack. The rumored cause was suicide or an accidental overdose of drugs or alcohol. No one was sure how long she had lain dead, alone in her apartment after her lover left for Paris to set up engagements for the small modern dance company she had struggled so hard to maintain. Trisler was only forty-five, just a little younger than Alvin.

There had been too many deaths in the last few years. Thelma Hill had died alone at home in a fire. Alvin's father was gone, as was his therapist, Hughes, Ellington, Minnie Marshall and Consuelo Atlas. Charles Mingus had died in January and Amos Alexander in late May in Navasota. "Man, I am tired of requiems," Alvin told a friend who complimented him on a solo he had choreographed for a commemorative program for Mingus that summer.

Alvin learned of Trisler's death in a phone call from New York to his hotel room in Antwerp. Two doors down the hall, Alvin's assistant, Mary Barnett, also received a call that afternoon but, like many others in the company, she hesitated at first to go to Alvin. For a time, he was left alone. There was stunned talk of the death at the theater that night. Then and later, however, Alvin registered almost no emotion. He did not attend a memorial service for Trisler, and he talked very little about her.

But he mulled the fact over in his mind that both Trisler and Horton had been younger than he when they died. How much life had he lived? How much life did he have left? When the company reached Paris, he let himself go, taking more drugs, drinking more and inviting Abdul, a young Moroccan man he met there, to come to America and live with him. When the company returned to New York and started rehearsing for the City Center winter season, Alvin began work on a new dance.

He had been listening to tape after tape of classical and popular music on the tour. Jazz piano music by Keith Jarrett seemed to flow out of every room where Alvin was, studio or office, as music always did before he started a new piece. Work began in mid-November, about three weeks before the City Center opening.

Rehearsal sessions started, now too, with Alvin padding into the studio barefoot or in socks, dressed in a baggy pullover and worn sweatpants. He greeted the dancers with the usual hello although without the joking change of voice he sometimes affected to make them laugh. Ordinarily he would sit down and motion the dancers closer to talk, and then bid them to "start doing some movement" that he first demonstrated, as the tape recorder clicked on. There was less conversation now. "Sometimes he'd sit, thinking, thinking," Barnett recalled. "They'd come in, but nothing broke his thought." Eventually he would let most of the dancers go, asking a few to stay and continue with him.

He sat on a bench as he normally did, his chin resting on his hand, his elbow on his knee as he watched, calling out a correction or instruction from time to time but for the most part a little quieter than usual. Barnett sensed in Alvin a greater degree of intensity, almost an obsession, about this piece.

Memoria is essentially a voyage for a woman accompanied by two men who support and frame her. There is a sense of fleeting relationships, of leaving earth but returning for a time, in memory perhaps.

Alvin placed the woman among couples at first and then with a larger group that was finally augmented by a wave of dancing teenagers in a vision whose grandeur he later admitted was inspired by cocaine. She is dressed in a soft, simple off-white gown adorned with a few white flowers at the shoulder. She returns in crimson, a blotch of red on a stage filled with soft colors until the children roar on in their blue jeans and shirts. Both the dance and the music build from a mood of somber yearning to frisky syncopation and finally to a surging, wild melodic joy.

There were hints that this was to be a dance about Trisler, although it took Alvin some time to realize that himself. He talked just a little about *Memoria* being a celebration of the woman many of the dancers had known as a teacher. He told the senior dancers small stories about her. "Her etherealness when she was onstage," Keith McDaniel said. "The passion she brought to her dancing." Allen recalled that Alvin talked about the dance in terms of "searching, suffering, and then joyousness at the end, when the freedom happens."

"One of the steps, he'd cover his ears," Allen said. "You knew he was hearing things and it was too much. He didn't want to hear any more."

He wove into the dance key phrases from the Horton technique and from the Trisler classic, the lyrical *Journey*. But *Memoria* can also be seen as a piece about a woman, a teacher, on her way through a life. The dance builds steadily to a climax in which the woman's body is lifted up above the crowd that has closed in around her in an unforgettable last image. The greatest beauty of *Memoria*, however, is the way the shifting groups and individuals are moved about in intricate flowing lines and circles, traveling so unerringly that the effect is as poignantly simple as anything in *Revelations.*

Alvin worked with the senior company, setting the movement and then paring it down. His rehearsals were usually fun. Donna Wood, who played the Trisler figure in the first New York performances of the dance, remembered that her private sessions with Alvin were grueling, with frequent repetitions of steps and phrases but with an exalting sense of the oneness of the dance and music.

There were two long stage rehearsals for the younger dancers, many of whom had studied recently with Trisler. It was a traumatic time for the twenty-two extras, who learned the steps and gestures Alvin had created for them from Waters and Kelvin Rotardier, the directors of the junior Ailey companies. They had been drilled to perfection, but once they were on the stage, dancing for "Mr. Ailey," there was a lot of bumping and some tears. Although Alvin attempted to put them at ease with jokes, his scrutiny was a little frightening, for he seemed to look into their midst without seeing the dance at all.

"We were very scared," Rodney Nugent, a student dancer who later joined the Ailey senior company, recalled. "Somehow the first-company people looked very big, even if they were not tall. And they were dancing movement that you never thought you'd be able to do, especially that fast." Jasmine Guy, another of the junior dancers, was nearly trampled as she sat in the wings watching, so mesmerized was she by the scene before her.

Alvin worked more quickly and surely than ever on the dance, which seemed to pour out of him. "It did come quickly, but it was very hard," Nugent said, "because he was really very fragile at that time. He was pushing himself, fighting to put it together. I think the form was very clear to him. The dance was about the deification of Joyce." Alvin referred frequently to Gary DeLoatch, one of the two men accompanying the woman, as a guide. Some dancers believed the two men represented Alvin and James Truitte, and that the second lead woman, danced by Allen, might be an angel. Others, irreverently, thought of the men as Trisler's estranged husband and her lover.

Alvin dedicated the season and the dance to "the joy . . . the beauty . . . the creativity . . . and the wild spirit of my friend Joyce Trisler." Kenneth Patchen's chill and wrenching poem, "In Memory of Kathleen," which was quoted in the program, suggested the depth of Alvin's desolation. "How pitiful is her sleep," the poem read. "Now her clear breath is still. There is nothing falling tonight, Bird or man, As dear as she. Nowhere that she should go Without me. None but my calling. O nothing but the cold cry of the snow."

Trisler had died alone. Somehow, Alvin felt responsible. He should have kept in closer touch with her. He should have been with her when she died. "We prayed that it was going to work," Wood said of the dance.

As stoical as ever, Alvin showed little response of any sort backstage on the night of the New York premiere, disappearing quickly from the theater after the program ended. Months later he would weep at what he had created. But not yet. The reviews were quietly positive and the audience responsive to the dance's elegiac glow. One day *Memoria* would become a beloved Ailey signature dance. For now, it was perceived as a touching response to the loss of a dear friend.

Back at the office, however, Alvin was behaving in erratic ways that were sometimes more frightening than any burst of temper. There were times when he sat for hours in his darkened office watching tapes of Sara Yarborough dancing. He had a new receptionist fired for mistakenly calling him "Mr. Alley." Other staff members, some of them longtime employees, were summarily dismissed for little or no discernible reason, although the wryly laid-back Hammond managed to rehire them quietly.

Sometimes Alvin arrived at the office dressed in peculiar outfits, once with his head covered by a knit ski mask in the middle of summer. He was looking even more disreputable than ever, a good thing, possibly, since he occasionally walked the entire distance from his apartment to the office with thousands of dollars in his pockets. There were telephone calls to the office from private detectives Alvin thought of hiring to look into mysterious apparent thefts by Abdul, the young Arab he had brought back from Paris. And Alvin decided to pamper himself with unrestrained shopping sprees and twenty-four-hour limousine service.

One frequent destination was the Nuyorican Poets Café on the Lower East Side, a small unfancy place of the sort where theatrical magic tends most to occur. Alvin and its director, Miguel Algarin, both drank in the same tawdry pickup bar near the Port Authority bus terminal on West Forty-second Street and had recognized each other at a poetry reading organized by Algarin one summer night at the Delacorte Theater in Central Park.

They bumped into each other again at City Center during an Ailey season. Alvin asked what Algarin, also a college professor of

English literature, did for a living. "I was really leery about telling him," Algarin said. "I too enjoyed being without—without the pretense of being a professor of literature. It was wonderful to be there just myself." Where did Algarin live? East Sixth Street, he told Alvin, not imagining that he would remember.

Around midnight that night, as Algarin worked on a script with the playwright Miguel Pinero in Algarin's street-level apartment, there was suddenly a noise at the window. Pinero paled, staring past Algarin out into the street, where a very large black man in a flowing caftan was peering into the room. "Oh, that's Alvin Ailey," Algarin said, laughing, and let him in.

The two became good friends. Algarin shared Alvin's love for theater, good writing and the seedy, teeming life of Times Square and the Blarney Stone bar where the two had first gotten to know each other by sight. "That was truly the element in which I think Alvin really socially thrived. He enjoyed unpretentious working-class places. There are Blarney Stones all over the city. This one was everything. You would have your drinks. All of the dancers and the artists and the hustlers were there. Clearly Alvin was not there to cast a ballet. No, it was his social milieu.

"The milieu that delighted Alvin and interested him was not, let us say, the salons of the rich, where we would go and hurry out as if there were a fire. It wasn't the parties after opening nights. Not because Alvin was too much of an artist or a genius to put up with society. The society he sought was on the street level. And it nourished him. All those great hot passionate jazz ballets had more to do with the social world of his street life than they had to do with the social world of the 1940s coquettes in some kind of Harlem speakeasy. Yeah, the frame became that. But the heat of it was like the world of the street, which he *really* loved."

His friendship with Algarin must have been a great relief for Alvin. Neither man was shocked by anything in the other's life. Neither expected anything of the other. They seldom even made plans to see each other. "Say that I were at the theater or at Sixth Street and I said to myself, damn, I should go and get Alvin. I wouldn't go to his house if it were after midnight. I wouldn't call him. There would be no point. I wouldn't think he was at the Russian Tea Room. I'd know to take a cab to Forty-second Street between Eighth and Seventh Avenue and if I was walking that route someone would say, 'Miguel! You're looking for Alvin, right?' Yes. 'He's at the bar.' This is the way."

Algarin instinctively understood the pressures Alvin felt. "It was the rags to riches story. You're in tatters. You're putting together something brilliant which is being held by the slightest glue, the strongest force being yourself. And what you generate grows into this *major* institution, multimillion-dollar budget, and en route it starts to choke you in a way. As it grows, there is a flank of administrators that comes between you and the dancers. There's a board of directors that comes between you and the administration and the dancers. There is a union that comes between you and rehearsal time. Mr. Balanchine once said he created his ballets around union time, towards the end. But before long these layers of bureaucratic functions become hurdles that you have to climb time and time again. The tresses become so long that the scalp feels the pull."

Alvin would go downtown to the café shaking with rage sometimes at his board and other problems. "What is that Greek story?" Algarin says. "The ball being rolled up the hill. And the moment Alvin let go it ran over him." At the café, he would watch the crowd of young people who stayed on to dance after the shows, pushing the chairs to the side to make a disco floor. Sometimes Alvin would walk out incognito onto the dance floor and move the dancers through choreographed disco moves, with none of them suspecting who he was.

One night he discovered Algarin's secondhand, patched-together light board, set up in a small back balcony that looked down on the theater. He dashed up and began to work a lush play of colored lights across the dancing bodies, light that was in throbbing symbiosis with the music's beat.

"Alvin would stand there yanking the goddamn lights and as the beat went he went with it. Bam bam bam bam. And of course the young people were in total ecstasy. And of course no one had any reason to know that a musical master was at the lights and that they were actually for the first time in their damned lives dancing to life's work by Mr. Alvin Ailey."

Algarin tried to stop Alvin, knowing that he was destroying the dimmer board that he had barely been able to afford and was inordinately proud of. "Oh, Miguel, have fun," Alvin told him when he complained, locking Algarin out of the balcony. This went on for several nights until, in a fury, Algarin roared onto the dance floor one night and was transfixed.

"Alvin was letting the mood of the music move him, and so it wasn't just some kind of madman crazed with buttons. It was lyrical manipulation of light, as if he were doing dance movement on the lights. Here was a bunch of ghetto kids dancing, but now it wasn't only the music. The lights had taken them too. Willie the soundman cut the sound for a moment, because it seemed to him that the lights were doing a magical reproduction of the sound and he wanted to see if it were true. And Alvin continued the lights, and this room erupted in cheers, screaming, and everyone danced more intensely. There was no music. So he had pulled it off. From that day on I let him destroy the board, without complaining. Which he did. Totally."

Alvin also terrorized Algarin's actors, stationing himself up in the balcony during late-night rehearsals before anyone could stop him and pitching cans and bottles down at actors he felt were not being honest or passionate enough. One actor in particular incurred his wrath as she rehearsed a love scene. "She was not focused. I think she was terrified. I screamed to Alvin to stop it." Couldn't Algarin see the woman was incompetent? Alvin asked. Algarin begged the actor to "show some activity onstage." The madman up in the balcony would not throw anything at her if she acted. And she did, at last.

"You see, Alvin believed at this point that he was God. The world had grown around him. He had gone into high gear. To grow from borrowing space to rehearse in to having these offices in this luxurious high-rise. Those extraordinary studios. It was beyond anyone's castle dreams. And then the people that started to come through. You'd go in and find Baryshnikov exercising. Makarova with Ivan Nagy. He was on Forty-fifth Street being very glamorous in what was probably some of the most glamorous studio space in the world. And then five blocks down he'd come to join me so we could go to our favorite cheap Irish bar where all the mad people of the world hung out. I think he wanted the glamour. It was just that along with it came a certain demeanor."

One night Alvin wandered in as Algarin was despondently trying to help Pinero find an ending for a play titled Nuyorican Nights. "I made a deal with Alvin that if I let him in he would move the cast around, I would send them home and we would go out and play." Algarin cued the sound to a song by Tom Waits called "Closing Time" and told Alvin to go to work.

He began immediately to arrange people on the little stage and tell them what to do. Algarin followed at his heels, pushing the dance captain to memorize every detail. Three minutes and twenty seconds later, at precisely the moment the song ended, Alvin finished putting together the dance that closed Nuyorican Nights. "I had tears in my eyes. I said, 'Oh, Alvin, you ended the play.' He said, 'Good, now send them home.' "

A few Ailey dancers went downtown with Alvin to the café, but no one else in the company seems to have known of this secret other life. Somehow Alvin was able to pull himself together when he worked in the studio, no matter how late he might have "played" or how irrational he appeared to the Ailey office staff. He was, after all, an actor.

He failed to convince everyone, however. Finally Barnett, Jamison and Waters took a stubbornly unheeding Alvin aside and talked to him about getting help. He turned away from them in disgusted disbelief.

Life went on, as it always seemed to do. And then, on March 9, 1980, New Yorkers awoke to the news that Alvin Ailey—the choreographer and founder of one of the world's great modern dance companies and a respected leader in the cultural life of the city—had gone mad.

twenty-eight

BREAKDOWN

The facts were simple. Alvin Ailey had been arrested at International House, a residence for graduate students at 500 Riverside Drive, just north of Columbia University, on the afternoon of March 7. He had been charged by the police with criminal trespass, harassment, disorderly conduct and resisting arrest after trying to force his way into the building in search of a friend living there. Admitted for observation at Bellevue Hospital, Alvin underwent psychiatric testing and was released a week later. The charges were dropped, but the news of the humiliating arrest began to spread, robbing him of the last vestiges of his cherished privacy.

There had been times when, for a few moments, Alvin almost defiantly laid open his life away from dance, arriving at a formal fundraising affair for the company, for instance, with a disreputable-looking date who seemed to have been picked up along the way. He wandered around the theater looking, as a friend put it sadly, like a battered alley cat.

One night when Alvin and several bar-cruising friends were leaving a place that Brother John Sellers remembered as a "slimy, slimy hole," someone spotted a board member coming out of the theater across the street. Be careful, Sellers warned Alvin, she may see you. "Let her see me," Alvin said. He didn't care if she did. Everybody had to have somebody, some life. "He *did* care," Miguel Algarin said. "At that moment he was grandstanding. He did care to keep those two things separate. And if he could help it he would not have had that person look at him. But it was important that he feel free enough to have his life."

That separation took literal shape in Alvin's notion at one point of renting the apartment next door to his and turning it into a kind of harem for his "night creatures." His own apartment would be retained as his everyday home. He would tear down the dividing wall and build a secret door beyond which would take place what Algarin called Alvin's "Arabian trap-door dreams." Those dreams, probably never very serious, were dashed when he was turned down for the second rental.

Alvin's two lives were joined in Abdul, the man Alvin was trying to reach at International House when he was arrested. Eighteen years older than the Moroccan, whom he believed to be even younger, Alvin had seemed to some to be genuinely in love with him, and he attempted to assume the roles of both mentor and lover. No one in Alvin's very small circle of confidants thought much of Abdul, whom they pegged as a hustler who had used Alvin to get to the United States. A slight and unprepossessingly scruffy man who looked younger than his thirty years, Abdul seldom took off the dark glasses that gave him a slightly sinister or at least disengaged look. He looked unsavory, his face obscured not only by the glasses but by a big mustache and fluffy hair that fell over his forehead and nearly to his shoulders.

Alvin enrolled Abdul as an engineering student at the Polytechnic Institute of New York and installed him in the apartment on Central Park West. But only months after his arrival in New York, Abdul sneaked out in the midst of a late-night party and moved into International House, where he had friends.

Alvin had grown suspicious of Abdul, although he fought hard to believe that on some level the Moroccan did love him. When he began to miss things around the house, he suspected Abdul of stealing them but later refused to believe that he could have been one of the "young men who take things" whom Alvin knew so well. He persisted in seeing the man as an innocent youth, possibly bisexual or even heterosexual, who had been driven away by Alvin's use of drugs and by his less reputable friends. His departure left Alvin deeply wounded.

Alvin's despair over all the deaths of the past few years was exacerbated by the growing demands of a career that had in many ways become less satisfying and by his inability to control the sexual and drug habits that had increasingly offered release from the difficulties of his work. Soon after Abdul disappeared, Alvin took a hammer to a marble-topped table he prized and smashed it into small pieces. He was observed pulling paper out of trash baskets in Central Park in the middle of the night. He had taken to shoplifting at the neighborhood supermarket, surprised when he was caught to discover that neither the store manager nor the police knew that he owned everything in the store. Riding in his rented limousine, he cowered at glowing red stoplights, sure they were a sign of danger.

Then, early on that March morning, Alvin called Sellers and asked that he accompany him uptown to find Abdul. Sellers refused. Alvin made his way alone to the back entrance of the residence hall and called Abdul repeatedly on the house telephone. When there was no answer, he cut across the block and entered from Riverside Drive into the handsome stone building. As luck would have it, the administrative offices had been moved into a single large room during renovations. The room was filled with people. Alvin walked over to the admissions area and asked fairly calmly for Abdul. Not getting an answer that satisfied him, he disappeared for a few moments and returned in an agitated state.

He began to shout, demanding that he be let into Abdul's room. Marian Sylla, a young staff member, called Abdul and told him that Alvin wanted to see him. It was not Alvin's first visit to the building that day. That morning and earlier in the week there had been shouted arguments conducted through the closed door of Abdul's room on the eighth floor. Abdul told Sylla that Alvin was crazy and to ignore him. She went back to Alvin and told him that his friend did not want to see him.

"He went ballistic," Sylla recalled. The building's security guards arrived, but they were not trained to handle such a disturbance, and someone called the police. By now, Alvin had charged out into the long, elegant old main lounge, watched from the door of their office by frightened staff members. In his rage, he threw a chair down a flight of stairs, breaking its legs. Suddenly the police were there, tackling Alvin to the ground, pulling his hands behind his back and handcuffing him. "He looked really miserable," Sylla said, her voice trembling at the memory of the pain she saw in his eyes. "His clothes started coming down and he had no underwear. A porter brought a blanket to cover him. I thought, 'My God, this is the great Alvin Ailey.' "

By now, it was midafternoon. Few of the residents were in the building, but a journalism student who lived there happened on the scene and called the story in to local newspapers. Most of the people standing around Alvin, screening him as he lay on the floor, did not at first realize who he was, and so, Sylla felt, there would otherwise have been a good chance of keeping the incident quiet. "He looked so sad, so beaten emotionally. He asked for the handcuffs to be loosened. They were too tight. But they didn't." At last, after what seemed a very long time, ambulance attendants arrived with a stretcher and took Alvin away, downtown to the grim psychiatric division of the city-run Bellevue Hospital, where he was met by Stanley Plesent and Paul Szilard. "Stanley, make them take these handcuffs off me," Alvin cried out. "I can't make these people take the handcuffs off, Alvin," Plesent responded gravely. But he promised to get a lawyer, and then Alvin was whisked off again, out of sight, into the turmoil of the hospital emergency room.

Abdul stayed on in New York for another few months before returning to Paris. He and Alvin never saw each other again. Alvin went back to work, seeming surprisingly unfazed by the incident. But James Truitte, for one, was worried. Meeting Alvin in a hallway at the Ailey headquarters soon after his breakdown, Truitte asked him how he felt. Fine, Alvin told him, adding that there hadn't been anything wrong with him in the first place. If you feel like that, my friend, Truitte said to himself, then there is something wrong. And early on the morning of April 30, the geyser blew again.

It had begun boiling again a few days earlier, when Alvin ran through the halls of his apartment house banging on doors and screaming "Fire!" late one night. No one is sure whether the rampage was set off by a small fire in his apartment that he set but then managed to put out, or if he was hallucinating. When police and firefighters arrived, Alvin watched from a bench across the street as they searched in vain for the fire.

A few nights later, at around 2:30 A.M., he raced through the building once more, pounding on doors to warn everyone that there was a fire. Doors opened and tenants, many of whom knew Alvin, poured out into the halls. On the twelfth floor, a woman opened her door to him. Knocked to the ground as he blindly pushed his way inside, she had him charged with assault. He had already called the fire department. There were several other calls. Six trucks raced to the building, but no fire was found.

Again, Alvin watched calmly from a park bench. But this time someone in the building pointed him out to the police, who recognized him and took him to St. Luke's Hospital for psychiatric observation. A few hours later, he was booked on burglary and assault charges and spent the rest of the night in jail.

There had been relatively little coverage of the first incident. This time, the tabloids went to town. "Alvin Ailey Runs Amok Again," a headline blared in the New York Post. Alvin's mother, worried already by the strange calls she had been receiving from her son, was summoned to New York. Meg Gordean, the company publicist, flew in from Washington to deal with the press. An informal committee had begun to meet after the first incident, made up of Dudley Williams, Judith Jamison, Masazumi Chaya and William Hammond, who was now executive director of the company. That Alvin needed help was clear, but they could not legally commit him. He had to sign himself in, and that, they saw, was not about to happen. Plesent had begun to look into treatment facilities and so, by the second arrest, they were prepared.

A deal had been negotiated with the district attorney that charges would eventually be dropped if Alvin agreed to commit himself to an institution Plesent had found in White Plains, the Cornell Medical Center New York Hospital Westchester Division. "Alvin was so taut and intense we had no idea what he was going to do," Hammond said. "We had debated who should tell him. Lula agreed to."

Why not be a man and choose to take care of yourself? Lula Cooper told her son as he stood near her in handcuffs in the tense courtroom. He agreed and told the judge that he was prepared to seek treatment, speaking so quietly, however, that the judge could not at first hear him. Then Alvin turned and walked out into a waiting ambulance. Outside the courthouse, his mother consoled the others. "Meg, relax," she reassured Gordean. "A great ballet will come out of this."

Alvin had been slightly cheered by the reputation of the Westchester hospital for treating the rich and famous. Politicians had gone there for drug treatment, Alvin had heard, and famous movie stars had dried out at the institution. But the trip by ambulance, strapped down and holding his mother's hand, was embarrassing as well as frightening.

As it turned out, Alvin was the doctors' best-known patient. "They were really wonderful with him there," Hammond recalled. "I think they were kind of intrigued by having a famous artist in their midst and having to bring him back to life."

The hospital, consisting mostly of handsome old buildings set into a green rolling landscape on which could be found a small golf course, a rugby field and a formal garden, had all the decorum and antique charm of an old spa or private boarding school. Alvin's room was small and sparely furnished, with a shared bathroom. The windows were unbarred, there were enclosed lawns where he could sit and soak up the sun without fear of discovery by the outside world or the temptation to bolt. Here, as one staff member put it, the idea was to learn both how to take care of oneself and how to be taken care of.

There were group therapy sessions and periodic consultations with medical doctors and psychiatrists, but for the first few weeks Alvin was sunk in so profound a depression that he scarcely noticed his surroundings. Eventually he began to be aware of other patients, encouraging those with an artistic bent to take that interest seriously. He began exercising and getting himself back into shape physically, and even participated in crafts sessions. He also revived enough to request, a little peremptorily, supplies of cigarettes, chocolates and books from the few friends he allowed to visit. His mother brought him a book of hers, *The Power of Prayer*. Back in Los Angeles, she told him, her church was praying for him.

Diagnosed as manic-depressive and put on lithium, Alvin returned to New York at the end of June. Jamison had taken over the company in his two-month absence, clearly an interim arrangement since she was preparing for a Broadway show. He had lost his apartment, but a board member found him one in a new building in the West Fifties called, ironically enough, the Encore. And the ranks closed behind him, with Plesent and Gordean making sure that he was protected from the media during the difficult first months after his release.

There were so many probable reasons for Alvin's breakdown that, in retrospect, it seems astonishing it took so long to happen—and that he was able to continue producing an amount and quality of work that would have consumed a healthy man. He had been drinking too much for at least two decades. His use of diet pills and other drugs, including, at the end, cocaine, had escalated in recent years. And the private life he sought to keep private was one many would find sordid, especially in a man who was in public life a role model, a visionary and a remarkably successful businessman in the most unbusinesslike of professions.

The young beauty who went to New York to perform on Broadway was not a sexual innocent. But there was then and continued to be a fundamental innocence in Alvin that manifested itself in his excited fascination, those early years in New York City, with what he referred to as "gutter" activities to a friend. No matter how promiscuously he behaved, in all of his addictions that haunting, troubling core of purity remained.

He trusted no one, essentially, but was curious about and open toward everything in the world around him. It was a lethal combination. His larger-than-life emotions and his easy superficial expression of them, with genuine eloquence or exuberant theatricality, served effectively to screen him and keep him private, giving him the isolation he craved his entire life. Everyone was his friend and he was a friend to all in his daily life, from stray animals to dancers he might abuse emotionally but cared greatly for and worried about. In turn, he was genuinely loved by even the most casual of acquaintances—so warm and funny and perceptive that he was irresistible.

But the pressure of a double life had long been building in him. Ivy Clarke had been troubled by his avid talk, poignantly naive at first, about what he thought of as the wicked ways of the theater folk around him. Soon he had embraced those ways. Nat Horne, a fellow cast member in *Jamaica* and an early Ailey dancer, later recalled his exasperation when he discovered that discarded champagne corks were the reason the toilet was frequently clogged when Alvin lived in his apartment house in the 1960s. Clarke felt a little uncomfortable with the offhanded way Alvin brought lovers home when he lived with her. Another roommate worried at some of the disreputable people he began to see hanging around outside the building where he and Alvin were living.

By the mid-1970s, Alvin's sexual encounters tended to be even more impersonal and impermanent, their chief emotion the thrill of danger. Did Alvin's promiscuity and his general secrecy about his life in general suggest that some part of this inherent innocent was appalled by his sexuality? Several old friends watched and worried, unable to stop what seemed to them profoundly self-destructive behavior.

"He could have had anybody he wanted," Mickey Bord said despairingly. "Especially when he was young. And he always picked on the crap. I always wondered. Was it because he thought so little of himself? Because he was maybe unsure and these people flattered him? But a lot of people flattered him. Everyone told him he was marvelous and wonderful. Why did he have to?"

"Alvin was extraordinarily talented. He could write, he could speak, he could act, he could dance. He just didn't want to live."

Algarin rejects the idea that Alvin acted out of shame. "Alvin's erotic sexual fantasy fulfilled itself in just the opposite ways that he fulfilled his artistic fantasy," he said. "In his artistic fantasy, there were studios, exquisite human bodies. But he would be attracted to a Puerto

Rican or a black man on the street sooner than to any of those males. His homoerotic fantasies were like an enormous physical release for him. His artistic fantasies were released completely within the strictures and disciplines of the company. His homoerotic fantasies were chaotic, sporadic, dangerous. How often, you know, was he not robbed? Not robbed physically at gunpoint or anything. But like you go and take a pee and you come back and find that your wallet has been rifled through. And the disappointment that comes, or the exhilaration that comes with the new meat every night.

"To say that Alvin's homoerotic fantasies were demeaning to his personal stature is precisely to have misread him. I don't think he did it because he had a low opinion of himself. I think he did it because there's something heat-wise, something hot and dangerous and exciting about it. And I don't think he felt himself demeaned by it."

Several Ailey dancers who felt close to Alvin talk of his developing illness and breakdown as simply a lack of ease in living, a condition of "dis-ease," as Keith McDaniel put it. Part of Alvin's love of danger had to do with drugs and seeing just how far he could go. By 1980, Alvin told Rodney Nugent in a movingly candid final interview for a video documentary that the former Ailey dancer was preparing, he was taking cocaine in Perrier in the morning and cocaine in champagne at night. "Everyone thought of cocaine as recreational in 1980," he said. "I became addicted."

"Alvin loved to get into trouble," Nugent says. "I really believe he wanted to be Isadora. He wanted to be exposed, found out."

That need to live dangerously can be a symptom of manic-depression, as can promiscuity. Alvin may have begun to suffer from the disorder in his late teens. Certainly the life of a dance company director in the 1960s and 1970s was prime fodder for a manic-depressive, a thing of drastic ups and downs into which Alvin threw himself for the most part with wily, vociferous gusto. What was clear, however, was that at heart Alvin was always a deeply lonely person. "I don't think he ever had fun with anybody," Paul Szilard said. "Everything was escape."

Success had come to him early, but it was a success he shrugged off almost superstitiously. "I don't think he ever really thought about what he was doing," Donna Wood said. "He just kept doing it, and he kept doing it, and he kept doing it. And I don't know if he realized he was getting anywhere. Yes, it was getting bigger. And yes, it was getting stronger. And yes, he had definitely gone from the Ninety-second Street Y to City Center to the Munich Opera House to you name it. But it's endless. It just keeps going. You go from New York to Ann Arbor and five years later you go back and they don't know who you are. So you start all over. You just keep doing. And I wonder sometimes if that didn't help kind of wear him into the ground."

By 1979, his little family had become a national cultural institution, and his dancers, young enough now to be his children, as Alvin observed to friends, were members of a profession. It might have helped if he could have kept the junior company as a workshop group with which to create new work and explore new forms of dance and music. But in a sense, Alvin had already begun to "lose" what he had made when Howard Squadron and Stanley Plesent entered his life in 1974 and it became clear it all had to be taken to another level. Al Holtz recalls how quickly the skepticism of major foundations died when they were approached by a businesslike board with businesslike records and plans for the future. How better could Alvin be served than by giving him the best possible instrument for his creativity and the freedom to use it?

He could choreograph to his heart's content now, torturously free to face the devil of his own and others' expectations—but only on union time and with two-year goals and unyielding budgets in mind. No more life-or-death plotting and planning as he padded from office to office in his stocking feet and practice clothes. Now all he had to do was show up at the cocktail parties of the rich and influential, dressed like the director of an important company worthy of investment. He was now indisputably a star. Increasingly, however, he had come to feel that his life was not his own.

"The board obviously was at times an obstacle on specific issues," Plesent said. "Perhaps just the fact of setting forth a budget. There was tension between the artistic role and the business side. But the streets are littered with the remains of dance companies that didn't make it.

"Alvin was angry at us because there was never enough money to do what he wanted to do. The good news was that over time—and I guess it was a function in part of how Alvin was feeling about the world and himself—Alvin kind of got it, that you could work with a board. There was a famous board meeting in the late 1970s. We were marking up the proposed budget for the year. I called Alvin and said, 'Look, the financial committee is meeting tonight. There will have to be cuts. Could you come and help us with this thing?' He came, and it was as productive a meeting as we ever had. Alvin was a thoroughgoing part of that meeting, without anger. He got it. At the end of the meeting I said to myself, 'The millennium has arrived.'

"Alvin had many frustrations, as all people and all creative people do. To some extent, the board became a symbol. The fact is, the board did the best it could. I don't know if any board ever does well enough for its artistic head."

There is an old saying that one must be careful what one wishes for. Alvin had gotten what he wanted, and there were times when he hated it and the Plesents of the world. Like most, this board of directors inhabited another world. For the most part, they were not friends. Some of their dealings with Alvin were ruthless and thoughtless, then and later, as fiscal prudence began to come first in this new age of dance. On the other hand, how many artistic directors of dance companies see the board chairman's duties as encompassing such tasks as getting them and their relatives out of jail or dealing with angry landlords?

Part of the problem was Alvin's vision of a large company with a repertory that was a world repository of dance. The state-supported European companies gave him all that he needed when he choreographed for them. Why couldn't he be treated that way in America? The company's impressive-looking Minskoff headquarters, so different from funky Fifty-ninth Street, fit into that vision. But Alvin never quite felt at home there. He wanted to be important and to be treated as such, but he also wanted to be able to joke with his dancers and wear whatever ratty clothes he had at hand. The board's goal was relatively uncomplicated: to keep the company going.

The fact that this contradictory but successful and genuinely important artist was also black—and a black man—added another layer of complication to the mix. And Alvin's now very public problems played into stereotypes of black men as creatures ruled by their natural impulses, without sufficient foresight or control to create anything as complex as a multimillion-dollar business.

But he had done that, persisting over a long and arduous time, at first intent on mere survival and then on proving, again and again, that he and his dancers were more than the success or failure of their latest work. With his vision of a company that would represent all of America and some of the best of its modern dance, regardless of the race of the choreographer, Alvin also did not fulfill the expectation that black achievement—or any activity by blacks—somehow represents the race. In addition, his dance and dancers were just too much fun to be art.

Audiences loved the bursting theatrical vitality and unabashed humanity of the "accessible" dance performed by the Ailey company in the late 1950s and the 1970s. It was true that with each succeeding generation of Ailey dancers, those qualities began unavoidably to spring less from the dances themselves and become more a matter of company style than of personal experience or of heart. But it is also true that dance has never been considered a theatrical art or even entertainment. And so, for some, whether Alvin's work was truly art was questionable.

The charge of commercialism was leveled against Alvin, his choreography and his company by people who were for the most part fair-minded and had a wide acquaintanceship with dance. Their criticism prompted a 1978 essay from Anna Kisselgoff in the *New York Times* that was a favorite of Alvin's, placing his work solidly within the framework of the larger dance scene in which it rightfully belonged but from which it was often implicitly excluded.

"With the 20th anniversary celebration of the Alvin Ailey American Dance Theater this season, it has been easy to look back nostalgically at the good old bad days," Kisselgoff wrote in the critical commentary "Has Ailey Really Gone Commercial?" "Two decades ago the Ailey company shared the mystique of commitment common to modern dance. It was the dedication of a small young troupe involved in the exploration of an evolving esthetic and a dance style. That commitment obviously cannot be reproduced by a company that is now established on a unique wave of popularity and by dancers who, rather than collaborate at creating the whole cloth of a new dance style, now put on that style as if it were a ready-made suit. Such progression—from struggle to accomplishment, from search to consolidation—is the path followed by all major dance companies in the last 20 years and it is not surprising that the Ailey troupe has gone the same way.

"Yet it isn't uncommon to hear the Ailey success story attributed to the company's going commercial. The corollary is that it has also gone 'showbiz' in the last decade. Both these assumptions are not only misplaced but seem directed at an organization that least deserves them." What, Kisselgoff wondered, did the charge of commercialism mean? "The broad appeal of the Ailey company should not be confused with Broadway's policy of presenting works out of box office considerations instead of an artist's need to express himself creatively. In fact, the record shows that Alvin Ailey has given more young choreographers—including black choreographers who have not had this wide an audience—a greater chance than any artistic director of a major company. . . . An artistic director who allows so many choreographers to express themselves—to fail as often as they succeed—is a very odd commercial specimen.

"It would be easy to reply that such choreographers are given this exposure because the public demands new works every season and that Mr. Ailey, by his own account, no longer has the urge to create all these premieres. Yet, there is no doubt that Alvin Ailey genuinely believes in the repertory concept, and he was the first to prove that it could work in modern dance as well as in ballet."

Kisselgoff went on to enumerate the reasons why commercialism might be an issue. Alvin and some of his choreographers used popular music. He had included "showbiz" elements as a comment on "showbiz" itself. The choreography danced by the company frequently incorporated popular dance forms. And there were perhaps too few social protest dances in this repertory that emphasized the black heritage.

Many of the solos created recently for the Ailey had been set to popular songs, but their weakness, Kisselgoff wrote, was that the dances tended merely to illustrate the lyrics and serve as vehicles for star dancers. "Yet 'Cry' has become a universal classic," Kisselgoff continued. "It is not the form but the quality that determines whether such dances are artistic creations. In the same way, as seen in this season's revival of his 'Flowers,' Mr. Ailey shows how the trappings of 'showbiz' can be used to artistic effect as a condemnation of 'showbiz' itself." The music might be rock, she continued, and the choreography for the ensemble might be in a "chorus-boy style," but Alvin had turned the style in on itself.

The company style was based on the techniques of Lester Horton and Martha Graham, but flavored with a kind of jazz-dance style seen frequently on Broadway and television and transformed by Alvin into something richer in works like *Night Creature*. And if recent dances in the Ailey repertory did not make one think or feel very deeply or measure up to his early classics, Kisselgoff added, some work by choreographers Alvin had chosen came close.

As to social commentary, "it is doubtful that Alvin Ailey, even in the beginning, conceived of his company primarily as a social protest group," Kisselgoff observed. "And yet he has never allowed that underlying concern to disappear. It is seen, deceptively, in such ostensibly comic pieces as George Faison's 'Suite Otis,' set to the pain of Otis Redding's songs. Black choreographers are the only choreographers today with a sense of humor. It is a bitter humor, often expressed in a gesture or attitude that a white audience cannot always grasp."

"What Alvin Ailey has just celebrated is 20 years of humanity. Other companies have stood for other things. But no other companies or their publics could have radiated the warmth on both sides of the footlights as the Ailey anniversary performance did on opening night."

That sense of familial affection made it both easier and more difficult for Alvin to return to the everyday life of his company and his school after his public disgrace. He moved back slowly, feeling naked and more than a little embarrassed. But he was welcomed warmly after some initial nervousness. On his first day back at the school, he was led about as if on a grand tour. "Alvin, look at what you have," someone told him. Raquelle Chavis was one of the students who watched as he passed. "I was scared," she recalled. "We'd heard about what happened. But he took my hand and it was soothing." Alvin bent down and picked the ten-year-old Chavis up, carrying her along as he walked through the studios. "He was like the Pied Piper. The kids started to flock around. They asked him how he was doing. But then he got exhausted and he had to leave."

To some, Alvin seemed a quiet ghost of himself. He continued to work, but it was not until 1984 that he created a major dance. That dance was *For Bird—With Love*, the piece that his mother had prophesied would come out of the misery of his breakdown.

twenty-nine

A FORMAL FEELING

Alvin settled into his new one-bedroom apartment at 301 West Fifty-third Street, within easy walking distance from City Center, the company headquarters. It was also all too near his old haunts in Times Square, though the building did have doormen to keep an eye on him. The drab modern building was a far cry from his magic lair on 107th Street, from which he had been evicted following the fire episodes.

Many of his possessions had been neatly unpacked and arranged in the new place when he arrived. His plants, beloved but only sporadically cared for, had been moved back from his office in the Minskoff, where his mother had taken them after Alvin's second breakdown. Despite these attempts by family and friends, the apartment was so devoid of charm or interest that Alvin never bothered to unpack the rest of his belongings. It didn't matter. He had no desire to decorate the place as he had done with such enthusiasm uptown. This was a stand-in for a home, a place to spend the time between company tours, trips abroad and long days at the Ailey dance center.

Alvin had been slowed, but his career and the company continued on in their habitually automatic-seeming way. The 1980s were a time of honors and rewards. There was a new level of public recognition of Alvin and his work toward the end of the decade. In a time of consolidation after long years of hopeful advance and the sudden flaring of

343

despair, the apartment was the perfect metaphor for a life lived with the formal feeling that, as Emily Dickinson observed, tends to follow great pain.

After the first tentative reconnoiterings of the office and studio, Alvin gradually became his old self. Things had gone almost too smoothly without him. Everyone was committed to keeping his company and school afloat, and the board was distracted by new problems. After a brief and unfamiliar period of solvency in 1979, the company was once more facing a mounting deficit. There had been no drop in giving after Alvin's public disgrace, but a City Center gala had been canceled because of Alvin's illness, as were several tour dates. And for the first time in the company's history, it had incurred a deficit during performing weeks—attributable, some board members suggested, to the impact of inflation.

Everything that could go wrong went wrong in 1980, Stanley Plesent recalled. Over the next decade the question was never whether the books would balance but by how much they didn't. Running the company had at least progressed from "coping day to day, to week to week, then month to month," as Plesent put it. At one point several worried dancers tried to help devise ways to raise money. The unspoken rule was that now more than ever Alvin must be kept as free as possible of worry over the company's financial burdens.

Judith Jamison, Dudley Williams and Masazumi Chaya had continued to work with William Hammond, and they kept things going well after Alvin's return to work. His personal bills had all been paid by the company, charged against his salary and freelance fees, during what Hammond described with typical discretion as "the time of Mr. Ailey's absence" in a memo to administrative staff members.

Friends rallied unobtrusively. Several of his old theater and school friends, now on the West Coast, called and wrote to Alvin to ask if they could help in any way. His lover of the mid-1960s volunteered an ear if needed. His old friend Clive Barnes wrote to remind Alvin that it was his achievements that were important, not his current troubles. And Alvin was surprised and a little embarrassed to be greeted by a wave of sympathetic applause as he walked to his seat at City Center that winter.

He approached his first postbreakdown premiere nervously. Would he still be able to choreograph, now that the tumult had been calmed by lithium? But he had no choice. A new work was required for the season. He had been thinking for some time of choreographing a dance set to the music of the jazz composer Pharoah Sanders. From those musings emerged *Phases*, danced to music by Sanders, Donald Byrd and Max Roach. Its tone was unexpected, for out of his troubles Alvin had come up with a clever, blithe little jazz party of a piece.

Creating a new dance for Jamison the following season was a more difficult task. Already feeling a little isolated by the attempts of company administrators to keep him free of as many daily problems as possible, Alvin was also about to lose Jamison to the Broadway theater. For all the ups and downs of their long relationship, she was a familiar face and a beloved performer who embodied the funky passion that had once identified the company. Yet nothing he had created for his dynamic superstar had lived up to *Cry*, and perhaps nothing ever would. It was clear that Jamison needed to move on. Nevertheless, he was upset when she told him she wanted to leave the company to star in the musical *Sophisticated Ladies*, which opened on Broadway in 1981.

Her farewell gift was another crowd pleaser, *Spell*, the quintessential gala canapé that winter season at City Center. Now billed as a guest artist, she was paired in the duet with Alexander Godunov, a dancer as easily flamboyant as she. The Russian ballet dancer, who later appeared in the film *Witness*, was tall, too, with long blond hair and a tempestuous stage presence that sent out sparks even when he was standing still.

Alvin had created an earlier solo for Jamison based on the legend of Marie Laveau, the nineteenth-century voodoo priestess of New Orleans. Now she played sorceress to Godunov's victim, rising up out of a billowing mist of dry ice and then locking him in an embrace as the mist again pushed up around them. Godunov, like Baryshnikov, hadn't a clue how to dance in the deceptively easy-looking Ailey style. And Jamison had been away from it for a time. But *Spell* was perfect gala-benefit flash, and the audience adored it.

Alvin created the season's other premiere for Mari Kajiwara. Concerned as always with making his dancers feel appreciated, Alvin was still keeping count of who had done what in recent years. It was time, he saw, for Kajiwara to have a dance of her own. *Landscape* was performed to a Bartok piano concerto filled with allusions to nature and dedicated to the Hungarian composer on his centenary and to Miloslav Kabelac, the Czechoslovakian composer, whose spirit, Alvin wrote in program notes, "soars above oppression."

In this single season, the company offered new dances in the idioms of ballet, jazz and modern dance. Alvin's balletic *River* was being performed for the first time by the Ailey dancers. *Spell* was pure jazz, and in *Landscape* Kajiwara's strong, supple modern-dance body arched and stretched eloquently in a ritual celebration of the earth that hinted at her almost intuitive appreciation of dance as an abstraction.

For all the warm accomplishment of his return to work, however, Alvin remained very much alone. Kajiwara was a loyal veteran in a company that was to some extent in transition, with half of its thirty-one dancers new or recent recruits. Most were very young and getting younger, it seemed, by the season. They could give little back to Alvin except devoted performing. Some of the women insisted on doing Alvin's nails for him, fussing over him when he was about to go out on a fund-raising expedition, as bedraggled as ever most of the time. Mickey Bord lovingly massaged his arthritic feet. But he had fewer soulmates— or what approached that for Alvin, friends in whom he could confide some of his dreams and laugh out his most far-fetched conceits.

By 1983, the year of the company's twenty-fifth anniversary, Alvin had become something of an elder statesman, although he was again at least sporadically involved in the sex and some of the drugs that had nearly destroyed him before. The year as a whole was satisfyingly active, with preparations for the anniversary and a big, splashy, twenty-six-character rock dance for the Paris Opéra Ballet that stunned Parisian audiences and critics. "The roar heard at the Paris Opéra several months ago was the sound, for better or worse, of the twentieth century crashing through the genteel building's once impenetrable walls," Sheryl Flatow wrote of *Au Bord du Précipice.*

Au Bord du Précipice followed a young rock singer through his rise and fall, surrounded by family, friends and milling fans who in the end, on the lookout for the next new star, nearly trample his dying body. It was the familiar territory of Alvin's 1971 *Flowers.* Once again, he had a sad and tawdry rock legend in mind. Although Alvin saw *Précipice* as "an abstraction" or at most "kind of a gangster ballet," its chief inspiration was Jim Morrison, the hard-living rock musician with the Doors who had died in Paris in 1970, at the age of twenty-six.

The other inspiration was Patrick Dupond, whom Alvin cast in the lead role, a strong technical dancer of great intelligence with a tough physicality and the delicately androgynous face of an angel. His flamboyance and outspoken irreverence made him the ballet equivalent of a rock star in Paris and around the world, and *Précipice* enhanced that reputation. His chest usually bared, playing a character identified simply as "Lui," Dupond ate up the stage with wildly abandoned virtuoso dancing highlighted by two fiery solos.

Précipice was part of an evening designed to expose audiences at the Opéra to new and adventurous dance. But the other pieces on the program—*Nouvelle Lune,* a gently contemplative modern dance work by Andrew de Groat, and Glen Tetley's sleek, fast-moving ballet *Voluntaries*—were the artistic equivalent of *The Sleeping Beauty* when compared with the torrent of shocking visual, musical and dance images that Alvin unleashed.

The audience cheered *Précipice.* Major critics applauded Dupond but lacerated the dance with shriveling Parisian invective. And Alvin muttered in print about having had to cut some extravagances because of "the old ladies of the Opera."

The theme of dances like *Flowers, Quintet* and *Précipice* was newly meaningful to Alvin after his own bout with drugs and the humiliation of his public breakdowns. In interviews in New York that followed the American premiere of the dance, he somberly alluded in passing to his own moments of feeling poised at the edge.

"What is ballet about?" Alvin wrote in notes to himself on *Précipice.* "Its theme is loneliness in the crowd—being at the edge & choosing either to fall or not—the man at the top—but lonely—& about drugs—drugs as a symbol of unrest in America—the malaise which came about [after] the deaths of John Kennedy & M. L. King. Eventually it is about the creative & talented individual—It is not a pretty ballet but not a sad one either—but perhaps a ballet about Spring—the Resurrection of the creative Spirit—in turmoil—I have worked for images experiences—America—the American dream of success—loneliness, desire, isolation, sex, desire, cruelty, ambition—Human beings caught in the act of living in their time—" Perhaps no dance could have lived up to all that. But in any case there was little feeling of personal truth to the piece, which at its worst paraded stock figures through a stock scenario.

Alvin had been making long lists of characters for many years, castoffs in an urban society who crowded the pages of his notebooks looking for release in his dances. He had given challenging roles in the ballet to Dupond and his partner, a rising star in the French company named Monique Loudières whom Alvin cherished as "a wonderful piquant little lady." Loudières played Elle, later identified in program notes as "His woman, his desire, his drug." But the other characters—among them Spoon (The Dream-Sewer), Gin (A Woman Worse Than She Should Be), Wolf, Speed and Sweet Thing (A Girl Who Should Be Home but Isn't)—did not find a home in *Précipice.*

His notes for the piece also include typically thoughtful references to his dancers. "Get color favorites from dcrs—their best colors," he reminded himself in preparation for costume discussions with Carol Vollet Garner, a frequent collaborator. And the dancers loved him. Alvin knew the steps he wanted, Dupond told an interviewer, which was hard at first. But he also proved to be very human, he added, which gave the French ballet dancers confidence.

Working at the Opéra gave Alvin a taste for the kind of grandeur and stability provided by state-supported European arts institutions, reinforcing his dream of someday having a company of the size and status of an established ballet troupe. The experience was not easy, however. Alvin theoretically had seventy-four dancers at his disposal in Paris, but they were just as busy as his own much smaller group.

"I spent 6 wks here in Paris—walking insecurely into a studio where at least some were waiting—the 1st few days Dupond, [Charles] Jude, [Michel] Denard, then Dupond in Italy for 2 wks," he wrote in notes that seem to have been intended for an article or published diary. "There have been frustrations beyond my normal torment while enduring the creative process. When I have been ready to make what I think would be a marvelous movement for Monique—she is somewhere in the vast caverns of the Opera rehearsing Bluebird—Claude's big moment came the day she was in Lyon giving Swan Lake—Charles & Florence I missed because of conflicting schedules—mine suddenly changed because of commitments to my own company on tour in America."

Alvin had invited his mother to France for the premiere at the venerable Paris Opéra and then a trip with him through Europe. Years later, Lula Cooper still recalled her surprise at seeing that someone had attempted to enliven one Alpine snowslope with bright plastic flowers. Alvin enlightened her. "They're real," he told her. "Here, flowers bloom in the snow."

Cooper saw something no one else did in *Précipice*. The piece was set to a score by Pat Metheny and Lyle Mays titled "As Falls Wichita, So Falls Wichita Falls." It was in Wichita Falls, Texas, she noted, that Alvin had found his father nearly a decade earlier, after years of silence. And for Cooper, at least one scene in *Précipice* resonated with the presence of that lost figure in Alvin's childhood.

"Alvin had all these people, even had a kid there that looked like him when he was coming up," Cooper said. "You'd swear he had the funeral. The men all dressed in black. And he had the idea in this thing that his daddy was being buried when it was pouring down rain. And the people were standing around with their umbrellas." She may have been right. Jotted down next to the names of the two dancers who played the parents of "Lui" were the descriptions "nun saint mother" and the considerably more distant "father uncle <u>suit</u>."

Back in New York, Alvin returned to his preparations for the upcoming anniversary and for the next year. With his usual awareness of what was happening in the larger dance world, he had invited a hot new young black postmodernist choreographer named Bill T. Jones to create a work for the company's spring season that gave a coolly hip twist to experimentation with form and structure and shook some sturdily held notions of what the Ailey company was all about. Danced to music by the art-rock composer Peter Gordon, *Fever Swamp* had six good-looking Ailey men, stylishly dressed in trousers and T-shirts and caps that were soon discarded, bouncing like boxers sparring playfully on a city street corner that just happened to be dotted with silver tubular trees backed by palm-tree projections.

Ballet steps were mixed with street-dance moves. Given Alvin's dislike of effeminate male dancers, it was not surprising that when the men sprung into one another's arms at one point the effect was of good humor and sleekly punchy energy. That effect was intensified when Alvin, always as interested in programming the audience as much as individual dances, later paired *Fever Swamp* with its opposite. Elisa Monte's *Pigs & Fishes*, a pulsing, roiling postmodernist ritual for women, was as sultry as *Fever Swamp* was cool.

Alvin flew to Italy that summer to work on *Escapade*, a piece that in retrospect seems much more a measure of his gifts than *Précipice*. Commissioned by the Aterballetto of Reggio Emilia, *Escapade* was set to glistening jazz music by Max Roach. Forming an inseparable whole with the easygoing score, it was one of Alvin's most appealing and quietly provocative dances. Sensuousness bubbled up through the outer skins of the dance and music in movement that allowed Alvin to explore some of the differences between modern and jazz dance and the ways the two could be combined.

When he returned to New York, Alvin appeared to be facing this twenty-fifth anniversary with something like serenity in the weeks before the winter season at City Center. He took time to be with the company's younger dancers as he negotiated appearances by the stars of other eras, striking up a warm friendship with the visiting father of Keith McDaniel, a favorite of Alvin's from Chicago. He was wryly amusing in a public appearance of the sort he loathed in a small ceremony in the theater lobby on November 30, the day of the opening

gala. Sporting his customary worn leather jacket and workaday trousers, Alvin accepted proclamations honoring him and the company
from Bess Myerson, cultural affairs commissioner for New York City,
and Kitty Carlisle Hart, chair of the New York State Council on the
Arts. Standing between these two glamorous women he felt, he told a
small crowd gathered for the event, like "a thorn between roses."

He had lost a little weight for the opening, at which, he assured
one reporter, he planned to "even do a few steps myself," though in
the end he relegated his dancing to the curtain calls. The gala, which
opened the season, is remembered by many as the best of the three
anniversary programs that Alvin put together.

It certainly was the biggest. Once again everyone, it seemed, had
returned to the fold to dance onstage with the Ailey company of 1983
in the three-and-a-half-hour celebration. Alvin had whipped up a con-
coction, set appropriately enough to Lionel Richie's "Can't Sit Down,"
that was danced by a company of former Aileyites that included James
Truitte, Charles and Ella Thompson Moore, and Dorene Richardson.
Carmen de Lavallade performed Lester Horton's delicately exotic *Sarong Paramaribo.* Dressed in tuxedos, Truitte and George Faison led
more former Ailey dancers in excerpts from *Night Creature.*

Diahann Carroll, who had starred in *House of Flowers,* was on
hand to talk about Alvin to a gala audience that was, unusually for
such an event, both high-spirited and high-powered. Dupond arrived
from Paris to join Donna Wood in *Pas de Duke,* and a giddy Natalia
Makarova introduced a duet from *The Lark Ascending,* danced by Ailey
alumni Sara Yarborough and Clive Thompson. Jamison darted across
the stage toward the end of *Cry,* performed for the occasion by three
dancers. But the frequent applause, shouts and hoots of affectionate
laughter that welled up from the black-tie audience threatened to blast
the theater down in the finale, when the closing section of *Revelations*
was danced first by the elders and then, in an encore, by the "kids," and
finally by both casts.

When at last it was time to call it a night, the entire evening's cast
partied onstage, joined by a jubilant Alvin, with cascades of streamers
pouring down on them from the flies. As the audience cheered them
on, the line that separated the viewer and the viewed seemed tenuous
indeed. Alvin had succeeded in welcoming everyone into his party,
proving, as Anna Kisselgoff put it in her review of the gala, that the
Alvin Ailey American Dance Theater was not a company but a school
of thought.

In the midst of all that whirl of activity, Alvin produced a small, not very important dance that became a favorite of Ailey aficionados. Set to a piano score by George Winston, *Isba* was a quiet, mysterious ritual for a male and female initiate of some magical and exotic religion and four tribal priestesses and a priest, dressed in long skirts, who spun, darted and held poses.

Isba fulfilled Alvin's obligation to create a premiere for the season. The dance was not exactly new in theme or look, but it was an eye-opener for at least one observer. "It made me realize what an unshak-able lyrical artist he was," Robert Greskovic, the New York critic and dance historian, said. "Ailey bought into all the politically aware stuff. He was aware. But at a basic level, everything was removed from those ordinarinesses of everyday life.

"What I loved about it was that I found all this depth in an auto-matic-pilot piece, a piece that didn't have any of the red flags that say 'Here's Important,' 'Here's Direction.' No one was going to call it a breakthrough piece, or hot. It was none of those things that make a masterpiece of the canon, but I couldn't dismiss it and I knew it wasn't dismissable. I realized what an amazingly truthful artist Ailey was."

It is a tribute that Alvin would probably have liked. Every work did not have to be *Revelations*. Even in the most ordinary of pieces, he had the gift of creating dance that both evoked and rose above the ordinary. There would be hits and failures over the next few years. But by 1983, he was in a position to rest a little on his laurels.

Alvin talked increasingly to friends of throwing it all over and escaping to some quiet, pretty place where he could do other things or nothing at all. He kept at the daily work of running a company, how-ever, at a soul-killing pace. There were always more dances to be made, more funds to be raised and more performances to be scrutinized and made better. His problems with his company were not unusual in mod-ern dance then or now. But it was almost as if Alvin imagined that everything—or perhaps just he himself—would disappear if ever he slowed down.

thirty

KANSAS CITY—AND BEYOND

Friends had noticed that Alvin seemed to be slowly winding down during the mid-1980s. He began to talk increasingly of feeling tired. His fingers were swelling badly and his arthritis grew more debilitating. It became harder and harder for him to walk. Stairs were an agony. As Masazumi Chaya took on increasing duties off the stage, he saw more of Alvin and watched his mostly matter-of-fact struggle with concern.

On tour in Japan in 1986, Chaya found a good acupuncturist to work on Alvin's knees. Alvin was reluctant. He was not eager to face the needles. But together they climbed six flights of stairs—Chaya worrying because he hadn't foreseen them—and settled into the office. The acupuncturist examined one knee and turned to Chaya. "He's old," he said in Japanese.

"What did he say? What did he say?" Alvin, then fifty-five, asked Chaya. The acupuncturist had commented on how old Alvin's knees were, Chaya responded. "The way he looked at me I could tell he knew what the man had said," Chaya recalled. "I thought he was going to get upset, but he was laughing."

And the company was slowing down, though just a little. It would not be performing at City Center in the spring of 1984 because of an announced inability to raise money for new productions, and in fact the 1983 season proved to be the last spring engagement at City Center.

But the announcement was misleading, for there was to be an impressive substitute for the jettisoned City Center season. On July 9, 1984, the Alvin Ailey American Dance Theater opened in an historic two-week engagement at the Metropolitan Opera House.

The Ailey company was the first black troupe to appear at the Met. Only one other modern dance group, the Martha Graham Dance Company, had ever played at the opera house, which was the summer home of the American Ballet Theatre and visiting foreign classical ballet companies. Alvin had, of course, worked there before as the choreographer of the benighted production of *Antony and Cleopatra* that had opened the theater in 1966 as well as the later production of *Carmen*. But the Met—all red and gold and filled with moneyed operagoers and haughty ushers—was a pinnacle to which most dance companies could not aspire.

The Met would produce the season, which meant that there was money for live music and the return of Brother John Sellers for *Revelations*. Alvin carefully chose a repertory of mostly big dances that would look at home on the large stage, although he also boldly programmed the slow-moving, intimate duet *Treading*, a favorite of his. It was an ideal time to present the full *Précipice* as well, in its American premiere. The Paris Opéra agreed to loan Patrick Dupond and Monique Loudières for the first week's performances, along with fifty-six costumes and two large backdrops. Also on loan was an intense young former Ailey dancer named Ulysses Dove, assistant director of the Opéra's modern dance wing, who helped Alvin restage the dance for the Met stage and contributed a churning ritual dance of his own, called *Night Shade,* to the season.

No one knew quite how the Met's generally staid audiences would respond to this interloper of a company, and the theater reduced its prices, from $50 for the most expensive ballet seats to a $30 that matched the top City Center ticket, in order to encourage a crossover audience. Alvin was calm as the season approached. Backstage on opening night as the audience filed in, he strode through the dancers' last, obsessive private moments onstage as they stretched, spun experimentally through a final turn or two and pushed their feet into the floor to stretch their arches.

The dark, cavernous wings at either side of the stage were filled with crew and Ailey staff. Dancers hung from light stands and grabbed hold of portable barres and any other stable, freestanding object to stretch against and curl around in last-minute warm-ups. In another few moments, the dancers onstage would take their places and freeze, to muted sounds of the orchestra and the swishing of the heavy curtain rising, revealing a black hole beyond that glittered with red exit signs and reflected light from the stage, afloat in a sea of shadowy, expectant bodies.

On the other side of the curtain, waiting for that moment in the last few minutes before the theater's chandeliers ascended and the lights dimmed, those who loved Alvin found themselves blinking back tears and swallowing hard as they looked around at the opening night audience and at the theater itself. "It was not possible to deny the remembrance of the mighty miles you travelled from that first 'Y' concert," Louise Roberts, director of Clark Center, wrote about that night to the man she had taught to budget his first concert. "Maybe some people were surprised by the size of the audience. Somehow I was not, just delighted. . . . Be proud, it's been twenty-five years well spent."

Alvin had sensibly opted for nearly unadulterated flash for the crucial opening night program. With its huge stage and chill, slightly antiseptic glamour, the Met was not as good a house for the company as City Center. The dancers had to force their projection at times in order to reach the upper regions of the 3,700-seat house. And it took them time to relax into *Night Creature* and *The Stack-up.*

Some noted that Talley Beatty's corrosive disco-pop dance about drug addiction and ghetto life had an uncharacteristically hard and frenzied look. There was a frenzy of a more natural kind in *Pas de Duke,* which Donna Wood and Patrick Dupond turned into a competition of virtuoso high-energy dancing. Then *Revelations* closed the evening on a note of simpler glory.

The applause that greeted the dancers in their final curtain calls on opening night would have done a City Center audience proud. Audiences continued to be large and enthusiastic throughout the season. They got a representative dose of Ailey styles, from the funk of Louis Johnson's goofy *Fontessa and Friends* to the lyrical sweetness of Billy Wilson's *Concerto in F* and the grandeur of *Memoria. Précipice* was the critical disappointment that some Ailey dancers had worried it might be. Clive Barnes weighed in with the cogent observation that "the story is carried, as it were, by the story itself, not by explicitly expressive choreography." But the season as a whole was a milestone in the company's history. In truth, the Met was most of all a symbol, but a potent one. The kid from Texas had climbed to another summit.

Yet he could find no rest up there. After a month of rehearsal in

September, Alvin and the dancers left for Kansas City for a two-week residency, and then flew off to Europe for a tour through Germany, Sweden, Denmark and Norway. Three days after flying out of Oslo, the company opened its winter season at City Center. In addition to a schedule that would have exhausted a man far younger and less worn out than he, Alvin was once more facing a troubling deficit. "Financial problems; we don't make money; deficit," Alvin wrote with weary succinctness in a notebook of the time.

He had been working lately, though, on a piece that provided more than enough creative fuel to keep him going. The dance was *For Bird—With Love*. He had dreamed of making it since the late 1960s, he told Chaya, who served as his rehearsal assistant. Over those years Alvin had been saving everything he came across on Charlie "Bird" Parker and had acquired boxes of records, books and articles on the great jazz alto saxophonist and model self-destroyer. The company had had a memorable first season the year before in Kansas City, Missouri, Parker's birthplace and one of the most important jazz centers in the nation from the mid-1920s through the 1930s. That legacy—and two dear new friends—were on Alvin's mind.

It had seemed an ordinary enough tour date when the Ailey dancers flew into Kansas City for performances at the newly restored, jewel-like little Folly Theater in September 1983. But to Alvin's unconcealed surprise, he was met at the plane by a shiny limousine and a hesitant young man named Allan Gray.

Gray had become involved in the engagement when the Gentlemen of Distinction, a group of black professionals that he had helped to found, decided to sell tickets to an Ailey program to raise funds for the group's community activities. The Gentlemen had approached the theater about tickets, with the idea that they would also get the city's black community interested in the performances. Suddenly, they had a block of five hundred seats on their hands, half the capacity of the Folly. The men were even more shocked to discover that a surprising number of Kansas City blacks had never heard of the choreographer or his company.

"Ever prideful, we didn't want to send the tickets back," Gray recalled with amusement. "So we took the challenge and decided we needed not only to market the performance but educate our community to the significance of Alvin as part of our history. We wanted to make sure that by the date of the performance, you would have had to have lived under a rock not to know that Alvin Ailey was coming or who Alvin Ailey was. We saturated every media source, every black community organization, every church group that was willing to listen."

A week before the performance, all five hundred tickets were gone and the men found themselves returning to the Folly to buy whatever tickets were still unsold. Then Gray, who knew almost nothing about American modern dance, set about preparing the right sort of welcome for this great American cultural figure and his world-renowned troupe. He arranged with a florist friend for flowers for the company and hotel fruit baskets for the dancers. In the process his friend, who also owned a limousine service, convinced him that Alvin must be met at the airport.

He had done a lot of promotions, the friend said, and knew that first impressions were lasting. Didn't Gray want to show that Kansas City knew how to do things with flair and class? Gray arrived at the airport in style to meet and escort Alvin into Kansas City, just as if he were a rock star.

"I didn't know Alvin used to just get on the bus with the rest of the company. There was this limousine sitting waiting for him. Not only did his mouth drop but many of the dancers were standing there, kind of envious. I remember him stepping back. Alvin would sort of tilt his head to the side and kind of give you a look once over. I remember him doing that and saying, 'So you're Allan Gray.' He said how glad he was to meet me, and I was kind of taken that he would be. Because here I was just trying to make him as comfortable and his stay as pleasant as possible. I never thought of this legend being happy to meet me."

Alvin stepped into the limousine, pulling Ailey dancer Marilyn Banks into the car behind him. Everyone relaxed a little when he suddenly asked where to get a good haircut in Kansas City. "So we're talking in the car," Gray remembered, "and Alvin kept sitting back and looking at me. I didn't feel uncomfortable. There was this immediate sense of connection. But it was odd. How do you act around a choreographer? I really didn't know much about him other than that he had created these wonderful dances that I had never seen.

"He was dressed in black. Black pants, a black shirt and a leather jacket. And his turned-over loafers. I always wanted to buy Alvin a new pair of shoes, because his feet hurt. He had this one pair of shoes he would wear with everything, whether it was casual or a tuxedo. They were truly worn. I remember at one point looking at those shoes and thinking about the streets where they had walked, in Paris, Copenhagen, Tanzania, Moscow."

In his innocent idealism, Gray had treated Alvin and his dancers with a courtesy and reverence to which they were unaccustomed. To add to that, the company performed to sold-out houses at the Folly, and to the kind of knowledgeable, proud and festive audiences that dancers dream of.

Alvin came to think of Gray as a son, although the soft-spoken young community developer had children of his own. And it was Gray who initiated the second of Alvin's Kansas City friendships—with Carol Coe, a small, round, no-nonsense black lawyer who had a great deal of Alvin's curiosity and zest for life and the same gutsy, unquenchable sense of humor. Gray had insisted that Coe attend a Folly performance. In a bad mood, she refused; she wasn't interested in going downtown to see people dancing, she said. But Gray prevailed, reminding her not only that she was always complaining about a dearth of black culture but that he had tickets to sell. "Okay," Coe told him at last. "If you put it like that."

Her mood did not improve at the performance. Seated at the back, she was disturbed by a big man who kept going in and out of her row. She glared at the man and asked why he didn't just sit down and enjoy the dancing. During intermission, she bumped into him again. Staring at the Alvin Ailey canvas tote bags on sale at the theater boutique, Coe commented to him that they were not worth the $25 that was being charged. To her surprise, the man handed her one and autographed it. It was Alvin, and at a party for the company later that night she got to know him a little better.

Coe would soon be traveling around the world with Alvin, often dropping everything at the last moment to join him and the company on their way to some exotic far-off place where, to Alvin's disgust, she wanted only to hang out in the theater and watch performances. Coe became his buddy, his shopping companion and an entertaining sidekick set loose in the tumultuous glory and disappointments of his world. She expected nothing of Alvin. She lived in a different world. But she understood and loved him in her own unconditional way. So did Gray, who over the next few years would help the Ailey company to develop a loyal following in Kansas City and a second home that felt at times like the early days of the Ailey company to Alvin.

The day after the company's gala opening at the Folly, Gray took Alvin across town to get his hair cut at the Ivy League Barbershop, across the street from Bean's Liquor Store in the heart of the city's black section. "We pull up in this stretch limo," Gray recalled. "It was like a scene out of a Pryor movie. All the 'fellas' on the block came out to check it out. It wasn't an everyday occurrence. Alvin and I go into the barbershop, with some of them following us in."

Inside, the television was on. An interview with Donna Wood was just beginning, and everyone was glued to the set. "Wow, this Donna Wood is a fox," somebody commented. Moments later, as the camera swung to shots of her and others dancing, another voice piped up: "Man, who is this cat Alvin Ailey? He got those fine sisters dancing around in tights. He's got to be one hell of a dude." One of the barbers pointed out that the man whose picture was just then flashing on the screen was at that moment sitting among them, quietly having his hair cut as his image answered a television interviewer's questions about what it meant to be "a choreographer."

Gray had been drawing Alvin out about his dream ballet and was at work gently planting the idea that Kansas City might be the perfect place for the premiere of a dance about the Bird. The conversation resumed when they left the barbershop. The Charles Parker Foundation was only six blocks away. Would Alvin like to drive over and check it out? A meeting was in progress when they arrived at the foundation, which housed Parker's archives. "Alvin got a chance to talk and he almost committed himself to doing this work," Gray said. "It was indicative of the snowball effect he was having on the community. These people were keeping Charlie Parker alive. Alvin had a chance to think about the piece."

Alvin also mused aloud about the possibilities of a residency in Kansas City, an extended period of performing during which he and his dancers would travel to community centers, schools and prisons to dance and talk about dancing. "Wouldn't it be great to get this many people out all the time?" Alvin had asked on the day of the opening. "Oh, yeah," Gray answered demurely.

"It amounted to the first of our sessions," Gray said. Not long after they first got acquainted, he and Alvin began to have long "what-if" conversations that Gray grew to think of as "dream sessions." What if there could be a Charlie Parker ballet? What if the company could establish some kind of special relationship with Kansas City? What if the city's children could study with Ailey dancers?

"He would call me late at night or early in the morning from all parts of the world and the country sometimes to talk," Gray recalled. "Just to talk. And I always knew when maybe he was struggling with something. He wouldn't talk with me about the problem. But he would talk. And sometimes I'd call him, too. The phone bills were horrendous. But we could draw on each other's strength.

"There would be times I knew that maybe he didn't know how he was going to get through the next period of his life, and I would feel the same way. I'd say, 'Gosh, Alvin, you've given me this big challenge here. I've got to raise all this money back here. And we want to do this and do this. And I'm fighting this battle here, that battle there.' "

Alvin would start out a session by talking about things he would like to see happen. He had always wanted to have a "people's gala," he told Gray, in which people from all walks of life would come to see his dances and then celebrate in a huge party like a minicarnival in Brazil. Wouldn't it be nice to establish a summer arts camp for children somewhere? Sometimes he would talk about frustrations with the board. There was never any real talk about personal problems. Gray sensed that Alvin had a need for privacy. Although they got to know each other better in later years, he felt that Alvin might be embarrassed by that private life and by his homosexuality.

Gray took it in stride that he was not invited to Alvin's apartment on his trips to New York, understanding that Alvin needed "a sanctuary, someplace where he could say no to people, someplace where if he wanted to yell and scream he could do that." The two would stuff themselves at Cabana Carioca, a brightly painted jam-packed little Brazilian restaurant not far from the Minskoff building and City Center, and talk for long hours. They'd walk uptown to the theater to see the company perform and then leave the theater together, chatting briefly outside the stage door before they went their separate ways.

But the two opened up to each other in the vivid shared life of their dream sessions. "We would go way out sometimes in our thinking. Because I think that he always knew that I wasn't going to say, 'Alvin, we can't do that.' So there was a sense of freedom. And then at the end of our talks, he'd always kind of say, 'Well, let's get back to what we really have to do.' With a sigh."

Coe watched the friendship grow and understood instinctively why the two were drawn to each other. "Alvin would say, 'They should have put red red green green.' And Allan would say, 'Well, put streaks of blue there, there, there.' And Alvin would go, 'Yeah!' He liked that feedback between them. And Allan understood a lot of what Alvin was going through.

"Alvin had a strange relationship with Allan. Sometimes it was as if he didn't want Allan to be too close to him, I think because he didn't want to disillusion him." Alvin sometimes called Coe after a dream session. "He'd say, 'Carol, what do you think? Allan's talking about doing this and this.' It was like, 'Do I dare get excited? Do I dare believe this guy is going to do this? Is it really going to happen?' And you'd say, 'Yeah, Alvin. They're really going to have a camp. They're really going to do this and that. There are people who want to do it.' It was like a childish thing. And sometimes you'd have to assure him that what he did was important and significant. But then if he ever thought he was important, he wouldn't have been Alvin Ailey. His ego did not get to that point."

In the early spring of 1984, Gray received an exciting call from William Hammond in New York. Would Kansas City be interested in establishing a second home for the Ailey company? It was a dream Gray had shared with friends and colleagues who had participated in the Folly gala the previous year. Alvin had entertained the thought of Ailey branches from the early years at Clark Center. And the establishment of second homes was now a popular and fashionable tactic among dance companies attempting to respond to dwindling resources as inflation shrank the financial bases in their home cities.

Kansas City was not the only city under consideration. Alvin had talked publicly late the year before about a second home in Miami. But he remembered the warmth of his company's reception in Kansas City.

Around the same time, Hammond received calls from arts leaders in Kansas City inquiring about the possibility of creating a formal relationship with the company. He flew out with Alvin, Stanley Plesent and others to discuss the idea with members of the city's arts and black communities. Kansas City seemed to be growing. There was no entrenched dance establishment there. And there was interest in bringing black culture, specifically, back to a city that was struggling to hold onto and celebrate its proud black cultural history.

A structure for a second home began to be worked out, program by program. There would be premieres, of course, with rehearsals to begin at City Center and finish in Kansas City. Dance classes would be taught by Ailey performers who would travel to high schools in the city. "We want to stimulate creativity, open doors and let young people see that we are real people just like them," Alvin told a local magazine interviewer. "Seeing us, they will push to really make it themselves."

A steering committee of seven organizations was formed with the encouragement of the city mayor and began to meet in July 1984. One member group was the Kansas City Ballet, a stylish young company headed by Todd Bolender, a former New York City Ballet dancer and a choreographer whose luminous *Still Point* had entered the Ailey repertory four years earlier. The Gentlemen of Distinction participated, as did the Kansas City Jazz Festival, representatives of the city, the black women's sorority Delta Sigma Theta and the Junior League.

As meetings continued, more and more individuals and groups signed on to help determine the feasibility of such a project and collaborate in its planning stages. Eventually the group became the Kansas City Friends of Alvin Ailey, a partnership unique in the cultural history of Kansas City, not only in its mix of arts and social groups but in its steadfastly multiracial composition. "We got bogged down a bit about how to organize and structure the group," Gray said. "There were also many political concerns. Here was this young guy, a black man for that matter, talking about setting up a second home for an international company, creating racial harmony, doing things in a nontraditional fashion. They were looking at me like, 'Who are you? And why are you here?'

"We naturally had people of color, people from many communities. There were arts people but also people who had never been involved in an arts group before. We said, 'You can come into this organization and make an impact immediately, see the benefit of your ideas, unlike a lot of organizations.' I think it was a natural reaction to the challenge to doing things the way they always had been done, which meant the way the white community had always done. But there was an unspoken agreement that in order for the partnership to succeed we had to operate on a basis of respect and mutual values.

"Everyone, regardless of class and position, had equal value. There was no right or wrong way to do things. With that message, we were able to openly discuss issues and find humor in our differences. We found the process equally as important as the product. And we found we were starting to look forward to getting together. Because we were friends."

The company was to arrive in Kansas City on September 28 for a two-week residency intended to lead to the formation of a second home. Six performances had been planned, with a glamorous four world premieres. Alvin had been pushing Judith Jamison to choreograph, and Jamison, whose presence was a magnet for fund-raising events among black women's groups in the city, would present her first major choreographic work here. Alvin had completed his new Charlie

Parker ballet, which was to be the centerpiece of the residency. And Ailey dancers would fan out to teach a total of twenty-three master classes and present twenty-four lecture-demonstrations in area schools and at the University of Missouri at Kansas City, in addition to special programs for families and blind children, gallery shows, fund-raising events and endless press conferences, panel discussions and receptions. Alvin was pushed into giving more speeches than he had ever made in so short a time.

One of the most ambitious events was a free Saturday dance program for handicapped children and adults from all over the city, performed in the three-thousand-seat outdoor Starlight Bowl by dancers from the Ailey company and the Kansas City Ballet as well as a group of local break-dancers. Alvin and the company had arrived in Kansas City in warm and sunny weather. But by the day of the outdoor performance, the temperature had dropped into the fifties, many degrees below the point at which the Ailey dancers could refuse contractually to perform. They arrived for morning rehearsal and huddled onstage under a gray sky, wrapped in coats and blankets, miserable and contentious, with Mary Barnett casting an appropriately cold eye on the concert presenters who were so mistreating her dancers.

By 11 A.M. it was clear that a little human intervention would be necessary for the stage temperature to rise to the required sixty-eight degrees by the 2 P.M. start of the show. A call went out to the president of the Kansas City Chiefs. Would it be possible to borrow the huge space heaters used on the sidelines of their football field? Someone found a truck and returned with six or seven of the heaters, which were wheeled into the wings. Parts of the set were hauled onto the stage to block the winds that billowed from the back. Gray watched Alvin, hoping that he didn't think his young friend had lost his mind. How could he possibly have scheduled an outdoor performance in late September?

The audience began to arrive around 1 P.M. The dancers disappeared into the dressing rooms, leaving behind Gray and others, including a stern Barnett, who looked ready to haul the dancers back onto their buses at any moment. The stage manager brought out a thermometer and set it on the stage. Eight more degrees to go, and if the temperature didn't rise to sixty-eight degrees by 1:45, the show would be canceled. At 1:30 the clouds broke, the sun began to come out and slowly the temperature climbed until, by showtime, it had reached sixty-nine degrees.

Standing at the back of the theater with Alvin as the show began, a worried Gray scanned the crowd, watching even lethargic faces light up as the performers danced. He was relieved by those smiles. He had wondered, too late, if the program would mean anything at all to this audience. Suddenly he felt a small hand grabbing at his. He looked down to see a boy looking up at him, silent but happy.

"I think it was one of those moments when I realized that this was something bigger than anything I'd ever imagined being involved in," he said. "And it really made me understand what it was about Alvin that could draw people into a common space in the universe where neither physical or economic or racial or educational impairments matter. We all became, during those moments that we watched his dance, one in our understanding of ourselves and of our place in the universe."

Kansas City began to claim the company as its own. There would be another, failed attempt to create an additional home in Baltimore. But something about the midwestern city enabled it to regard Alvin with awe and yet accept him as family. His fund-raising duties were at least as arduous here as at home. Gray searched the streets for Alvin on more than one occasion when he fled from some promised commitment. He had to make excuses for his friend when Alvin refused to make even brief public comments at a fund-raising event, then watch as he sidled up to the microphone anyway and proceeded to charm the assembled guests at greater length than anyone had hoped for or expected.

The company opened the season with a "Best of Ailey" program, then turned up the heat with second-night world premieres of dances by Donald McKayle and Loris Anthony Beckles, one of Alvin's young choreographic finds. The premiere of Jamison's *Divining*, a sultry, seething tour de force of a dance, set to drum music, got the lyrical company star Donna Wood moving with an unaccustomed ferocity. But the cornerstone of the relationship between Kansas City and the company was set with *For Bird—With Love*, which had its premiere on October 6 at the Folly Theater in a gala benefit for the Friends.

The work ran a long seventy-five minutes, seemingly a life poured out onstage unmediated by an intervening choreographic editor. *For Bird—With Love* was filled with raw power, a cry rising up from smoky jazz clubs and lonely hotel rooms. The title role and piece itself were a gift for Gary DeLoatch, a popular dancer who played Parker as an unforgettable mix of sweetness and despair. The other lead role was danced by Dudley Williams, a mysterious, omnipresent deus ex machina in a variety of guises.

This was DeLoatch's moment. A breezily cheerful senior company member, he seemed able with very little visible effort to breathe poignant dramatic life into the most abstract of dance roles. He was a dancer whom Alvin adored, in part because he saw himself in DeLoatch and could hear his own voice in his dancing. He and DeLoatch had similar senses of humor, too. "Gary could make Alvin cheer up on a bad day in a minute," Sharrell Mesh Alexander, a former Ailey dancer, recalled. " 'Ey, what's up Big Al?" DeLoatch would say. "Nuttin' much, man," Alvin answered.

Alvin had never created a major role for DeLoatch in the five years he had been with the company. Now, he was not only the tortured central figure in an ambitious new piece but a surrogate Alvin.

It was clear to DeLoatch and others who loved Alvin that he was reliving his life in the dance, one of his most powerful and accomplished narrative pieces. "It was as if he were purging himself of all the things that had happened and putting them in the piece," Coe said. Some scenes seemed to allude directly to Alvin's past. One, involving a straitjacket, had the immediacy of something created by a man who knew the helpless feeling of arms pulled tight by handcuffs.

Much of the dance's darkness was eventually edited out as Alvin cut the piece down to a more manageable and upbeat forty-five minutes over the following year. But it was as if a dam had been worn away with the new work, rather in the way *Blues Suite* and *Revelations* had allowed Alvin to pour out his past and his wry affection for the world that had made him what he was. *For Bird—With Love* enabled Alvin to articulate the pain that in part drove him as an artist.

Like Alvin, Parker was a "junior." The two shared certain creative traits, among them styles that are technically fresh but focused on feeling, as the jazz historian Barry Ulanov put it. Alvin managed to choreograph, Ulanov observed, as if his dancers were somehow free to improvise in the manner of jazz musicians. Parker was a largely self-taught artist, like Alvin, although his music was a driving discipline and obsession to a degree that dance was not for Alvin.

Parker, too, had been brought up by an extremely attentive mother, a relationship on which one fellow musician blamed a long, wildly self-destructive addiction to heroin and alcohol that left Parker penniless and then dead at the young age of thirty-four. "I think he got the habit because he didn't learn how to cope," a musician who played with Parker in Jay "Hootie" McShann's band said. "He couldn't fit into society, 'cause evidently his mother had babied him so much, that he thought he was expecting that from everybody else in the world." And both knew the pain of the artist as historical outcast, not in the nourishing way, written so large, of romantic legend, but in the grinding poverty of means and begrudging respect of a nation of pioneers historically uncomfortable with and too busy for art as much more than a badge of gentility or entertaining relief from hard work. On one of his worksheets for the new dance, Alvin wrote out poetry that made him think of Parker. One recurrent image is from Charles Baudelaire. "Exiled on earth among the shouting people," the lines read, "his giant wings hinder him from walking."

In its final form, *For Bird—With Love* took Parker from his childhood to club life to physical and emotional collapse, ending with a startling shift to a happy apotheosis in which Alvin seems to be exclaiming that "Bird Lives!" through the joy of his music. The score is an adroitly sewn together suite of pieces by Parker, Dizzy Gillespie, Count Basie and Jerome Kern, with original music by Coleridge Taylor-Perkinson. At the beginning and end, the action takes place under huge blown-up photographs of Parker, the first on a poignantly inscribed identity card that appears to have been issued by police after an arrest.

Unlike *Précipice,* the Parker piece can be appreciated best by someone with a knowledge of the subject. Alvin weaves together a small-town kind of life not unlike that of Navasota, Texas, with the hurly-burly of the teeming clubs and brothels of Kansas City in the 1930s, where Parker got his start as a teenaged saxophonist. He creates a sense of the city's community of musicians, although not Parker's angry distance from many of his colleagues.

Each member of the large cast had a character. Williams modeled himself after Perky Perkins, a club owner who limped and walked with a cane. Alvin produced a cane from the many props he had brought to rehearsal and told the dancer to walk back and forth while he carefully timed the walks and the entrances of other dancers as Williams passed by.

"We all got a chance to contribute what the person was underneath the situation," Williams said. "It was like we lived with Bird and so we knew how each person would react. We talked. He gave us names. Each character had a name. Sarah Vaughan. Billie Holiday. We all got a chance to contribute. Alvin allowed us to do that. It was a very very special piece for all of us."

Parker's almost demonic connection to his instrument and his music is also present in *For Bird—With Love,* as is the terror of waking up the "morning after." Alvin even refers to Parker's habit of carrying his saxophone in a cloth sack, which doubles as the swaddling clothes in which Parker lies as an infant. And Williams even acts out an oedipal relationship with DeLoatch's character.

This is theatrical dance, rooted in the Ailey blend of ballet and jazz and modern dance body lines and techniques, that is securely anchored in an actual place and time. It is tempting to imagine that Alvin's stay in Kansas City gave him a more immediate feel for his characters and story.

For all the demands for Alvin's time at the troupe's new second home, he could look back on Kansas City as something of a respite from the fast-changing kaleidoscope of new hotel rooms, new theaters, the same old dancers' problems and the extra edge of nerves a New York season generally inspired in all. There was a kind of ingenuous freshness to Kansas City that amused and appealed to Alvin.

"He was real tired," Coe said. "He liked coming to Kansas City because it was almost like starting over. He would say how gentle Todd Bolender's girls were with their feelings. And they respected him as the master. They'd say, 'Mr. Ailey, Mr. Ailey, am I doing this right?' Or he would say, 'Now, dear, what was that you just did?' and their little faces would just sink." When Alvin sternly asked his own women dancers whose ballet they thought they were dancing, they just went ahead and danced it again right for him. "But these girls were so young and tender."

Another chance at a kind of starting over presented itself in September 1985, when Alvin became the first choreographer to be awarded a Distinguished Professorship at City University of New York, at a yearly salary of $60,000. He was to help set up a dance program at the Borough of Manhattan Community College, a gleaming new school with a high proportion of minority students, built near the southwest tip of the city in an area of bleak warehouses and artists' lofts.

Although there was talk of Alvin teaching regular technique classes and participating in several seminars a year, his job was chiefly to bring some much-needed glamour and inspiration to educationally impoverished young lives. His touring schedule alone obviously meant that Alvin could not be a steady presence at the school, and Jamison and Ailey alumnus John Parks dealt with the details of the programming.

Alvin had lost none of the love for creating projects that had both delighted and exasperated Edele Holtz in the early Clark Center days. He dove into the details of a dance curriculum for college and visiting high school students, coming up with an eight-point plan that dealt with everything from the design of the dance department logo to performances by guest modern and African dance companies and programs by student choreographers and performers.

He was very specific about what he wanted. "Alvin *insisted* that the second semester of a two-semester course in dance history should be a history of black dance," Dawn Lille Horwitz, who headed the dance faculty, recalled with affectionate laughter. "If you had sneezed you would have missed the whole history of the Romantic ballet." Soon after, Alvin put together a program for an ambitious cable television series for 1987 that examined black concerns in dance in nine one-hour shows that made use of the school's well-equipped media laboratory.

Traveling with the company in Australia, Alvin flew to New York from Melbourne to be present at the start of the seven-week semester—and to finish preparations for a two-week tour of China to be sponsored by the United States Information Agency, the first performances in that country by an American modern dance company.

While in New York, Alvin attended to some professorial duties, and then flew on to Kansas City for a few days. He bought a bottle of the city's famed Gates Barbeque Sauce to season his food in China and, talking with Coe, he had a sudden inspiration. "Coe, I'm leaving for China on Friday," he told her. "Why don't you come?" It was only a few days before departure, but Coe found her passport and was ready to go when the State Department told her that she had to have a formal invitation. There was a great deal of backing and filling until at last Coe was told nothing could be done unless Alvin called them himself.

Alvin was surprised. "Honey, is that all we got to do?" he asked her. Still a little in awe of Alvin's clout, as he himself could be, Coe watched how government officials scrambled into action after the master made his wishes known. "The Chinese Embassy called me back from New York and said Coe can go," she said, laughing.

Alvin flew back to New York from Kansas City for the last of his classes at the college, and was in his usual disarray on the eve of his departure. "I wake up before the alarm stings my ears—indeed I have not really slept all nite—having gotten home later than I wanted to from the evening students convocation at the college," he wrote in the first (and last) entry of a journal entitled "To China and Back." "Kelvin's group had danced among a flurry of student activist speeches & I had spoken also (too long) in my usual improvisatory style & ended up signing autographs for an hour & a half. They like me at the college. The students are enthusiastic about my presence."

At 6 A.M. he was up and staggering around the apartment doing all his packing for the trip to China in the few hours before the airport limousine was due to arrive. Hammond had planned to be there at 8:30 to collect Alvin and then Plesent, who was coming along for the first week of the tour. "Somehow by 8:15 I am washed, bathed, & packed & ready to go—this has happened very often in my lifetime—in many hotels in many countries—too tired or busy to pack the nite before & ending up doing it at the last minute. Indeed I have been proud of the fact that I could pack in 45 mins & be downstairs composed & waiting for bus, taxi or whatever."

Wearily, he admitted to panic, though, and a sense of exhaustion from the return of his arthritis. "I leave the apt a mess—also not unusual in my many trips," he wrote later, tucked into a seat on a Northwest Airlines jet for the thirteen-hour trip to Tokyo, where the company was to change planes for Beijing. "My knees are painful as I drag the heavy bags to the elevator and to the car. Bill is uncharacteristically dressed in jeans & open dress shirt. Stanley is in tie, shirt—a real lawyer look." Having decided to "look formal in China," Alvin had brought along an equally uncharacteristic four suits, one of them a new Willi Smith corduroy, he noted with something like pride, as well as shirts and ties.

"As I write this after the 11th hour of flite I wonder how much more of my life I want to spend on the airplanes of the world—or is it only this particular direction I am reacting to—the Orient?" Then "6:10 NY time," the diary ends, "still enroute to Peking from Tokyo—it is now 24 hours since my getting up in New York and starting to pack for this trip—"

There was, at least, a day of rest before a group trip to the Great Wall and the Ming Tomb, the first of many activities planned for Alvin and the dancers. The following day, he and the company gave a master class and lecture-demonstration to the eager but shy young students of the Beijing Dance Academy, who performed for the Ailey dancers. And then, on November 1, the company opened in the first of ten historic performances in China.

As had been the case with the Soviet tour, Alvin was faced with stringent restrictions on what he could present. There were to be no dances about drugs, alcohol, sex or religion. "Well," Alvin quipped, "that's my whole repertoire." In the end, he was allowed to present *Night Creature, Cry, Memoria* and, of course, *Revelations,* as well as Billy Wilson's spring-drenched Gershwin piece, *Concerto in F.* It was a good balance of prettiness and intense drama, although this new and unfamiliar kind of dance reduced some Chinese audiences to giggles in the packed theaters where the company performed in Beijing, Nanchang (where performances were at the Railroad Workers' Cultural Palace) and Shanghai. Once again, the dancers noted, there seemed to be an instinctive understanding of what the works were about and even a surprised recognition of part of one Ailey score as a familiar Chinese song.

Alvin returned to New York to good and bad news. The company had received a $300,000 grant from Philip Morris Companies, the largest ever made to a dance company by a corporation. The money was earmarked by Philip Morris for national, European and Asian touring over the next two years. At home, however, there was the usual worry about finding enough money to pay the bills and the consequent redeploying of school and office personnel, along with an even more terrible new worry.

The specter of AIDS had begun to settle over the company, soon to claim two of the best-loved young members of the administrative staff. "I want to take this opportunity to again thank you & your company for all you have done for me," one of them wrote in a loving Christmas message to Alvin, thanking him, too, for the fact that "while I fight the biggest battle in my life the comfort that you are there is most appreciated!"

thirty-one

UP AND DOWN, AGAIN

With the company busy on a national tour, Alvin flew off to Copenhagen in late January 1986 to work again with the Royal Danish Ballet,
for whom he had staged *Memoria* in 1981. The Danes had asked him
back to teach the company *The River.* They also commissioned a large
group dance called *Caverna Magica,* which Alvin had already begun
work on using student dancers from the Ailey school in New York. A
celebration of "the anticipation of spring," as Alvin subtitled it, the new
piece was set to a New Age electronic score by Andreas Vollenweider.
But once in Copenhagen, among dancers for whom he had a special
affection, Alvin decided to choreograph a second new piece, *Witness,* a
solo for senior ballerina Mette Honningen.

He was intrigued by Honningen, a dancer of somewhat chill perfection. Alvin's mischievous pleasure in tweaking his nose at authority
was likely set off by his sense that she was not one of the more favored
members of the company at the time. In *Witness,* all attention was on
Honningen in the role of a woman making a joyous peace with grief as
she moves among three benches on a stage lit with rows of candles,
dancing to a recording by Jessye Norman and a chorus singing a spiritual, "My Soul Is a Witness for My Lord."

Alvin was fine at first in Copenhagen. He had been dieting again
and was looking lean and handsome. He had also taken to dressing

somewhat more stylishly than usual, although his pants cuffs still hung down unhemmed. But, always bad about taking medicine, he had gone off his lithium. This was probably not Alvin's first lapse, nor would it be his last. Mickey Bord had returned to work for the Ailey company as promised after her retirement from teaching. Helping to clean up Alvin's office later that year, she was startled to find not only unopened presents from three Christmases ago but a steamer trunk full of bottles of untaken medicine.

Alvin began to do odd things, although seldom in the rehearsal studio. His behavior became even more markedly peculiar when Paul Szilard, who had accompanied him to Denmark, left to take care of some European touring business. In New York, he had already slipped a bit. Friends noticed he was drinking a little, and the disreputable hangers-on from other years were seen once again waiting for Alvin by the stage door at City Center. Now it seemed he might again be taking drugs.

There had been trouble at his hotel, the elegant old Hotel d'Angleterre, where Alvin was sometimes to be found wandering around public spaces in bed clothes and his stocking feet. Even those who knew Alvin best found it hard to be sure what was normal and abnormal disorder in him. It wasn't until he began obviously stepping over the line that the Danes were frightened. Szilard was called.

"We all did love Alvin, even despite all the problems," Frank Andersen, then director of the Danish company, said. "He was very special. He did something for us that none of us will ever forget. It was my first season as director and he said, 'Of course I'll come.' He was the first choreographer I spoke to after I was appointed. And *Witness* came out of the blue, a gift. It was very important for me and for the company to have two creations and *The River*. And we had a lot of fun. It was just toward the end."

Alvin seemed somehow to have convinced himself that the Danes wanted him rather than Andersen to direct the company. Passing a senior dancer backstage one day, he told the man that he didn't like him and so would not allow him to dance *Don Quixote*, a nineteenth-century ballet that Alvin had nothing to do with. He declared outright during a stage rehearsal that he would make a better director than Andersen. And scattered notes to himself from the time, written in the racing print of his manic days in the late 1970s, suggest that Alvin was also obsessed by the idea that the great Danish classical dancer Erik Bruhn must be brought back to Copenhagen to direct the company.

He began to abuse Honningen verbally in rehearsal, berating her for lackluster dancing in the vulnerable days just before the March 22 premiere. Backstage before the first performance, he told her that he didn't know why he had created the solo for her. Szilard reassured the weeping ballerina that Alvin loved her. She went on in the solo and it was a great success, as were the other Ailey pieces on the program. But Alvin had left the theater earlier that evening and returned to the hotel, and the audience cheered in vain for him to take a curtain call with the dancers.

Szilard persuaded Honningen to return with him to the hotel, where he talked Alvin into coming down to meet with her in the bar. Alvin kissed her and took her back to his room, where he presented her with one of several fur coats he had bought that day. Another coat went to an unimpressed Szilard. "Give it back," Alvin told him the next day. "I know you hate it."

Soon after, Szilard heard Alvin call out to him from the adjoining hotel room late at night. "He told me he felt very bad," Szilard recalled. "I asked him if he had taken his pills, but he had thrown them in the toilet." William Hammond was called in New York. Could he bring some lithium to Copenhagen? But Alvin was beyond such help, and Szilard and Hammond began to talk of flying him home. In the middle of all this, Alvin's mother called Szilard in the middle of the night to ask what was wrong with her son. His troubles had been kept quiet in both Denmark and New York, but Lula Cooper had not lost her sixth sense about Alvin. She was told not to worry. "Alvin loved her, but he always said not to let her come," Szilard said.

Rumors abounded in the Copenhagen ballet community, and there was a very oblique passing reference to Alvin's sickness in one city newspaper. For the most part the company managed to hush talk about his problems. Ves Harper, Alvin's early costume designer, had been working in London during the breakdown but heard about it when he returned to his home in Copenhagen. Had there been some problem with Mr. Ailey? he asked a colleague. Oh, you know how these artists are, Harper was told. The Danes had loyally closed ranks around Alvin.

He dedicated the performances of *Caverna Magica,* the second premiere, to "the good, sweet and warm people of Copenhagen, especially to those at The Royal Theatre with many thanks for making me a part of their wonderful extended family." His affection was reciprocated. On his return to New York, Alvin had called a friend in the Danish company, Andersen's secretary Vibeke Poulsen, to reassure her that he was feeling better. He received a fond letter from her in mid-April thanking him for the call and "for being you, for two marvellous months and for leaving three beautiful ballets behind you." The performances, she added, had been sold out almost every night, which was unusual for a triple bill.

"We miss you," Poulsen continued, in a letter that suggests how lovingly thoughtful Alvin could be even in distress. "It is so strange not to see you daily. But it is comforting to 'feel' you around in so many special ways. . . . Daily, I enjoy your flowers, the little black boy figure and the boxes, both here and at home. Also, Frederik is happily wearing the clothes you gave him.

"As you will understand, you are in our hearts and minds and you have a very enthusiastic audience in the Royal Theatre. So, we are very grateful to you.

"We can hardly wait to see you again here in Copenhagen in September—or perhaps May as you mentioned to me on the phone? May is the real month of arrival of the spring, perhaps not warm, but nevertheless the first blossom of leaves and flowers do start—all very light, pastel shades of colours. Come and see for yourself." She closed by sending "much love from your R.D.B. friends," including Honningen, Poulsen and her little son, Frederik, and other fond signatories.

Alvin pulled himself together enough to engage in the typical flurry of activity at home. He joined the dancers for a three-week tour of Japan and Hong Kong, followed in mid-August by a European tour that took the company to Athens and performances in the ancient outdoor Herod Atticus. With his love for the theatrical moment, Alvin never lost his delight in the effect of great lights sweeping out over the six-thousand-seat amphitheater and across the nightscape of ruins beyond following the performance.

The company returned to national touring, with the year's second stop at Kansas City and a culminating winter season at City Center. *Caverna Magica,* whose American performances Alvin had tried unsuccessfully to get the Kansas City Friends to help underwrite, was a centerpiece of the New York season. This time, sadly, it was dedicated to Ron Bundt, the second young member of the Ailey administration to succumb to AIDS in 1986.

The amorphous new dance was not a success, despite its lush use of swirling lights and costumes. Critics praised the company's strong dancing, however, especially that of April Berry, the ballet's tall, thin, becaped central goddess, and Gary DeLoatch as a male initiate, this time given unusually lyrical dancing in an all too familiar Ailey ritual dance. *Witness,* performed by Marilyn Banks, fared better. The hit of the season was Alvin's new *Survivors,* for which Mary Barnett was given credit as cochoreographer the following year for her work on the opening and closing of the dance.

Survivors was danced to an eloquent, throbbing drum and vocal score composed by the jazz drummer and composer Max Roach, who had donated his services. With singing by Abbey Lincoln (then known as Abbey Lincoln Aminata Moseka), the music and dance reached a kind of symbiotic relationship that suggested heat and light, darkness and the persistence of belief, in a portrait of a political prisoner and his wife that was inspired by Nelson and Winnie Mandela.

Nelson Mandela had long wandered through Alvin's notebooks, a real-life character in search of a dance, and Alvin had been reading about him recently. Worldwide rallies in July were timed to coincide with the imprisoned South African leader's sixty-seventh birthday. The celebrations in South Africa were quashed, however, and Mandela's friends were not allowed to visit him in his dank cell at the Pollsmoor Maximum Security prison just outside Cape Town. A month later, it was learned that he had tuberculosis.

Alvin's intense feelings about racial equality were more clearly stated in *Survivors* than ever before, although in a powerfully stylized way. Here it was Dudley Williams to whom Alvin had given a chance at an unusual role. Williams's containment of emotion perfectly matched the physical control of his dancing in the role of a powerful man who watches the passing parade from behind shadow prison bars, a parade led by the wife with whom he yearns to be reunited. In another inspired bit of casting, the small, delicately pretty Sharrell Mesh was surprisingly implacable as Winnie Mandela.

Alvin's subject matter and storytelling in *Survivors* were strong enough to draw bomb threats in a theater in Clearwater, Florida, where the company was performing the dance on tour two years later. But the piece was a more complex and subtle work than *Masekela Langage,* which it most closely resembled in theme, and a more distanced dance than any of Alvin's previous message pieces. *Survivors* was an expression of hope, fear, rage and despair that could have come only from a mature choreographer.

That distance and maturity did not make it any easier for Alvin to deal with a company filled with eager young dancers all jostling for his attention and approval. He and Mary Barnett, who had been pressed into service as his associate artistic director, had fallen into familiar roles. Alvin was the kind but not entirely approachable father. Barnett, who left the company the following year, had become the omnipresent martinet-mother, unnerving even Alvin with her intense devotion to duty and her willingness to take over chores.

One must be either infantile or extremely mature to live through the kind of extensive touring done by the Ailey company. Everyday personality clashes and problems that might blow over quietly in the studio at home are intensified by living close nearly twenty-four hours a day on tour, as the company did during national and foreign engagements that accounted for eighteen of the dancers' forty-five weeks of work in 1987.

Tensions came to a boil in May as the company crisscrossed the country. When the dancers landed in Chicago for eight days, Alvin decided to try to do something about the unhappiness he had sensed among them for many months. He had long ago realized that to run a dance company democratically was not possible. He called a company meeting in the hotel room of Masazumi Chaya, who had stopped performing the year before and had become Alvin's assistant.

The meeting soon degenerated into an impassioned gripe session, complete with tears, over the allocation of roles. Alvin tried to explain that he chose dancers because he wanted to see them perform those roles rather than because one dancer was necessarily better or worse than another. Instead of soothing the dancers, the meeting made them more upset. Finally, a tired and disconsolate Alvin left for a late-night takeout dinner with Chaya.

"He was so disappointed, so sad," Chaya said. "I kind of understood how the dancers felt. But at the same time, you have to work under direction. I always wanted to do the *Backwater* guy in *Blues Suite,* but Alvin didn't see me doing it. That you have to accept."

A month later, Alvin received a three-and-a-half-page letter, typed single spaced, from an outspoken young company member intent on helping him identify problems and find "constructive solutions" for them. There was insufficient artistic direction. Too many of the dancers—some of them identified by name in the directive—had deteriorated into useless lumps of flesh with less than functioning brains, the letter continued, because of Alvin's neglect. Some of the accusations were well reasoned. Most were merely the age-old complaints of dancers. Williams had made many of the same points years before in a similar letter at a very different time. But here the tone bordered on condescension, and it came from a relatively new young member of the company, who nonetheless did not lose his job with the Ailey troupe.

Not all the dancers were so lordly. "Forgive me also for resenting you and the company, thinking that it was your fault that I was so lost and unhappy," a dancer leaving the company wrote to Alvin in 1987 after a hoped-for last conversation did not materialize. "I see now that the condition of my life was and is all up to me. Thank you for your generosity, and the laughs we shared." Alvin, who sometimes wept when favorite performers quit, kept the two letters.

But it was a good time, too. On June 7, Alvin received the 1987 Samuel H. Scripps American Dance Festival Award in a solemn but joyful ceremony at Duke University in Durham, North Carolina, where the summer festival had moved ten years earlier from Connecticut College in New London. Established in 1981 and named after a colorful philanthropist with an interest in lighting design, the award was the richest in American dance, carrying with it a cash prize of $25,000. Asked by a reporter how he would spend the money, Alvin said he might go up and sit on a mountaintop and think about an autobiography. The one just published by Paul Taylor, he added generously, was so wonderful. Or he might do what he had done in the old days and plow the money back into the company.

The festival, where Alvin had presented the premiere of *Masekela Langage,* had played an important part in encouraging modern dance in America. The Scripps "Sammy," as it was nicknamed, had a cachet that the older dance awards that Alvin had already received did not. And the words of the citation must have meant a great deal to him, for all the lightness of tone and the humor with which he responded.

> To Alvin Ailey, dancer, teacher and choreographer, whose work is generated from the heart and powered by passion; he stands as a model of artistic integrity. An American, informed by the Black experience, Mr. Ailey's choreography presses through cultural lines and speaks a universal language. His dances, whether sassy, sad, witty or lyrical, have brought joy and a sense of purpose to people throughout the world. Alvin Ailey's consistent artistic achievements have insured him a place as a giant in the history of American modern dance.

Harry Belafonte was on hand to present the award to Alvin, and he drew frequent laughter from the crowd that packed the college theater. Describing Alvin as a "restless, forceful, energetic and sometimes intimidating human being," Belafonte talked of their battles in *Sing, Man, Sing*. "I sang and he danced," he said. "He didn't think I sang well enough, and I didn't think he danced well enough."

Then it was time for the presentation, and Alvin entered the stage, looking almost roly-poly in his tuxedo next to the elegantly svelte Belafonte. The audience rose in waves throughout the cavernous old theater in a noisy standing ovation. "Thank you very much," Alvin boomed out at last over the upraised, smiling faces. "Aren't you sweet."

He had not prepared a speech, he said. But his comments were vintage Ailey: teasing, eloquent, comfortably discursive and with a slight gadfly edge. He talked of his company, of dance history and of his origins. He talked of not wanting to be caged by his color. The audience hung on every word, with a stillness occasionally broken by laughter and applause. It was only later—after the last curtain call for the performance of *Revelations* and after the last frenzied, loving cheers, after the champagne and strawberries under the trees outside the theater in the humid night air, after the newspaper accounts and the passing-along of quips from the always quotable Alvin Ailey—that one bittersweet, surprising comment stood out. He was now a part of Isadora Duncan, of Martha Graham, of Ted Shawn and Asadata Dafora, he had said. He was a part of Lester Horton, too. It was clear that not until now, despite the years of accomplishment, did he feel he had joined the ranks of modern dance.

Alvin returned to the Horton fold five months later when he attended a reunion in Los Angeles with many of the dancers he had known at the Horton studio. He himself had suggested the reunion when some of the "kidlets" visited him backstage after an Ailey performance in Los Angeles. His Horton friend from early New York days, Lelia Goldoni, had gone on to a career in theater and film, and she seized the occasion to tape interviews for *Genius on the Wrong Coast*, a documentary about Horton that was released in 1994.

Alvin seemed almost apathetic, however, at the reunion. He would ordinarily have been moving from friend to friend, eager to catch everything that was going on. Now he sat quietly, receiving those friends. His face had begun to take on a grayish, crumbling look, with glittering eyes that seemed to stare out from some long distance inside of him. In retrospect, Goldoni wondered if Alvin somehow sensed there would not be many more chances for him to see them all and that the reunion would be a way to say good-bye.

The pace of work had not slowed. Alvin's dreams of reviving lost dances and his love for Dunham had come together in the ambitious *Magic of Katherine Dunham* program, which would offer a demonstration of Dunham technique and eleven pieces, drawn from traditional African, Caribbean and American black dances, that had not been seen since the 1960s. (These included *Afrique, Los Indios, Nanigo, Choros, Shango, L'Ag'ya, Fieldhands, Plantation Dances, Flaming Youth, Barrelhouse* and *Cakewalk.*) They not only were being revived for the company by Dunham and a small army of her former dancers, but were to be performed with reconstructions of the original sets and costumes designed by John Pratt, Dunham's husband, that had played an important role in establishing her as a consummately theatrical artist. Epitomizing Dunham's dances, the costumes were beautiful things in themselves, departures from their Afro-Caribbean influences that did full justice to the originals.

Dunham, at seventy-five a seductive grande dame with a voice like warm honey and the manner of a drill sergeant, was a formidable teacher who expected total commitment. There was, after all, only one Dunham. Traces of her great stardom—as well as her breath-catching beauty—still clung to her, although she had not been onstage in many years and now had trouble walking. Her work was an important but overlooked part of the nation's cultural history. But the exhaustive preparations for *The Magic of Katherine Dunham* were fraught with drama and cost overruns. And Dunham's demands and high expectations were like red flags to the independent-minded Ailey performers, many of whom found it hard to understand why they were suddenly being force-fed history and a foreign-feeling, difficult technique that did not seem particularly transferable to other dances in the repertory.

They could not escape her. Blown-up photographic portraits of Dunham hung in the studio. She conducted rehearsals with the help of early Dunham dancers who in varying degrees seemed to worship her and consider her word unquestionable law. Yet the years were gone when Dunham—or George Balanchine or Martha Graham—could cow a dancer with a single glance. Dancers were still relatively poorly paid. That hadn't changed. But now they were more highly trained and competitive. Alvin had an eye for the performer who didn't fit the mold, and so the Ailey troupe was a less heterogeneous group than many, with allowances made for dynamic performers cursed with less than perfect bodies that would have cost them jobs in many other companies. Like the sleek beauties who otherwise filled the profession, however, these performers had an at least superficial sense of their own worth. The old fear tactics didn't work with them. They hadn't taken the dancer's "course in knee-bending," as one longtime observer of the scene put it.

An attempt had been made to prepare the Ailey dancers for Dunham with lectures, slide shows and films, all of which the older dancers tended to ignore. The younger dancers were more malleable, but they grumbled. "I thought if I saw *Stormy Weather* one more time, I was going to lose it," a new company member groaned, talking of one of the Hollywood musicals in which Dunham starred. This was old history. What did it have to do with them?

Not everyone felt the same. April Berry, whose mother had died before the rehearsal period, was initially drawn into the work by the quietly expressed concern of Dunham and Glory Van Scott, one of the assisting Dunham dancers. And although company members would later amuse Alvin on tour with their apt imitations of the old-timers, a few dancers were delighted by their strong personalities and their energy, and intrigued by how differently each taught the technique.

Alvin had wanted the dancers to start learning the Dunham technique early in the summer of 1987 so they could get it solidly into their bodies before the City Center season in December. The touring schedule prevented that, but eventually they got a hefty eight weeks of Dunham classes and rehearsals, in days that often ran straight through from 10 A.M. to 9 P.M. Dunham kept a mostly firm grip on the sessions, rehearsing from her wheelchair or leaning against a barre, looking glamorous in her functional, flowing pants and tops and turban. Sometimes she would surprise the dancers with her digressions, stopping midpiece to talk to them about life. "She'd ask to see *Nanigo* and the guys would start and then she'd stop them in the middle of a jump or an arabesque and start talking about AIDS and cats," Raquelle Chavis recalled. "Everyone had to stop dancing and come around."

Dunham's dances required strong ballet skills, but generally her technique stressed weight, gravity and the isolation of body parts in motion, all antithetical to the lighter, flowing look of ballet. Returning to ballet classes in preparation for performing Billy Wilson's comparatively airborne *Concerto in F,* the dancers found that after weeks of digging into the ground for Dunham, it was physically painful to soar. Faced with complaints, Alvin asked for patience from his dancers. Miss Dunham was, he reminded them, their history.

Certainly there was an air of extra importance to the rehearsals, as if history were in fact being made. Students on their way to and from classes crowded around the studio door to catch a glimpse of this legend. Alvin often slipped into the huge airy room and sat on a bench to watch, accompanied sometimes by Harry Belafonte, whose wife had performed with Dunham. Journalists came and went during the last few weeks. Photographers and videotapers threaded through the dancers, creating archival records of an event that Alvin was determined would live on long past the season. There were fewer and fewer comments from Dunham about "elephant" landings and "ducklings" stepping out of line. There were even times when everyone in the studio, visitors and workers, would suddenly burst into song as Dorothea Freitag, the tiny, effervescent rehearsal pianist, rollicked through the scores for the program's exuberant closing *Barrel House* and *Cake Walk.*

The Magic of Katherine Dunham was a popular and for the most part a critical success. Unsurprisingly enough, given the differences in generational perspectives, the choreography looked less exciting on the Ailey dancers than what the cheering audiences of the 1940s and 1950s had seen, among them a young boy in an elegant Los Angeles theater who suddenly understood the power and beauty of being black. For all her academic work in anthropology and the disciplined performing her dances required, Dunham was about theater and the selling of a dance. Her concerts had been revues, performed by dancers intent on seducing their audiences. The Ailey dancers, although far less distant and cool than their counterparts of the time, came out of a culture steeped in irony.

The Dunham performances significantly outsold other programs in the City Center season. The project proved to be much more expensive than anyone had foreseen, however, running $100,000 over its $300,000 budget even with costs minimized by tactics like the establishment of an in-house costume shop that was "just a cut above loving hands at home," as Peter Brown, the company's general manager, put it.

Alvin was obsessed with the idea that everything had to be perfect, from the dancers to the sets and costumes. Watching those earlier performances in Los Angeles, he had understood "that black people could do things that were wonderful and elegant and meaningful and physical and theatrical," he told partygoers after the opening performance of *The Magic of Katherine Dunham* in St. Louis in 1989. Even more important, perhaps, that realization planted the idea that "the dances that my family did at our home in Texas, those social dances, were beautiful marks of our own culture."

But $7,700 for two chandeliers for the set, and $4,170 for moss for *L'Ag'ya?* A twenty-four-hour limousine and a room for Dunham at the expensive Crillon or Georges V when the company performed in Paris? It didn't matter if there was not enough money for these niceties for Dunham on tour in Europe, Alvin told an irritated Szilard. She deserved them all—although Szilard eventually won out.

In the midst of all this tumult, Alvin had become a Buddhist, like Dunham and Van Scott, converting shortly before the start of rehearsals for *The Magic of Katherine Dunham*. He had had talks about religion with Dunham, whose worldview was a startling combination of mysticism and extreme practicality, on visits with her in her home in East St. Louis. Sensing some need in Alvin, Van Scott encouraged him to learn about Buddhism. "I could see he was a little sick," Van Scott said. "He needed peace. I was one of the people who was with him as he went through Shakubuku, the ceremony to become a Buddhist. He understood he needed something and it gave him some comfort." But he soon lapsed. "He tried real hard to keep up with it," Van Scott said. "But it's a demanding practice. You have to chant twice a day. And Alvin was under an enormous amount of pressure."

Not only was he worried about the Dunham program and its cost, but there was also the company's need of new facilities to be considered. The Minskoff building had been sold and the Ailey lease would be up in May 1989. The company could not stay there under the kind of conditions negotiated originally during a real estate slump.

There had been talk of buying into the famous 890 Broadway building once owned by Michael Bennett and now the home of the Eliot Feld Ballet and the American Ballet Theatre, which were pushing the Ailey company to make a decision. The purchase price would have been $1.1 million for about five thousand square feet of raw space. The company eventually pulled out, concerned about raising the extra money to buy and renovate the space. Burdened by these ongoing worries, Alvin lost his temper during the company's December season at City Center and ended up in the Page Six gossip column of the *New York Post* for slamming the phone down on Dina Merrill, the wealthy socialite and sometime actress, who was angry at him for denying permission to a company member to dance at a benefit she was chairing.

Time seemed to be drawing in on Alvin as one year ended and the next began. He had been thinking of buying a home, possibly a handsome gray-stone row house at 419 Convent Avenue at 148th Street, catty-cornered from homes that were owned and were being refurbished little by little by Mary Barnett and by Sylvia Waters and her husband, Chauncey Jones, all of whom urged Alvin to join them in that elegant outpost of serenity in the noisy, hurried city. He had also been talking with Gary DeLoatch, Judith Jamison and William Hammond about their condos and co-ops and the neighborhoods in which they lived. Perhaps he should flee to San Francisco, he told friends, or a pied-à-terre in Paris. Or what about just going somewhere to fish?

Alvin was thinking again about writing an autobiography and had begun making notes for the book, jotting down public milestones and private events with an almost desperate desire, it seemed, to let everything hang out to air. Defiantly, he was determined to release his private life. In January 1988, he began the first of several confessional sessions with A. Peter Bailey, the writer he had chosen as his collaborator.

Meetings with old friends rekindled buried emotions. After a relaxed, far-reaching conversation with Carmen de Lavallade for the book, Alvin startled his long-ago muse by suddenly pulling a gold bracelet off his hand and giving it to her. To her astonishment, her name was engraved inside. "I didn't know what to do," she recalled. "I don't know how or when he got it. He said, 'Oh, you can make it smaller.' "

In March, Alvin went off to Italy to create an unmemorable new dance in his water vein, *La Dea della Acqua,* and to stage *Streams* and *Memoria* for the ballet company at La Scala Opera House in Milan. He always enjoyed working with foreign companies and La Scala was no exception, although he was now nearly crippled by his arthritic knees and found it difficult to get up and move around in rehearsals.

The ballerinas fascinated him. "So sweet, so lovely, so feminine," he told friends back in New York. "Oh, cara bella!" He loved the fuss that was made over him, Waters said. "And he loved being appreciated in the world." Somehow, in foreign settings, the acclaim seemed more believable, and it came not only from audiences and critics but international ballet stars as well.

"Caro Maestro," the Italian prima ballerina Carla Fracci wrote Alvin from Genoa in a breathless, childlike printed hand on March 29, the premiere of his ballets at La Scala. "In Genoa Giselle I wish to be near you to night. It 20 years that I hope to be on stage dancing for and with you—You have for me 'the touch of the poet' what I love most in our world. con Amore Carla."

Alvin returned to New York in April to face the problem of the company's new home and an assignment to create a worthy successor to *For Bird—With Love* for the Kansas City season in November. A thirtieth-anniversary television program and gala loomed in December.

The burdens were sweetened by the news in early August that he would be one of five artists to receive the Kennedy Center honors that year, chosen by theater trustees for lifetime contributions to "American culture through the performing arts," as the citation read. Now fifty-eight, Alvin was the youngest artist ever to be given the award, which he shared that year with Myrna Loy, George Burns, Alexander Schneider and Roger Stevens, the theatrical producer, first director of the National Endowment for the Arts and a prime mover in the establishment of Kennedy Center.

There was still a new dance to be made. Much of the work on the Kansas City premiere was done in Paris in October, in rehearsal time grabbed during the company's successful season at the Palais des Sports—a success that inspired one newspaper to observe in a headline that "Le dieu noir mene la danse a Paris." But the new work, *Opus McShann,* had the look of a pièce d'occasion and was not of the caliber of *For Bird—With Love.*

The bawdy new dance was intended as an introduction to the Parker tribute and was to be part of a Kansas City trilogy. The piece was built around the figure of Jay "Hootie" McShann, the jazz pianist, singer, composer and bandleader, to whose music the dance was performed. Played by Williams in purple top hat, tie and tails, McShann wandered through scenes of Kansas City life in the mid-1930s, the era when he had arrived there and worked as a "whorehouse pianist" playing the brothel music that helped to develop the aggressive, bouncy "Kansas City style" of jazz.

Opus McShann gave Alvin a chance to summon up scene after scene of vibrant period life on the seamier side of town. The dancers got to look gorgeous and shake it all out in lavish costumes by Randy Barcelo, the designer who had costumed the Parker piece. Parker could be seen among the characters, along with Mary Lou Williams.

The McShann piece was recognized from the first as a suite of scenes and dances rather than an integral whole, including a boisterous Lindy Hop that Alvin had invited veteran Savoy Ballroom dancers Frankie Manning and Norma Miller to choreograph. A sudden sober scene late in the dance, in which Alvin exorcised childhood fears of the Ku Klux Klan and suggested a bleaker side of life for blacks in the 1930s in Missouri, struck most viewers as jarringly unexpected. And when the dance was presented on its own, without *For Bird—With Love* to follow it as planned, its last moments mystified audiences as they watched DeLoatch methodically put on the suit he wore in the Parker piece. Still, there was a poignantly tender love duet for André Tyson and Mesh, so strong as Winnie Mandela in *Survivors*, as well as a steamy striptease solo for the ladylike Berry and a knockabout number for two drunks danced to perfection by DeLoatch and Carl Bailey.

Alvin took time off from rehearsals for the City Center season to fly to Washington, D.C., on December 3 for the Kennedy Center gala. His mother had flown in from Los Angeles the afternoon before and was waiting excitedly for him at the fashionable Ritz Carlton Hotel, where rooms had been booked for the entire Ailey party.

"Alvin had a big, big room," Lula Cooper recalled. "With a living room and a bedroom, because people were forever in there interviewing him." She was staying across the hall, but the two spent a good deal of time in his fancy suite. "Mama," he told her teasingly, "we're going to have to soak everything we can to get out of this place when we get ready to leave."

Like wide-eyed children, they explored the rooms together and wondered at all their accoutrements. The handsome locked cabinets in each room were miniature bars, they discovered, and even Alvin was a little bemused by the free meals and twenty-four-hour limousine service provided them. In spite of themselves, they were relieved when the desk clerk reassured them as they checked out that everything was indeed on the house. She could have left with a whole suitcase full of those little liquor bottles in the cabinets if she had only known, Cooper observed regretfully long after the event.

Alvin and his mother were persuaded to join several of the Ailey dancers at a disco that night, drinking the dancers' beer as they watched them let loose on the dance floor. A little later, Alvin sidled out into the night on his own, with Mickey Bord trotting faithfully behind him. Ducking into a nearby boîte, they were greeted by a glamorous woman seated at the bar who seemed to have a yen for Bord. Years before Alvin had teasingly urged Bord to go up onstage with others in the audience and join in the nude writhings in an Off-Broadway play, *Dionysus '69*, which they had gone to see together. Now he whisked Bord out of the clutches of the woman, a transvestite, and shooed her back to her hotel.

The festivities—a day-and-a-half-long blur of elegant reception rooms and heavy plate silverware, of famous faces and exquisite clothes, of overheated rooms and increasingly fixed smiles—had gotten off to a formal start on Saturday night with a black-tie dinner in the Benjamin Franklin Room at the State Department, given by the Kennedy Center trustees, where the honorees received their decoration, a medallion hanging on long multicolored ribbon.

Alvin had rented a floor-length mink for his mother, his date for the two days, and picked out a dress for her. "Girl," he told her, "you got to wear something shiny." A tall, slender, natural clotheshorse, Cooper returned to his room in all her finery and whirled about the floor on Saturday afternoon. "Ooh, look at Miss Lula," he exclaimed affectionately to visiting friends. "That chick's really dressed up."

Cooper was her irrepressible self even in these august surroundings. There had been a long wait in the lobby of the State Department as security guards checked the guests and ushered them through electronic barriers before they boarded the elevator for the reception room. There was another wait upstairs at the receiving line. But as Alvin and his mother entered the room, Alvin wearing a kente-cloth scarf over his tuxedo, Cooper made a beeline for George Burns as he stood flicking ash from his trademark cigar over the antique furniture and lush rugs. She asked him for the cigar and declared to a delighted reporter that she had promised it to her pastor back home.

The mood was both solemn and giddy throughout the evening. Dunham and Agnes de Mille, both previous Kennedy Center honorees, were interrupted in conversation by a reporter who asked if they were talking about dance. No, Dunham told her, the topic was life. Alvin and his mother had a heady extended conversation with the actress Kathleen Turner, whom he immediately liked. Secretary of State George Schultz managed to link the arts and American diplomacy in a speech, talking of the nation's recent refusal to let Palestine Liberation Organization leader Yasser Arafat enter the United States. De Lavallade, drawing murmurs for the flowing gold wrap her husband had designed for the occasion, sounded a gentler note in an after-dinner toast to Alvin that touched upon their days together at George Washington Carver Junior High and Thomas Jefferson High School in Los Angeles.

Alvin was subdued during much of the weekend, feeling tired and unwell. He was worried about his interrupted work on the anniversary gala and depressed, he told a reporter on Saturday night, because his dance company was facing a $700,000 deficit and a homeless future. The company might not even be able to continue past the spring, he added. But most of all, he was stunned at the idea of having been given the Kennedy Center award at such a young age. Honorees were traditionally much older. He had so much more to do, he told Coe, who had traveled to Washington for the event. Why was he being given this?

It couldn't have raised Alvin's spirits to hear the honorees' contributions to national culture sloughed off by President Reagan as being "more precious than rubies" in a speech at a shrimp and white wine reception in the Blue Room at the White House the following afternoon. The day had begun with a brunch at the hotel that was an almost unbearable jam of celebrities packed into a small space. There was still the ceremony at Kennedy Center to go, and a dinner after that.

But Alvin was touched by Dunham's participation. He and Arthur Mitchell had long talks together. Most of all, his mother was so very happy and proud. Friends noticed him looking lovingly at her, resplendent in the finery he had chosen for her. To some extent, he lived the event through her. And she was fascinated by it all, particularly the reception and dinner at the White House on Sunday.

"We went there in a limousine," Cooper recalled. "We had to give them identification. A man opened the gate and we drove right up to the White House, with the gate slamming behind us. A man in a red coat came up to the car, standing so straight, with his uniform and his cap. And he said, 'Alvin Ailey and Lula Cooper, how are you today?' He shook hands with us and said he would be our escort for the evening. He took my coat and I didn't see it anymore until I got ready to leave."

Everywhere they walked in the White House there seemed to be portraits of presidents on the walls, their eyes all following Cooper as she passed. "Boy, that was some place. Scary. All those presidents looking just like they looked. I went up to look at President Lincoln, he was just sitting there. And President Kennedy had his arms like he wanted to have a baby in there rocking."

Then, at last, the honors were given out in a program at Kennedy Center that night. Alvin and his mother sat with the other honorees and their dates in a center box next to the one occupied by President and Mrs. Reagan. Cooper felt numb but grateful at this acknowledgment of her boy, rousing herself to wave at appropriate moments to the audience and to the dancers on the stage. At one point one of her new shoes, kicked off because it was too tight, rolled down past Alvin's seat. To her embarrassed relief it was gathered up and gravely handed back to her by one of the escorts standing in the box.

She cried a little, sitting behind her son, at the public tributes to him from famous people like Walter Cronkite, host of the event, who described Alvin as a choreographer who had "helped free blacks from the cage of tap-dancing." Then Cicely Tyson stepped onto the stage, looking glamorous in her black and white evening gown and sounding more than a little emotional as she remembered the first time she had seen Alvin dancing, in *House of Flowers,* and how unforgettable a performer he had been.

Alvin breathed a little harder, his eyes cast down, as she mentioned his greatest ballets. There was laughter as she described his matter-of-fact approach to choreography, with Reagan bending to look around his wife and smile at an unseeing Alvin. A screen was lowered for well-chosen scenes from his life and work: a young Alvin dancing, an even younger fat-cheeked little boy smiling out at the world a little shyly, a handsome teenager in football regalia and an exotic-looking youngster posing at the Horton studio.

Alvin beamed down on the ensuing ovation with his "aren't you sweet" smile and nod. He jumped to his feet as Dunham was wheeled out to introduce the closing section of *Revelations,* listening intently as if she were bestowing a benediction, his eyebrows rising slightly at her description of him as "a genius." Leaning forward, he watched her being wheeled off, as if to will her back onstage. And then *Revelations* was performed, followed by exultant curtain calls before a cheering audience, Alvin laughing and waving to his performers as they raised their arms to him. "Every dancer was crying," Sharrell Mesh Alexander recalled. "We were so proud of him. So proud of him."

Back at the White House afterward, dinner was served in the Grand Foyer on tables laid out in Christmas reds and greens. Burns and Loy bowed out before the end of dinner, and Alvin and his friends left soon after for more disco partying.

Reality intruded the following morning, when they all left for New York. Alvin was now feeling so sick that he had to steel himself to get through the festivities for the company's thirtieth anniversary three days after Kennedy Center, as well as the conferral on him of a Handel Medallion, New York City's highest cultural honor, a few days after that.

For some time he had been having trouble swallowing, which made eating difficult. He continued to be troubled by arthritis. And it was hard to feel optimistic about the company's future, a mood he did not hesitate to share with the public in a series of articles that appeared in New York in December, prompted both by the honors he was receiving and by the anniversary season.

An upbeat salute to Alvin appeared on the front page of the *New York Times* Arts and Leisure section the Sunday of the Kennedy Center honors, with Anna Kisselgoff describing Alvin as "the great anomaly of

American dance for the past 30 years." "At a time when nearly all the arts turned toward abstraction, not to speak of inaccessibility via trendy minimalist and conceptualist currents, Mr. Ailey insisted on celebrating the human spirit," Kisselgoff wrote. "Communication with the widest audience possible was his goal, harmony was his idea. Paradoxically, the odd man out has also been phenomenally 'in.' "

Society had changed in many ways, Alvin commented to Kisselgoff, but his vision had remained the same: "I am trying to show the world we are all human beings, that color is not important, that what is important is the quality of our work, of a culture in which the young are not afraid to take chances and can hold onto their values and self-esteem, especially in the arts and in dance. That's what it's all about to me."

When asked about the theme of the artist's loneliness in his dances, Alvin spoke with poignant simplicity of the part the public doesn't see, a part that may be dying inside as each autograph is signed. "You can't get away from yourself," he told Kisselgoff. "It is a troubled sleep." She pointed out that the inner struggle for balance was manifested in the company's precarious financial situation, in a time when Alvin was at the peak of his powers and the company had gained such an international reputation that it was the only American dance troupe asked to perform in Paris the next year in the city's celebration of the bicentennial of the French Revolution.

Many factors had played a part in the Ailey company's unimaginable success. Alvin's exposure to Horton, the loving early encouragement of friends and his own charisma, intelligence, shrewdness and talent as a choreographer had all simmered into the rich broth that was his company. He had come along on the tide of the civil rights movement in America, and had chosen to create a company that performed a wide repertory of dances in the enduring ballet model rather than his work alone in the way of most modern dance directors. Now the Alvin Ailey American Dance Theater was indisputably one of the most successful dance companies in America.

In thirty years, the Ailey company had performed in forty-eight states and forty-five countries across six continents. The roster of dancers had jumped from seven to twenty-eight. The troupe now had an annual budget of $6.7 million, less than the major ballet troupes but a great deal more than the annual national mean of $1.6 million for dance companies determined by the National Endowment for the Arts. And the Ailey company's ratio of earned to contributed income, always a measure of financial stability, was an extremely healthy 75 to 25 percent, with corporate donations up to $1.85 million. Alvin and the company had come far and done so much better than many other popular American dance troupes. Yet so little had changed. In interviews whose headlines were eerily prescient—"Dancing in the Dark," one in the *New York Post* read, ALVIN AILEY FEARS THAT THIS SEASON MAY BE THE LAST ONE—Alvin talked more believably than ever before of a sense that his company was about to go under.

But he summoned up the old gala spirit for the season's opening program at City Center. Since the opening night benefit was being taped for a television special to be called "Bill Cosby Salutes Alvin Ailey," there was money for a real party. Directed by George Faison, who had moved on from Ailey to a successful career on Broadway and television, the gala was also a good deal sleeker and slicker than past anniversaries.

Cosby was a good-natured presence throughout the evening, dressed in orange tights and a stocking cap as a dancer more aspiring, he told the audience, than perspiring. His wife, Camille Cosby, put in an appearance, as did popular New York television anchors Sue Simmons and Yolanda Watts, actors and singers, and a slew of city, state and corporate representatives. Cooper had stayed on in New York for the gala and appeared with all her usual flair in the closing curtain bows at the end of the evening, glancing proudly from time to time at Alvin, who wore his Kennedy Center decoration over a well-cut suit.

He had danced out onto a strobe-lit stage for the finale along a path of rose petals strewn before him by a capering Cosby. Standing before a throng of three generations' worth of Ailey dancers whom Faison had blended ingeniously into the fast-moving three-hour show, Alvin spoke for a few moments, looking as close to tears as he claimed to be. After fond tributes to de Lavallade and his mother, he talked of the past, of the urgency he felt about preserving the heritage of modern dance, and of a promising but perilous future, in a tone that hit the perfect balance of teasing and solemnity.

He'd had a ball, he said. But, in the end, the thirty years had been all about "family." "These people always came back, no matter how they left—whether I fired them, or they got mad at me, or they decided to go and have babies, or do Broadway shows, or become choreographers, like Miss Jamison and her new company, which we're so happy about," he said, gesturing toward the smiling dancers who clustered around him, a few in tears. "No matter what's happened, we've always come together—the school, the offices—everybody knows it's their home. That is the essence of what we're about, the distilling of the spirit through movement."

He talked of the black choreographers—Talley Beatty, Louis Johnson and Donald McKayle—who had inspired him when he first arrived in New York. Then Alvin turned to tease James Truitte about his penny-pinching ways as manager of the company in the 1960s. How times had changed. "Anyway, I don't want to talk too much," he said. "My heart is full. I am overwhelmed by these people—it's always been the people."

The last of the year's festivities took place on December 13, when Alvin and his mother were called to Gracie Mansion, the official home of the mayor of New York City, for the ceremony at which he and the year's other recipients were awarded their Handel Medallions for cultural achievement.

Four nights later, Szilard received a frightened phone call from Alvin. He was feeling very sick, he said. Could Szilard help him get to a doctor? His own was out of town for the weekend.

Szilard called his doctor, who arranged for a room at Lenox Hill Hospital. He picked Alvin up in a cab and they drove to the hospital, across town on the Upper East Side, where Alvin was admitted immediately. His illness could no longer be ignored. He had pulled himself together emotionally many times—but now he faced another, even harder challenge.

ᴸ

thirty-two

"SO EASY TO BREAK,
AND YET SO STRONG"

Worried by Alvin's lack of energy and the way he seemed to be failing, Paul Szilard had been trying to get Alvin to go to his doctor for over a year. But Alvin resisted. He had his own doctor, he said, afraid, possibly, of what he would find out. And the news was not good.

In addition to his arthritic pain and exhaustion, Alvin told Dr. Albert Knapp, Szilard's physician, he had been having increasing difficulty eating because it was so painful. Alvin was diagnosed with pneumonia, which antibiotics cleared up. Tuberculosis was suspected, but after a battery of tests Knapp, a gastroenterologist, discovered that Alvin was infected with cytomegalovirus, or CMV. A common herpes virus, CMV is normally kept in check by the body's immune system.

The virus is often found in gay men, whether sick with AIDS or healthy. "When one's immune system is no longer working, the virus can run amok and start destroying tissue," Knapp said. "In Alvin's case, the virus was probably all over his body but was heavily concentrated in the esophagus or food pipe. The result was an esophagal ulcer that perforated through into the adjoining trachea or wind pipe. The resultant abnormal connection fistula was the cause of his initial pneumonia. It was very painful."

Knapp asked Alvin if he could test him for the human immuno-deficiency virus, or HIV, the virus that causes AIDS. Alvin resisted at first—he had never had the test, he said—but finally gave in. The result, as Knapp had expected, was positive. And given the CMV, very little could be done medically for Alvin short of keeping him alive and functioning as best he could.

His stay at Lenox Hill was kept a secret, although Masazumi Chaya sent him an affectionate New Year's note. "Season went very well," Chaya reported. "All the dancers did wonderful job. They danced beautiful, and all the review was great. Of course we all missed you very much. Please take care."

Chaya had watched with helpless concern as an obviously frail Alvin pushed himself through a difficult season, coughing his way through Italy and having to leave early during performances that December at City Center. A photo session for Alvin and the company had been scheduled on the day Alvin was hospitalized. Chaya was asked to accompany the dancers. "My mind was not there at all. When I was growing up I experienced an earthquake. It was almost the same feeling of Alvin not being there that time. I was standing, but I had no idea where I was standing. That kind of scared feeling. The dancers were just doing a beautiful job, but that was the only thing I kind of held on to, because my feet were not quite on the ground then."

Alvin spent many long days in near-silence in Room 7623 of the Uris Pavillion, alone with a feisty English-born private-duty nurse named Anne McKnight whom Knapp had recommended. McKnight understood that this fascinating new patient needed to get through a profound emotional trauma. Alvin was finally facing something he could not talk, charm or work his way out of.

"He wanted to be isolated," McKnight recalled. "He really did not want anybody to know anything. Everyone thought they were his friend and maybe they were. But to me he was a very private person. And I think he realized that from this point on his privacy was taken away and also, in a way, his life. I think he realized it was all over, because of the illness."

At first, Alvin talked to McKnight only of how pleased he had been by the Kennedy Center honor, describing the ceremonies, parties and the famous people he had met in Washington a few weeks earlier. She enjoyed his gossip and shared his exuberant sense of humor. And although they were new friends, she felt immensely proud of him and glad that he had had this well-deserved adulation, however uncomfortable it also seemed to make him.

Slowly he began to tell McKnight about his life. She could see how hard it was for him to open up to her. But gradually he did, telling her about his early life and his mother, his work and the people he had loved, often in an uncharacteristic near-murmur as McKnight sat beside him in the quiet, dimly lit room on her twelve-hour shifts.

"In the beginning, it took many days to build up his trust. His mother was very dominant in his life and he was reticent about saying a lot about his illness, to protect her. His mother knew. She never admitted it. I think he knew his mother knew. It was a very big game."

Yet McKnight watched something good happening to him in the hospital. Difficult as it was for Alvin to reveal himself, it was becoming a little more difficult for him to hide.

The ward nurses made much of him, cosseting him like briskly protective surrogate mothers. McKnight suggested he might like a videocassette recorder in his room, and the head nurse managed to find him one. He and McKnight watched videotapes of dance performances together. Although well read and interested in the arts and the world around her, McKnight had had relatively little exposure to dance. A fan of the English Royal Ballet and Dame Margot Fonteyn, she happily discovered a new world of modern dance with Alvin, looking and listening to him talk about what they were seeing. He reran a tape of the Kennedy Center honors many times. They had passionate discussions about writers and politicians. She listened to him talk about company problems and his feelings about his board of directors.

"He exposed me to books and people I had never heard of. He told me things I never knew existed. He might talk for one hour out of the twelve. But if I could get him to talk, I would."

Gradually, too, Alvin began to respond to this entertaining angel of mercy, a comfortably plump blonde whose speech was peppered with "dahling" and whose explosive laughter was very like his own. She was touched. She had assumed he might prefer a black nurse. And she fell into step with Alvin's childlike excesses. "He was so impossible," McKnight said with gusto. "He drove me crazy." He called her Miss Anne and she called him Mr. Ailey, but she soon became "Nurse Ratchet" because of her insistence on such nuisances as medicine-taking and short walks down the hospital corridor. She could make him smile simply by suggesting that "a spot of tea," sipped sitting up in a chair in his room, might be the perfect cure for a minor ailment of the moment.

"At first I was not treating AIDS, only auxiliary problems. That was the dance we played. He thought he could pull this on me because of who he was. But not me, dahling! I told him that he was ridiculous, that I wouldn't listen to that nonsense. He was furious I was trying to get him well. He was in such denial about his illness. But you see, I wanted him to live."

Alvin left the hospital on February 3, having worked out a plan to keep in touch weekly with Dr. Knapp, calling in when he was out of town to report on whether or not he was taking his medicine. "It was no secret to me that Alvin had had problems with that in the past," Knapp said. "He and other people told me that he had neglected his health for years and that he was seen by a variety of society doctors who just pandered to him. Alvin was very naive about that. He just was not discriminating.

"I honestly think that people who are very famous get the worst care. But if you take certain medications chronically, you have to take them chronically. And Alvin pulled it off. He did it. He would miss a couple of weeks here and there and I gave him hell. But most of the time he would call and say, 'Hi, I'm here, I took my two pills each day and I checked them off on the little list you gave me.' "

The company announced that month that Alvin would take a partial leave of absence. He needed to rest after the thirtieth anniversary season, it was said, and he had obligations to attend to in Europe. He talked to few people about the results of the HIV test or his feelings about this confirmation of long-held suspicions. Szilard believed that Alvin had already known what was wrong with him. "Another doctor told him, or perhaps just said that he suspected it," Szilard said. Certainly there had been talk among his friends about that possibility as early as 1985, when Alvin began to look ill.

Judith Jamison, now working with a small dance troupe of her own, took over the directorship of the company with Alvin for three months. But he was fully active by late February, flying off to California to accept an award and then on to Honolulu for a week's vacation. By early May he was touring again with the dancers and was on hand later that month, dressed in business suit and tie, to mug with students for newspaper photographers covering the formal unveiling of the space that had just been found for the Ailey school and companies.

In a three-year search for a new home, William Hammond had

come upon space in a former warehouse two blocks from Lincoln Center at 211 West Sixty-first Street that already housed several dance studios. It would be free in April 1989. As large as the company's combined space at the Minskoff, the new headquarters would have the great advantage of being on a single floor, with four good-sized, airy studios at one end and offices at the other. The landlord had agreed to take care of renovations that would then be paid for over the fifteen years of the lease.

Alvin kept up with day-to-day obligations, appearing at fund-raising events, working on a proposal for an inner-city residency in Baltimore and consulting with the dean overseeing the dance program at the Borough of Manhattan Community College. He met with choreographers and watched rehearsals at the Minskoff headquarters, sometimes lying on the floor when he felt too tired to sit up. At times, he stretched out on a couch outside the studios.

It was hard now not to notice how sick he looked. Even his facade slipped from time to time. Lois Framhein, who worked with the company in the 1970s before joining City Center, had smiled at him backstage at the theater one day and asked how he was. "I'm terrible," he answered uncharacteristically. "What a shitty life." At a mid-June tribute to Pearl Primus at Aaron Davis Hall, a theater complex on the City College campus in Harlem, an acquaintance who greeted him warmly was astonished when he gazed right through her, gaunt and lost in another world. And yet he talked excitedly about the future.

Harry Rubenstein, Joyce Trisler's companion and the director of her company after her death, encountered Alvin on the street outside the Minskoff later that month. "Where are you going?" Alvin asked. Rubenstein told him that he and the friend he was with were about to have a quick beer together. "He didn't even invite himself," Rubenstein recalled. "He came along." They ducked into a nearby restaurant, where Alvin kept the conversation going for a long two hours. He talked eagerly of moving to Paris and of having a very large company in the future. "I think his vision was of something like the New York City Ballet," Rubenstein said. "I think it was mostly the idea of the success. I told him he was crazy." Finally it was time to leave, and as Rubenstein and his friend turned away toward Eighth Avenue, he looked into Alvin's eyes. "There was such a sadness there, such a deep sadness. I felt he knew he was very sick and just wouldn't accept it."

On June 20, Alvin flew down to Haiti to a birthday party for Katherine Dunham at her plantation near Port-au-Prince. He had expected to hook up with a friend along the way but arrived by himself and seemed a little lonely. Troubled, Dunham felt a pall hanging over him. But home in New York again, there were last-minute details to work out about the company's appearance in Paris at the Grand Palais des Champs Élysées in La Danse en Revolution, a three-month celebration of the bicentennial of the French Revolution. Three Ailey classics—Donald McKayle's *Rainbow 'Round My Shoulder* and Alvin's *Memoria* and *Revelations*—were selected for a weeklong engagement that opened on July 17. The international roster of companies also included the Paris Opéra Ballet and school ensemble, Maurice Béjart's popular Ballet du XXe Siècle, the sensuous Spanish dance troupe of Antonio Gades and the Moiseyev Folk Dance Ensemble from the Soviet Union.

"I never saw him so nervous," Chaya recalled. "Opening day, he thought everything was wrong. Nothing was right, from costumes' color to dancer to sound. On and on. Mari [Kajiwara] came to help me and we sat there wondering what to do. I had to convince Alvin to come see the performance." Chaya huffed and puffed, imitating Alvin's strenuous resistance to the suggestion. But Chaya prevailed, and Alvin was on hand to see the company received as exuberantly as it had ever been. At some point in the ongoing applause, the audience began to cry out rhythmically, "Al-vin! Al-vin!" He came out onstage to even wilder cheers, and then turned to thank his dancers and Chaya. "Oh! All the hard work," Chaya said, sighing happily at Alvin's acknowledgment of it.

The company applauded Alvin as he boarded the bus that was to take them back to the hotel after the performance. Although Knapp had insisted he return to New York, Alvin decided to remain with his dancers and travel on to performances in the south of France before going home. "He was so happy," Chaya said.

On his return, there was an interesting project to discuss with Allan Gray, who had consulted with Alvin earlier that year about a program to be organized by the Kansas City Friends of Alvin Ailey. Starting in mid-June that year, fifty to sixty preteens had begun to study dance at AileyCamp, a model program carefully designed to enhance the children's self-esteem and critical thinking.

This time it was Gray who had initiated a dream session. The program would be for children selected by local organizations on the basis of their need for such a program. Looking ahead, he told Alvin, he could see national possibilities for AileyCamp and, in fact, such a program was begun in New York in 1991. Eventually, both the Kansas City and New York camps became geared toward children likely to drop out of school or to become involved in other antisocial behavior, with some contact maintained after the summer.

Gray and the other Friends were intrigued by how readily other applications could be found for elements of the arts. One dance exercise evolved into a test of spatial relationships. "The children start to see movement differently," Gray said. "But they also start seeing how their bodies have to react differently to different situations. They later tie that into control and learning what discipline it takes to think through a program, make strategies and then be prepared physically to carry them out. And they tie that into how you have to be mentally prepared but also educationally prepared if your strategy is to complete school. So you have this kind of linkage."

Gray was heartened by the transformations he saw in the children. "It's incredible to see how these kids come in like raw recruits and leave very much in touch with who they are. Many of the kids realize for the first time they have control of their lives. They don't have to react to the outside world or their families."

Gray was not surprised that Alvin was interested in the program when they met in New York just before the camp started in Kansas City. He was taken aback, however, by the ferocious pace of office activities at the Minskoff, where the day-to-day lives of the company and school had been further complicated by the necessity to work in temporary studios before the move uptown. And he was concerned about Alvin. Ceaseless demands were being made on his attention at a time when he looked very sick, although he reassured Gray that he had simply had a brush with tuberculosis.

Never able to resist becoming involved in new projects, especially those with the kinds of social goals that were close to his heart, Alvin began to ask Gray questions and offer specific, minutely detailed proposals for the camp. It was too bad he had to go to Paris, he told Gray, just when the camp was in session. Then suddenly, as it was about to end, Alvin decided to fly out to Kansas City for the performance that closed the camp session.

He asked Gray not to tell anyone that he was coming, and Gray went so far as to arrange for a seat distant from his own and at the back of the auditorium so that none of his friends would see Alvin. The children danced, recited poems they had written and acted out skits about dealing with everyday life problems. The performance ended with acknowledgments of people who had helped to support the camp. Then, sensing Alvin wanted to be introduced to the children, Gray announced that he was in the theater. There was a roar of applause from them. "You would have thought Michael Jackson had been introduced," Gray recalls. "They just mobbed him. His arms were filled with kids. They had never met him, but to them he had become this superstar, I guess."

Alone later with Carol Coe, Alvin talked emotionally of how loved he had felt by the Ailey campers and how much the program exemplified his own ideas about the importance of keeping dance from becoming too elitist. "I think he was at peace with himself," Coe said. "No matter what happened to Alvin Ailey, somewhere out here in America there would be kids learning, going to Ailey camp, dancing Alvin's stuff."

Alvin, Gray, Coe and a group of friends went off after the performance to a jazz club where they had dinner and talked for hours. Coe had broken her arm and Alvin was concerned. "Gee, you look terrible," he told her. "We need a trip. Why don't we go to the Bahamas?" Coe agreed immediately and the two set about attempting to coax Ulysses Dove, the former Ailey dancer who had worked with Alvin in Paris on *Précipice* and later choreographed for his company, to join them. A friend had just died and Dove was inconsolable. They would cheer him up, they thought. But Dove decided against the trip, so Alvin flew off with Coe for a week lazing on the beach in Nassau, shopping avidly together and searching for a villa to rent as a refuge for dancers.

She could see that Alvin was depressed. He talked to her defiantly about a plan to get the board to pay him royalties for his ballets. He had been putting his money from awards and commissions back into the company for too long, he said. He had started to fly first class. "I asked him why and he said that after all these years he thought he deserved to fly first class and stay in first-class rooms." He was tired, he said, of subsidizing the company.

When he returned to New York, Alvin worked out an agreement with Harold Levine, the company's new board chairman. He would now license his dances to the foundation governing the company. He would be paid a yearly salary of $100,000, in addition to his rent and other apartment expenses. He would be paid royalties of $200 for each performance of *Revelations* and $100 for other dances, as well as percentages from the net profit of other Ailey foundation projects. His travel, rooms and per diem allowance would be upgraded. All of this would be in effect through December 31—and renegotiated after—when Alvin was to take a sabbatical or step down as director of the company. He needed to find himself and, Hammond felt, he also worried about providing for his mother's future.

Still, Alvin was frequently reminded of why he had loved his work. Dressed in one of his best suits, he clowned with delighted children at the school one Saturday morning in an informal ceremony at which he was presented with an appreciation award from their parents. The new headquarters on West Sixty-first Street had begun to take shape, and Chaya took Alvin to see where his office would be. As Chaya pointed out its planned features, Alvin seized his hand and told him to leave the building with him.

The startled Chaya followed in tow as Alvin walked up the street to a housing project for low-income families. He went into the security office and introduced himself. A school was opening down the block that would be for everybody, he told the wary guards, especially the children of the project. And it was not meant only for people who wanted to be dancers. Would the children come? The guards were stunned. What was this man talking about? Alvin handed out brochures, and suddenly they became interested. "It was so funny," Chaya recalled. "We stayed about half an hour. And by the end of that half hour, I think everybody was so excited about the school. Then Alvin suddenly decided, 'Let's go.' " And out the two men trotted.

A big, welcoming back office had been reserved for Alvin, with a bank of high, small-paned windows that looked out on green trees. But Alvin never saw the room completed. Chaya kept a sort of vigil, screaming furiously at staff members and workmen when he saw the office was being used for temporary storage. "Then our stage manager came and sort of made it nice. We made sure flowers were put there all the time for whenever Alvin could come."

By autumn, Alvin had become so weak that he was forced to return to Lenox Hill, where he was readmitted on September 19. There had been one short, stabilizing hospitalization in the spring, so at first this visit seemed almost routine. "It started out as an attempt to treat for a recurrent CMV infection once again and either clear or at least stabilize him as much as possible," Knapp said. "But after the first two or three weeks we realized we were getting nowhere and the decision was made, with Alvin, basically just to keep him comfortable. He knew we were being very aggressive. But he was no man's fool."

There was an attempt at first to keep people from visiting Alvin, who was very depressed. His condition was kept secret. No public mention of the hospitalization was made, even when stories appeared rather ghoulishly in mid-October in two daily city newspapers about charges that Alvin was a no-show at the Borough of Manhattan Community College. And when Lula Cooper flew in from Los Angeles, she was unable to find her son's name in the hospital's register of patients, for he had been checked in as Charles Gordon.

Impatiently, Cooper changed all that, urging Alvin to receive visitors and welcoming them herself with a warmth and concern that at least one dancer found unforgettable. "Mrs. Cooper took care of people," Sarita Allen remembers. "She ordered all this food. She told stories about Alvin. When we'd come up with sad faces, she'd look at us like, 'Hey, y'all, how are you today? Hungry? Want to eat something?' "

Dance posters, reviews and photographs of Alvin and his dancers taken that summer on a shoot in Central Park were taped to one wall of Room 7622, a comfortable private room with light filtering in from a window that overlooked Park Avenue. Alvin had insisted on returning to the seventh floor of the hospital's Uris wing but ended up in a different room, which gradually took on almost a party atmosphere.

Szilard came by each day, visiting only if Alvin wanted him but always checking with the nurses to see if anything was needed. Chaya came every morning and evening, before and after work, slipping unobtrusively into Alvin's room to ask if he could help in any way. Jamison was a daily presence, as was little Sharrell Mesh, now retired from the company, married and living in New Jersey. "Pretty Sharrell," as Alvin called her, came in the morning and remained through the day at Alvin's bedside, often just sitting quietly beside him. "I think she was very good for him," Alvin's nurse, Anne McKnight, said. "He could see what he had produced."

Mesh had left the company a few months before and heard about Alvin's condition only when Donna Wood called and encouraged her to visit. Mesh found Alvin in his room with Denise Jefferson, the head of the Ailey school. "Denise said, 'Oh, look who's here! Sharrell!' Alvin hadn't been speaking but he said my name. I hugged him. I tried not to react.

"It was important for me to be there. I knew the company was out of town. I hoped to be some comfort to him and his mother. I thought I'd give her—and Alvin—a break. I read the Bible to him. We'd talk about choreography, about his having seen Billie Holiday and Marilyn Monroe. He was a great storyteller."

Alvin's mind was often on his dancers, in all three of the Ailey companies. He and Sylvia Waters had long been worried about the stiff feet of one of Alvin's favorite dancers in the Repertory Ensemble. "He's really working on them, Alvin," Waters reported one day at the hospital. "He's dancing like a poet." Alvin nodded. "He has beautiful feet," he said serenely.

Alvin's mother seldom left his side. She needed, McKnight sensed, a good deal more support than she was admitting. Calvin Cooper had flown in, with a saddened Fred Cooper staying behind in Los Angeles, and McKnight was touched by the quiet ways in which Alvin's younger brother helped out. Coe flew in several times, as did Gray. Soon dancers and company personnel were flocking to Uris 7622.

McKnight admitted to feeling a little jealous. "I had been used to being alone with Mr. Ailey," she said ruefully. "Now I had to relinquish my relationship. It was hard. I had been crazy about him. I had been through a lot with him. But I met these marvelous, interesting people.

"He was terribly sick. And I think he felt, The hell with it. For some reason he gave up. But the people who came to see him never did."

Chaya was cheered by Alvin's attempts to spruce up for his visits. "He was so *cute*. Each time I visited, I had to call before. He wanted to change to pants and a shirt." He tried to encourage Alvin to begin work on his next ballet. How about doing the Josephine Baker piece he'd long thought of? He brought photographs and books on Baker to the hospital so that Alvin could begin his research. Alvin did continue to work, occasionally driving Chaya and Szilard into paroxysms of frustration with his obstinacy on certain issues. But there were calmer times. The subject of *Night Creature* arose during one program-planning session. "Alvin, it's such a really beautiful opener," Chaya said. "It's a beautiful piece." To Chaya's astonishment, Alvin agreed. "I know," he told Chaya, adding that he loved the dance. "When I heard that from him it made me so happy," Chaya said. "He never really said that. I always wanted to ask him, 'Alvin, do you *like* your ballets?'"

The two talked of plans for the future. Alvin was once again thinking of starting a new company, this time in Paris or San Francisco where there were people who had a lot of money, he said, and who loved his work. The dancers in the present company would just have to be let go.

Was he really prepared to start from zero, Chaya asked Alvin, and train a whole new group of dancers? He was, Alvin said, but did Chaya know where he could find good ones? Yes, Chaya said. Alvin asked where they were. " 'In the Ailey company,' I said. He laughed. 'Ah, ha, ha.' He said to me he wanted to find out who Alvin Ailey really was. His name showed up on coffee cups and towels. But if he started from zero, he would know every step he took. He would know who Alvin Ailey is."

Why not take six months off each year instead? Chaya proposed. He loved Paris. Why not live there part of the year? And when he returned to the studio in New York, what about giving himself first pick of dancers and rehearsal hours for once? Chaya would change the system, he promised. Alvin need only let him know when he was ready to work.

If the emaciated man before them was almost unrecognizable to some visitors, Alvin was often his exuberant old self, particularly with Coe and Gray. "We really need to call Allan," he told Coe at one point. "He'll come up here and make us laugh." Gray said he would not be able to get to New York until the following week. Alvin and Coe told him that was not good enough, and he flew up the next day.

That night, Alvin decided to celebrate with a few "beeeeers," as he drawled the word out. Gray drew the line at that. What would McKnight say if she knew? They could not drink in a hospital. "Oh yes we can," Alvin told him, and the hapless Gray found himself going across the street for a six-pack of beer, which Alvin drank from his hospital cup, pretending it was apple juice. Maneuvered later into the same position, his brother did manage to fool Alvin into drinking fruit juice instead of beer.

For all Knapp's experience with the sick and dying, the doctor found himself greatly moved by Alvin's behavior. He could be impossibly nasty at times, refusing treatment and knocking medicine out of McKnight's hand. But it was always hard to remain angry at him for long. "He realized the terminal nature of his illness and faced it bravely," Knapp said. "Though he was in pain, he kept his sense of humor and remained on the whole a cooperative patient. He could easily have committed suicide, or done something stupid, when he found out he was sick, but he continued to work hard. There was a steady deterioration, but each time Chaya would come by the hospital, Alvin would scream that he had to see the program for tomorrow, or the next week.

"He never really complained or bemoaned his fate. He did have the occasional temper tantrum so typical of an artist, but it was more for attention-getting purposes. But besides little things like that, he was a real sweetie. His cool courage really impressed me. He had made his share of prior mistakes in life, but I think he made up for it by the way he faced his final moments. He was a portrait of bravery."

It was difficult, though, for those who loved Alvin to keep their courage up. Mickey Bord, one of the people he asked for toward the end, came squirreling over to the hospital bearing his favorite chocolate cake and a bouquet of roses. She had been talking with Cooper daily but had waited to visit until Alvin wanted her. "I had no idea how sick he was," Bord recalled. "He was lying in bed and I kissed him and asked how he was. 'Where did you come from?' he said. I told him from the school. He said, 'I'm coming back with you to the school now.' I told him they didn't need him. That everything was under control and he should just stay there and rest. I stayed there about twenty minutes, with Mrs. Cooper and Calvin."

She managed to hold back her tears until she got back to the school, where she bumped into Meg Gordean, the company publicist. Then she began to cry and couldn't stop. "Alvin's dying, isn't he?" Bord said. Gordean gently said yes. Why hadn't she told her? "No one here could tell you," Gordean said.

Alvin was slipping in and out of consciousness by the last week of November. One night Mesh was afraid to be with him by herself and she called Donna Wood, who joined her in the room. But she kept returning. In happier times, she had loved to run her fingers through his thick, soft hair during idle moments in rehearsals. Now, there were sadder attentions to pay: "I'd wipe his mouth. His tears. I felt I needed to be there. I knew I was losing him. I guess that was my way, so small, of thanking him for what he did for us."

Lula Cooper swung gallantly into action for her son on Tuesday that week, appearing at the formal opening of the new Ailey facilities on West Sixty-first Street. Stylishly dressed and charming the assembled reporters, students and dancers with her off-the-cuff speech and commanding presence, she showed no sign of worry. The only reference to Alvin's absence was made in passing by Harold Levine, who remarked simply that Alvin was sick and unable to be present.

Alvin had slipped into a coma when Szilard visited that Thursday, on November 30. Szilard called out to him that he was there, and thought Alvin's head turned toward him a little, as if he heard. On Friday at noon, Gordean received a call from Laura Beaumont, the company's young director of public relations and marketing. The two had been planning to visit Alvin together that afternoon. "Alvin is dying," Beaumont said. "Start calling people and getting press kits ready." Gordean began hunting down dance writers and assembling press material to put into kits over the weekend. At 4:55, her phone rang. It was Beaumont again. Alvin was dead.

Alvin's mother, Sylvia Waters, Jamison and Chaya had been with Alvin when he died, standing and sitting around his bed in prayer. McKnight and Knapp stood nearby. Alvin began to breathe hard, almost as if he were gasping for life. After he was still, there was a last, false breath.

Cooper bent over Alvin, looking at her son's face, lovingly obdurate even at his death. "You damned fool," she remembered thinking, "here I am as old as molasses and you done gone so young. Who is going to take care of me?" But all she said aloud was "He's gone, that's all." She sat down and began to cry in what Waters described as her inward way. Jamison held on to Alvin's hand. Then McKnight returned with a nurse and gently asked everyone to leave the room while they laid Alvin's body out. The group went back in for a last look, and then it was time to go home.

Word of Alvin's death had started to filter out by the time they descended to the hospital lobby. Calvin Cooper was there, choking with tears, having run to the hospital after hearing the news over a radio. A friend of George Faison was waiting to sneak the group out a back way, avoiding reporters waiting at the hospital's front entrance. They drove back to the Westbury Hotel, where Cooper had a room.

At Sixty-first Street, the shocked and tearful senior company had been told to finish rehearsal and go home when the news arrived that Alvin was dying. As news of his death spread through the school, students emptied quietly into the halls, some of them in the midst of a *Memoria* rehearsal, until Denise Jefferson told them to return to work. Several former company members had gathered at the headquarters as if not sure where else to be at such a time.

There was no one to talk to the media. Gordean arrived to find television cameramen piling into the building. Who would talk to the reporters? Beaumont asked worriedly. "Put on your lipstick, Laura, and go for it," Gordean told her. The women took reporters into the reception room and began to talk to them about Alvin. "We tried not to make it horrifying," Gordean said. "We talked about his past, how he hated wearing shoes." At about 7 P.M. the school was closed. Gordean and Beaumont took a cab to the Westbury, where Philip Morris, a major corporate contributor to the company, had booked a conference room and put together a huge spread of food. The place was jammed with dancers, family and friends of the company.

Knapp made himself available to the press soon after Alvin's death, announcing that he had died of terminal blood dyscrasia, a disorder affecting the bone marrow and red blood cells. The disease, essentially a kind of umbrella term for any abnormal condition of the blood, had in fact been a partial cause of death. Alvin had asked the doctor not to disclose that he had had AIDS, which troubled many young company members and friends.

"My answer to them was that everyone is entitled to privacy," Knapp said. "Furthermore, Alvin was from a different generation—a child of the 1930s and the Great Depression—with both a different mind-set and values. He was eccentric and perhaps outrageous in some ways, but when it came to certain aspects of his life he was both very private and perhaps prudish. Complicating the issue was the fact that Alvin dearly loved his mother and did not want her to be embarrassed by the social stigma of the disease."

Ellis Haizlip had approached Sylvia Waters before Alvin's death and asked if he could plan Alvin's funeral. She asked Lula hesitantly, concerned that such a question might upset her. "I know, I've been thinking about it, little girl," Cooper told her. "Don't you worry." The day after Alvin's death a committee was formed to plan a service. It was decided that the funeral would be held at the Cathedral of Saint John the Divine, a huge, handsome Episcopal church on 112th Street where Duke Ellington and other prominent black achievers had lain in state.

The cathedral was large, it was near Harlem and its priests were not traditionbound, or at least not entirely. "Ellis had me talking to the Most Very Reverend This One and the Most Very Reverend That One, and they were swingin'," Waters recalled. "I really enjoyed them as people." Haizlip had told her not to be talked into "having choruses and 'that stinking incense,'" as he put it. As it happened, one of the ministers, Reverend Dr. Robert Polk, who officiated at the service with the Very Reverend James Parks Morton, dean of the cathedral, and Canon Joel A. Gibson, had known Alvin since the company's earliest days and had visited him at the hospital.

In the end, the reverends prevailed, and the scent of incense floated through the church, together with a northern kind of churchly choir music, adding a bit of formal seasoning to the family feeling of a memorial service on December 8 that Haizlip named "A Celebration of Alvin Ailey Jr. Going Home." The church was crowded with an estimated forty-five hundred people: family, friends, students, dancers and company personnel, the media, politicians, arts figures and those who simply loved the Alvin Ailey American Dance Theater and wanted to pay their respects to the man who had made it possible.

As reporters moved through the crowd, students talked about the man who knew all their names. A City Center crew member, one of thirty who had shown up for the service, spoke simply of having been touched by Alvin. Clive Thompson, an Ailey dancer from the late 1960s, told an interviewer that "coming into the bosom of Abraham, which was Alvin to me, I realized how wonderful, how proud, how positive it is to be black in America." Mourners walked slowly past the open casket at the back of the church. Alvin was dressed in a dark gray suit with his scarf of kente cloth draped around his neck. His face looked softer and less exhausted than it had in years.

Watching the long line of people filing past her son, so handsome and so soon to leave her that she wanted to crawl into the casket with him, Lula Cooper noticed an odd figure lurking at the back near the door of the church. "She was a Caucasian girl, kind of tacky. I went to her and told her I was Alvin's mother. That girl just hugged me. 'You don't know what Alvin done for people like me,' she said. 'We were hungry. He'd reach in his pocket and give us money.' She was young. Her name was Hallie. I told her why not go up to the coffin? She said it was too late. That she had just wanted to come."

Gradually, mourners made their way into the pews. As the last rows of the great, shadowy cathedral filled, the beat of Max Roach's drums began, stately yet lilting. Alvin's coffin, covered now in purple and red brocade, was wheeled to the altar with a line of mourners walking slowly behind. Led by Alvin's mother and brother, they wound up the long, long center aisle. The line grew as it moved forward, swelling as dancers and company employees, choreographers and colleagues of other years, were pulled gently in by the marchers. Someone reached out for Ivy Clarke, and she slipped into the group as it passed by her.

At last the cathedral was still. One after another, speakers climbed the steps of the ornate carved pulpit, beside which stood a handsome portrait of Alvin looking a little consideringly out into the crowd. Stanley Plesent read a telegram from President George W. Bush that eulogized Alvin as "a man of gentleness and vision." There were comments from David N. Dinkins, New York's first black mayor, and Polk, who talked affectionately of hearing Alvin at work planning a European tour once when the company "couldn't afford to get to J.F.K."

Maya Angelou, Alvin's friend from Los Angeles days, compared his death to the fall of a great tree in a forest. John Parks and Mari Kajiwara had returned to the company to dance the *Fix Me, Jesus* duet from *Revelations* on a wooden stage erected behind the coffin. And then nine dancers filed on for *I Been Buked,* the opening section of *Revelations,* their bodies frozen at the start, some biting back tears. From the mass of mourners, Arthur Mitchell watched with a clenched jaw. Keith McDaniel, looking more than ever like a young Alvin, tilted his tear-stained face back in pain, his lips moving to the words of the spiritual. Leaving the stage at the end, the performers reached out and held hands in the way dancers often do to guide one another when entering or leaving an unfamiliar performing space. Here, at that moment, the gesture had an almost unbearable extra poignancy.

"Remember me as a sunny day that you once had along the way," Ashford and Simpson sang in a song created for the service. And then Carmen de Lavallade, as chic as ever and speaking with a grand simplicity, talked of how like the cathedral Alvin had been, down to the last shard of stained glass, "so easy to break, and yet so strong." Looking out over the sea of upturned faces, she addressed the young people in the crowd, urging them not to let go of Alvin's legacy. "He gave you an open chest of gems and jewels," she said softly. "And all you have to do is dip your hand in and take. You take, and you use, and then you pass on, as he is passing on now. Support each other. And not selfishly, but generously, as Alvin has."

Dudley Williams danced *A Song for You,* seeming to sing silently to himself the refrain "I love you, in a place where there's no space or time." At times, dancing Alvin's choreography, he seemed to reach out toward the coffin, surrounded by candles and banked flowers. At the end, he quietly blew a kiss to it and walked quickly off.

Donna Wood had come back to perform the close of *Cry,* suddenly flooding the church with a joyous abandon that shot through the ceremony like a penetrating shaft of sunlight. Dancing as she had never quite danced before, she was sending Alvin home, as she put it. Cooper, her crumpled face nearly covered by a black veil, smiled and unconsciously beat time with her gloved hands.

Jamison maintained an almost icy control until the last moments of her commemoration, when her voice began to tremble a little. Alvin, she said, had given her "legs until I could stand on my own as a dancer and a choreographer." "He made us believe we could fly." At last, the music of *Rocka My Soul* started for the closing dance in *Revelations.*

And as the dancers started to move to its steady beat, Cooper began to clap. Calvin Cooper joined her, and slowly the rhythmic clapping spread along the line of speakers, through the solemn-looking ministers and out into the rows and rows of mourners, gradually filling the cathedral with its sound.

Alvin's body was flown back to Los Angeles for a service at the First Baptist Church of Artesia, where the Coopers worshiped, followed the next day by a ceremony in the small, airy chapel at Rose Hills Memorial Park in Whittier, the cemetery where Alvin is buried. Friends were there from the Horton days. Former Ailey dancers were there. Jasmine Guy, who had been a student performer in the first *Memoria*, had asked to sing "His Eye Is on the Sparrow" at the cemetery service. Polk was there to speak, as were Hammond, Gray and Stanley Plesent.

Alvin was buried on December 13 on a grassy, sunlit hillside in a plot marked by a flat polished stone with his photograph and the inscription, "Beloved Son Alvin Ailey, Jr., 1931–1989, Forever in our hearts, the Cooper Family." The spot is hard to find in that immense cemetery but once found, it is a place that breathes with a soothing peace.

AFTERWORD

Lula Cooper visited every weekend, sometimes in a limousine hired with all her old panache. Often, she brought flowers to replace those that were cleared away each Friday. "I bring a towel and sit down and say, 'Hey, kid, what's going on? I know you busy today, doing a ballet in heaven.' You may think I'm crazy, but every time, after I sat there for a while, about twenty ants came out and rolled over the stone. I'd think, 'That's Alvin's company.' They were dancing. And the last little one to leave was Alvin."

Judith Jamison was named artistic director of the Alvin Ailey American Dance Theater on December 20, and two years later Masazumi Chaya was named associate director. Carol Coe, who married despite Alvin's dire warnings that she was not the marrying kind, had a daughter on June 6, 1990, whom she named Ailey Phillips Pope. And around that time, Cooper came across an elegant shawl Alvin had bought for her and hidden in her closet as a surprise.

There is now an Alvin Ailey Street in the still-tiny town of Rogers, Texas, a market road crossing the railroad tracks that bisect the town. In New York City, a block of West Sixty-first Street has been renamed Alvin Ailey Place.

Lula Elizabeth Cliff Ailey Cooper died on May 13, 1994. She is buried next to her son.

EIGHT MAJOR WORKS BY ALVIN AILEY

BLUES SUITE, first performance March 30, 1958, at the Kaufmann Concert Hall of the Ninety-second Street YM-YWHA, New York. Choreography, Alvin Ailey; decor and costumes, Geoffrey Holder; lighting, Nicolai Cernevitch; music arranged and composed by Paquita Anderson and José Ricci. Paquita Anderson, piano; José Ricci, flute and drums.

The musical heritage of the southern Negro remains a profound influence on the music of the world . . . during the dark days the blues sprang full-born from the docks and the fields, saloons and bawdy houses . . . indeed from the very souls of their creators. . . .

Performers: Clarence Cooper, Nancy Reddy, Julius Fields, Lavinia Hamilton, Tommy Johnson, Audrey Mason, Charles Moore, Charles Neal, Dorene Richardson, Liz Williams (*Good Morning Blues*); Claude Thompson (*Smokedream*); Reddy, Hamilton, Mason, Richardson (*Fare Thee Well*); Reddy, Thompson (*New Broom*); Fields, Hamilton, Johnson, Mason, Moore, Neal, Richardson, Williams (*Sham*); Reddy, Hamilton, Mason, Williams (*Careless Love*); Cooper and company (*Jack of Diamonds*).

REVELATIONS, first performance January 31, 1960, at the Kaufmann Concert Hall, Ninety-second Street YM-YWHA, New York. Choreography, Alvin Ailey; music, traditional; costumes, Laurence Maldonado; lighting, Nicola Cernovich. Music performed by the Music Masters Guild Chorus of the Harlem Branch YMCA, Frank Thomas, director.

This suite explores motivations and emotions of Negro religious music which, like its heir the Blues, takes many forms—"true spirituals" with their sustained melodies, ring-shouts, song-sermons, gospel songs, and holy blues—songs of trouble, of Love of deliverance.

Performers: *Pilgrim of Sorrow:* The company (*I been buked*); Nancy Redi (*Weeping Mary*); Redi (*Poor Pilgrim*); Joan Derby, Minnie Marshall, Dorene Richardson (*Round About the Mountain*); Merle Derby (*Wonder Where*); the company (*Troubles*). *That Love My Jesus Gives Me:* Marshall, Herman Howell (*Fix Me*); the company (*Honor, Honor*); J. Derby, Jay Fletcher, M. Derby, Nathaniel Horne (*Wade in the Water*); Redi, J. Derby, M. Derby, Marshall, Richardson (*Morning Star*); the Chorus (*My Lord What a Morning*); Gene Hobgood, Horne, Howell, Fletcher (*Sinner Man*). *Move, Members, Move!:* Hobgood, Redi and the company (*Precious Lord, God A Mighty, Waters of Babylon, Elijah Rock!*).

QUINTET, first performance August 28, 1968, at Church Hall Theatre, Edinburgh Festival, Scotland; American premiere January 27, 1969, at Billy Rose Theater, New York. Choreography, Alvin Ailey; music, Laura Nyro; costumes, Matthew Cameron and George Faison.

Little girl of all the daughters, you were born a woman not a slave! . . .

Performers in American premiere: Sylvia Waters, Linda Kent, Michele Murray, Consuelo Atlas and Alma Robinson (*Stoned Soul Picnic*); Murray and Waters, Kent, Robinson and Atlas (*Luckie*); Robinson (*Poverty Train*); Kent and Murray, Atlas and Waters (*Women's Blues*); Atlas (*December's Boudoir*); Waters, Robinson, Kent, Murray and Atlas (*The Confession*).

MASEKELA LANGAGE, first performance on August 16, 1969, at Palmer Auditorium, Connecticut College, New London; New York premiere November 21, 1969, at Brooklyn Academy of Music, Brooklyn, New York. Choreography, Alvin Ailey; music, Hugh Masekela; costumes, Christina Giannini; lighting, Gilbert Hemsley.

Five dances with prologue and epilogue based on the music of South African trumpeter Hugh Masekela.

Performers in New York premiere: the company (*Prologue-Sobukwe*); Judith Jamison, Kelvin Rotardier, Renee Rose, John Medeiros, Sylvia Waters, Harvey Cohen (*Fuzz*); Rotardier and the company (*Babajula Bonke*); Michele Murray and Medeiros, Cohen (*Morolo*); Jamison (*Bo Masekela*); Rose, Medeiros, Cohen, William Hansen (*U-Dui*); George Faison and the company (*Mace and Grenades*); the company (*Epilogue-Sobukwe*).

CRY, first performance May 4, 1971, at City Center, New York. Choreography, Alvin Ailey; music, Alice Coltrane ("Something about John Coltrane"), Laura Nyro ("Been on a Train") and the Voices of East Harlem ("Right on, Be Free"); lighting, Chenault Spence.

For all Black women everywhere—especially our mothers.

Performer: Judith Jamison.

NIGHT CREATURE, first performance by Alvin Ailey American Dance Theater on April 22, 1975, at City Center, New York. Choreography, Alvin Ailey; music, Duke Ellington ("Night Creature"); costumes, Jane Greenwood; lighting, Chenault Spence.

"Night creatures, unlike stars, do not come out *at night—they come* on, *each thinking that before the night is out he or she will be a star."*—Duke Ellington.

Performers: Tina Yuan and Dudley Williams, with Enid Britten, Charles Adams, Mari Kajiwara, Warren Spears, Estelle Spurlock, Elbert Watson, Sarita Allen, Masazumi Chaya, Beth Shorter, Michihiko Oka, Jodi Moccia and Melvin Jones (*Movement 1*); Yuan and Kelvin Rotardier, with the company (*Movement 2*); Yuan and Williams, with the company (*Movement 3*).

MEMORIA, first performance November 29, 1979, at City Center, New York. Choreography, Alvin Ailey; music, Keith Jarrett ("Runes—Solara March"); assistant to Mr. Ailey, Mari Kajiwara; costumes, A. Christina Giannini; lighting, Chenault Spence.

This work is dedicated to the joy . . . the beauty . . . the creativity . . . and the wild spirit of my friend Joyce Trisler.

> *How pitiful is her sleep.*
> *Now her clear breath is still.*
> *There is nothing falling tonight,*
> *Bird or man,*
> *As dear as she.*
> *Nowhere that she should go*
> *Without me. None but my calling*
> *O nothing but the cold cry of the snow.*
> > *—Kenneth Patchen*
> > *(In Memory of Kathleen)*

Performers: *In Memory . . . In Celebration*: Donna Wood, with Alistair Butler and Gary DeLoatch, and Sarita Allen, Marilyn Banks, Linda Spriggs, Michihiko Oka, Keith McDaniel, Ronald Brown, Sharrell Mesh, Pat Dingle, Danita Ridout, Masazumi Chaya, Milton Myers, Otis Day (Alvin Ailey American Dance Theater); Carl Bailey, Marsha Clark, Susan Dillen, Jeffrey Ferguson, Arrow Holt, Regina Hood, Norman Kauahi, Diane Maroney, Lauren Overby, Ted Pollen, George Randolph, Eugene Roscoe, Awa Rostant, Hideaki Ryo, Elizabeth Sung and Leslie Woodard (Alvin Ailey Repertory Ensemble); Wally Alvarez, Basil Baker, Courtney Connor, Joseph Garcia, Jasmine Guy, Raymond Harris, Barbara Koval, David McCauley, Cheryl Ann Penn, Renee Robinson, Steven Rooks, Cheryl Lynn Ross, Elizabeth Roxas, Ronnell Seay, Robert Smith and Victoria Williams (American Dance Center Workshop).

FOR BIRD—WITH LOVE, first performance October 6, 1984, at Folly Theater in Kansas City, Missouri; New York premiere December 12, 1985, at City Center.

Choreography, Alvin Ailey; assistant to Mr. Ailey, Masazumi Chaya; music, Charlie Parker, Dizzy Gillespie, Count Basie, Jerome Kern; original music composed, assembled and conducted by Coleridge-Taylor

Perkinson*; set and costumes, Randy Barcelo; lighting, Timothy Hunter.

From all of us forever touched by his magic.

Performers: Gary DeLoatch (*"Bird," A man, a musician; Alto Sax*); Carl Bailey (*Trumpet*), Kevin Brown (*Tenor Sax*); Daniel Clark (*Piano*), Ralph Glenmore (*Drums*) and Jonathan Riseling (*Bass*) (*Men Close to Him—Musicians*); Marilyn Banks, Barbara Pouncie, Neisha Folkes and Debora Chase (*Women Close to Him—3 Singers and a Pianist*); Dudley Williams (*The Man Who Came Before, A Club Manager*); Patricia Dingle and April Berry (*Two Chorus Girls*).

Overture*. Prologue*. Kansas City Roots: "Let Jesus Come In"*; "Tismaswing"*; An Interview; "Way Back Blues." The Street That Never Sleeps—52nd St., Birdland, Minton's, The Royal Roost, The 3 Deuces, Billy Berg's . . . : "The Song Is You"; "A Night in Tunisia"; "Be-bop"; "Lover Man"; "Cherry Red"; "Birds of Prey"*; "Embraceable You"— "The Healing."* Bird Lives!*

MEMBERS AND GUESTS OF THE ALVIN AILEY AMERICAN DANCE THEATER THROUGH 1989

Loretta Abbott, Charles Adams, Alvin Ailey, Sarita Allen, Barbara Alston, Christopher Aponte, Adrienne Armstrong, Takako Asakawa, Consuelo Atlas, Carl Bailey, Marilyn Banks, Nerissa Barnes, Mary Barnett, Mikhail Baryshnikov, Talley Beatty, Don Bellamy, Yemina Ben-Gal, April Berry, Marla Bingham, Shirley Black-Brown, Frederick Bratcher, Enid Britten, Glen Brooks, Roman Brooks, Kevin Brown, Ronald Brown, Delores Brown, Eileen Bushman, Alistair Butler, Sergio Cal, Leu Camacho, Donato Capozzoli, Kevin Carlisle, Lazarro Carreno, Bill Chaison, Marie-Dominique Chaize, Debora Chase, Raquelle Chavis, Masazumi Chaya, Daniel Clark, Hope Clarke, Harvey Cohen, Georgia Collins, Duane Cyrus, Otis Daye, Mario Delamo, Carmen de Lavallade, Gary DeLoatch, Joan Derby, Merle Derby, Betsy Dickerson, Patricia Dingle, Ulysses Dove, Robert du Mee, Ronald Dunham, Patrick Dupond, Michael Ebbins, Lyn Elam, Charles Epps, George Faison, Louis Falco, Ronni Favors, Cliff Fears, Valerie Feit, Julius Fields, Alphonso Figueroa, Jay Fletcher, Neisha Folkes, Gene Gebauer, Ray Gilbert, Frank Glass, Ralph Glenmore, Miguel Godreau, Alexander Godunov, Meg

Gordon, Altovise Gore, Connie Greco, Paul Grey, Marey Griffith, Lavinia Hamilton, William Hansen, Lee Harper, Raymond Harris, Nicky Harrison, Avind Harum, Dana Hash, Thelma Hill, Nat Horne, Paul Hoskins, Herman Howell, Christopher Huggins, Carmen Hylton, Judith Jamison, Bobby Johnson, Tommy Johnson, Wesley Johnson III, Melvin Jones, Michael Joy, Mari Kajiwara, Norman Kauahi, Linda Kent, Christina Kimball, Barbara Koval, Beth Lane, Cristyne Lawson, Keith Lee, Bernard Lias, Anita Littleman, Maria Llorente, Monique Loudières, William Louther, Ed Love, Max Luna III, Aubrey Lynch II, Bobbi Lynn, Deborah Manning, Diane Maroney, Minnie Marshall, Don Martin, Audrey Mason, Clover Mathis, Eleanor McCoy, Keith McDaniel, John Medeiros, Leonard Meek, Hector Mercado, Sharrell Mesh, Jan Mickens, Sharon Miller, Jodi Moccia, Steven Mones, Charles Moore, Ella Thompson Moore, Elbert Morris, Delila Moseley, Christa Mueller, Michele Murray, Milton Myers, Charles Neal, Rodney Nugent, Michihiko Oka, Richard Orbach, Nat Orr, Ernest Pagnano, Miriam Pandor, Carl Paris, John Parks, Kenneth Pearl, Cynthia Penn, Stanley Perryman, Joan Peters, Michael Peters, Toni Pierce, Harold Pierson, Margaret Pihl, Dennis Plunkett, Barbara Pouncie, Robert Powell, Don Price, Lucinda Ransom, Gail Reese, Dwight Rhoden, Desmond Richardson, Dorene Richardson, Danita Ridout, Jonathan Riseling, Alma Robinson, Mabel Robinson, Renee Robinson, Paul R. Roman, Freddy Romero, Renee Rose, Kelvin Rotardier, Elizabeth Roxas, Alton Ruff, David St. Charles, Ruthlynn Salomons, Mariko Sanjo, Dana Sapiro, Leland Schwantes, Ramon Segarra, Geri Seignious, Desire Sewer, Lynn Seymour, Maxine Sherman, Beth Shorter, Michele Simmon, Joy Smith, Stephen Smith, Warren Spears, Linda Spriggs, Estelle Spurlock, Sally Stackhouse, Rosemarie Stevenson, Gregory Stewart, Carol Straker, Danny Strayhorn, Lynne Taylor, Barbara Ann Teer, Ilene Tema, Glen Tetley, Nasha Thomas, Claude Thompson, Clive Thompson, Mel Tomlinson, Sally Tramell, Joyce Trisler, James Truitte, Marvin Tunney, Matt Turney, André Tyson, Desire Vlad, Jacqueline Walcott, Sylvia Waters, Elbert Watson, Melinda Welty, Myrna White, Dereque Whiturs, Dudley Williams, Liz Williamson, Broderick Wilson, Lester Wilson, Morton Winston, Donna Wood, Peter Woodin, Sara Yarborough and Tina Yuan.

ALVIN AILEY AMERICAN DANCE THEATER REPERTORY 1958–1989

1950s

Alvin Ailey (*Ode and Homage; Blues Suite; Ariette Oubliee; Cinco Latinos; Sonera*)

1960s

Alvin Ailey (*Revelations; Gillespiana; Knoxville Summer of 1915; Creation of the World* [new version]; *Three for Now—Modern Jazz Suite; Roots of the Blues; Hermit Songs; Been Here and Gone; Reflections in D; Labyrinth; Rivers, Streams, Doors; Light; The Blues Ain't; My Mother, My Father; The Twelve Gates; Riedaiglia; Quintet; Masekela Langage*)

John Butler (*Letter to a Lady*); Lester Horton (*Variegations; To José Clemente Orozco,* from *Dedications in Our Time; The Beloved*); Glen Tetley (*Mountainway Chant*); Talley Beatty (*Toccata; Congo Tango Palace; The Road of the Phoebe Snow; Come and Get the Beauty of It Hot; Black Belt*); Anna Sokolow (*Rooms*); Joyce Trisler (*Journey; Dance for Six*); Louis Johnson (*Lament*); Paul Sanasardo (*Metallics*); Geoffrey Holder (*The Prodigal Prince*); Lucas Hoving (*Icarus*); Robert Schwartz (*Scrum*); Pauline Koner (*Poeme*); Michael Smuin (*Panambi*); Richard Wagner (*Threnody*)

1970s

Alvin Ailey (*Streams; Gymnopedies; Flowers; Archipelago; Choral Dances; Cry; Mary Lou's Mass; Myth; The Lark Ascending; Shaken Angels; Love Songs; Hidden Rites; Such Sweet Thunder; Night Creature; The Mooche; The Blues Ain't; Sonnet for Caesar; Sacred Concert; Black, Brown and Beige; Pas de Duke; Three Black Kings; Passage; Memoria*)
Miguel Godreau (*Paz*); Geoffrey Holder (*Adagio for a Dead Soldier*); John Parks (*Black Unionism; Nubian Lady*); Kelvin Rotardier (*The Cageling; Child of the Earth*); Brian McDonald (*Time Out of Mind*); May O'Donnell (*Suspension*); John Butler (*According to Eve; Carmina Burana; After Eden; Portrait of Billie; Facets*); Katherine Dunham (*Choros*); Donald McKayle (*Rainbow 'Round My Shoulder; Blood Memories; District Storyville*); Ted Shawn (*Kinetic Molpai*); Marlene Furtick (*How Long Have It Been*); José Limón (*Missa Brevis*); Norman Walker (*Clear Songs After Rain*); Janet Collins (*Canticle of the Elements; Spirituals*); John Jones (*Nocturne*); Pearl Primus (*Fanga; The Wedding*); Milton Myers (*Echoes in Blue; The Wait*); Lester Horton (*Liberian Suite*); George Faison (*Gazelle; Hobo Sapiens; Suite Otis; Tilt*); Louis Falco (*Caravan*); Lar Lubovitch (*The Time Before the Time After [After the Time Before]; Les Noces*); Dianne McIntyre (*Ancestral Voices*); Jennifer Muller (*Crossword*); Rudy Perez (*Countdown; Coverage II*); Rael Lamb (*Butterfly*); Eleo Pomare (*Blood Burning Moon*)

1980s

Alvin Ailey (*Phases; The River; Landscape; Spell; Satyriade; For Bird— With Love; Isba; Précipice; Survivors; Caverna Magica; Witness; Opus McShann*)
Ulysses Dove (*Inside; Night Shade; Bad Blood; Vespers; Episodes*); Kathryn Posin (*Later That Day*); Todd Bolender (*The Still Point*); Elisa Monte (*Treading; Pigs and Fishes*); Billy Wilson (*Concerto in F; Lullaby for a Jazz Baby*); William Chaison (*Places*); Choo San Goh (*Spectrum*); Louis Johnson (*Fontessa and Friends*); Rodney Griffin (*Sonnets*); Talley Beatty (*The Stack-up; Blueshift*); Bill T. Jones (*Fever Swamp*); Gary DeLoatch (*Research*); John Butler (*Seven Journeys*); Loris Anthony Beckles (*Anjour*); Donald McKayle (*Collage*); Judith Jamison (*Divining*); Bill T. Jones and Arnie Zane (*How to Walk an Elephant*); Jennifer Muller (*Speeds*); Katherine Dunham (*The Magic of Katherine Dunham*); Rovan Dean (*From the Mountains of Taubalu*); Donald Byrd (*Shards*); Kevin Rotardier (*Tell It Like It Is*); Barry Martin (*Chelsea's Bells*); Lester Horton (*Sarong Paramaribo*)

CHAPTER NOTES

one "BUSY AS SOON AS HE WAS BORN"

General sources:
Jacqueline Quinn Moore Lathem, "A Biographical Study of the Lives and Contributions of Two Selected Contemporary Black Male Artists—Arthur Mitchell and Alvin Ailey — in the Idioms of Ballet and Modern Dance, Respectively" (dissertation submitted in partial fulfillment of the requirements for the degree of Doctor of Philosophy in Dance and Related Arts in the Graduate School of Texas Woman's University, College of Health, Physical Education, and Recreation, 1973).

Handwritten notes Alvin Ailey made for an autobiography, File 0289, Alvin Ailey Archives, Black Archives of Mid-America, Inc., Kansas City, Missouri.

Sources for information on Ailey's childhood in Rogers, Texas:
Interviews with Pam Crow, Bill D. Douglas, Lula Cooper, Matty Duckens, Eddy Duckens, Reverend Sylvester Duckens, Billy Ray Crow, Clyde McQueen, Rusty Graham.

Sources for material on Texas history:
Collection of Roy Elliot Goodwin, town historian of Navasota, Texas.
Archives of the *Navasota Examiner.*

two A LIGHT AND SHADOWED PARADISE

General sources:
Lathem, "A Biographical Study."
Ailey autobiographical archival notes.
Alvin Ailey and A. Peter Bailey, *Revelations: The Autobiography of Alvin Ailey* (New York: Birch Lane Press, Carol Publishing Group, 1995).

Sources for information on Ailey's childhood in Navasota, Texas:
Interviews with Lula Cooper, Ruby Alexander Phillips, Roy Elliot and Margaret Goodwin, James Henley, Evelyn Ashford, Darcell Jackson, Clark J. Whitten, Onella Travis, Walter William Travis, Ruby Hunter, Sandy Neblett, Matty Duckens.
Maya Angelou, *I Know Why the Caged Bird Sings* (New York: Random House, 1970), pp. 3–4.
Quotations from Ailey on childhood loneliness: Lathem, "A Biographical Study," pp. 447, 443.
Quotation from Ailey on scene at Dew Drop Inn: Lathem, "A Biographical Study," p. 447.
Quotation from Ailey on life after departure of Chicano family: Ailey autobiographical archival notes.
Reference to childhood sexual experience with a girl: Ailey and Bailey, *Revelations*, p. 21.

Sources for information on Navasota history:
"The Navasota Bluebonnet 1854–1954" and other materials in the collection of Roy Elliot Goodwin, town historian of Navasota. I am also indebted to Mr. Goodwin for his tours of Navasota and surrounding countryside, and his introductions to townspeople who knew Alvin Ailey and Lula Ailey.

three LOVE AND NEED AND GROWING UP

General sources:
Lathem, "A Biographical Study."
Ailey autobiographical archival notes.
Ailey and Bailey, *Revelations.*

Sources for information on Los Angeles history:
Keith E. Collins, *Black Los Angeles: The Maturing of the Ghetto, 1940–1950* (Saratoga, Calif.: Century Twenty One Publishing, 1980).

Lawrence Brooks de Graaf, "Negro Migration to Los Angeles, 1930 to 1950 (dissertation, University of California, Los Angeles, 1962. Reprinted by R and E Research Associates, Saratoga, California).

Interview with James Truitte.

Sources for information on the lives of Lula and Alvin Ailey in Los Angeles:

Interviews with Lula Cooper, Ella Hurd and Bob Harris.

Transcript of an interview by A. Peter Bailey with Lula Cooper, File 0459, Alvin Ailey Archives, Black Archives of Mid-America, Inc., Kansas City, Missouri.

Quotation from Ailey on dancing of Gene Kelly: Lathem, "A Biographical Study," p. 457.

Quotation from Ella Hurd on Ailey's moodiness: Lathem, "A Biographical Study," p. 464.

Quotations from Lula Cooper on Fred Cooper's return to Los Angeles: A. Peter Bailey archival transcript of interview with Lula Cooper, p. 45.

Reference to Ailey's avoidance of sounds of lovemaking: Ailey and Bailey, *Revelations*, p. 37.

Sources for information on Ailey's junior high school days:

Interview with Blanche Sutton.

School programs, yearbook photos, papers from collection of Blanche Sutton.

four APPROACHING CENTER

General sources:

Lathem, "A Biographical Study."

Ailey autobiographical archival notes.

Ailey and Bailey, *Revelations*.

Sources for information about Ailey's teenaged years:

Interviews with Lula Cooper, Don Martin, Blanche Sutton, Ella Hurd Harris, Cristyne Lawson, Gladys Nelson, David McReynolds, Thurston Carlock, Carmen de Lavallade, Arthur Reynolds.

Ailey autobiographical archival notes.

Ailey and Bailey, *Revelations*.

Lathem, "A Biographical Study."

Collection of materials on Thomas Jefferson High School and George Washington Carver Junior High School, Blanche Sutton.

Source for information on the Ballet Russe de Monte Carlo: Jack Anderson, *The One and Only: The Ballet Russe de Monte Carlo* (New York: Dance Horizons, 1981).

Sources for information on Katherine Dunham:
Interviews with Glory Van Scott, Katherine Dunham.
Walter Terry, *I Was There: Selected Dance Reviews and Articles—1936–1976* (New York: Audience Arts, Marcel Dekker, 1978), p. 64.

Source for information on Jack Cole:
Glenn Loney, *Unsung Genius: The Passion of Dancer-Choreographer Jack Cole* (New York: Franklin Watts, 1984).

five   "HARD TIMES BUT THE BEST TIMES"

General sources:
Lathem, "A Biographical Study."
Ailey autobiographical archival notes.
Ailey and Bailey, *Revelations.*

Sources for information on Lester Horton:
Larry Warren, *Lester Horton, Modern Dance Pioneer* (Princeton, N.J.: Dance Horizons/Princeton Book Company, 1991).
"The Dance Theater of Lester Horton," *Dance Perspectives* 31, Autumn 1967; reprinted by permission of Dance Perspectives Foundation Inc. (© all rights reserved).
Genius on the Wrong Coast, a film by Lelia Goldoni, Green River Road Productions, 1993.
Interviews with Lelia Goldoni, Bella Lewitzky, Frank Eng, James Truitte, Don Martin, Carmen de Lavallade.
References to Lester Horton's work with Michio Ito and props: *Dance Perspectives,* pp. 6, 31.
Quotation of Horton's film scenario: Warren, *Lester Horton,* p. 108; reprinted by permission of Princeton Book Company.
Reference to Horton's costume building: *Dance Perspectives,* p. 57.
Anecdote about Ruth St. Denis's visit to Horton studio: Warren, *Lester Horton,* p. 186.

six STUDIO DAYS

General sources:
    Lathem, "A Biographical Study."
    Ailey autobiographical archival notes.
    Ailey and Bailey, *Revelations.*

Sources on Horton and his studio:
    Warren, *Lester Horton.*
    Dance Perspectives.
Joyce Trisler collection of Horton material at the Dance Collection, New York Public Library for the Performing Arts, Lincoln Center, New York.
    Lelia Goldoni, *Genius on the Wrong Coast.*
    Interviews with Lelia Goldoni, James Truitte, Don Martin, Frank Eng.
    Review of Lester Horton company in New York City: P. W. Manchester, *Dance News,* May 1953.

Sources on Ailey in the late 1940s and 1950s:
    Ailey autobiographical archival notes.
    Warren, *Lester Horton.*
    Loney, *Unsung Genius.*
    Interviews with Marjorie Berman Perces, David McReynolds, James Truitte, Cristyne Lawson, Carmen de Lavallade, Don Martin, Maya Angelou, Ruth Beckford, Anna Halprin.

    Source for university semester dates: Report cards and other college papers, Alvin Ailey Archives, Alvin Ailey American Dance Center, New York; reprinted with permission.
    Quotation from prose poem ("You know the type—you've seen them . . .") by Ailey: Uncatalogued material [UCLA Bruins three-ringed notebook] in the Alvin Ailey Archives, Black Archives of Mid-America, Inc., Kansas City, Missouri.
    Source for information on Ailey's shift at Greyhound Bus Station in San Francisco: Ailey and Bailey, *Revelations,* p. 53.
    Reference to Lon Fontaine: Ailey and Bailey, *Revelations,* pp. 53–55.
    Description of *Liberian Suite:* Warren, *Lester Horton,* p. 166.
    Description of Jack Cole by John Martin: Loney, *Unsung Genius,* p. 14.
    Description of Ailey's work in *Lydia Bailey* by Jack Cole: Lathem, "A Biographical Study," p. 484.

seven FILLING LESTER HORTON'S SHOES

General sources:
　　Lathem, "A Biographical Study."
　　Ailey and Bailey, *Revelations.*
　　Ailey autobiographical archival notes.
　　Notebooks in Alvin Ailey Archives, Black Archives of Mid-America, Inc.

Sources for information on Horton's death:
　　Interviews with Frank Eng, Don Martin, Lelia Goldoni, Carmen de Lavallade, James Truitte.

Sources for information on Ailey's first work at the Horton studio:
　　Interviews with Frank Eng, James Truitte, Don Martin, Lelia Goldoni, Carmen de Lavallade, Lula Cooper.
　　Joyce Trisler collection, Dance Collection, New York Public Library for the Performing Arts, Lincoln Center, New York.
　　Reference to Ailey's copying Horton's way of working: Lathem, "A Biographical Study," p. 488.
　　Ailey's description of *Morning Mourning* as "fantastically strange . . .": Lathem, "A Biographical Study," p. 490.
　　Reviews of *Morning Mourning* and *According to St. Francis*: Patterson Greene, " 'Choreo '54' Stimulating," *Examiner*, June 1954; Albert Goldberg, "Lester Horton Group Offers 'Choreo '54,' " *Los Angeles Times*, June 5, 1954; copyright 1994, Albert Goldberg; reprinted with permission. Russ Burton, " 'Choreo '54' Stimulating," *Daily News*, June 1954; David Bongard, "Introduce 'Choreo '54,' " *Herald*, June 1954; Walter Terry, "Dance: Jabcob's Pillow Festival," *Herald Tribune*, July 23, 1954.

eight COMING OF AGE IN NEW YORK

General sources:
　　Lathem, "A Biographical Study."
　　Ailey autobiographical archival notes.
　　Ailey and Bailey, *Revelations.*

Sources for information on House of Flowers:
　　Interviews with Glory Van Scott, Arthur Mitchell, Carmen de Lavallade, Geoffrey Holder, Herbert Ross.

Lewis Funke, "Capote's Flower People," *New York Times*, September 17, 1967.

Sources for information on Ailey's life in New York in the 1950s:
Interviews with Carmen de Lavallade, Geoffrey Holder, Michael Shurtleff, Mickey Bord, Arthur Mitchell, Arthur Reynolds, Cristyne Lawson, Lelia Goldoni.

Letter from Dr. Judith Ginsberg, executive director, Covenant Foundation, June 22, 1993.

Description of duet danced by Ailey and de Lavallade in *House of Flowers*: Ailey and Bailey, *Revelations*, p. 74.

Reference to Truman Capote's attempt to give Ailey his Rolls Royce: Ailey and Bailey, *Revelations*, p. 75.

Quotation of review by Carl Van Vechten of Ailey's dancing: Carl Van Vechten, *The Dance Writings of Carl Van Vechten*, ed., with introduction by Paul Padgette (New York: Dance Horizons, 1974), p. 44; reprinted with permission of Princeton Book Company.

Quotation referring to dance in New York in the 1950s: John Martin, "The Dance: Season Turns to Concert Artists," *New York Times*, February 7, 1960.

Reference to Ailey's reluctance to choreograph *Sing, Man, Sing*: Ailey and Bailey, *Revelations*, p. 79.

Reference to Ailey's attitude toward Walter Nicks' choreography for *Sing, Man, Sing*: Lathem, "A Biographical Study," p. 507.

Quotation from Ailey letter about Cristyne Lawson: Lathem, "A Biographical Study," pp. 508–509.

Sources for information on New York theater and dance in the 1950s:
Richard Long, *The Black Tradition in American Dance* (New York: Rizzoli, 1989).

Interviews with Arthur Mitchell, Donald McKayle, Sophie Maslow, Charles Queenan, Geoffrey Holder, Claude Thompson, Louis Johnson, Joe Nash, Charles Blackwell, James Truitte, Talley Beatty, Mary Hinkson, Richard Shepard, Michael Shurtleff, Alex Dube, Ivy Clarke, Anna Sokolow, Walter Nicks.

Quotation from John Martin referring to what black dancers ought to perform: Long, *The Black Tradition*, p. 24.

American Dance Festival: The Black Tradition in American Modern Dance, published in 1993 by the festival, Durham, North Carolina.

American Dance Festival: African-American Genius in Modern Dance, published in 1994 by the festival, Durham, North Carolina.

Alvin Ailey Archives at the Alvin Ailey American Dance Center.
Martin Duberman, *Stonewall* (New York: Penguin Books, 1994).

nine THE FIRST CONCERT

General sources:
Lathem, "A Biographical Study."
Ailey autobiographical archival notes.
Ailey and Bailey, *Revelations.*

Sources for information on Jamaica:
Interviews with Cristyne Lawson, Lena Horne, Nat Horne, Sherman Sneed, Mickey Bord, Charles Blackwell, Louis Johnson,
References to Lena Horne and Josephine Premice camps in *Jamaica* and to Horne's nickname for Ailey: Ailey and Bailey, *Revelations,* p. 82.

Sources for information on Ailey's life in the mid- to late 1950s in New York:
Interviews with Dorene Richardson, Ella Thompson Moore, Dan Butt, Geoffrey Holder, Mickey Bord, Louise Roberts, Claude Thompson, Charles Blackwell, Milton Katselas.
Quotations from Liz Williamson referring to Ailey casting and costuming of first concert: "Continuing Revelations," a seminar at the New York Public Library for the Performing Arts, Lincoln Center, New York, May 1992; reprinted with permission.
Program notes for the first performance of *Blues Suite,* March 30, 1958, at the Ninety-second Street YMHA.
Quotation from John Martin review of *Blues Suite* premiere: John Martin, "The Dance: Review III," *New York Times,* July 6, 1958.
Quotation from Doris Hering's review of *Blues Suite* premiere: Doris Hering, *Dance Magazine,* May 1958, pp. 65–66.
Programs and letters from collection of Dorene Richardson.

ten SONGS OF TROUBLE, SONGS OF LOVE

General sources:
Lathem, "A Biographical Study."
Ailey autobiographical archival notes.

Ailey and Bailey, *Revelations.*

"Continuing Revelations" seminar.

Interviews with Charles Blackwell, Herbert Ross, Cristyne Lawson, Ella Thompson Moore, Dorene Richardson, Claude Thompson, Lelia Goldoni, Mickey Bord, Norman Singer, Alwin Holtz, Edele Holtz, Marianna Gates, Matt Turney, Gary Harris, Nicholas Cernovitch, Ves Harper.

Review of *El Cigaro*: P. W. Manchester, *Dance News,* February 1959.

Reference to Ophelia Wilkes as inspiration for the "woman upstairs" in *Blues Suite*: Ailey and Bailey, *Reflections,* p. 91.

According to program notes for the second Ailey concert at the Ninety-second Street Y, Ailey cut Ernest Parham's dance and his own *Beguine* quartet from the reworked *Cinco Latinos* and added two new dances he had choreographed. *El Cigaro* was the renamed Horton *Rumba* from the first performance.

Review of Ailey's "Mistress and Manservant": Selma Jeanne Cohen, *Dance Magazine,* March 1959.

Account of the Here-U-R: Jennifer Dunning, "A Ma-and-Pa Restaurant for Jacob's Pillow Dancers," *New York Times,* August 21, 1979.

Description of response to *Creation of the World*: Lathem, "A Biographical Study," p. 524.

Description of *Blues Suite* beginning "motivations and emotions of Negro religious music": program copy.

Ailey's description of childhood impressions of the blues: Ailey and Bailey, *Revelations,* p. 97.

Description of response to *Revelations*: "Continuing *Revelations*" seminar.

eleven REVELATIONS

General sources:

Lathem, "A Biographical Study."

Ailey autobiographical archival notes.

Ailey and Bailey, *Revelations.*

"Continuing Revelations" seminar.

Interviews with Nat Horne, Donald McKayle, James Truitte, Claude Thompson, Dudley Williams.

Quotation from Ailey on the essence of dancing: Walter Sorell, "Style, Essence, Allusion, A Talk with Alvin Ailey," *Dance Magazine*, August 1963, p. 47.

Reference to Ailey's changing ending of *Revelations*: Ailey and Bailey, *Revelations*, p. 100.

Quotation from Anna Kisselgoff review of *Revelations*: Anna Kisselgoff, "Ailey's Fusion of Jazz, Modern and Ballet," *New York Times*, December 13, 1981.

Dudley Williams's comments on *Revelations*: "Continuing Revelations" seminar.

Linda Kent's comments on *Revelations*: "Continuing Revelations" seminar.

Quotation from Ailey on humor in dance: notes on file in the archives of the Alvin Ailey American Dance Theater; reprinted with permission.

twelve A NEW YORK FAMILY

General sources:

Lathem, "A Biographical Study."

Ailey autobiographical archival notes.

Ailey and Bailey, *Revelations*.

Notebooks in the archives of the Alvin Ailey American Dance Theater; reprinted with permission.

Interviews with Paul Szilard, Edele Holtz, Charles Blackwell, Michele Murray, Ves Harper, Ella Thompson Moore, Hilary Ostlere.

Reviews of *Three for Now*: Selma Jeanne Cohen, *Dance Magazine*, January 1961; Walter Terry, *New York Herald Tribune*, November 28, 1960; Louis Horst, *Dance Observer*, January 1961.

Reviews of *Knoxville: Summer of 1915*: Selma Jeanne Cohen, *Dance Magazine*, January 1961; Walter Terry, *New York Herald Tribune*, November 28, 1960.

Review of *Gillespiana*: Walter Terry, *New York Herald Tribune*, July 23, 1962.

Sources on Clark Center:

Interviews with Al Holtz, Edele Holtz, Ivy Clarke, Mickey Bord.

Programs, brochures and announcements for Clark Center and personal correspondence from the archives of Al and Edele Holtz.

thirteen BACK TO ACTING, ON TO ASIA

General sources:
Ailey autobiographical archival notes.
Lathem, "A Biographical Study."
Ailey and Bailey, *Reflections.*
Interviews with Michael Shurtleff, Milton Katselas, Dustin Hoffman, Daniel Nagrin, Maxine Glorsky, Linda Kent, Naomi Nomikos, Vinnette Carroll, Lawrence Hatterer, M.D.

References to Ailey's shared birthdate with Robert Duvall and to Ailey's assessment of reviews for *Call Me by My Rightful Name* as "terrible": Ailey and Bailey, *Reflections,* p. 83.
Quotations from reviews of *Call Me by My Rightful Name*: Howard Taubman, *New York Times,* "Theatre: Young Triangle," February 1, 1961; Richard Watt Jr., "The Arrival of a New Dramatist," *New York Post,* February 1, 1961; Whitney Bolton, " 'My Rightful Name' Is a Spellbinder," *Morning Telegraph,* February 1, 1961.
Review of *Roots of the Blues, Dance News,* January 1962.
Review of *Roots of the Blues* at Jacob's Pillow: Lillian Moore, "Dance: Jacob's Pillow Dance Festival," *New York Herald Tribune,* July 1960.
Analysis of *Black Nativity* by Arnold Rampersad: Arnold Rampersad, *The Life of Langston Hughes* (New York: Oxford University Press, 1986), vol. 2, p. 347.
Diaries and notes written by Ailey from the Alvin Ailey Archives, Black Archives of Mid-America, Inc.
Material on Ailey's plans for the 1962 Asian tour: Notes written by Ailey from the Alvin Ailey Archives, Black Archives of Mid-America, Inc.
Quotation beginning "The cultural heritage of the American Negro . . .": Program notes for the Alvin Ailey American Dance Theater season in October 1964 at the Shaftesbury Theatre in London, England.

fourteen "HOT AND PERFECT"

General sources:
Diary of Asian tour written in 1962 by Ailey, File # 0840. Alvin Ailey Archives, Black Archives of Mid-America, Inc.

Material on the tour from the Alvin Ailey Archives, Black Archives of Mid-America, Inc.

Notes and correspondence from the archives of Edele and Al Holtz.

Interviews with Mickey Bord, James Truitte, Carmen de Lavallade, Don Martin, Ella Thompson, Charles Reinhart, Ves Harper, Ivy Clarke.

Quotation beginning "The elegant nineteenth century gilt and plush atmosphere . . .": "Pitt Street's Deep South," *Sydney Morning Herald*, February 3, 1962; reprinted with permission.

Ailey's estimation of the number of people in the audience for the first performance in Sydney: Ailey and Bailey, *Revelations*, p. 104.

Review beginning "The American Dance Theatre show . . .": Frank Harris, "Cheers for U.S. Dancers," *Daily Mirror*, February 5, 1962.

Quotation beginning "Half-savage jazz rhythms . . .": Norman Kessel, "Lament of the Blues," *Sun*, February 5, 1962; John Fairfax Publications.

Quotation beginning "Judging by the reactions of the audience . . .": Roland Robinson, quoted in Arthur Todd, "Two-Way Passage for Dance," *Dance Magazine*, July 1962, p. 39.

Reference to reception of the Ailey company in Rangoon: Ailey and Bailey, *Revelations*, p. 105.

Reference to Ailey audiences' fear of terrorists in Saigon: Ailey and Bailey, *Revelations*, p. 106.

Reference to Ailey's proposals for future tours: Todd, "Two-Way Passage," p. 41.

Reference to behavior of American soldiers in Saigon: Lathem, "A Biographical Study," p. 548.

Reference to aircraft carrier docked near dancers' hotel in Saigon: Ailey and Bailey, *Revelations*, pp. 106–107.

Quotation from review in Philippines beginning "He uses the human body . . .": Rodrigo Perez III, *The Manila Times*, March 1962; reprinted with permission.

Quotation from Ailey interview in *South China Post-Herald* beginning "The best of everything . . .": *South China Post-Herald*, March 1962.

Description of Brother John Sellers's singing beginning "A contortionist of a singer . . .": "Dynamic Dancing with a Difference," *China Mail*, April 10, 1962.

Quotation from Alvin Ailey interview in *Djakarta Daily Mail:* "American Dance Company in Bandung and Jakarta," *Djakarta Daily Mail,* March 22, 1962.

Reference to review by Elise Grilli: Elise Grilli, "Fine Dance Company from U.S.," *Japan Times,* April 24, 1962.

Quotation from review by Masao Kageyasu beginning "The unusual length . . .": Masao Kageyasu, "Overwhelming Negro Ballet Full of Extravagance and Dynamism," *Sankei Shimbun* (Evening), April 21, 1962.

Quotation from review by Taiji Miyagishi beginning "The Queen de Lavallade . . .": Taiji Miyagishi, "Enraptured the Audience," *Tokyo Shimbun* (Evening), April 21, 1962.

Reference to State Department spokeswoman's assessment of tour: Todd, "Two-Way Passage," p. 39.

Ailey's comment on Asian knowledge of American blacks: Todd, "Two-Way Passage," p. 40.

Ailey's description of American dance scene: Todd, "Two-Way Passage," p. 41.

fifteen PROPHETS WITH LITTLE HONOR

General sources:
   Materials from the archives of Edele and Al Holtz.
   Lathem, "A Biographical Study."
   Ailey autobiographical archival notes.
   Ailey and Bailey, *Revelations.*
   Archives of the Alvin Ailey American Dance Theater.
   Interviews with Edele and Al Holtz, Sylvia Waters, Michael Shurtleff, Michele Murray, Ves Harper, Talley Beatty, Geoffrey Holder, Brother John Sellers, James Truitte.

Review of Ailey company 1962 performances at American Dance Festival at Connecticut College, beginning "The chances are, however . . .": Allen Hughes, "Dance: Influence of Ethnic Traditions," *New York Times,* July 23, 1962.

Sources on Rebekah Harkness:
   Craig Unger, *Blue Blood* (New York: William Morrow & Co., Inc., 1988).
   Review of *Feast of Ashes* beginning "So far I know Ailey's

work . . .": Peter Williams, "Two Looks at Harkness," "First Look," *Dance & Dancers*, April 1965, p. 16.

Sources on Tiger Tiger Burning Bright:
Gay Talese, "The Soft Psyche of Josh Logan," *Esquire*, April 1963; reprinted with permission.

Reference to the other actors' behavior toward Ailey: Lathem, "A Biographical Study," pp. 561–62.

Reference to Ailey's response to Claudia McNeil: Ailey and Bailey, *Reflections*, p. 85.

Reference to Ailey's breakdown during rehearsals: Gay Talese, p. 84.

Critical reference to *Light*: James Felton, "Ailey Dance Theater Offers Superb Program," *Evening Bulletin*, November 4, 1963.

Sources for information about My People:
John Edward Hasse, *Beyond Category: The Life and Genius of Duke Ellington* (New York: Simon and Schuster), pp. 350–51.

Ailey's comment about invitation to choreograph *My People*: "Ailey Talks," *Dance & Dancers*, April 1965, p. 33.

Reference to Ailey's temper tantrum in Brazil: Ailey and Bailey, *Revelations*, p. 110.

Report on Alvin Ailey Dance Theater performance in Brazil: "Big Festival Views Alvin Ailey Dancers," *New York Times*, September 6, 1963.

Alvin Ailey's codirector on *Jericho–Jim Crow* was William Hairston.

Sources for information on Langston Hughes and his theatrical productions and writing:
Rampersad, *The Life of Langston Hughes*.

Langston Hughes's description of *Tambourines to Glory* beginning "a singing, shouting, wailing drama . . .": Rampersad, *The Life of Langston Hughes*, vol. 2, p. 255.

Langston Hughes's description of *Jericho–Jim Crow* beginning "a serious but entertaining play . . .": Rampersad, *The Life of Langston Hughes*, vol. 2, p. 364.

Langston Hughes's description of the subject of *Jericho–Jim Crow* beginning "young people of all racial and religious backgrounds . . .": Rampersad, *The Life of Langston Hughes*, vol. 2, p. 371.

Quotation from reviews of *Jericho–Jim Crow* beginning "incredible heights . . .": Rampersad, *The Life of Langston Hughes*, vol. 2, p. 372.

sixteen BACK ON THE ROAD AGAIN

General sources:
  Lathem, "A Biographical Study."
  Ailey autobiographical archival notes.
  Ailey and Bailey, *Revelations.*
  Unger, *Blue Blood.*
  Interviews with Edele and Al Holtz, James Truitte, Anna Sokolow, Talley Beatty, Clive Barnes, Brother John Sellers, Dudley Williams.

Quotation from review beginning "outwardly conforming people . . .": Billie Burke, " 'Stark' Art by Dancers," *Daily Telegraph*, February 4, 1965.

Ailey on *Rooms* beginning "has a kind of linear sculpture . . .": James Mellen, "Rooms," *Nation*, February 6, 1965; reprinted with permission.

Reviewers' comments on decline in Ailey's performing: Jacqueline Maskey, *Dance Magazine*, August 1964; Allen Hughes, "Shades of Blue," *New York Times*, September 2, 1964.

Reviewer's comment on Truitte's performing at the Delacorte: Jacqueline Maskey, *Dance Magazine*, August 1964.

Reviews of the 1964 London season: Peter Williams, "Blues and All That Jazz," *Dance & Dancers*, November 1964; Richard Buckle, "In a Friendly Fashion," *Sydney Morning Herald*, October 22, 1964; A. V. Coton, "Expressive Dancing by Negroes," *Daily Telegraph and Morning Post*, October 22, 1964 (© The Telegraph plc, London, 1964).

Review quotation beginning "By his use of back projections . . .": Peter Williams, "Blues," *Dance & Dancers*, November 1964, p. 22.

Review quotation beginning "There is no such thing as Negro dance . . .": Williams, "Blues," p. 21.

Review quotation beginning "The path on which he is travelling . . .": Williams, "Blues," p. 23.

Review quotation beginning "One of the most odd aspects of Ailey's work . . .": Clive Barnes, "Blues and All That Jazz," *Dance & Dancers*, November 1964, p. 25.

Review quotation on Dudley Williams's "elusive, unobtrusive brilliance": Barnes, "Blues," p. 25.

Ailey quoted on *Rooms* in interview in Sydney: "Jazz Ballet 'A Shocker,' " *Australian*, February 3, 1965.

Ailey on the two different audiences in Sydney: Lathem, "A Biographical Study," p. 590.

Ailey quoted on *Rooms* in interview in Melbourne: Howard Palmer, "Top-line Ballet Off Program," *Sun*, February 26, 1965.

Ailey quoted on working with the Harkness "kids": "Ailey Talks," *Dance & Dancers*, April 1965, pp. 32–33.

Account of Harkness Ballet 1965 Paris season beginning "For a brand-new ballet company . . .": Cynthia Grenier, "A Glittering Paris Debut," *New York Herald Tribune*, March 13, 1965.

seventeen "THREW ALL DANCE CLOTHES INTO WASTEBASKET"

General sources:

Archives of Al and Edele Holtz.

Ailey notes for an autobiography, Alvin Ailey Archives, Black Archives of Mid-America, Inc.

Alvin Ailey Archives, Dance Collection, New York Public Library for the Performing Arts, Lincoln Center, New York.

Lathem, "A Biographical Study."

Interviews with Al Holtz, Edele Holtz, James Truitte, Brother John Sellers, Dudley Williams, Linda Kent, Sylvia Waters.

Christopher is a pseudonym.

Quotation from review of March 23 Alvin Ailey American Dance Theater (AAADT) performance in London beginning "As an occasion . . .": A. V. Coton, "Rare Negro Dancing by United States Company," *Daily Telegraph and Morning Post*, March 30, 1965 (© The Telegraph plc, London, 1965).

Quotations from review of AAADT Copenhagen season beginning "Especially during the first part . . .": Svend Kragh-Jacobsen, "American Dance Acrobats," *Berlingske Tidende*, April 20, 1965.

Quoted phrase describing AAADT as "this formerly unknown American Negro group" in *Variety*: "American Negro Dance Troupe Now Touring Europe, Ailey Group Very Big," *Variety*, June 23, 1965.

eighteen BACK IN BUSINESS, SEVERAL TIMES

General sources:

Judith Jamison, *Dancing Spirit: An Autobiography*, with Howard Kaplan (New York: Doubleday, 1993).

Olga Maynard, *Judith Jamison: Aspects of a Dancer* (Garden City, New York: Doubleday, 1982).

Archives of Lula Cooper.

Archives of Al and Edele Holtz.

Archives of the Alvin Ailey American Dance Theater.

Alvin Ailey Archives, Dance Collection, New York Public Library for the Performing Arts.

Lathem, "A Biographical Study."

Interviews with Judith Jamison, Donald McKayle, James Truitte, Al Holtz, Edele Holtz, Arthur Mitchell, Herman Krawitz.

Quotation from article on the making of the opera *Antony and Cleopatra* beginning "Too much water . . .": Hans W. Heinsheimer, "Birth of an Opera," *Saturday Review,* September 17, 1966.

nineteen AFRICAN ODYSSEY

General sources:

Archives of Al and Edele Holtz.

Alvin Ailey Archives, Black Archives of Mid-America, Inc.

Archives of the Alvin Ailey American Dance Theater.

Alvin Ailey Archives, Dance Collection, New York Public Library for the Performing Arts, Lincoln Center, New York.

Lathem, "A Biographical Study."

Interviews with Al Holtz, Edele Holtz, James Truitte, Ivy Clarke, Dudley Williams, Clive Barnes, Gil Shiva, Brother John Sellers.

Quotation from Clive Barnes review beginning "When is Mr. Ailey . . .": Clive Barnes, "Dance: Ailey Troupe in Amsterdam," *New York Times,* September 12, 1967.

Information on Carl Goldman and quotation from Martin Duberman: Martin Duberman, *Stonewall* (New York: Penguin Books, 1994), pp. 63–64.

Quotation from review by Clive Barnes beginning "It must be quite a new experience . . .": Clive Barnes, "Dance: Ailey Troupe in Amsterdam," *New York Times,* July 12, 1967.

Quotation from review by Meir Ronnen of AAADT performances in Jerusalem beginning "There is no doubt a great deal of sympathy here . . .": Meir Ronnen, "Alvin Ailey and Some Negro Myths," *Jerusalem Post,* August 18, 1967; reprinted with permission.

Account of arrest of Ailey: Ellen Cohn, "Ailey, Arsonist," *New York Times Magazine*, April 29, 1973.

Anecdote about dimming of streetlights in African towns during AAADT tour: Alvin Ailey, "African Odyssey," *Dance Magazine*, May 1968, p. 53.

Ailey's comment on African response to AAADT repertory beginning "I only wish . . .": Ailey, "African Odyssey," p. 53.

Quotation from President Leopold Senghor about AAADT repertory beginning "You have discovered . . .": Ailey, "African Odyssey," p. 86.

Interpretation by Ghanaian audience member of *Metallics* beginning "to be about a shy person . . .": Ailey, "African Odyssey," p. 53.

Ailey's comment about the "unusual beauty" of the Congolese: Ailey, "African Odyssey," p. 87.

Ailey's comments about colonialism: Ailey, "African Odyssey," p. 88.

Quotations from review by Togbi Yao in *Sunday Mirror* in Accra beginning "Something breathtaking . . .": Togi Yao, "It Was a Sight to Live for a Life Time," *Sunday Mirror*, October 29, 1967; reprinted with permission.

twenty BUDGETS, BOARDS AND TWO GOOD-BYES

General sources:

Archives of Al and Edele Holtz.

Alvin Ailey Archives, Black Archives of Mid-America, Inc.

Alvin Ailey Archives, Dance Collection, New York Public Library for the Performing Arts, Lincoln Center, New York.

Archives of the Alvin Ailey American Dance Theater.

Interviews with Al Holtz, Edele Holtz, Sylvia Waters, James Truitte, Ivy Clarke, Norman Singer, Linda Kent, Gil Shiva, Talley Beatty.

Conversation with Sidney Poitier.

Ailey's characterization of 1968 as the year "we spent more than we had": Maynard, *Judith Jamison, p. 227.*

Quotation from review by Clive Barnes of AAADT season at Hunter College beginning "Without question . . .": Clive Barnes, "Alvin Ailey's Troupe at Hunter," *New York Times*, January 20, 1968.

Quotation from review of AAADT performance of *Black Belt* at

Edinburgh Festival beginning "The piece has ceased . . .": Nicholas Dromgoole, "More Alvin Ailey Wanted," *Sunday Telegraph*, September 15, 1968 (© The Telegraph plc, London, 1968).

twenty-one AN ANGER IN THE AIR

General sources:

Alvin Ailey Archives, Black Archives of Mid-America, Inc.

Alvin Ailey Archives, Dance Collection, New York Public Library of the Performing Arts, Lincoln Center, New York.

Archives of Al and Edele Holtz.

Interviews with Ivy Clarke, Mickey Bord, Meg Gordean, Sylvia Waters, Al Holtz, Edele Holtz, Talley Beatty, Charles Reinhart, Norman Singer, Harvey Lichtenstein, Michele Murray, Linda Kent, George Faison, William Hammond, Kelvin Rotardier, Dudley Williams.

Quotation from account by society columnist Suzy of open rehearsal by AAADT: Suzy Says, "Beaming in the Rain," *Daily News*, June 19, 1968.

Quotation from review by Frances Herridge of AAADT performance at Billy Rose Theater beginning "The material is so theatrical . . .": Frances Herridge, "Alvin Ailey Turn at Billy Rose," *New York Post*, January 28, 1969.

Quotation from review by A. V. Coton of AAADT performance of *Quintet* at Edinburgh Festival beginning "five very worldly wise ladies . . .": A. V. Coton, "Attractive Dancing in a Ballet," *Daily Telegraph and Morning Post*, September 15, 1968 (© The Telegraph plc, London, 1968).

Quotations by Ailey about deceptive success of AAADT, being a black choreographer and black art in interview with Ellen Cohn beginning "Everybody thinks I've got it made . . .": Ellen Cohn, "I Want to Be a Father Figure," *New York Times*, April 13, 1969.

"Instructions: How to Play the Drums," poem by Ailey, from the archives of the Alvin Ailey American Dance Theater.

twenty-two CLIMBING

General sources:

Alvin Ailey Archives, Black Archives of Mid-America, Inc.

Hasse, *Beyond Category.*

Interviews with Harvey Lichtenstein, Dudley Williams, Ivy Clarke, Masazumi Chaya, Sylvia Waters, Louise Roberts, William Hammond, Dennis Nahat, Cynthia Gregory, Maxine Glorsky, Calvin Cooper, Charles Reinhart, Pearl Lang, Anna Kisselgoff, Meg Gordean.

Quotations from essay by Deborah Jowitt on AAADT at the Brooklyn Academy of Music beginning "Ailey has always been an extremely stylish choreographer . . .": Deborah Jowitt, *Dance Beat: Selected Views and Reviews, 1967–1976* (New York: Marcel Dekker, Inc., 1977), p. 104; permission granted by the author and *The Village Voice.*

Quotations from essay by Clive Barnes on AAADT season at the Brooklyn Academy of Music beginning "Ailey is black and proud of it . . .": Clive Barnes, "A Great Lesson in Race Relations," *New York Times,* April 26, 1970.

Quotations from Ailey on dissolving his company beginning "a constantly worsening situation . . .": Anna Kisselgoff, "City Ballet and Musicians Talk; Ailey May Disband His Troupe," *New York Times,* April 23, 1970.

Quotation from Joseph Gale on announced disbandment beginning "The death of the AAADT would be . . .": Joseph Gale, "Dance: Ailey's Decision," *Newark News,* May 10, 1970.

Quotation from Judith Jamison on difficulties of AAADT Russian tour, beginning "It was the *blues* . . .": Jamison, *Dancing Spirit,* p. 125; reprinted with permission.

In his Russian diary, Ailey refers to the year James Truitte left the company as 1967. Truitte left in 1968.

Anecdote about Russian ballerina describing sexy duet as something "we do in bed" from: Anna Kisselgoff, "Ailey Dancers Set Russians Cheering," *New York Times,* January 21, 1971.

Description of Ailey signing autographs in orchestra pit on closing night in Leningrad: Kathilyn Solomon Probosz, *Changing Our World: Alvin Ailey, Jr.* (New York: Bantam, 1991), p. 57 (© 1991 by Angel Entertainment, Inc.).

twenty-three FAMILY MATTERS

General sources:
Alvin Ailey Archives, Black Archives of Mid-America, Inc.
Archives of Al and Edele Holtz.

Lynn Seymour, with Paul Gardner, *Lynn, The Autobiography of Lynn Seymour* (London: Granada, 1984).

Maynard, *Judith Jamison.*

Jamison, *Dancing Spirit.*

Interviews with Ivy Clarke, Lynn Seymour, Norman Singer, Al Holtz, Lula Cooper, Judith Jamison, Linda Kent, Masazumi Chaya, Calvin Cooper, Lois Framhein, Raquelle Chavis, Sharrell Mesh Alexander, Pearl Lang, William Hammond, Meg Gordean, Sylvia Waters, Sarita Allen, Mickey Bord, Dudley Williams, George Faison.

Comment from Ivy Clarke on the attendance at the AAADT ANTA season beginning "The next night . . .": Ellen Cohn, "Ailey, Arsonist," *New York Times,* April 29, 1973.

Comment from Ailey about the effect of long-term touring on personal relationships: Ailey and Bailey, *Revelations,* p. 125.

Lynn Seymour's reaction to her role in *Flowers* and Ailey comment to Lynn Seymour beginning "Just remember . . .": Seymour, *Lynn,* pp. 249–50.

Lynn Seymour's description of opening night mishap and quotation beginning "The curtain went up . . .": Seymour, *Lynn,* p. 250.

Quotation from Judith Jamison on dancing *Cry* beginning "my lungs were on one side . . .": Jamison, *Dancing Spirit,* p. 133.

Description of Jamison's turban in *Cry* as a "black woman's stately tiara": Maynard, *Judith Jamison,* p. 140.

Quotation from Marcia B. Siegel review of *Cry:* Marcia B. Siegel, *Boston Herald Traveler,* June 8, 1971, reprinted with permission of the *Boston Herald.*

Quotation from Anna Kisselgoff review of AAADT spring season 1971 at City Center beginning "One thing was clear last night . . .": Anna Kisselgoff, "Premiere of *Choral Dances* by Ailey," *New York Times,* April 21, 1971.

Ailey's comment on his dancers' role in *Mass* beginning "second class performers . . .": Anna Kisselgoff, "Ailey Dancers to Give Mary Lou's Mass," *New York Times,* December 9, 1971.

Quotation from Charles Mingus on Ailey's *Mingus Dances:* Barry Cunningham, *New York Post,* October 20, 1971.

Ailey's comment about Mary Lou Williams's score for *Mary Lou's Mass:* Anna Kisselgoff, "Ailey Dancers to Give 'Mary Lou's Mass,' " *New York Times,* December 9, 1971.

Description by Clive Barnes of Consuelo Atlas in *Myth* beginning

"Miss Atlas, superbly womanly . . .": Clive Barnes, "Dance: Playfully Seizing on a Ritual," *New York Times*, December 16, 1971.

twenty-four "THE BOARD" ARRIVES

General sources:
Alvin Ailey Archives, Black Archives of Mid-America, Inc.
Maynard, *Judith Jamison.*
Jamison, *Dancing Spirit.*
Interviews with Ivy Clarke, Norman Singer, Dudley Williams, Peter Koepke, Brother John Sellers, William Hammond, Miguel Algarin, Stanley Plesent, Lois Framhein.

Ailey's comments about AAADT deficit to Ellen Cohn beginning "Compare that with any ballet company . . .": Ellen Cohn, "Ailey, Arsonist," *New York Times Magazine*, April 29, 1973.
Ailey's comments on the AAADT joining City Center as a resident dance company: Anna Kisselgoff, "Ailey Joins City Center," *New York Times*, August 4, 1972.
Headline phrase "tough assignment" in review of Virgil Thomson's *Lord Byron*: Anna Kisselgoff, "Ballet in 'Byron': A Tough Assignment," *New York Times*, April 22, 1972.
Ailey's comments to Chinese journalists beginning "We are very lucky . . .": Anna Kisselgoff, "Ailey Gets Informal Bid to Visit China," *New York Times*, May 21, 1973.

twenty-five "DADDY WORE KHAKI PANTS"

General sources:
Archives of the Alvin Ailey American Dance Theater.
Alvin Ailey Archives, Black Archives of Mid-America, Inc.
Hasse, *Beyond Category.*
Mark Tucker (ed.), *The Duke Ellington Reader* (New York: Oxford University Press, 1993).
Rampersad, *The Life of Langston Hughes,* vol. 1.
Interviews with Al Holtz, Lula Cooper, Talley Beatty, Linda Kent, Herman Krawitz, Sarita Allen, Fred Benjamin, Sylvia Waters, Edele Holtz, Ella Thompson Moore, Eddy Duckens, Meg Gordean, Masazumi Chaya.

Comment by Janet Collins to Anna Kisselgoff beginning "I was always an enigma . . .": Anna Kisselgoff, "Collins and Primus in Ailey Spotlight," *New York Times*, May 15, 1974.

Anecdote about Ailey and Donald Byrd beginning "I don't know if you're a dancer . . .": Probosz, *Changing Our World*, pp. 74–75 (© 1991 by Angel Entertainment, Inc.).

Quotation from review by Arlene Croce beginning "At one time 'Revelations' was plausibly the signature work . . .": Arlene Croce, *Afterimages* (New York: Alfred A. Knopf, 1977), pp. 26–32; permission granted by Arlene Croce.

Quotation of phrase "to stay just this side of schlock" from Marcia B. Siegel review: Marcia B. Siegel, *Watching the Dance Go By* (Boston: Houghton Mifflin, 1977), p. 182.

Quotations from essay by Marcia B. Siegel on AAADT and effects of touring beginning "The business of performing night after night . . .": Marcia B. Siegel, *At the Vanishing Point* (New York: Saturday Review Press, 1972), pp. 152–53; permission granted by Marcia B. Siegel.

Headline "New Dances, Same Old Steps," *Christian Science Monitor*, May 1973.

Quotation from review of AAADT by George Gelles beginning "The works are pale . . .": George Gelles, *Washington Star-News*, August 25, 1973.

Information on Carl Goldman's death: Duberman, *Stonewall*, p. 64.

twenty-six ELLINGTONIA

General sources:

Alvin Ailey Archives, Black Archives of Mid-America, Inc.

Alvin Ailey Archives, Dance Collection, New York Public Library for the Performing Arts, Lincoln Center, New York.

Interviews with Stanley Plesent, Sylvia Waters, Dudley Williams, Mikhail Baryshnikov, Anna Kisselgoff.

Ailey's comment from interview with Ellen Cohn beginning "I know it sounds so corny . . .": Ellen Cohn, "Ailey, Arsonist," *New York Times*, April 29, 1973.

Works commissioned by AAADT for "Ailey Celebrates Ellington" from new choreographers were Raymond Sawyer's *Afro-Eurasian*

Eclipse, Cristyne Lawson's *Still Life,* Dianne McIntyre's *Deep South Suite,* Alvin McDuffie's *New Orleans Junction* and Gus Solomons Jr.'s *Forty.* Works by Alvin Ailey were *Black, Brown and Beige, Three Black Kings, The Mooche, Night Creature,* and *The River* (performed by American Ballet Theatre). Works by guest choreographers were *The Road of the Phoebe Snow* (Talley Beatty), *Liberian Suite* (Lester Horton), *Caravan* (Louis Falco) and *Echoes in Blue* (Milton Myers).

Mikhail Baryshnikov's description of feeling like "a cow on ice" in *Pas de Duke*: Mikhail Baryshnikov, *Baryshnikov at Work* (New York: Alfred A. Knopf, 1976), pp. 205–207.

Ailey's comments to Joseph H. Mazo about his fantasy programming for "Ailey Celebrates Ellington" beginning "Maybe you shouldn't say this . . .": Joseph H. Mazo, "Alvin Ailey's Dance Tribute to the Duke," *New York Times,* April 13, 1975.

Ailey's comment about goal of "Ailey Celebrates Ellington" beginning "What I really want to do . . .": "Ailey Celebrates Ellington" reprinted from Playbill®, City Center season, May 1976; used by permission.

Joseph H. Mazo's assessment of relationship between Ailey and Duke Ellington beginning "For the next few years . . .": Joseph H. Mazo, "Alvin Ailey's Dance Tribute to the Duke."

twenty-seven "NONE BUT MY CALLING"

General sources:

Alvin Ailey Archives, Black Archives of Mid-America, Inc.

Alvin Ailey Archives, Dance Collection, New York Public Library for the Performing Arts, Lincoln Center, New York.

Maynard, *Judith Jamison.*

Ailey and Bailey, *Revelations.*

Interviews with Mickey Bord, Sylvia Waters, Sarita Allen, William Hammond, Edele Holtz, Paul Szilard, Masazumi Chaya, Ivy Clarke, Meg Gordean, Donna Wood, Dorene Richardson, Ella Thompson Moore, Carmen de Lavallade, Mary Barnett, Harry Rubenstein, Mari Kajiwara, Ronald Nugent, Keith McDaniel, Miguel Algarin.

Estimate of AAADT box office revenue: Probosz, *Changing Our World,* p. 66.

Ailey's comment in announcing loss of AAADT season at the New

York State Theater beginning "It is sad and frustrating . . .": "Ailey, Citing Costs, Drops Lincoln Center Season," *New York Times,* June 29, 1977.

Ailey's account of problems of AAADT season in Rio de Janeiro beginning "I felt a lot of rage . . ." and quotation from local reporter beginning "the uncommon fact . . .": David Vidal, "Alvin Ailey Dance Company Encounters Problems on Brazil Tour," *New York Times,* July 8, 1978.

The guest performers at the AAADT twentieth-anniversary gala at City Center also included Loretta Abbott, Altovise Gore Davis, George Faison, Linda Kent, Hector Mercado, John Parks, Kenneth Pearl, Lucinda Ransom, Alma Robinson, Kelvin Rotardier, Sylvia Waters and the company's rehearsal director, Mary Barnett.

Ailey's comments about AAADT New Year's Eve performance in Rabat: "Notes on People," *New York Times,* December 6, 1978.

Ailey's comments on winning Capezio Award beginning "well, nervous . . ." and "people in this country equate . . .": "Notes on People," *New York Times,* April 24, 1979.

Ailey's comment on dance company financing beginning "Not very dignified . . .": Anna Kisselgoff, "Where Should the Money Come From?" *New York Times,* May 6, 1979.

Ailey's comment, "Man, I am tired of requiems,": Maynard, *Judith Jamison,* p. 211.

Abdul is a pseudonym.

Kenneth Patchen's "In Memory of Kathleen" is quoted from the program notes for *Memoria.* Kenneth Patchen, *Collected Poems of Kenneth Patchen* (© 1939 by New Directions Pub. Corp. Reprinted by permission of New Directions).

twenty-eight BREAKDOWN

General sources:

Interviews with Brother John Sellers, Miguel Algarin, William Hammond, Meg Gordean, Marian Sylla, James Truitte, Ivy Clarke, Nat Horne, Mickey Bord, Keith McDaniel, Ronald Nugent, Paul Szilard, Donna Wood, Stanley Plesent, Raquelle Chavis.

Notes written by Ailey on file in the Alvin Ailey Archives, Black Archives of Mid-America, Inc.

Visit to the Cornell Medical Center New York Hospital Westchester Division and interviews with Juliet Goldsmith about the history of the institution and the kinds of treatment offered there and with Brad Perry, M.D., about the treatment of manic-depression.

Ailey's comment about "young men who take things": Ailey and Bailey, *Revelations*, p. 141.

Story about Ailey's fear of traffic lights: Ailey and Bailey, *Revelations*, pp. 139–41.

Description of scene during Ailey's second incident: Patrick Doyle and Fred Kerber, "Arrest Ailey in Rampage," *Daily News*, May 1, 1980; Joanne Wasserman, "Alvin Ailey Runs Amok Again," *New York Post*, May 1, 1980.

Information about Ailey holding mother's hand in ambulance: Ailey and Bailey, *Revelations*, p. 133.

Quotations assessing charges against Ailey of commercialism: Anna Kisselgoff, "Has Ailey Really Gone Commercial?" *New York Times*, December 17, 1978.

twenty-nine A FORMAL FEELING

General sources:

Interviews with William Hammond, Mickey Bord, Stanley Plesent, Clive Barnes, Robert Greskovic, Lula Cooper, Keith McDaniel.

Notes written by Ailey on file in the Alvin Ailey Archives, Black Archives of Mid-America, Inc.

Description of reception of *Au Bord du Précipice* at the Paris Opéra: Sheryl Flatow, "Enfant Terrible," *Ballet News*, July 1983, p. 21.

Ailey's description of *Précipice*: Jennifer Dunning, "Ailey Company to Open at the Met," *New York Times*, July 8, 1984.

Ailey's comments about having to streamline *Précipice* because of "the old ladies of the Opéra": E. J. Dionne, "New Alvin Ailey Dance Shakes Paris," *New York Times*, April 16, 1983.

Ailey's description of Monique Loudières: Jennifer Dunning, "Ailey Company to Open," *New York Times*, July 8, 1984.

Patrick Dupond's comments about Ailey: Rob Baker, "Dupond Dances Ailey's Precipice," *Daily News*, July 8, 1984.

Account of Ailey's twenty-fifth anniversary proclamations from the City of New York: "New York, New York Honor Alvin Ailey," *New York Times*, December 1, 1983.

Ailey's talk of his weight loss for anniversary celebration: Diana Maychick, "Alvin Ailey Has Eyes on a Second City," *New York Post*, November 28, 1983.

Account of anniversary gala program: Anna Kisselgoff, "Dance: For Alvin Ailey, 25th Anniversary Gala," *New York Times*, December 2, 1983.

thirty KANSAS CITY—AND BEYOND

General sources:

Interviews with Masazumi Chaya, Jane Hermann, Allan Gray, Carol Coe, William Hammond, Barry Ulanov, Dudley Williams, Laura Beaumont, Dawn Lille Horwitz.

Programs, feature stories, letters and notes written by Ailey on file in the Alvin Ailey Archives, Black Archives of Mid-America, Inc.

Review quotation beginning "the story is carried . . .": Clive Barnes, "Ailey's French Connection," *New York Post*, July 12, 1984.

Information about second home for Ailey company in Miami: Diana Maychick, "Alvin Ailey Has Eyes on a Second City," *New York Post*, November 28, 1983.

Quotation from Ailey beginning "We want to stimulate creativity . . .": Laurie Larson, "Leap Year," *Boulevard*, September 1984.

Musician's description of Charlie Parker beginning "I think he got the habit . . .": Nathan W. Pearson Jr., *Goin' to Kansas City* (Urbana: University of Illinois Press, 1987), p. 210.

thirty-one UP AND DOWN, AGAIN

General sources:

Interviews with Sharrell Mesh Alexander, Paul Szilard, William Hammond, Frank Andersen, Ves Harper, Masazumi Chaya, Ellen Jacobs, Lelia Goldoni, Raquelle Chavis, Glory Van Scott, Katherine Dunham, Sylvia Waters, Mary Barnett, Carmen de Lavallade, Lula Cooper, Mickey Bord, Arthur Mitchell, Meg Gordean.

Programs, letters written to Ailey and notes written by Ailey on file in the Alvin Ailey Archives, Black Archives of Mid-America, Inc.

Quotation about the "course in knee-bending": Ellen Jacobs, in a conversation in 1993.

Peter Brown on "loving hands at home": Quoted from "Alvin Ailey: Blue Chip Dance Company," fund-raising brochure put out by AAADT in 1987.

Ailey quoted that "black people could do things . . ." and "the dances that my family did . . .": videotaped coverage of "La Boule Blanche" in St. Louis in 1989, provided by Katherine Dunham.

Anecdotes about Lula Cooper asking George Burns for cigar and conversation between Katherine Dunham and Agnes de Mille at the Kennedy Center Honors weekend: Barbara Gamarekian, "Kennedy Center Honors 5 in the Performing Arts," *New York Times*, December 5, 1988.

Descriptions of guests and speeches at the Kennedy Center Honors reception on Saturday night: Carla Hall and Kara Swisher, "Artistry, Honor and a Starry, Starry Night," *Washington Post*, December 5, 1988 (© 1988, *The Washington Post*; reprinted with permission).

Interview quotations from Ailey on thirtieth anniversary: Ailey notes for the speech, Item 0512, Alvin Ailey Archives, Black Archives of Mid-America, Inc.

Figures on AAADT number of performances and dancers, budget and earned income: "Alvin Ailey, Blue Chip Dance Company," proposal for a 1988 fund-raising report.

thirty-two "SO EASY TO BREAK, AND YET SO STRONG"

General sources:

Interviews with Paul Szilard, Albert Knapp, M.D., Masazumi Chaya, Anne McKnight, Dawn Lille Horwitz, Harry Rubenstein, Katherine Dunham, Allan Gray, Carol Coe, Lula Cooper, Sarita Allen, Sharrell Mesh Alexander, Sylvia Waters, Calvin Cooper, Meg Gordean, Laura Beaumont.

Programs, letters and other papers on file in the Alvin Ailey Archives, Black Archives of Mid-America, Inc.

Sources for description of Ailey's memorial service in New York:

"Celebration of Alvin Ailey Jr., Going Home," Public Broadcasting Service, WNET-TV New York; reprinted with permission from the Educational Broadcasting Corporation, Thirteen WNET.

Jennifer Dunning, "4,500 People Attend Ailey Memorial Service at St. John the Divine," *New York Times*, December 9, 1989.

Pallbearers for Ailey's funeral in Artesia, California, were Allan Gray, Stanley Plesent, Masazumi Chaya, Ulysses Dove, George Faison, Harold Levine, Donald McKayle, Arthur Mitchell, Kelvin Rotardier, and Brother John Sellers.

INDEX